MICROCOMPUTER APPLICATION

A HANDS-ON APPROACH TO PROBLEM SOLV

Dr. A.C. MANOHARAN
Computer Sc Dept.
CSU

MICROCOMPUTER

APPLICATIONS
A HANDS-ON APPROACH TO PROBLEM SOLVING

Larry Joel Goldstein

Goldstein Software, Inc.

University of Maryland

ADDISON-WESLEY PUBLISHING COMPANY

Reading, Massachusetts • Menlo Park, California
Don Mills, Ontario • Wokingham, England • Amsterdam
Sydney • Singapore • Tokyo • Madrid • Bogotá
Santiago • San Juan

Sponsoring Editors: Cindy Johnson; Chris Williams
Development Editor: Darlene Bordwell
Technical Editor: Michael Rogers
Copy Editor: Stephanie Argeros-Magean
Production Administrator: Marcia Strykowski
Technical Art Consultant: Loretta Bailey
Text Designer: Roy Howard Brown
Vignette Writer for Chapter Openers: Patricia Mandell, Mandell Features
Cover Designer: Marshall Henrichs
Illustrator: Textbook Art Associates
Part Opener Photos: Frank Siteman
Layout Artists: Lorraine A. Hodsdon; Melinda Grosser
Manufacturing Supervisor: Hugh J. Crawford

Library of Congress Cataloging-in-Publication Data

Goldstein, Larry Joel.
  Microcomputer applications.

  Includes index.
  1. Microcomputers—Programming.   2. Computer programs.
I. Title.
QA76.6.G627   1987   005.265   86-3517
ISBN 0–201–15392-0

Reprinted with corrections, March 1987

CDEFGHIJ–DO–8987

For Sandy,
who brings sunlight and
music into my life

PREFACE

The Purpose of This Book

In the span of a decade, the microcomputer has developed from a sophisticated plaything to a problem-solving tool of incredible significance—such significance, in fact, that today's students in all disciplines are required to be computer-literate, with increasing emphasis on microcomputers and their applications. This book is meant to provide such microcomputer literacy.

In this book I have attempted to tell the story of the microcomputer revolution and to describe contemporary microcomputers as problem-solving tools. To be sure, I have described microcomputers in terms of the traditional hardware–software dichotomy. However, I have heavily emphasized the role of application software in solving problems, especially in a business context.

In reading this book the student will learn the history of the microcomputer revolution, microcomputer hardware and how it functions, and the main categories of application software (word processors, spreadsheets, and database managers). The book emphasizes hands-on use of the programs to solve actual problems.

It seems to me that too many textbooks on microcomputing place an undue emphasis on learning technical skills necessary to master one or more particular software packages. This emphasis is unfortunate, since rapid change in the microcomputer world will make most of these packages obsolete very quickly—perhaps even before the student has a chance to apply knowledge of the packages in a business setting. Instead, beginning microcomputer courses that emphasize the general principles of microcomputing and the generic strategies for applying microcomputers to the solution of problems will help students to better grasp the ideas behind all software packages, and will give them much more flexibility in the real world. That flexible approach is taken in this book.

However, this is not to say that microcomputer courses should be so general that they exclude hands-on experience with software packages. "Learning by doing" is an important strategy in any microcomputing course, and accordingly I have included hands-on exercises, application projects, and command descriptions for a number of the most popular software packages.

Features of the Text

This book is designed as a textbook for use in lecture or laboratory courses and incorporates the following student-oriented features:

1. Easy-to-read, conversational tone.
2. Chapter-opening vignettes describing typical applications of microcomputers in the real world.
3. Review questions (Test Your Understanding) testing students' knowledge at the end of every section.
4. Hands-on exercises designed to develop technical facility with microcomputer software.
5. Extensive chapter review materials, including chapter review questions, lists of key terms, and discussion questions.
6. Application projects designed to develop problem-solving skills using application packages.

Teaching Aids

An Instructor's Manual, created by Dana Johnson of North Dakota State University, is available for use with the text, as is a test bank of approximately 450 questions, compiled by Todd Waymon of Montgomery College. The test bank is available in both written and floppy disk format to coordinate with the text.

Coordinating Software

This book can be used with or without accompanying software. For courses without a laboratory component, the book can be used for teaching general principles of microcomputers and application software. For courses with laboratory components, the book provides problems for the student to solve using a microcomputer, and command tables for many of the most popular application packages, including the following:

WordStar
Microsoft Word
Lotus 1-2-3
SuperCalc 3
dBASE III
R:BASE 5000.

Purchasing most of these software packages represents a major threat to student budgets. As an alternative, I have provided inexpensive, full-function software that can be used with the book. Using this software, the instructor can create a turnkey system giving each student his or her own software and manuals to use, either in a university laboratory or on student-owned microcomputers. The software consists of the GoldWord™ word processor and the GoldSpread™ spreadsheet. Each of these is a full-function package, identical to the versions being distributed commercially. (See "Software," page x, for details on these packages.)

Acknowledgments

Any project of this scope can be accomplished (at least within a finite time span) only with the help of many people. My heartfelt thanks go out to everyone who had a role in making it possible, including Peter Welcher for his work in designing and implementing GoldSpread™; Fred Mosher for his work in designing and implementing GoldWord™; and the staff of Goldstein Software, Inc. for their hard work and dedication above and beyond the call of their jobs. In developing colorful application projects for the text, I had the benefit of input from David L. Sayers of Auburn University; Robert Schaffer of California State Polytechnic University; and Gary Trennepohl of Texas A & M University. I would also like to thank John Connolly and Wayne Oler of Addison-Wesley for their support of my work; Cindy Johnson for her editorial support and sharp insights; Pat Mallion for her enthusiasm and cooperation in developing the book; Marcia Strykowski for her careful production supervision; and Stephanie Argeros-Magean for her excellent copyediting job. Finally, a special note of thanks to Darlene Bordwell, developmental editor on the project, who did a magnificent job of giving direction and life to the project and who acted as my alter ego throughout.

Silver Spring, Maryland   L.J.G.

SOFTWARE OPTIONS

Word Processors

GoldWord™, a "what you see is what you get," full-function word processor.

Features

- automatic paragraph reform
- command-driven for rapid typing
- italics and boldface displayed on screen (with graphics card)
- extensive document formatting options
- complete set of block operations
- search and replace function
- supports most popular printers
- user-friendly command structure
- on-screen help available

Requirements

- 256k IBM PC or compatible
- one disk drive or hard disk
- graphics card needed to display italics

Wordstar 3.3 Educational Version, developed by MicroPro, has all the regular word processing features of full-function WordStar, including access to file management commands while editing, advanced search and replace options, and write excerpt to a new file. Limited to a maximum document length of five pages; does not support CorrectStar, StarIndex, SpellStar or MailMerge.

Spreadsheets/Integrated Packages

GoldSpread™, a powerful integrated package supplying spreadsheet, data management, and graphics.

Features

- 8096 rows by 256 columns
- full support for financial, scientific, data management, and logical functions
- macro capability
- easy-to-use pop-up menu design
- on-screen help
- supports all Lotus 1-2-3 release 1-A commands and functions; allows you to read Lotus 1-2-3 worksheets
- produces output that can be input to Lotus 1-2-3 release 2
- allows you to use templates (including macros) designed for use with Lotus 1-2-3.

Requirements

- 256K IBM PC or compatible
- one disk drive or hard disk
- graphics card needed to display graphics

Preview II, an on-line tutorial introduction to the most important applications on the microcomputer: word processing, spreadsheets, database management, and business graphics. The thoroughly class-tested package shows how to create and print up to five-page documents, use a 16-column by 25-row spreadsheet, build a database with up to 10 entries, and create bar charts and line graphs. Available in Apple and IBM versions, Preview II is free to all adopters of this book.

Database Management

dBASE III Plus, Educational Version, free to adopters of this book. This package handles a broad range of applications—mailing lists, labels, accounting systems, and inventory management systems. The package offers the choice of either Assistant, a pull-down menu system featuring context-sensitive help, or dBASE, the powerful procedural programming language. Although files cannot exceed 31 records, up to 10 database files can be opened at once, thereby demonstrating the capabilities of a fully relational system.

REVIEWERS

Thank You

We would like to thank the following people for reviewing the text and command tables. Their generosity with praise, criticism, and fertile ideas has helped to mold and polish the project.

Warren J. Boe
University of Iowa

Darrell Couch
Florida State University

Geoffrey Crosslin
Kalamazoo Valley Community
   College

John P. Gallagher
Duke University

Ella Paton Gardner
George Mason University

John P. Grillo
Bentley College

Richard Hartley
Central Michigan University

Peter L. Irwin
Richland College

Dana Johnson
North Dakota State University

Rose M. Laird
Northern Virginia Community
   College/Annandale

Richard A. Lyczak
University of New Hampshire

Jeff Mock
Diablo Valley College

Steve Murtha
Tulsa Junior College

David B. Newhall
Bentley College

Neal L. Snyder
Wright State University

Richard D. Spinetto
University of Colorado, Boulder

Maureen Sprankle
College of the Redwoods

John Stephan
Columbia Business School

Tim Sylvester
College of DuPage

Lou Tinaro
Tidewater Community College

Todd Waymon
Montgomery College

F. M. White
Catonsville Community College

Gail J. Yaverbaum
Temple University

Chi-Chung David Yen
Miami of Ohio University

NOTE TO THE STUDENT

This book was written with you, the student, in mind. It has many features designed to assist you in learning about microcomputers and application software. Before beginning to read, you should pause to look at the organization of the book and its various study aids.

How This Book Is Organized

This book is organized as a text for a course. However, you may use it for self-study as well.

The book is divided into three parts. Part I covers microcomputer hardware and operating systems, illustrates how microcomputers work, and prepares you to run application programs.

Part II discusses the main categories of application software: word processing, spreadsheets, and database management. The features of application software are described, as well as the operation of several commercially available software packages, including the software packages you can purchase with the text.

Part III discusses additional application software, including graphics and special utilities, as well as such important issues in microcomputing as data security and copy protection.

Study Aids

Section Study Aids. You will find the following helpful study aids included in each numbered section:

- *Test Your Understanding,* a series of questions located at the end of each section, helps you check your understanding of the material discussed in the section.
- *Hands-on Exercises,* designed to develop your problem-solving ability using an application software package, are contained, where appropriate, at the end of the chapter.
- *Margin Maxims,* placed throughout each section, summarize main points of the discussion and give you helpful guidelines on good microcomputing habits.

- *Command Tables,* located throughout the chapters relating to application software, summarize commands for sample programs. You can use the tables as quick references when studying or working at your microcomputer, or to compare structures of different programs.

Chapter Study Aids. Each chapter begins with a vignette describing a real-life application of microcomputers.

At the end of each chapter, you will find these learning aids:

- *Chapter Review Questions,* cumulative questions that recap the material in the entire chapter.
- *Key Terms,* a list of all important terms introduced in the chapter. For definitions of these terms, consult either the text of the chapter or the glossary.
- *Discussion Questions,* extensive, open-ended questions that your instructor may use as essay assignments or for class discussion.
- *Application Projects,* hands-on projects you can carry out using an application software package. Whereas the Hands-on Exercises at the ends of sections stress mastery of technical details of application software operation, the Application Projects are open-ended and give you an opportunity to solve problems from beginning to end.

The Hands-on Approach to Microcomputing

While you read, study, and work at your microcomputer, do as many of the Hands-on Exercises and Application Projects as you can. In order to learn about application software, you must use it to solve problems. The more hands-on experience you have, the better. Feel free to experiment with the software and to use it to solve problems that come up at school, at home, or on the job. You, too, can be a part of the microcomputer revolution!

L.J.G.

CONTENTS

I

The Principles of
Microcomputers

1 The Microcomputer Revolution

A Case Study: Canadian Pacific Rail

Stretching coast to coast through Canada's glorious mountains and plains, from St. John's, New Brunswick, to Vancouver, British Columbia, are the lines of the Canadian Pacific Railroad, in operation since 1885.

Although the railroad is an old one, some things continue to change. CP Rail, for instance, has entered the computer age, at first with large mainframe computers and terminals, and today with smaller but more powerful microcomputers. As is the case at many other companies throughout North America, micros are transforming the way work is being done at CP Rail.

One of the most dazzling feats microcomputers perform is to help with the dispatching of trains. Dispatchers manage the movements and clearances of trains over hundreds of miles of track. Following complex safety rules, they must keep trains from colliding or running onto a section of track under repair. In the past, the task was handled with a handwritten log.

Now the job is handled by an IBM PC and a program that "knows" all the rules, a program that has the potential to save lives, as well as millions of dollars through the elimination of jobs.

Jack Rutko, a dispatcher in CP Rail's Saskatoon, Saskatchewan, station, uses the program every day. "The computer to us is the best thing since sliced bread," Rutko says.

On the microcomputer screen, commercial freight trains moving into or out of the 720 miles of track he dispatches are shown as color-coded bars. Each time he issues a dispatch, Rutko keys in the information, and the colored bars advance onscreen, so he can see at a glance which sections of track are busy and where each train is currently located.

Like air traffic controllers, dispatchers work under a great deal of pressure and try to picture mentally what the traffic situation is at all times. "Now with the computer and a color monitor, the picture is always there right in front of you," Rutko says. The microcomputer is also much speedier. "The computer saves us time, and it relieves a lot of pressure," Rutko says.

Perhaps most important, all the rules are programmed in, "So there's less chance for us to make a mistake," Rutko says. In the past, human errors were probable when the handwritten system was used. "I could have two trains go head on, or two trains tail-end each other," Rutko says. Since the program has been in use, there have been fewer dispatching mistakes.

All in all, this single microcomputer program makes CP Rail a much leaner, meaner machine. "Let's put it this way," Rutko says. "The Canadian National Railroad, which is our competition, wishes they had this program."

SINCE THE DAWN OF TIME, numbers and data have been calculated and analyzed. More than five thousand years ago, the Chinese and the Egyptians used mathematics to solve problems related to commerce and agriculture. Relying on manual calculations, they were able to devise calendars that predicted the correct time to plant their fields and harvest their crops.

For thousands of years, calculations and data analysis continued to be done by hand. One can only marvel at these achievements, which were due as much to incredible perseverance as they were to academic brilliance. For instance, Johannes Kepler's laws governing the motion of the planets around the sun were the result of 40 years of observations and calculations. In his diary, Kepler complained of individual calculations taking as long as 80 hours!

In the last decade, microcomputers have become a commonplace problem-solving tool. They perform calculations and data analysis—tasks formerly done by hand or, in the last few decades, by large, so-called "mainframe" computers. Microcomputers perform an incredible array of tasks in businesses, schools, and homes. They can place in the user's hands analytical power only dreamed about a few years ago. One of today's more powerful microcomputers can perform all of Kepler's calculations in a few hours! A microcomputer scientific workstation sitting on a desk can provide as much (or more) computing power as was available in the computers that monitored the first manned space flights.

Today's microcomputers put a wonderful problem-solving capability into your hands. In this book, you will learn how to use this power to solve problems that you will meet in your professional life. This book will explain the principles of microcomputer operations and how to use the most important types of application programs.

Chapter 1 introduces microcomputers, their history, and the types of problems they can solve.

1.1 The Microcomputer Revolution

The microcomputer is a versatile problem-solving tool. Although the first microcomputers were built as recently as the mid-1970s, there are already thousands of problems that they can solve. For example, they can be used to:

write business letters
develop a financial analysis of a project

prepare graphs for a report

schedule jobs and monitor progress at a construction site

transmit a report electronically to another office

design an automobile on a screen

use reference material stored in another computer to research a legal opinion

assist in making a medical diagnosis

Moreover, new applications are being invented almost daily.

The introduction of microcomputers into our society has been so rapid and pervasive that it has been called the **microcomputer revolution**. Microcomputers are everywhere. They have invaded our offices, our factories, and even our homes. We are affected by them daily during work as well as leisure hours. Computer stores sell the latest in microcomputers and their related equipment, and even general retailers have joined the fray. Newspapers advertise seminars devoted to applications of the latest software. Local bookstores sell books on programming and microcomputer applications. School boards debate the best approach to introduce computer literacy to their students. Small businesses as well as large struggle to cope with the rapid changes necessitated by the microcomputer revolution. In just a few years, microcomputers have changed the way we work, play, learn, and think.

The Impact of Technological Change

Throughout history, technology has sparked profound changes in society. The bulk of these changes can be traced to a small number of inventions, at most a handful in each century. A list of such might be endlessly debated, but here are a few candidates that would be chosen by most:

Gunpowder, invented in the twelfth century by the Chinese, changed the nature of warfare and, with it, the political and social organization of the world.

Moveable type, invented by Johannes Gutenberg in the fourteenth century, led to the widespread circulation of books and the information they contained.

The *electric light* freed human activities from the natural cycle of light and darkness.

The *telephone* allowed people to communicate with each other over great distances.

The *automobile* gave people tremendous mobility, which led to major changes in where they lived, worked, and shopped.

Television conveyed visual information into households through-out the world and became a major force in molding public opinion, tastes, and knowledge.

The microcomputer certainly belongs on this list. Indeed, the microcomputer is probably the single most important technological development to occur in this half of the twentieth century. As a result, major social changes have followed. Decades-old job categories are being eliminated and new ones are taking their place. Home computers perform as tutors as well as entertainers. Computer crime has generated the need for new laws. Before the computer revolution has run its course, its effects on society will be as far-reaching and profound as the impact of the telephone or the automobile.

What Is a Microcomputer?

A **microcomputer** (also called a **personal computer** or a **desktop computer**) is a computer small enough to fit on a desk top. Although its name might suggest that a microcomputer is a single device, it actually consists of a number of separate components that work together as a **microcomputer system** in much the same way that the components of a stereo system work together. A typical microcomputer system is illustrated in Figure 1.1.

The system components, which are interconnected by cables, include the following:

- **Keyboard**. Resembling a typewriter, this component allows the user to communicate information to the system.
- **Monitor**. This component resembles a television set and is used to display information.
- **System unit**. This is the central control unit for the system. It contains electronic circuitry for performing data manipulation and **memory** for holding data that is being manipulated.
- **Data storage devices**. These devices store information on a long-term basis (for example, when the computer is turned off). The most common data storage devices are diskettes and hard disks, although other devices are in common use as well.
- **Printer**. This component produces printed copies of data.

This list represents only the most common components. Microcomputer systems are quite flexible and generally allow for extensive user customization. Installing additional circuit cards (see Chapter 3) to the system unit allows you to add new system components, such as a **mouse** or a **light pen** for pointing to the screen, a **plotter** for making high quality graphics, or a **controller**

Figure 1.1 A typical microcomputer system, including monitor, keyboard, diskette drives, printer, and diskettes.

device, which allows the microcomputer to control an instrument such as a thermostat or a burglar alarm.

The physical components of a microcomputer system are collectively called **hardware**. By contrast, **software** refers to the medium containing the sets of instructions that tell the hardware how to perform particular tasks. A set of instructions for performing a task is called a **program**. The instructions are generally stored in advance in a data storage device, rather than being passed to the microcomputer one at a time. On command, the system unit reads the instructions from the data storage device and carries them out. The process of carrying out the instructions in a program is called **running the program**.

The Acceptance of Microcomputers

Within a remarkably short time, microcomputers have changed their status from new invention to standard problem-solving tool. Their acceptance can be traced to a number of factors, among them:

1. **Problem-solving capability**. Microcomputer software solves problems. This book will survey some of the software available for use with a microcomputer.

2. **Cost**. Microcomputers are relatively inexpensive. Moreover, their cost continues to decline, so that increasingly greater problem-solving capability can be bought for decreasing price.

3. **Size**. Microcomputers are small in size and can be accommodated within most work environments.

4. **Speed**. Microcomputers process data with amazing speed. They can perform hundreds of thousands of operations per second and can retrieve a piece of data from memory in less than one millionth of a second.

5. **User friendliness**. Developers have gone to great pains to make microcomputer software easy to use. In order to use a microcomputer, you do not need to be a computer scientist and you do not need to have any knowledge of electronics.

The History of Microcomputing

Microcomputing is a very young field that is still changing rapidly. In order to make sense of the field as it exists today, it helps to know something about its history.

The first electronic computers were built in the 1940s. By the early 1970s, they were in common use in large businesses, the government, and the military. Even the cheapest computer was expensive and required a large area and a special staff to operate it. The largest computers (like the ENIAC, shown in Figure 1.2) were called **mainframes** and typically cost more than a million dollars. Designed for use by a major company or a government installation, they were housed in a large room, and required special electrical cabling and air conditioning.

In the 1970s, smaller computers, called **minicomputers**, were introduced. However, these still cost from $50,000 to $250,000

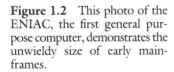

Figure 1.2 This photo of the ENIAC, the first general purpose computer, demonstrates the unwieldy size of early mainframes.

Figure 1.3   Semiconductor chips. (Photo courtesy of Motorola, Inc.)

and were designed for use by a department of a large company or by a small company. The average minicomputer was about the size of an office desk.

The Birth of Microcomputing. In the late 1960s and early 1970s, engineers made great strides in reducing the size of electronic components. They developed the **semiconductor chip** (see Figure 1.3), which was about the size of a fingernail and could contain hundreds of transistors. The semiconductor chips enabled engineers to miniaturize the circuitry contained in all electronic devices. Most importantly, it produced a new generation of mainframes and minicomputers with increased capabilities, greater speed, and smaller size.

In the early 1970s, semiconductor technology progressed to the point where the circuitry for the "brain" of a computer (the **central processing unit** or **CPU**) could be manufactured on a single semiconductor chip. These miniaturized computers were called **microprocessors** and were manufactured by corporations such as Intel and Motorola.

These microprocessors made it possible for the first time to build a computer that was small enough to fit on a desk top and inexpensive enough for an individual to afford. By the mid 1970s, several such microcomputers were available to consumers. The first microcomputers were sold in the form of kits, designed for electronic hobbyists. To the amazement of all (especially the microcomputer designers!), these kits sold like wildfire. It seemed that many people were intrigued with the idea of having their own computer.

The earliest microcomputers could not do very much. In fact, faulty components kept many of them from working at all. And when they were functioning, making them do anything was a complicated affair that involved entering programs as mind-numbing sequences of 0's and 1's.

In order for microcomputers to become problem-solving tools, a number of hurdles needed to be overcome. The first was to simplify the programs for the machines. One step in this direction was taken by a young Harvard drop-out named Bill Gates, who wrote a version of the programming language BASIC for one of the earliest microcomputers. BASIC had been introduced at Dartmouth College in the mid-1960s by John Kemeny and Kenneth Kurtz. By the mid-1970s, it was a popular programming language on mainframe computers. Gates's version of BASIC evolved into the programming language automatically included with most microcomputers. Gates founded a computer company called Microsoft, Inc., which has become one of the major producers of software for microcomputers.

In 1977, Stephen Jobs and Stephen Wozniak, two microcomputer enthusiasts, working in a garage, designed their own microcomputer. This was to be named the Apple and their fledgling business was to become the Apple Computer Corporation. Business grew at an unprecedented rate. In no time, Apple was selling hundreds and then thousands of machines per month. Figure 1.4 illustrates the Apple II.

One reason behind Apple's success was the availability of a number of useful application programs. The most important of these was the spreadsheet VISICALC. (Spreadsheets will be fully discussed in Chapters 7, 8, and 9.) VISICALC allowed accountants and financial planners to automate many of the calculations that they were accustomed to doing on adding machines, or with pencil and paper. Hours of calculations were thus completed in a matter of seconds. Such raw power did much to convince people that microcomputers were real problem-solving tools—not toys.

At about the same time as the introduction of the Apple II, a number of other microcomputers appeared on the market. One of the most popular was Tandy Corporation's TRS-80. By the end of 1980, several hundred thousand microcomputers were in use, and Apple and Tandy were the two largest manufacturers, each with about a 25 percent share of the market.

Figure 1.4 The Apple II microcomputer.

The Spread of Microcomputers. Early microcomputer users banded together into groups to exchange ideas and to share solutions to problems. They dreamed up new applications of microcomputers and often wrote their own software to solve problems. A strong spirit of adventure encouraged users to feel they were participating in a major intellectual turning point in computer use. Part of the excitement was created by the unusual mixture of people who participated. In addition to computer scientists and engineers, physicians, business people, and students became microcomputer enthusiasts, at work as well as home. All were interested in the same goal: using microcomputers to solve problems.

Before long, the early microcomputer users were bringing their microcomputers to work. They became gurus to whom all levels of workers came to for advice: Which microcomputer should I buy? Which printer will work best with my microcomputer? How can I get this word processing program to work with my microcomputer?

Many application packages began to appear around 1980. First generation programs for word processing, data management, spreadsheets, and communications allowed novice users to experience the power of microcomputing. To be sure, these programs were primitive compared with the ones that followed, and to use them often required a long training period and great perseverance. However, in spite of their flaws, the early application packages brought microcomputing closer to the ultimate "information consumer." Moreover, they created a demand for more powerful packages that would be easier to use.

Three distinct markets for microcomputers emerged: schools, homes, and businesses. The education market was initially dominated by Apple computers. The home market, which featured lower-priced computers capable of providing entertainment as well as more serious applications, was dominated by Apple, Commodore, and Atari. This book will not discuss computing in the education and home markets, except for an occasional tangential reference. Rather, it will concentrate on the third market, computers in business.

At first, major corporations viewed microcomputers as toys—and compared with the power available in their mainframe computers, they were. However, most corporations underestimated the significance of bringing computing power down to the level of the individual worker. This view abruptly changed in 1981 when International Business Machines (IBM), the largest computer company in the world, introduced its own microcomputer, dubbed the IBM PC ("PC" being the abbreviation for personal computer). The fact that IBM, a company of such corporate prestige, would enter this market convinced businesses that the microcomputer was more than a passing fad. Within a short time, the microcomputer was recognized as a productivity tool to be used by workers at all levels to process, store, retrieve, and analyze information. Almost every business could find a legitimate place for the microcomputer.

IBM's hold on the marketplace was so great that their personal computer immediately set a standard for the young industry. IBM designed its computer with a completely open architecture. That is, IBM published the circuit diagrams and the details of the internal programming of its machine. This made it simple for outside companies to design hardware add-ons and software for the IBM machine. Hundreds of companies have followed this path.

Some companies have concentrated on building add-on circuit boards to add memory, communications facilities, and other hardware features to the IBM PC. Others have concentrated on hardware development. Yet others have built machines that are functionally identical to IBM's machine, in the sense that they can use the same hardware and software as the IBM. Such computers are said to be

Not now with PS/2

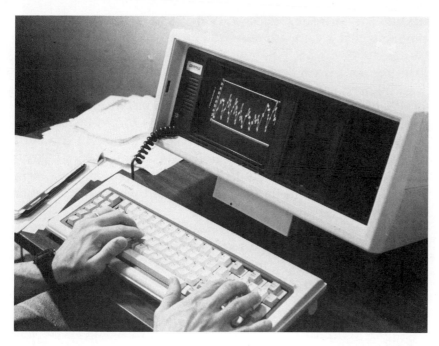

Figure 1.5 The COMPAQ portable microcomputer.

compatible. As of this writing, approximately 70 percent of all microcomputers being sold are either IBM PC's or IBM compatible.

A number of the companies manufacturing IBM compatibles have achieved extraordinary successes. The most notable is COMPAQ Computer Corporation, a company originally founded to produce a portable version of the IBM PC (see Figure 1.5). COMPAQ immediately thrived and within five years of its founding became one of the top 500 industrial corporations in the United States.

The Industry Grows Up. In the years between 1981 and 1986, microcomputers became an important tool in the workplace. Businesses, both large and small, recognized that workers who perform routine tasks increased their productivity when aided by microcomputers. In 1985, the U.S. Bureau of Labor estimated that 56 percent of all technical workers, 37 percent of managers, and 39 percent of professional workers had microcomputers. By 1990, the corresponding figures are projected to be 76 percent, 64 percent, and 64 percent.

The microcomputer business has gone from a $1 billion industry in 1981 to a $5 billion industry in 1985. The growing industry has been characterized by increasingly sophisticated technology and falling prices. Operating speeds and available memory continue to increase, while software developers are producing programs that accomplish more and are easier to use.

In 1978, the TRS–80 was equipped with 4,096 characters of main memory, expandable to 16,384. In 1981, IBM's original PC was equipped with 16,384 characters of main memory, expandable to 589,824 characters. By 1985, the minimum memory available on any of IBM's personal computers was 262,144 characters. Moreover, COMPAQ's 286 Deskpro computer could be equipped with as many as 8,388,608 characters. As a consequence of such expanded memory, software developers have been able to design programs that have many more features and which are far easier to use.

Computer speed has also increased dramatically over the years. Compared with the first personal computers, program execution speeds have increased by more than a factor of 20. Computations and data processing tasks that would have taken hours only ten years ago (if they could be done at all) can now be accomplished in seconds.

Long-term storage has increased in both size and speed. The original personal computers were equipped with cassette tape units that required as long as 10 minutes to load, even for a simple program. Today, cassette units have been replaced by floppy diskette drives and hard disks. A recent model diskette drive can store as many as 512 pages on a single diskette. The hard disk on IBM's PC AT computer can store more than 15,000 pages.

Competition and improvements in technology have brought down the prices of microcomputers by 20 percent each year. Automation has made it possible to assemble microcomputers in larger quantities for less money. Moreover, new semiconductor technology has enabled designers to construct computers using fewer chips, which lowers both the cost and the power requirements.

The price decreases in some system components have been breathtaking. The price of semiconductor chips for 64,000 characters of memory has fallen from $100 in 1981 to $4 in 1986. A 10-million-character hard disk storage unit that was $3,000 in 1981 could be bought for $400 in 1985.

Such price reductions and improvements in technology have led to increased computing power in the average machine. In 1984, IBM introduced its IBM PC AT, a model having about four times the computing power of the original IBM PC. Successors to the PC AT will probably increase computing power by a factor of 5 to 10. The microcomputer of today is already more powerful than the mainframe computers of the 1950s and 1960s. And there is no end to the improvements in sight.

Section 1.1: Test Your Understanding

1. What is a microcomputer?
2. What is the difference between hardware and software?
3. List the main components of a microcomputer system.
4. List six applications of microcomputers.
5. What is a semiconductor chip?
6. What role have semiconductor chips had in the development of the microcomputer?
7. What was the first major piece of microcomputer application software?
8. Explain the reasons for making microcomputers "user friendly."
9. What will be the percentage of workers who will use microcomputers in 1990?
10. Explain the role of Apple in the microcomputer revolution.
11. What is BASIC?

1.2 Microcomputer Applications

Section 1.1 briefly discussed the history of the microcomputer and the dimensions of the microcomputer revolution. But what is all the fuss about? Why are microcomputers so popular that they are purchased by the millions? What do they really do? To answer these questions, let's look at how the power of a microcomputer is applied.

Application Programs

Microcomputers are useful to millions of people because they can be made to run programs that perform tasks. A program that performs tasks is called an **application program**.

For example, a word processing program is an application program that inputs, edits, and prints out documents such as letters, memos, and reports. A spreadsheet is an application program that manipulates numeric data, related to inventory or financial analyses, for example. A graphics package is an application program that displays graphs and charts on a screen and then prints them out.

At the start of the microcomputer revolution, there were few application programs. However, as people from wider-ranging fields began to use microcomputers, they realized that routine tasks could be handled easily by using an application program. As a result, an almost spontaneous outpouring of creativity led to the development of a vast array of application programs. Some of them performed tedious tasks, such as printing payroll checks or mailing labels. Others, however, performed highly complex functions, such as medical diagnosis. Almost any task involving the manipulation of information became a candidate for an application program.

You might ask, "Why go to the trouble of describing a task to the computer? Isn't it simpler to just perform the task myself?" The answer is, "Usually, no." Here are some reasons why:

1. The typical microcomputers can manipulate data at the rate of hundreds of thousands of instructions per second. For example, a microcomputer can easily maintain a mailing list of 100,000 names—a difficult task to do manually.

2. Microcomputers perform data manipulations with great accuracy. The computer does not get bored or tired. It simply executes the instructions it has been given. If you had to perform the same task a thousand times, you would almost surely get bored and make mistakes.

3. Modern storage devices allow microcomputers to manipulate vast arrays of information. For example, you can refer to a 100,000-word computerized dictionary to check your spelling or you can maintain 100,000 pages of business records on a single hard disk. If you want to locate a particular document among those 100,000 pages, the computer can do it in a matter of seconds—whereas it might take you an hour or more.

Application Programs for Business

This book will concentrate on application programs for business. The majority of these programs fall into one of the following categories:

- Word processors
- Spreadsheets
- Database managers
- Graphics
- Communications
- Integrated software

We will later explore each type of program in detail. For now, let's examine a brief description of each category of program.

Word Processor. A **word processor** is a program for manipulating text. Such a program allows you to type a document (say a letter

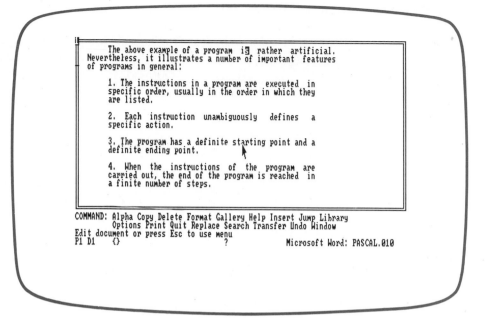

```
      The above example of a program is rather artificial.
Nevertheless, it illustrates a number of important features
of programs in general:

      1. The instructions in a program are executed  in
      specific order, usually in the order in which they
      are listed.

      2.  Each instruction unambiguously   defines   a
      specific action.

      3. The program has a definite starting point and a
      definite ending point.

      4. When the instructions of  the  program  are
      carried out, the end of the program is reached  in
      a finite number of steps.


COMMAND: Alpha Copy Delete Format Gallery Help Insert Jump Library
         Options Print Quit Replace Search Transfer Undo Window
Edit document or press Esc to use menu
P1 D1    {}                        ?              Microsoft Word: PASCAL.010
```

Figure 1.6   A screen display from the word processing program GoldWord.

or a report) into the microcomputer's memory. You may view the document on the screen as you type. (See Figure 1.6.)

You can move directly to any point within the document to add or delete, to copy, or to move sections of text. You can save the document for later retrieval or you can print it. Some word processors can number sections and footnotes automatically, and some even incorporate spelling checkers.

Spreadsheet.   A **spreadsheet** program turns the microcomputer into an accountant's worksheet. It can be used to plan budgets, to do accounting tasks, and to analyze investments. Figure 1.7 illustrates a typical display from such a program.

A spreadsheet allows you to define relationships between numbers. For example, one entry can be defined as the sum of a certain column of numbers. As numbers in the column are changed, the sum is automatically updated. This feature thus allows you to analyze various possibilities. (What will happen if interest rates rise to 12 percent? Fall to 9 percent? Remain at 10.8 percent?)

A microcomputer can keep track of a spreadsheet containing hundreds (or thousands) of interrelated entries.

```
 D15: 3500                                                                READY


                A               B                 C               D
  1                                            JAN 86          FEB 86
  2    ===========================================================================
  3    EXPENSES
  4
  5    Payroll
  6
  7                        President          $6,000.00       $6,000.00
  8                        SrProgrammer       $4,000.00       $4,000.00
  9                        Programmer             $0.00       $3,000.00
 10                        ProgrammerPT(3)      $900.00       $1,350.00
 11                        Documentation      $1,500.00       $1,500.00
 12                        ExecSecy           $1,400.00       $1,400.00
 13                        Secretary          $1,200.00       $1,200.00
 14                        ClerkPT(3)         $1,000.00       $1,000.00
 15                        MarketingDir       $3,500.00       $3,500.00
 16
 17    Total Payroll                         $19,500.00      $22,950.00
 18    Payroll Tax
 19                        Social Security    $1,374.75       $1,617.98
 20                        Unemp. Comp.         $643.50         $305.10
 16-Apr-86   03:37 PM
```

Figure 1.7 A screen display from the spreadsheet program Lotus 1-2-3.

Database Management. In many business settings you need to deal with sets of data. For example, the personnel office has a data sheet for each employee, and the order department generates an invoice for every order placed. These collections of employee records and invoices can be easily maintained in the long-term storage of a microcomputer.

When necessary, such collections of data can be analyzed or updated by using a **database management program**. This program allows you to add the data for a new employee or a new invoice, determine the number of employees within five years of retirement, or calculate the total amount of all unpaid invoices. (See Figure 1.8.)

Graphics. **Graphics** programs allow you to create images on a screen and to print such images with a printer or plotter. The most common graphics required by business are those depicting numeric relationships: bar charts, line graphs, pie charts, etc. Many programs are available for creating such graphics.

Integrated Software. Frequently, data created by one program is used as input to another program—for instance, a graph is designed to depict numeric information found in a spreadsheet. Software developers have met such requirements by creating **integrated software packages**, which include several applications within a single program. A single such package may include a spreadsheet, word processing, graphics, data management, and communications. Integrated packages allow for easy manipulation of data in several different applications. Moreover, they allow the user to learn one consistent set of commands for accomplishing a variety of tasks.

Communications. In recent years communications and computers have become intertwined. It is only natural that the millions of computer users all over the world should be able to communicate with one another. For example, a branch office in Omaha might require data from the memory of the company's main computer in Manhattan. Using a communications program, the branch office's computer can "talk" to the main computer and obtain the data.

You can use communications programs to access information in distant computers. Much of this information is organized into computerized libraries on various subjects. These collections of information are called **databases**. You can subscribe to such databases for a fee, which is based on the length of time the

Figure 1.8 A query being entered into a database management program.

```
SELECT ALL FROM transx WHERE tdate = "03/13/85"
transid    empid      custid      prodid   units       price            tdate
--------   ---------- ----------  -------- ---------   ----------------  --------
    4792       129        102 CX3020        5           $2,575.00 03/13/85
    4865       102        102 MB3020        5           $1,975.00 03/13/85
    4874       102        102 MB3030        5           $2,350.00 03/13/85
    5009       131        107 MB3000       25           $1,620.00 03/13/85
    5010       131        107 PX3040       25           $2,790.00 03/13/85
    5051       129        104 MB3000       25           $1,800.00 03/13/85
    5052       129        104 CX3000       10           $1,800.00 03/13/85
    5065       160        106 CX3000       50           $1,750.00 03/13/85
    5070       129        104 PB3040       10           $2,250.00 03/13/85
    5071       129        105 CX3000        5           $1,900.00 03/13/85
    5086       160        106 PX3040       10           $2,900.00 03/13/85
```

computer spends searching through the database information. One example of a database service is The Source, which allows you access to many databases, including The Official Airline Guide, which is the master schedule for commercial airline flights. By subscribing to The Source, you can browse through listings of available flights and compare fares among competing airlines. You can even make reservations and pay for them using a credit card.

Electronic mail is another application of communications programs. Commercial services such as MCI Mail and Western Union's Easylink provide electronic "mailboxes" into which people can deposit mail. Using electronic mail, you can receive memos, reports, and sales information from anywhere in the world. The sender can deposit the mail at any time, and you can "pick up" your mail by using a communications program to transmit the contents of your mailbox to your computer.

Programming a Microcomputer

You can purchase programs to perform a wide range of tasks. For example, such programs can tutor you for the Scholastic Aptitude Test (SAT), manage your stock portfolio, type a term paper, or calculate your tax return.

Every program consists of a sequence of steps that tells the computer what to do. These steps may involve various functions, such as the following:

- Display data (such as an SAT question) on a screen.
- Obtain data (the answer to the question) from the user.
- Respond to the data (right or wrong answer) the user provided.
- Draw graphs on a screen (to plot the daily fluctuations in the price of a stock).
- Print data on paper (to print out your tax return).
- Save data for later retrieval (to store a copy of your unfinished term paper for later completion).

The process of telling the computer the program steps to perform is called **programming**. Programs are written in a **programming language**, which is in a form resembling written English. The instructions in the programming language are then translated into machine language instructions that the computer can execute directly. There are dozens of programming languages available for use on microcomputers. The most common one is BASIC, which was mentioned earlier in the chapter.

Some application programs can themselves be regarded as programming languages. As we shall see, you can record sequences of spreadsheet instructions into a program that you can run whenever you wish. Similarly, you can record a sequence of instructions as a program for a database management system.

   This book will not be concerned with the type of programming needed to write an application program. However, it will discuss how to write programs that use various application programs as programming languages.

Section 1.2: Test Your Understanding

1. What is a program?
2. What is meant by "running a program"?
3. For each of the tasks listed in items a) through f) below, indicate the type of application software you would use (word processing, spreadsheet, database manager, graphics, communications).
   a) Analyze the results of a population study.
   b) Plan the budget for a new office building.
   c) Obtain information in THE SOURCE database.
   d) Use an automatic teller machine to make a bank deposit.
   e) Write a novel.
   f) Plot the movement of the price of Apple Computer Corporation stock.
   g) Keep a record of the contents of a warehouse.
   h) Balance your checkbook.
4. Explain the operation of a word processor.
5. Explain the operation of a graphics program.
6. What is an integrated program?

KEY TERMS

microcomputer revolution	light pen	microprocessor
microcomputer	plotter	compatible
personal computer	controller device	application program
desk-top computer	hardware	word processor
microcomputer system	software	database management
keyboard	program	program
monitor	running the program	graphics program
system unit	mainframe computer	integrated software package

communications program	mouse	programming
database	minicomputer	programming language
data storage device	semiconductor chip	
printer	central processing unit (CPU)	

CHAPTER REVIEW QUESTIONS

1. Explain the function of a spreadsheet.
2. What is a word processor?
3. Give an example of how a communications program may be applied.
4. Give an example of how a graphics program may be applied.
5. What is an integrated program? Describe some advantages offered by such programs.
6. What advantages do microcomputers distributed throughout a company offer when compared to the mainframe computers housed in a data processing department?

7. Suppose that you want to address an envelope. Is it more efficient to use a computer program (and a printer) or to address it by hand?
8. Same question as 7, but you have 10,000 envelopes to address.
9. Same questions as 7, but you have 10,000 envelopes to address every month.
10. Based on your answers to questions 7 through 9, what conclusion can you draw about the type of tasks that may be efficiently computerized?

DISCUSSION QUESTIONS

1. A consulting company is working on a project to analyze the market for real estate in a city 100 miles away. Discuss the various application programs that could be used by the company in this project.

2. How would you use a microcomputer in your everyday life?

Information Management

In organizing. All organizations face problems in managing information. For example, the organizers of the 1986 Live Aid rock benefit for Ethiopia famine relief faced a mammoth problem of information management. They needed to coordinate scheduling hundreds of performers—on two stages—half a world apart. Furthermore, they needed to broadcast the concert, live and on tape, for sixteen consecutive hours around the world. Using Apple microcomputers, the program Jazz, and a 1,000-row grid listing the performers who would be on stage every minute of the broadcast, computer-literate students at Drexel University helped the concert organizers keep the program under control, making sure that last-minute replacement acts were entered and script changes made. (J. Langevin/Sygma)

In retail. Microcomputers revolutionized the retailing industry, providing a way to track inventory and sales at the point of purchase. This tracking system eliminates excessive time spent in order processing, greatly simplifies inventory control, and helps employees work more efficiently. (Courtesy of International Business Machines Corporation)

In athletics. Professional sports organizations have discovered the value of microcomputers and database management programs for tracking and organizing statistics regarding team members and rivals. (Courtesy of International Business Machines Corporation)

Graphics: Getting a Message Across

In manufacturing. Manufacturers in all industries find computer graphics programs invaluable in designing products, ranging from auto parts to textiles. (Courtesy of International Business Machines Corporation)

In construction. Graphics programs were used to create this blueprint on-site during a construction project. (Courtesy of Hewlett-Packard Company)

In education. Microcomputers play an increasingly large role in education, especially in teaching the handicapped. At the National Institute for Deaf Children in Paris, a deaf child working with a therapist matches his speech to a prototype pattern displayed on an IBM PC screen. This visual feedback helps the child adjust his vocal pitch until he makes the correct sound. (Courtesy of International Business Machines Corporation)

In business. A presentation—whether to clients or to employees—requires a professional level of quality and attractiveness. To prepare an impressive presentation, business people create useful, informative graphics on a microcomputer screen using graphics software. (Courtesy of International Business Machines Corporation)

The graphics are then photographed on screen using a color film recorder, a machine containing a high-quality 35mm camera. The film is then processed into 35mm slides, which are assembled into a cohesive visual exposition. (Darlene Bordwell, Boston)

Business people who use graphics that they create themselves develop much more effective presentations. Graphics help emphasize major points in a colorful, easily understood way and may make an innovative or controversial idea more palatable. (Darlene Bordwell, Boston; graphic images courtesy of Hewlett-Packard Company)

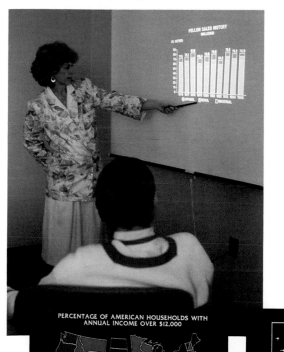

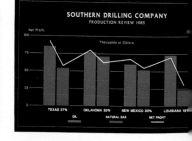

Communications

In trading. Microcomputers and data communication programs keep the wheels of commerce turning. Worldwide commodity price quotes and other trading information are transmitted from the offices of commodity news services, and are received by brokerages via communication programs and telephone lines, or with a satellite dish antenna. (Courtesy of Knight-Ridder Newspapers, Inc.)

A stockbroker then reads the latest stock price information to advise clients on selections. (Courtesy of the Allied Corporation)

The client's order to buy or sell is transmitted to the floor of a regional exchange or to the national New York Stock Exchange, where the brokerage firm's representative is posted. Computer displays showing stock prices are constantly updated. Once the transaction is made, it is recorded, again through the use of computers. (Courtesy of the New York Stock Exchange)

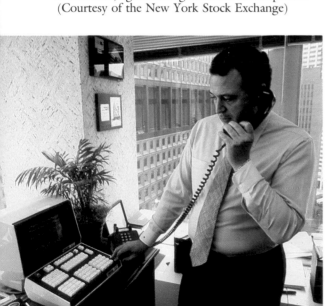

2 Problem Solving with a Microcomputer

A Problem-Solving Tool You Can Bank On

You have just started a brand new job. You are issued a microcomputer and taught how to use Lotus 1-2-3, a program that combines a spreadsheet, database management, and graphics. Now what? How will you put these tools to work to help you sell more mortgages or to keep track of invoices?

A key issue today in microcomputer training is making sure that employees learn not only how to use a microcomputer and a program but how to use a microcomputer to solve their own particular business problems, whether that involves identifying potential markets in the hand-tool business or finding a better way to make hotel reservations.

To that end, many companies have set up what they call microcomputer information centers, their role being to manage the use of microcomputers in the company. Typical services would be choosing the right hardware and software needed to do a job, teaching employees how to use microcomputers, and installing equipment. In the past, many microcomputer information centers taught employees how to operate their microcomputers and run a program—nothing else. They were on their own when it came to figuring out what to do next. Today's businesses have moved to training that emphasizes ways of using the microcomputer to solve problems.

Bank of New England in Boston, Massachusetts, New England's second largest bank holding company, uses case studies in its training to show its employees—from lenders and credit analysts to trust officers—how the microcomputer might be used in their jobs. For example, when a lender wanted to know how to calculate the cash flow of a potential loan customer, the bank developed spreadsheet models using Lotus 1-2-3.

Jim Trenz, a lender at BNE in a specialized group that handles oil and gas and utilities loans, has been using an IBM PC for several years to help him analyze and calculate loan figures. After his training, he worked with a BNE analyst to develop a Lotus 1-2-3 spreadsheet model that would analyze the cash flow of a potential customer and calculate loan payment schedules. "Speed is the main advantage of using the model," Trenz say. Trenz now uses an IBM PC AT, an even more powerful microcomputer, that allows him to analyze loans that involve up to 50 oil wells.

Even with rapidly changing oil and gas prices and interest rates, all Trenz has to do is plug the new numbers into his spreadsheet and in a matter of minutes the new loan picture emerges. "I can have a very fast analysis available for anybody who would need it in the bank," Trenz says. In the past it would take a lender using pencil and paper over two weeks to calculate loan figures for fifty oil wells. With Lotus and the microcomputer, it takes a couple of days to enter the myriad figures needed into the spreadsheet, but once they are entered, the program calculates the loan figures in a zippy 20 minutes.

CHAPTER 1 DESCRIBED the microcomputer revolution and some of the resulting application programs being used in business. The next few chapters will lay a foundation for the more detailed study of application software that will appear later in the book.

As has already been mentioned, microcomputers are problem-solving tools. Any problem solving that involves a microcomputer has four basic components:

1. **Hardware**. The physical components of a computer system, consisting of monitor, keyboard, printer, and so forth. If you are to use a microcomputer to solve a problem, your hardware must be sufficiently capable. The amount of memory, the sizes of data storage devices, the speed of the computer, and the speed and quality of your printer are all factors that determine whether you can solve a particular problem.

2. **Software**. Another name for the programs that tell a computer system how to carry out a particular task. There are tens of thousands of application programs available. For any particular task, there are often a dozen or more programs from which you can choose. As a problem solver, you must be able to select the most appropriate application program for a particular problem and learn to use that program.

3. **Data**. The information manipulated by a program. Data can consist of a mailing list, a report, or accounting information. As a problem solver, you must be able to determine and locate the data you need. Data may be located in paper documents, microcomputer storage, or in the data banks of a large computer. As part of your problem solution, you must get the data into your microcomputer in a form that your application program can use. This can involve typing the data into your computer, transmitting data from one computer to another, and rearranging the data into a form your application program can use.

4. **User**. The problem solver in the problem solution. The user must determine the amount of time available to solve the problem, choose the best application programs, supply any necessary data, and direct the activities of the program.

The interaction between these four components is illustrated in Figure 2.1. It can also be summarized by a simple equation:

Hardware + software + data + the user = problem solution.

This chapter will now begin to explore each of the four components of problem solving on a microcomputer.

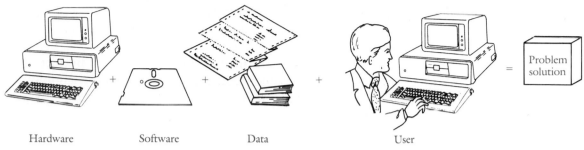

Hardware   Software   Data   User

Figure 2.1   The problem-solving equation.

2.1 Microcomputer Hardware

Microcomputer hardware must be matched to the task it is to perform. On the one hand, the hardware must be powerful enough to solve the problems you give it. Just as you would not use a garden spade to dig the foundation of a house, you cannot use a small home computer to manage a mailing list of 100,000 names. On the other hand, it is a tremendous waste of resources to use hardware that is too powerful to solve a simple problem: It does not take a $10,000 scientific workstation to balance your checkbook!

This section will survey the parts of a microcomputer system and how each one contributes to the solution of a problem.

Understanding hardware and how to use it is the first component in solving a problem with a microcomputer.

The Organization of a Microcomputer System

As explained in Chapter 1, a microcomputer system is assembled from components in much the same way that a stereo system is. The organization of a typical microcomputer system is shown in Figure 2.2. The parts of a microcomputer system fall into seven categories:

1. Processing unit
2. Random access memory (RAM)
3. Read-only memory (ROM)
4. Secondary storage
5. Input devices
6. Output devices
7. Option cards

All of the hardware contained in a microcomputer system is crucial to the function of application programs. Chapter 3 will look more closely at each component of a microcomputer system; for the moment, the focus will be on the kinds of memory contained within a microcomputer, how memory and data are stored, and how you can use this information to solve business problems.

One type of memory contained in your microcomputer is called **random access memory (RAM)**, also known as **primary memory, short-term memory,** or **high-speed memory**. RAM holds the program currently being executed by the user, as well as the data being manipulated.

It is important to know how much memory a particular application program requires, since RAM must be big enough to hold the program. In planning your microcomputer system, an important step is to survey the application programs you are likely to want to use and the amounts of RAM they require. You must then equip your computer with enough RAM to accommodate the largest of these programs.

RAM can be accessed very quickly. It usually takes only about one millionth of a second to read (or write) a character from (or to) primary memory. Offsetting this high-speed access, however, is the fact that most types of primary memory are erased as soon as electrical power is turned off. This means that RAM is not suitable for long-term storage of programs or data.

RAM is constructed from semiconductor chips. Some of these chips are located on the circuit board of the processing unit, which you will learn more about in Chapter 3. Memory capacity can be increased by adding RAM chips on optional circuit cards, as illustrated in Figure 2.3.

The second type of computer memory, called **read-only memory (ROM)**, contains important programs for operating the

Random access memory (RAM) holds the program currently being executed and the data the program is manipulating.

Read-only memory (ROM) operates the microcomputer's system devices. It cannot be altered.

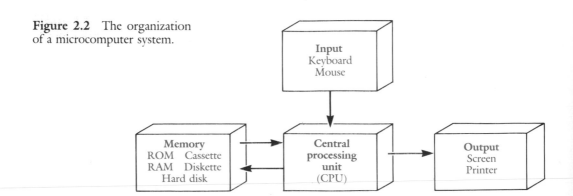

Figure 2.2   The organization of a microcomputer system.

Figure 2.3   RAM on an optional circuit card.

microcomputer's system devices. These programs are recorded in ROM at the factory and cannot be altered by the system user. Application programs use ROM programs to access the various system devices.

Secondary storage is a third type of memory used for permanent storage of programs and data. Items from secondary memory must be loaded into RAM before the computer can use them. The most common secondary memory devices are diskette drives and hard disk drives.

A **floppy disk drive** reads and writes information on flexible **diskettes**, which can hold anywhere from 160,000 to 1,200,000 characters. A **hard disk drive** reads and writes information on a **hard disk**, which is permanently sealed within a chamber in which it rotates at very high speed, as shown in Figure 2.4. A hard disk can store from 10 million to 100 million characters of data and provide much quicker access times than can a floppy disk drive. However, hard disks are more expensive than diskette drives. Problems that require large amounts of data may make the added expense worthwhile when the savings in time is considered.

Problems that access large amounts of data frequently can be handled more quickly with a hard disk.

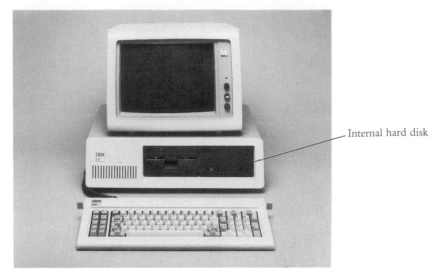
Internal hard disk

Figure 2.4 An internal hard disk.

Accessing Data from Memory

Access of data from secondary storage devices is much slower than access from primary memory. However, the slow speed is compensated for by the ability to use secondary storage for long-term storage and to store large quantities of data.

At the present time, there is no single type of memory that has rapid access and a long-term storage capability, and is cheap enough to store large quantities of data. Therefore computer designers equip their machines with several types of memory and so take advantage of the merits of each type. RAM size and secondary memory requirements are key elements to consider in the hardware segment of the problem-solving equation.

User Communication with a Microcomputer

The keyboard is only one way of communicating with the microcomputer.

There are many input devices that you can use to transmit information to the computer. The most common device used in business applications is the keyboard. However, there are others that will be discussed later, including the mouse, light pen, digitizing pad, and scanner. Your choice of input device will depend on the particular problem you are solving, the amount of data, its form, and the amount of time available for input.

The computer communicates information to the user via an output device, such as a **monitor** (also called a **screen**). In addition, most microcomputer systems use a **printer** to supply output information on paper. You must choose an output device appropriate for the particular problem you are solving, based on the desired form and quality of output, its volume, and the speed with which it must be produced.

Collectively, input and output devices are called **input-output devices** (or **I/O devices** for short). They are also called **peripheral devices**, or just **peripherals**.

Section 2.1: Test Your Understanding

1. What is an input device? An output device? Give some examples of each.
2. What is RAM?
3. What is secondary memory? Give some examples.
4. What are the advantages of primary memory? Its disadvantages?
5. What are the advantages of secondary memory? Its disadvantages?
6. Compare the amounts of information, in characters, which can be stored on a diskette and on hard disk.
7. What is the function of ROM?

2.2 Software and Data

The second component in solving a problem on a microcomputer involves **software**, and the third involves **data**. These two ingredients must work closely together to perform tasks on the microcomputer.

A **computer program** consists of a sequence of instructions for the computer to execute. At one extreme, a program can be designed by a user wanting a custom solution. More often, users simply choose an existing package that has the tools required to solve their problem. For example, as described in Chapter 1, there are application programs that would be particularly useful in various phases of business. Each application package brings a finite set of capabilities. Choosing the right package depends on understanding how it works and what the options are. Some packages allow more sophistication than others but may be more difficult to use. Finding the right package for the problem is thus a major consideration in solving the problem.

Understanding software is the second component in solving a problem with your microcomputer.

Finding the Right Application Package
There are many different application packages that can be used for most problems. You can survey packages listed in software direc-

tories or read reviews in microcomputer journals. When choosing a program, you must consider the following factors:

- Will the program run on your computer system? All programs are designed with particular hardware configurations in mind. You must make sure that the configuration of your machine is one on which the program can run.
- What are the inputs and outputs of the program? You must check that the program can perform the data manipulations you require and that it can use the data that you provide.
- Is the program easy to use? How long will it take you to learn the program?
- Will you have to make major alterations in any procedures you are currently using in order to collect, manipulate, or act on data?

Designing a Microcomputer System

When you are planning the purchase of a microcomputer system, consideration of the hardware to buy should be the last step in your design process. You should begin by analyzing the problems you plan to solve using the microcomputer system. Then, you need to determine the type of application software that can be used to solve these problems. Next, you should choose the actual software packages that best suit your needs. Finally, you should choose hardware that best functions with that application software.

Running a Program

When programs are not being used, they are usually stored in some form of secondary storage, such as on a diskette. If you want to run a program, you must give a command that specifies the name of the program and where it is located. In response, the computer does the following:

1. The computer reads the program from secondary memory into RAM.
2. The computer executes the program's instructions.
3. When the program ends, the RAM occupied by the program and data is released for use by the next program. Figure 2.5 summarizes this process.

Data

The third component in a problem solution is data. There are several questions that you must answer about your data. What data will the program need as input? What is the source of the data?

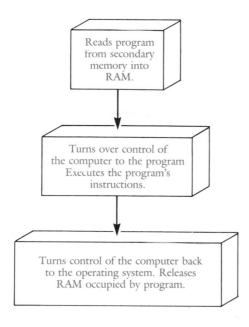

Figure 2.5   Running a program.

How will the data be input into the computer? Who will do the inputting? What data manipulation must be performed? What format will the output data take?

Efficient manipulation of data can help you solve a problem quickly

Types of Data. Programs can manipulate several distinct types of data. Data consisting of normal text characters (letters, digits, punctuation marks, and such common symbols as #, $, %) are called **alphanumeric data**. The text of a business letter would be an example of alphanumeric data. Data consisting only of numbers are called **numeric data**. Any number—5, 15.875, 0.00025, or 127,850—would thus be classified as numeric data. Data consisting only of letters are called **alpha data**. For example, an alpha data response to a question might be indicated by typing the letters "Y" or "N." Data consisting of visual displays or symbols, such as a bar chart or a company logo, are called **graphics data**.

Data Manipulation within a Program. Many types of data manipulation can be performed on a microcomputer. The type of manipulation depends on the type of data. Manipulations of numeric data include arithmetic operations and numeric comparisons, as well as data formatting (for example, number of significant digits, alignments of decimal points). Manipulations of alphanumeric data would include sorting (arranging data into alphabetical order, or by length of the first word), formatting (in lines of a given length

A solution is only as good as the data it's based on.

according to specific capitalization rules), and encryption (translating data into coded form). Even graphics data can be manipulated. This would include the rotation, enlargement, shrinking, and superpositioning of any visuals on your monitor.

Data Input and Output. Some programs provide data within the program instructions themselves. More often, however, a program can get its data from external sources. Such external data are called **program input**. This input may result from user action while the program is running (such as a document typed into a word processor). Input may also consist of data that has been previously stored on a diskette or hard disk. This is the case when an accounting program reads a payroll file that was previously saved on diskette.

The results of data manipulation are usually provided as **program output**, which either is given directly to the user (via the screen, printer, or some other output device) or is saved in a secondary memory device (for later output to the user or for later input to another program).

A computer can manipulate only the data that you give it. The output is only as good as the input. There is no way for a computer program to compensate for missing or incorrect data. Accordingly, you must incorporate into your problem solution procedures for checking that your data is complete and accurate.

Section 2.2: Test Your Understanding

1. Explain how a program runs.
2. What are the various types of data? List them and provide examples for each.
3. What is program input?
4. What is program output?
5. Give examples of data manipulation for numeric data.

2.3 The User

The user is the most crucial factor in the solution of a problem.

The fourth component in a problem solution is the **user**. The user has complete control over when and how a problem is solved. The microcomputer puts power in the hands of the user and performs tasks that would be impossible for one person to do, such as adding and computing ratios of large numbers of figures on a continuous basis. The user's role will pervade the entire text, but this section analyzes the user's role in interacting with the microcomputer.

Problem Description and Analysis

As the user of a microcomputer system, you are responsible for problem description and analysis. Most problems are not presented in a form that allows you to immediately apply a computer for their solution. Rather, most problems require you to describe them in clear terms, fill in missing information, and develop a method of solution.

In developing a solution method that involves a microcomputer, you must decide the role that the computer is to play, the information you have available to input to the computer, and the information you wish the computer to derive for you. From these facts, you must decide which application package is suitable for solving your problem.

User Interaction with the Microcomputer

The user interacts with the computer in numerous ways and on a multitude of levels. First of all, the user gives the commands to initiate and interrupt programs and to perform system housekeeping functions such as formatting disks and copying or erasing files.

A program requiring user participation is called an **interactive program**. One of the significant features of microcomputing is its emphasis on interactive programs. This is one of the reasons the application of microcomputers is often called **personal computing**, and microcomputers are called **personal computers**.

During program execution, the user can provide input data from the keyboard. The user may respond to program requests for information: What is the name of the file containing the letter you want to edit? Which drive is the payroll data on? The user may also input such data as a memo or some accounting information, which the program then manipulates. In other cases, the user may need to respond to an error condition: Is the printer turned on? Is the diskette in the wrong drive? Such interactions with the computer make the user the most vital part of the problem-solving process.

The User Interface

The process whereby the user communicates with the computer is called the **user interface** or the **human interface**. The human interface of an interactive program can range from quite simple (using typed communications) to very elaborate (using a mouse, light pen, and graphic representation of commands).

Interactive computing stands in sharp contrast to **batch processing**, which is commonly used for data processing in mainframe and minicomputer installations. In batch processing, a number of programs are input to the computer at the same time and the computer runs them in sequence without further human interaction. This approach to computing is suitable for large-scale data processing (for instance, if you need to prepare 100,000 insurance policy bills), but runs counter to the philosophy of the microcomputer as a tool to be used by individuals to solve problems.

In the early days of microcomputers, both the machines and the programs were designed without much thought being given to the human component. Designers and manufacturers assumed that users would adjust to the "needs" of the computer. Complex commands to input data were often unintelligible and hard to remember. However, it didn't really matter since the early microcomputer users were enthusiasts with engineering or science backgrounds who pursued microcomputers as a hobby.

As microcomputers became part of the office environment, managers and workers alike pleaded for machines and software that were easier to use—in other words, microcomputers and software that were **user-friendly**.

Since 1980, manufacturers have made great strides in introducing user-friendliness into the world of microcomputers. A great

Figure 2.6 The graphics interface of the Apple Macintosh microcomputer.

Figure 2.7 Using a mouse with an Apple Macintosh.

deal of thought has gone into making the command screens of programs appealing and intuitive by making the keystrokes that activate commands suggestive of the command (such as using S for Save). Each step in this direction broadens the appeal and usefulness of the microcomputer. Less training is required as the accessibility of the technology increases.

Some microcomputers use **graphics interfaces** to achieve user-friendliness. One such microcomputer is the Apple Macintosh, which presents commands and programs as pictures called **icons**. Figure 2.6 illustrates the graphics interface of the Macintosh. Instead of typing a command on a keyboard, you point to the appropriate icon with a device called a **mouse**, shown in Figure 2.7. On the Macintosh screen, the mouse is represented by an arrow, which replicates the motion of the mouse itself. To execute a command, you point the arrow to the corresponding icon and click one of the buttons on the mouse.

Today's computer manufacturers continue to lavish attention on the human interface and to experiment with many new interfaces. It does not by any means appear that the end of the user-friendliness story has been written.

User Responsibilities in Problem Solving

The control and power you have in using a personal computer carries with it many responsibilities. As the primary user, you are responsible for the full range of the problem-solving process. This includes the following:

- Formulating the problem
- Deciding which data to use
- Verifying the accuracy and consistency of the data
- Deciding on the method of problem solution
- Choosing the necessary hardware configuration
- Choosing the application program that will best effect the solution
- Inputting the data to the computer
- Interacting with the application program to solve the problem
- Interpreting the output of the application program
- Formulating the solution of the problem
- Circulating the solution to your colleagues and interpreting it for them

This role will demand many skills and a broad range of knowledge. You must combine careful problem analysis and meticulous attention to detail with knowledge of application programs and interpersonal communications skills. It is precisely this broad interplay of skills that makes personal computing challenging and exciting.

Adjusting to the Microcomputer

If you are comfortable using your microcomputer, you will have a better chance of solving your problems successfully.

A microcomputer takes some getting used to. You must practice in order to be comfortable with it, just as you are with a pencil and paper, or with a book. At first, a microcomputer may be intimidating. After all, it is a complex, powerful tool with many do's and don'ts associated with it. However, you can make your microcomputer easier to deal with by bearing in mind certain factors.

Computers can't think. If you have used an application program that interacts extensively with the user, it is easy to believe that computers "think." The give and take between computer and user has many of the qualities of human conversation. Furthermore, the seeming ability of the computer to draw conclusions resembles human reasoning. However, computers don't think, at least not in the same sense that humans do.

Actually, computers are rather stupid machines. They slavishly follow whatever instructions are set forth for them by their programmers. Their seeming ability to reason and make choices is not the result of any thinking, but rather an automatic response planned by a programmer. Computers do no have the ability to fill in missing information; only humans do. We can understand a conversation in which we don't hear all the words and we can understand written text with missing or misspelled words. A computer can only manipulate the data that it is given. If the data is faulty, then the computer cannot generate valid data from it. Because computers cannot think, you must be careful to spell out your commands in detail, which will be frustrating if you are a beginner. You must also remember that there is no way for a computer to interpret what you mean if your commands are incorrect or incomplete.

Ordinary use can't hurt the computer. Novices worry about harming a computer by giving incorrect instructions. Well, dismiss the thought from your mind! Short of physical abuse, you can do nothing to harm a microcomputer. If you make an error, you can simply interrupt the computer program, cancel the incorrect command, and then give another command. Occasionally, you may give a command that "hangs the computer up," that is, the computer refuses to respond to your commands. If this happens, just turn off the power and restart the computer. Don't be afraid of such hang-ups; they don't hurt the computer in any way.

Computers rarely make mistakes. Although it is possible for a computer to make a mistake, it is very unlikely that an error will go undetected. The microcomputer continuously checks on the operation of its components and the integrity of the data in memory. If the computer detects a malfunction, it will signal that there is a problem and indicate the nature of the problem. But even this is very rare. Microcomputers are highly reliable and can perform faithfully for months or years without making any errors.

Section 2.3: Test Your Understanding

1. What is the human interface?
2. What is an interactive program?
3. What is batch processing?
4. Why are microcomputers often called personal computers?
5. Explain what the term user-friendly means.
6. What is a graphics interface?
7. Can computers think? Explain your answer.
8. Do computers make mistakes? Explain your answer.

2.4 Problem Solving on a Microcomputer

In the preceding sections, you were introduced to the four components involved in the solution of a problem on a microcomputer. Now think about how these four components come together to solve a problem. There are four steps that you must follow when solving a problem using an application program:

1. Choose an application program.
2. Run the application program.
3. Use the application program to solve the problem.
4. Exit the application program.

Let's see what is involved in each of these steps by considering the following task: You must prepare a letter to be sent to the 1,000 members of your professional organization. Note the role played by each of the four components (hardware, software, data, and the user) in the problem solution.

Step 1: Choose an Application Program

The problem to be solved involves manipulation of textual material, and the programs that handle such manipulations are word processors. However, the particular problem at hand imposes certain requirements on the word processor you select. All word processors have the ability to prepare letters. However, since the letters are to go to your professional peers, they should be printed on letterhead stationery by a printer capable of high-quality print. If your computer system has such a printer, you must then choose a word processor capable of using it.

Since the same letter must be addressed to 1,000 people, the word processor must have the ability to merge the names and addresses that are stored on a diskette in a mailing list file. Not all word processors have the ability to handle form letters. So you must consider only those word processors having this capability. Even with these restrictions, there are many word processors from which you can choose. You should not base your choice solely on a single application. Also consider the other applications you may later require. Such applications will impose additional requirements on the word-processing program and narrow the choice still further.

Once all requirements have been met, you should consider other factors, such as the quality of documentation and the ease of learning and using the package.

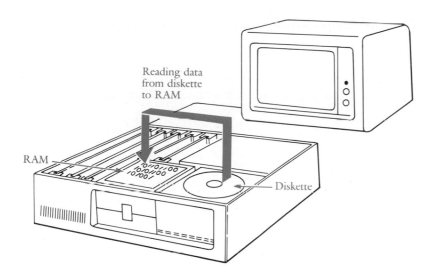

Figure 2.8 Reading a program into RAM.

Step 2: Run the Application Program

When a word-processing program is not in use, it is stored on a diskette or on a hard disk. To run the program, the microcomputer must copy the program into RAM. If the program stored on a diskette, you must first insert the diskette containing the program into a diskette drive. No corresponding action is necessary if the program is stored on a hard disk.

Next, you must type the appropriate command that will tell the microcomputer to run the word-processing program. The program will then be read from diskette or hard disk into RAM. This process is illustrated in Figure 2.8. Control of the microcomputer is now turned over to the word-processing program. That is, the microcomputer is told to carry out the instructions of the word-processing program.

Step 3: Use the Application Program to Solve the Problem

Once the application program is running, you must use its commands to solve your problem. Most programs begin with the following sequence of screens: title screen, copyright notice, command screen. Figure 2.9 illustrates the command screen of WordStar, a popular word-processing program. The commands are summarized at the top of the screen. If you want to prepare a letter, the first command will be to press the D key, for "open a document file."

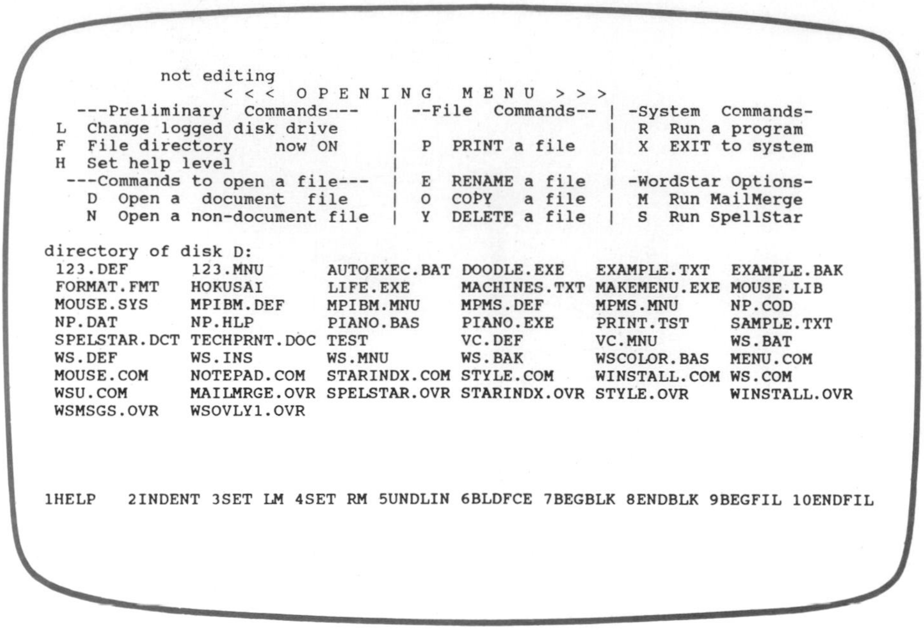

```
          not editing
                < < <  O P E N I N G   M E N U  > > >
   ---Preliminary Commands---  | --File Commands-- | -System Commands-
L  Change logged disk drive    |                   | R  Run a program
F  File directory    now ON    | P  PRINT a file   | X  EXIT to system
H  Set help level              |                   |
   ---Commands to open a file--- | E  RENAME a file | -WordStar Options-
   D  Open a document file      | O  COPY   a file  | M  Run MailMerge
   N  Open a non-document file  | Y  DELETE a file  | S  Run SpellStar

directory of disk D:
123.DEF        123.MNU        AUTOEXEC.BAT DOODLE.EXE   EXAMPLE.TXT  EXAMPLE.BAK
FORMAT.FMT     HOKUSAI        LIFE.EXE     MACHINES.TXT MAKEMENU.EXE MOUSE.LIB
MOUSE.SYS      MPIBM.DEF      MPIBM.MNU    MPMS.DEF     MPMS.MNU     NP.COD
NP.DAT         NP.HLP         PIANO.BAS    PIANO.EXE    PRINT.TST    SAMPLE.TXT
SPELSTAR.DCT   TECHPRNT.DOC   TEST         VC.DEF       VC.MNU       WS.BAT
WS.DEF         WS.INS         WS.MNU       WS.BAK       WSCOLOR.BAS  MENU.COM
MOUSE.COM      NOTEPAD.COM    STARINDX.COM STYLE.COM    WINSTALL.COM WS.COM
WSU.COM        MAILMRGE.OVR   SPELSTAR.OVR STARINDX.OVR STYLE.OVR    WINSTALL.OVR
WSMSGS.OVR     WSOVLY1.OVR


1HELP    2INDENT 3SET LM 4SET RM 5UNDLIN 6BLDFCE 7BEGBLK 8ENDBLK 9BEGFIL 10ENDFIL
```

Figure 2.9   The command screen for the WordStar word-processing program.

Figure 2.10   WordStar's editing screen.

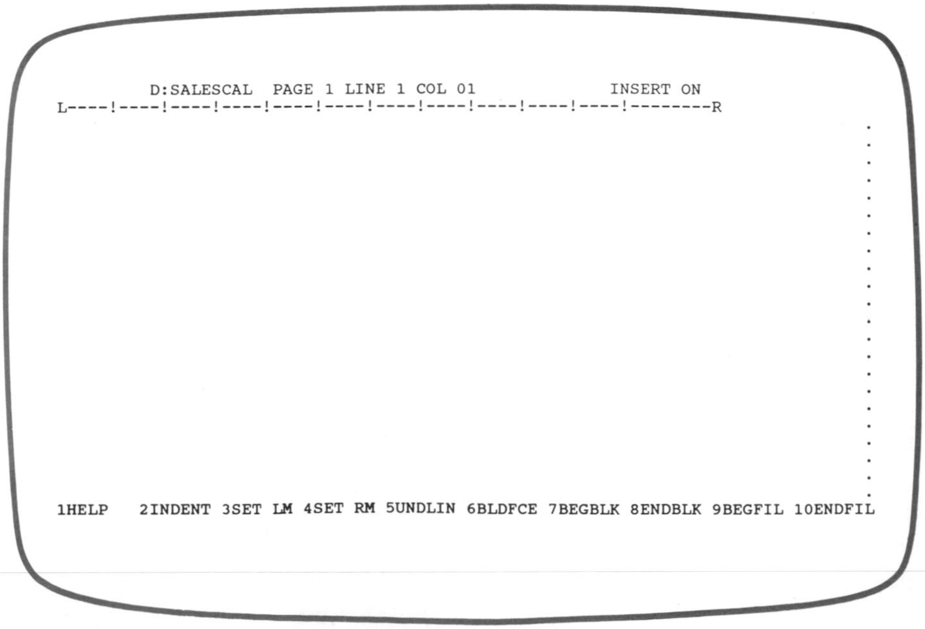

```
        D:SALESCAL  PAGE 1 LINE 1 COL 01             INSERT ON
  L----!----!----!----!----!----!----!----!----!----!--------R           .
                                                                          .
                                                                          .
                                                                          .
                                                                          .
                                                                          .
                                                                          .
                                                                          .
                                                                          .
                                                                          .
                                                                          .
                                                                          .
                                                                          .
                                                                          .
                                                                          .
                                                                          .
                                                                          .
                                                                          .
                                                                          .
     1HELP    2INDENT 3SET LM 4SET RM 5UNDLIN 6BLDFCE 7BEGBLK 8ENDBLK 9BEGFIL 10ENDFIL
```

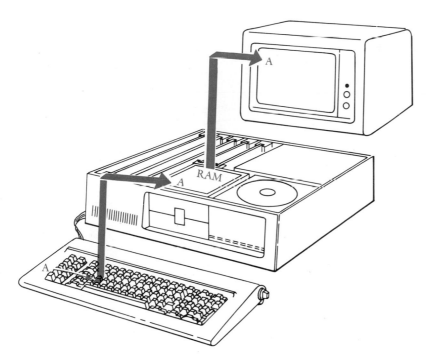

Figure 2.11 Entered text is displayed on a screen and stored in RAM.

In response, the program displays a new command screen with a split screen, as shown in Figure 2.10. At the top of the screen is a summary of the commands you can use to edit your letter (delete a word, move to the end of the letter, move to the next line, insert a standard paragraph already stored on disk, and so forth). Your letter will appear in the bottom portion of the screen.

You may now begin to type your letter. As you type, the characters are displayed on the screen and are also stored in RAM. This process is illustrated in Figure 2.11. The WordStar program allows you to correct errors, add or delete text, change the page layout, and so forth. With each change in the letter, the screen (and the copy in RAM) is updated. You would also at this point include a command to obtain the appropriate name and address from a data file. These commands will be executed later, as part of the printing process.

When you are finished with your letter, you may give a command to save it on a secondary storage device, as shown in Figure 2.12. The letter will thus be copied from RAM to the diskette or hard disk you specify. At a later time, you may recall the letter from secondary storage for further editing or for printing. When you give the command to print the letter, WordStar obtains a name and an address from the designated data file, inserts them onto the letter and then transmits a copy of the letter from RAM

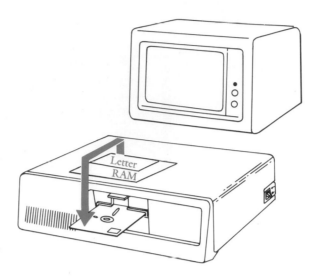

Figure 2.12 Saving a letter on a secondary storage device.

to the printer. The program also sends control codes to the printer that will format the letter (its margin widths, line spacing, and so forth) exactly the way you specify. Figure 2.13 shows a letter being printed.

After printing the letter, WordStar obtains a second name and address from the data file and prints the letter again, this time using the new name and address. The entire sequence is repeated for each of the 1,000 names in the data file. After all the printing is finished, the command screen shown in Figure 2.9 is redisplayed. WordStar is ready to accept a new command (for example, to prepare a new letter).

Figure 2.13 Printing a letter.

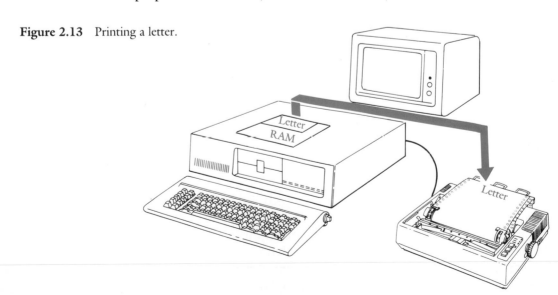

Step 4: Exiting the Application Program

When you are finished with your letters, you must give a command to end the program. This is done by typing X (for EXIT) from the main menu. WordStar then relinquishes control of the microcomputer and turns it over to a program called the **command processor** (sometimes called the **system monitor**). This program simply sits and waits for new instructions (such as the command to run another program).

A Session with a Microcomputer

The sequence of four steps that has just been illustrated may be repeated with a number of different programs at a single session at the computer. For example, after ending the word-processing session, you might use a graphics program to draw some diagrams for a presentation. You might then return to the word-processing program to make some alterations in the letter you previously entered. In conclusion, you might use a spreadsheet to work out some financial projections.

Section 2.4: Test Your Understanding

The questions below refer to the letter used in the example in Section 2.4.

1. Explain the role of hardware in preparing the letter.
2. Explain the role of software in preparing the letter.
3. What role did the user play in preparing the letter?
4. Identify the data used in connection with the word-processing program.
5. What manipulations of data were performed by the word-processing program?
6. What input operations were performed by the word-processing program?
7. What output operations were performed by the word-processing program?

KEY TERMS

hardware	user	short-term memory
software	random access memory (RAM)	high-speed
data	primary memory	memory

read-only memory (ROM)   software   personal computer
secondary storage   data   user interface
diskette drive   computer program   human interface
diskette   alphanumeric data   batch processing
hard disk drive   numeric data   user-friendly
hard disk   alpha data   graphics interface
monitor   graphics data   icon
screen   program input   mouse
printer   program output   command processor
input-output (I/O) device   stored program concept system monitor
peripheral device   interactive program
peripheral   personal computing

CHAPTER REVIEW QUESTIONS

1. Explain the steps needed to solve a problem that uses an application program.
2. What devices are available for program input?
3. Explain why most early microcomputer programs were not user-friendly.
4. What is a mouse?
5. Explain how a graphics interface can be used to make programs more user-friendly.
6. What are some consequences of a program that is not user-friendly?
7. What are some typical data manipulations performed by software?

DISCUSSION QUESTIONS

1. In recent years, monitors that produce green or amber images have become popular. What does the use of such monitors have to do with user-friendliness?
2. Discuss some aspects of computer equipment design that might contribute to its user-friendliness.

3 Microcomputer Hardware

The Perfect Problem-Solving Tool

At Pfizer, scientific equipment has come a long way from the laboratories of the mid-nineteenth century. Pfizer, a multinational corporation whose drug products are well known, uses the most modern technology available.

Today that includes microcomputers. Each microcomputer is tailored to the needs of the employee who uses it.

Dr. Roger Sachs, Pfizer's vice president of regulatory affairs and clinical safety, uses a Compaq Deskpro 286, a high-speed IBM compatible. Sachs's job is to monitor and distribute drug safety information, to make sure others in the company get the latest data, and to ensure that company products meet Food and Drug Administration regulations. Sachs reads and assimilates countless reports and data tabulations, which requires fast machinery. "The Compaq is important to my job because, first of all, it's fast," Sachs says. They often need results quickly.

Sachs's Compaq has a 30-megabyte hard disk and two diskette drives. This large chunk of added memory gives him additional speed in handling information, or in transferring data from diskettes. "The hard disk transfers information much faster than the floppy drive does," Sachs says.

Other components of Sachs's computer system are a color monitor, on which he interprets color-coded spreadsheets, and a high-quality dot-matrix printer, the speed of which he also finds essential. Rather than edit a document onscreen, he prefers to edit on paper. With his microcomputer system, he can spit out rough drafts quickly for editing and finalizing.

Finally, Sachs's computer is connected to a centralized company modem, which means he has access to data kept on a large corporate mainframe. He can send mainframe data to his Compaq for more convenient examination or manipulation. For example, if he wants to examine the data in one of the many drug-safety related databases stored on the mainframe, Sachs transfers the file via modem to his Compaq and examines it in his office, saving delays in locating paper files or obtaining a computer printout from a corporate management information department.

The hookup to a company modem also allows Sachs to send and receive messages (called electronic mail) through his microcomputer. He sees electronic mail as useful and convenient, because it has cut out a lot of "telephone tag" with his colleagues. Using his microcomputer, Sachs can can be sure his message gets to the right person.

Hardware + software +
data + the user =
problem solution.

A S A MICROCOMPUTER USER , you may think that you don't need to be concerned with hardware, just as you don't need to know how an internal combustion engine works to drive a car. In a limited sense this analogy applies. However, you need to know something about your car's operation in order to maintain it properly, to drive it safely, and to recognize signs of trouble. In a similar vein, you should familiarize yourself with the basics of what goes on "under the hood" of a microcomputer. This knowledge can help you understand how your application programs work, what they can do, and how to keep yourself and your microcomputer out of trouble.

You may one day want to put together a microcomputer system for use at home. Such a home system could work out a personal budget for you or help you to do your taxes. The applications you intend to use will affect your choice of hardware. Similarly, when you put together a microcomputer system for office use, you will need to consider specific applications so that you purchase the best hardware to help you do the job. Some problems will be unique to your particular business; others will be more universal.

In any event, when you are confronted with a task or problem, you must first analyze all the components of the problem-solving equation, which we introduced earlier.

The first component of the equation is hardware. This consists of:

- the processing unit
- RAM
- the keyboard
- the monitor
- secondary storage
- the printer

Figure 3.1 shows the hardware in a microcomputer system and its interconnections. This chapter will discuss each part of the microcomputer system in detail, particularly its function and availability, and how it works.

3.1 The Processing Unit and RAM

The processing unit and RAM are the most fundamental components of a microcomputer system. They are also the most mysterious, since they consist of complex electronic circuits that are intelligible

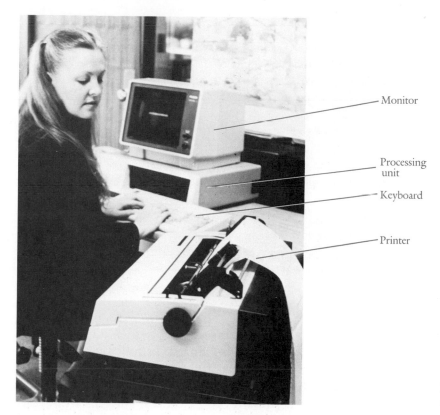

Monitor

Processing
unit

Keyboard

Printer

Figure 3.1 The hardware of
a microcomputer system.

only to someone with a technical background. However, understanding how these circuits operate is quite simple.

The Processing Unit

The **processing unit** consists of the circuitry necessary to manipulate
data and to control the various components of the system. The
processing unit, hidden from view within a case, usually consists
of a number of semiconductor chips mounted on a single **circuit
board** (often called the **mother board** or the **system board**).
Figure 3.2 shows the mother board of the IBM PC and its main
parts, namely

- the central processing unit (CPU)
- the bus
- the system clock
- the expansion slots
- the expansion boards
- read-only memory (ROM)
- random access memory (RAM)

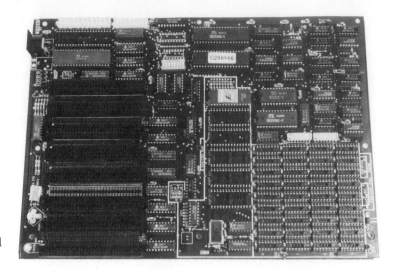

Figure 3.2   The mother board of the IBM PC.

The circuitry in the processing unit is incredibly complex. Thanks to the microminiaturization made possible by semiconductor technology, each chip on a typical mother board contains tens of thousands—or hundreds of thousands—of transistors. The lines engraved on the mother board carry electrical currents from place to place on the board. Contrast today's technology with that of the 1950s, when the amount of circuitry contained on the mother board would have taken up a large room.

Let's look at the function of each part of the mother board.

The Central Processing Unit. If you picture a microcomputer system as a human being, the **Central Processing Unit, CPU** would represent the "brain." The CPU is responsible for carrying out program instructions. It is contained in a single semiconductor chip called a **microprocessor**. As is true with different models of automobiles, different types of microprocessors vary widely in their capabilities. In the IBM PC, for example, the microprocessor is an Intel 8088 chip, shown in Figure 3.2; in the Apple Macintosh it is a Motorola 68000.

The Bus. If we think of the CPU as the brain, then the **bus** of a microcomputer can be called its "nervous system." An electronic pathway connecting all of the important components of the processing unit, the bus allows information to be passed between the components, from the central processing unit to RAM or from RAM to the disk drives, and so forth. Referring again to Figure

3.2, you can see the bus and the expansion slots of an IBM PC and how they fit on the mother board.

The System Clock. The **system clock**, a crystal that vibrates at a frequency of several million times per second, synchronizes the internal operations of the processing unit. The clock frequency sets the "beat" at which operations within the computer take place, much as a metronome sets the pace for a musician. All operations take a certain number of full clock beats, never fractions of a clock beat. The clock speed varies from system to system. In an IBM PC, the clock frequency is 4.77 megahertz, or 4.77 million beats per second. (Hertz is a unit of frequency measure, with one Hertz equaling one cycle per second.) In a Compaq Deskpro, the clock is dual-speed and can be set to run at either 6 or 8 megahertz. Higher clock speeds of 10 to 20 megahertz will probably be used in future microcomputers.

The Expansion Slots and the Expansion Boards. Optional devices can be connected to most microcomputers. You can add disk drives, hard disks, and a variety of other components. Of course, each added device comes with its own circuitry, which must mesh with the circuitry of the microcomputer. Usually, the circuitry for a device is contained on an **expansion board** (also called a **controller card** or **interface card**), which plugs into one of the expansion slots in the processing unit. Some expansion boards contain additional memory, whereas others provide circuitry to control system devices such as floppy disk drives, hard disks, printers, monitors, or communications devices. Some expansion boards combine a number of different functions, so that you may add a number of devices to your system using a single expansion slot.

The optional device is connected to the expansion board with a cable. The microcomputer operates the device by sending signals along the bus to the circuit card, which then sends the appropriate commands to the device. Figure 3.3 illustrates an expansion board for a hard disk.

RAM

As previously mentioned, RAM is used to store the program you are running and the data you are manipulating at the current moment. In most microcomputers, a certain amount of RAM is located on the mother board. The precise amount varies with the brand and model of computer.

As microcomputer programs become more complex, they require ever increasing quantities of RAM in order to run. Many

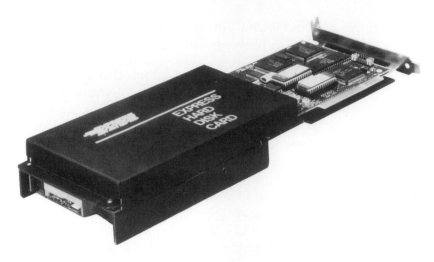

Figure **3.3** An expansion board for a hard disk.

of the application programs you will be using require more RAM than fit on the motherboard. To use such programs, you will need to add RAM contained on memory expansion cards.

Binary Numbers. All information, including programs and data, to be stored in a computer is converted to **binary numbers**, which consist of the numbers 0 and 1 in a limitless variety of sequences. Here are some examples of binary numbers and their decimal equivalents:

Binary number	Decimal equivalent
101	5
1101	13
10011001	153
00001111010101010	7850

Circuit designers use binary numbers because it is easy to build circuits to manipulate such numbers. In this circuitry, the presence of an electrical current is indicated by a 1 and the absence of current is indicated by a 0.

A single binary digit (a 0 or a 1) is called a **bit**. A sequence of eight binary digits (eight bits) is called a **byte**. Here are some examples of bytes.

00001111
10101101
11110011
11111111

In decimal terms, a byte represents a number between (and including) 0 and 255. For instance, 00000000 represents the decimal number 0, 10101101 represents the decimal number 173, and 11111111 represents the decimal number 255. Inside a microcomputer, most binary manipulations are performed on bytes or sequences of bytes because most microprocessors are built to handle byte-sized pieces of data.

Measuring Memory. The size of memory (RAM or secondary) is measured in bytes. You might expect computer memories to come in "round numbers" such as 1,000 bytes or 500,000 bytes. Such assumptions are the result of prejudices that have developed from years of working with the decimal system. In computer work, most important sizes are related to powers of 2. The closest power of 2 to 1,000 is 2 to the 10th power, or 1024. Computer memories are measured as multiples of 1024 bytes. This amount of memory is usually denoted as 1K from the Greek "kilo," which means thousand. Here are some common memory sizes expressed in K and their equivalents in bytes.

$$64K = 64 \times 1024 \text{ bytes} = 65,536 \text{ bytes}$$
$$256K = 256 \times 1024 \text{ bytes} = 262,144 \text{ bytes}$$
$$512K = 512 \times 1024 \text{ bytes} = 524,288 \text{ bytes}$$
$$1024K = 1024 \times 1024 \text{ bytes} = 1,048,576 \text{ bytes}$$

The last quantity of memory, 1024K, is referred to as a **megabyte**. These numbers are all powers of 2, as you can see in Table 3.1. The number of bytes of RAM is either a power of 2 or a low multiple of a power of 2 (say, $3 \times 2^{16} = 3 \times 64K = 192K$).

The first microcomputers had 4K of RAM, which was expandable in 4K increments. By 1980, the typical microcomputer

Table 3.1 Powers of 2

n	2^n	n	2^n
0	1	9	512
1	2	10	1024
2	4	11	2048
3	8	12	4096
4	16	13	8192
5	32	14	16,384
6	64	15	32,768
7	128	16	65,536
8	256		

contained 16K of RAM, expandable to 64K. When IBM released its personal computer in 1981, the minimum memory was 16K with a potential expansion to 576K. This upper limit was raised to 640K about a year later. Newer microcomputers, such as the Compaq Deskpro 286, can have as much as 8 megabytes (or 8 × 1,048,576 bytes) of RAM.

Microcomputer users are equipping their machines with increasing quantities of RAM. A 1985 survey of business users revealed that the average amount of RAM in corporate microcomputers was 419K.

The increase in available RAM has stemmed from two factors. First, programs have become more complex and require more RAM to run. Second, RAM has experienced dramatic price declines due to both improved manufacturing technology and intense competition among semiconductor manufacturers. The cost of 64K of RAM was about $100 in 1981; in 1986 it was under $4.

RAM and Application Software. A program is stored in RAM while it is being executed. Depending on the program, different amounts of RAM are required. The word processor WordStar requires only 64K of RAM to run. However, the more complex word processor Word requires 348K. The amount of RAM a program requires is an important consideration (but not the only one) in determining whether you can run it on your microcomputer.

Representing Data in Memory. As has already been mentioned, all data within the computer, both numeric and text, are represented in binary form. When we type data into the computer's memory, we use our own language—letters, digits, punctuation marks, and symbols—to express the data. The computer translates our language into binary form so that it can perform data manipulations. When outputting data, binary numbers are translated back into standard decimal numbers and text.

There are many schemes for representing numeric data in binary form. As an application user, it is not usually necessary for you to know or to care about how this is done. Your only concern should be that your application programs can accept numeric data in standard decimal form and perform the usual arithmetic operations. However, if you can understand how a microcomputer represents text internally, it will help you to understand why word processors and other text manipulation programs work the way they do.

Microcomputers use a byte to store a single character. There are about 2,000 characters in a double-spaced, typewritten page, which means that 64K bytes of RAM are enough memory to store about 32 pages of text. Since a byte can have 256 different values (from 0 to 255), there are 256 different characters that can be represented by the various byte values—more than enough characters to represent all of the standard symbols on a typewriter with quite a bit of room to spare.

Virtually all microcomputers use the **ASCII system** (the American Standard Code for Information Interchange) to represent characters as bytes. In this system, each character is assigned a particular byte, called its **ASCII code**. For instance, the letter **A** is assigned the byte 65 (or rather its binary equivalent, which is 10000001); the letter **B** is assigned the byte 66 (or, in binary, 10000010); the symbol (is assigned the byte 40 (or, in binary, 00101000).

H 41

H 40 in EBCDIC

Table 3.2 lists all ASCII codes from 32 to 128 and their corresponding characters. ASCII codes 0 through 31 correspond to various control characters, such as a line feed that tells the printer to start a new line, or a form feed that tells the printer to start a new page.

Only the ASCII codes 0 through 127 are universally agreed-upon. Most microcomputers use ASCII codes 128 through 255 to represent additional characters, but there is no universal agreement on which character each code represents. The character set used by IBM in its microcomputers is very popular. It is shown in Table 3.3.

Memory Addresses. RAM can be thought of as a sequence of boxes, with each box capable of storing a single byte. Each box is called a **memory location** and is identified by an **address**, which tells the computer its location within RAM. The diagram in Figure 3.4 illustrates this concept.

Memory Address	Contents
15842	1111 1111
15843	0000 1011
15844	1011 0001
15845	1110 0000
15846	1100 0001
15847	0110 0010

Figure 3.4   Memory addresses and memory locations.

The CPU uses addresses to read and write data into memory locations. A typical instruction might tell the CPU to write the byte 00001111 into the memory location number 5781, as shown in Figure 3.5. Don't confuse the address of a memory location

10100110

Table 3.2 ASCII codes for standard characters

ASCII value	Character	ASCII value	Character	ASCII value	Character
032	(space)	064	@	096	`
033	!	065	A	097	a
034	"	066	B	098	b
035	#	067	C	099	c
036	$	068	D	100	d
037	%	069	E	101	e
038	&	070	F	102	f
039	'	071	G	103	g
040	(	072	H	104	h
041	)	073	I	105	i
042	*	074	J	106	j
043	+	075	K	107	k
044	'	076	L	108	l
045	-	077	M	109	m
046	.	078	N	110	n
047	/	079	O	111	o
048	0	080	P	112	p
049	1	081	Q	113	q
050	2	082	R	114	r
051	3	083	S	115	s
052	4	084	T	116	t
053	5	085	U	117	u
054	6	086	V	118	v
055	7	087	W	119	w
056	8	088	X	120	x
057	9	089	Y	121	y
058	:	090	Z	122	z
059	;	091	[	123	{
060	<	092	\	124	¦
061	=	093	]	125	}
062	>	094	∧	126	~
063	?	095	—	127	△

Courtesy of International Business Machines Corporation.

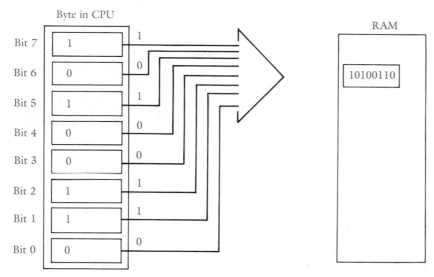

Figure 3.5 Writing a location in memory.

with its contents. In the above example, 5781 is the address specifying where in RAM the byte is located. The contents of the memory location (that is, the data stored there) is the byte 00001111. Similarly, you can read the contents of the CPU's internal storage locations from a specific location in memory.

In running a program, the CPU continuously reads and writes memory locations in RAM. For example, if you are using a word-processing program to prepare a document, the program keeps a copy of the document in RAM. As you type portions of the document, they are written to RAM and your monitor. The contents of RAM are changed to reflect changes you make in editing the document. Moreover, as you move through the document, the program updates the text on the monitor by reading the contents of the document from RAM. Typically, a word processor keeps only 15–50 pages of a document in RAM at a time. Any parts of a document that cannot be fitted into RAM are kept in secondary storage, and are copied into RAM as they are needed for editing.

As an application programmer, you don't need to keep track of how a program uses RAM or specific memory addresses. That's automatically taken care of by the program. But, as usual, it helps to have some idea of what is going on "under the hood."

The Volatility of RAM. RAM is **volatile**. This means that RAM is erased as soon as the computer's power is turned off. This might not seem like much of a problem, but consider that even a

Table 3.3 IBM character set for ASCII codes 128 through 255

ASCII value	Character	ASCII value	Character	ASCII value	Character	ASCII value	Character
128	Ç	166	a̱	204	╠	242	≥
129	ü	167	o̱	205	═	243	≤
130	é	168	¿	206	╬	244	⌠
131	â	169	⌐	207	╧	245	⌡
132	ä	170	¬	208	╨	246	÷
133	à	171	½	209	╤	247	≈
134	å	172	¼	210	╥	248	°
135	ç	173	¡	211	╙	249	•
136	ê	174	«	212	╘	250	·
137	ë	175	»	213	╒	251	√
138	è	176	░	214	╓	252	ⁿ
139	ï	177	▒	215	╫	253	²
140	î	178	▓	216	╪	254	■
141	ì	179	│	217	┘	255	(blank 'FF')
142	Ä	180	┤	218	┐		
143	Å	181	╡	219	█		
144	É	182	╢	220	▄		
145	œ	183	╖	221	▌		
146	Æ	184	╕	222	▐		
147	ô	185	╣	223	▀		
148	ö	186	║	224	α		
149	ò	187	╗	225	β		
150	û	188	╝	226	Γ		
151	ù	189	╜	227	π		
152	ÿ	190	╛	228	Σ		
153	Ö	191	┐	229	σ		
154	Ü	192	└	230	μ		
155	¢	193	┴	231	τ		
156	£	194	┬	232	Φ		
157	¥	195	├	233	Θ		
158	Pts	196	─	234	Ω		
159	ƒ	197	┼	235	δ		
160	á	198	╞	236	∞		
161	í	199	╟	237	∅		
162	ó	200	╚	238	ε		
163	ú	201	╔	239	∩		
164	ñ	202	╩	240	≡		
165	Ñ	203	╦	241	±		

Courtesy of International Business Machines Corporation.

momentary power outage (during a thunderstorm or if someone trips over the power cord) can be enough to erase RAM (along with the many hours of work it took you to create the data in it).

Because RAM is volatile, it is good practice to regularly save any data in RAM (say, every 15 minutes) on either disk or hard disk. Moreover, in installations where losing even an hour's worth of data is intolerable, it is common to install uninterruptible power sources that supply battery-generated power within thousandths of a second after the regular power supply is interrupted.

Don't lose your data; save your files every 15 minutes.

Section 3.1: Test Your Understanding

1. List the main components of the processing unit.
2. Explain the function of the central processing unit.
3. Why does a microcomputer need a system clock?
4. What is an expansion slot? What is its function?
5. Give three examples of specific expansion cards.
6. True or false: Microcomputers use the decimal system to work with numbers. Explain your answer.
7. What are ASCII codes? Why are they used?
8. Explain the difference between a bit and a byte.
9. Explain the difference between a memory location and its contents.
10. What does it mean to say that RAM is volatile?
11. How many bits are in 64K of RAM?
12. How many bytes are in 192K?

3.2 The Monitor and the Keyboard

Two of the most prominent components of a microcomputer are the monitor and the keyboard. As you learned in Chapter 2, the keyboard is an input device, a mechanism through which you enter data directly to the microcomputer. The monitor, which resembles a TV screen, acts as an output device because it displays on its screen the data you entered via the keyboard. The monitor also allows you to display output data, such as the computer's response to your input. (Monitors are also referred to as video displays, terminals, CRTs, and simply screens. For our discussion we will refer to them as monitors.)

The Monitor

The **monitor** of a microcomputer system resembles a television set. All monitors share one important feature: they allow display of text output. However, there are a variety of monitor types that introduce additional features. This section surveys the various types of monitors and describes the advantages and disadvantages of each.

Monitor Types. Computers use many different types of monitors, depending on the application and the particular display requirements.

Monochrome monitors are capable of displaying only a single color. Although older monitors use white lettering on a black background, studies of human factors have shown that green or amber letters on a black background lead to much less eyestrain when viewed for long periods of time. Accordingly, most monochrome monitors being manufactured today are of this type—either green or amber screens.

A color monitor is capable of displaying many colors. The least expensive color monitors accept a "composite signal" from the processing unit. In these composite monitors, the colors are premixed in much the same fashion as they are in a television set. The more expensive color monitors are the RGB (Red-Green-Blue) monitors, so-called because they use three colors—red, green, and blue—as a basis for all blended colors.

Color can be used in many clever ways to call attention to data and to provide a more user-friendly interface. However, color monitors can be hard on the eyes when used for long periods of time.

Display Adapter Cards. A monitor is managed by video controller circuitry within the processing unit. In some microcomputers, such as the Macintosh, the video controller circuitry is found on the mother board. This design limits the type of display to one that can work only with the computer manufacturer's circuitry. In other microcomputers, including the IBM PC and most of its compatibles, the video controller circuitry is placed on an expansion card, which is called a **display adapter card**. An example is illustrated in Figure 3.6. This design is very flexible since it does not fix in advance the type of monitor you must use. It also allows you to update your computer to use more advanced monitors as they become available.

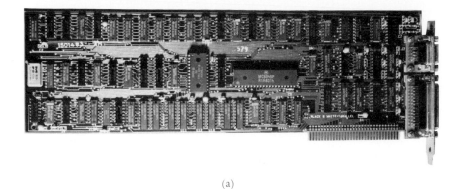

(a)

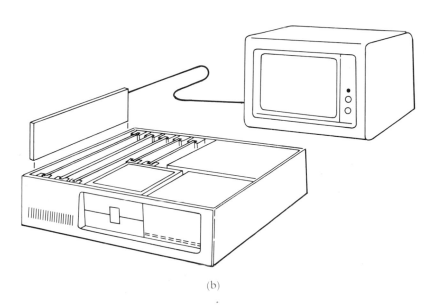

(b)

Figure 3.6 (a) A display adapter card (b) connected to a microcomputer.

To demonstrate this flexibility, let's look at the four video display adapter cards IBM offers.

1. *Monochrome display adapter*. This adapter card allows display of high-resolution text on monochrome monitors. The displayed text features clear, crisp letters. However, this adapter does not allow you to display graphics.

2. *Color/graphics adapter*. This adapter card supports color monitors, either RGB or composite. It allows display of up to four colors at time. It supports both text and graphics, but its letters do not have the high quality produced by monochrome display adapters.

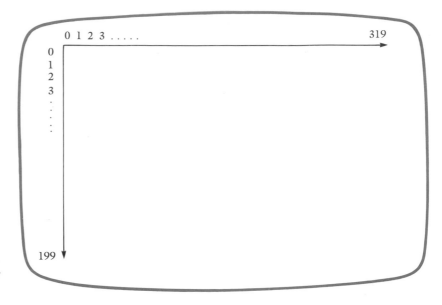

Figure 3.7 The monitor image is made up of a rectangular grid of pixels.

3. *Extended graphics adapter (EGA)*. This adapter provides both high-quality monochrome text and graphics output and high-quality color text and graphics output in 16 colors.
4. *Professional graphics adapter*. This adapter provides extremely high-quality color text and graphics output and is suitable for demanding scientific and engineering applications, such as computer-aided design.

In addition to these adapters from IBM, there are many display adapters available from other manufacturers for use in the IBM PC and its compatibles. Many of these third-party display adapters can function as either a monochrome or a color/graphics adapter.

Screen Resolution. Monitors produce images as collections of dots. The individual dots are called **pixels** (which is short for picture elements). The monitor image is divided into a rectangular grid of pixels, as illustrated in Figure 3.7. The size of the grid is called the **screen resolution**. The capabilities of a particular display adapter determine the possible screen resolutions. Some display adapters permit only a single resolution, such as that of the Macintosh. Others allow for several different resolutions. For example, IBM's color/graphics adapter allows screen resolutions of 200 rows by 640 columns of pixels (**high-resolution mode**) and 200 rows by 320 columns of pixels (**medium-resolution mode**).

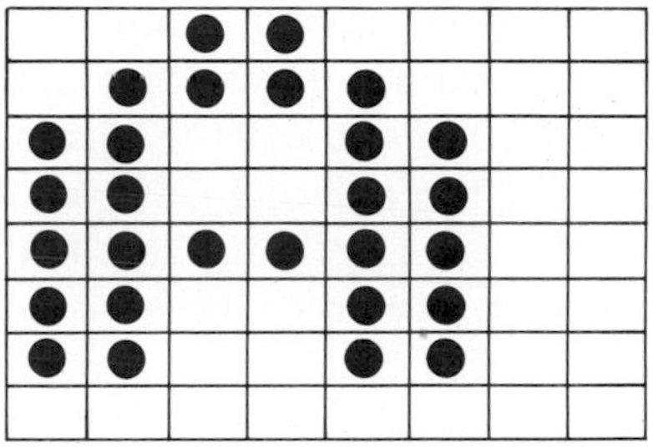

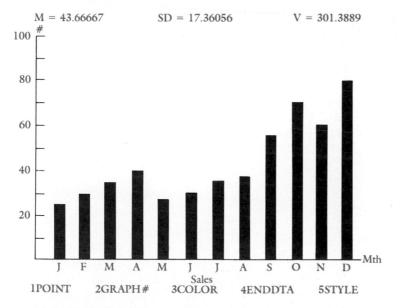

Figure 3.8 The letter "A" constructed with pixels.

All data, text, or graphics displayed on a monitor are composed of pixels. Figure 3.8 shows the letter "A" constructed with pixels. Figure 3.9 demonstrates how a bar chart may be constructed with pixels. These images are enlarged so you can see the individual pixels, which you cannot easily distinguish when you look at an image on your monitor.

The higher the screen resolution, the higher the quality of the display. In higher resolutions, letters appear crisper and graphics appear clearer. A display adapter with higher-resolution is more complex and hence more costly than a lower-resolution adapter (all other features being equal). However, a higher resolution monitor produces clearer, crisper images that are easier to read.

M = 43.66667   SD = 17.36056   V = 301.3889

Figure 3.9 A bar chart constructed with pixels.

Display Modes Each display adapter offers one or more **display modes** that control the nature of data that can be displayed (text and/or graphics), the resolution, and the allowable colors.

The simplest mode, the one offered by all display adapters, is **text mode**, the mode for displaying standard text. Text mode divides the screen into a certain number of lines, with each line divided into a fixed number of columns. You can display a single character at each row-column position. A typical arrangement is 25 rows and 40 or 80 columns.

The resolution in text mode determines how many pixels are used for each character. For instance, if the resolution is 350×720 and there are 25 lines of 80 characters each, then each character is displayed in a rectangular grid $350/25 = 14$ pixels high and $720/80 = 9$ pixels wide. If the resolution is 320×200 and there are 25 lines of 80 characters each, then each character is displayed in a rectangular grid that is $200/25 = 8$ pixels high and $640/80 = 8$ pixels high. Naturally, the higher the resolution, the higher the quality of the characters. Some text display modes allow a variety of colors, but others allow only two-color (monochrome) characters.

An alternative to the text display mode is the **graphics mode**, which is provided by many display adapters. In a graphics mode, the program is given control of all the pixels of the screen. Each pixel can be turned on or off and, depending on the mode, can be made to display a pixel in any one of a number of colors.

Table 3.4 summarizes the display modes provided by the various display adapters for the IBM PC.

Find out which display adapter is used in your computer. It is often necessary to install software that works with your particular display adapter, usually by running an installation program in which

Programs using graphics may require a special display adapter.

Table 3.4   Display modes for various IBM PC display adapters

Display Adapter Type	Display Modes
Monochrome	Text only
Color/graphics	Text
	320×200 4-color graphics
	640×200 2-color graphics
Enhanced graphics	Text
	320×200 4-color graphics
	640×200 2-color grpahics
	640×350 16-color graphics
	640×350 monochrome graphics

Figure 3.10   The keyboard of the IBM PC.

you select a display adapter from a menu of choices. If your display adapter is not listed or if it is not compatible with one listed, you may not be able to run the program on your machine.

The display adapters listed in an installation program are determined by the display requirements of the program. For instance, the program may need to display graphics, in which case it can be used only with a display adapter having graphics display modes. This would rule out the IBM monochrome display adapter, for example. Once you install a program for a display adapter, you can pretty much forget about display adapters and display modes. The program will automatically select display modes as it runs.

The Keyboard

The **keyboard** of a microcomputer resembles a typewriter keyboard. One difference is that the keystrokes appear on a monitor instead of on paper. Actually, the keyboard of a microcomputer is a high-tech wonder all its own. Most keyboards contain their own microprocessors to help decode the keystrokes and to hold keystrokes until the processor unit reads them.

As a user, you will spend many hours with your microcomputer keyboard. Figure 3.10 will acquaint you with a typical keyboard. Refer to it as you read this section.

You can think of your keyboard as a typewriter keyboard, but keep in mind the following important differences:

1. The letter el (l) and the number one (1) are typed with two different keys. On many typewriter keyboards, you are forced to use the lowercase el as the numeral one. This is not true on a microcomputer keyboard. A computer cannot tolerate any ambiguities. When it processes digits and letters, the computer must know whether you meant to type an el or a one. To

Use the numeral one (1) when indicating a number, and the letter el (l) when indicating a letter. These characters are not interchangeable and the computer will not differentiate between them.

resolve any potential ambiguity, two different keys are provided.

2. A microcomputer keyboard contains symbols not found on
most typewriters, such as

These symbols are part of the standard ASCII character set
that you will find useful in computer work.

3. Most microcomputer keyboards have **cursor motion keys** that
you use to direct the cursor. The cursor is the symbol on the
screen which is used to indicate position of the next typed
character. These keys are usually designated with arrows
indicating the direction of cursor motion, either left, right, up,
or down.

4. Many microcomputer keyboards have **function keys**. These
programmable keys can be defined within a program. For
example, a word processor program may define function key
1 as the command "Save the current file," function key 2 as
the command "Edit a new file," and so forth. The number of
function keys varies with the keyboard.

5. Microcomputer keyboards have a number of keys that generate
control signals to the computer. The most important of these
is the key marked **ENTER** or **RETURN** (sometimes indicated
by a bent left arrow). This key is normally used to indicate
the end of a line. Also, after you type a command or a data
input, you must press <ENTER/RETURN> to tell the
computer that the line is complete. Before pressing <ENTER/
RETURN>, you may use the **BACKSPACE key** to correct
all or part of the line. By backspacing over a character you
erase it. You may backspace over all or part of a line and then
replace the erased characters with corrected ones. (Throughout
this book, words in brackets (⟨⟩) refer to a key or a combination
of keys that execute a command.)

6. The **ESCAPE key** sends a particular control signal to the
computer. Many programs use the ESCAPE key to tell the
computer to cancel the current command.

7. Microcomputer keyboards usually have one or more **control
keys** that are used in connection with other keys. For instance,
the IBM PC and compatibles have keyboards with **CONTROL**
(marked CTRL on some keyboards) and **ALTERNATE**

(usually marked ALT) **keys**. These keys are used in combination with other keys to generate control key combinations. For example, to generate the combination <CONTROL-C>, you hold down <CONTROL> and press <C>.

8. Some microcomputer keyboards feature **numeric keypads** that resemble the key layout of a calculator. Such keypads facilitate entering numeric information into programs such as spreadsheets. Note that the numeric keypad and the cursor motion keys share the same keys on the keyboard shown in Figure 3.10. The two functions of the keys are shifted using the **NUMLOCK key**. Press <NUMLOCK> to use the keypad as a calculator and press it again to use the cursor motion keys.

Section 3.2: *Test Your Understanding*

1. Explain why some monochrome screens have green or amber characters.
2. List some applications in which a color monitor would be superior to a monochrome monitor.
3. What is the difference between a text mode and a graphics mode?
4. What is a pixel?
5. What is the resolution of a display?
6. How is the position of the next character to be typed indicated?
7. What happens if a display screen fills up during an input operation?
8. What is the function of the ENTER/RETURN key?
9. What are the function keys?
10. Give two examples of how function keys might be used in a word-processing program.
11. What is a numeric keypad? What types of program are most likely to use a numeric keypad?

3.3 Secondary Storage—Diskettes

Since RAM is erased when the power is turned off, a microcomputer must have a means for long-term storage of data and programs. The most common storage device is the **disk drive**.

Figure 3.11   A diskette drive.

How a Disk Drive Works

A disk drive reads and writes data onto flexible disks called **floppy diskettes**. A disk drive consists of a device to hold the diskette, a motor to rotate the diskette, and electronics to read and write on the diskette; these components are shown in Figure 3.11. A disk drive is small enough to fit into the same cabinet as the processor unit. In fact, some recent models of half-height disk drives are so small that as many as four disk drives can fit into a typical microcomputer cabinet.

A disk drive can access a single diskette at a time. The diskette is inserted through a slot in the front of the drive. Flipping the lever on the drive door activates a spindle that grabs the diskette and holds it so that the diskette can spin without slipping. To read and write on the diskette, the disk drive rotates the diskette at about 300 revolutions per minute.

A disk drive reads data from and writes data to a diskette via **read/write heads** that are mounted on arms that allow the heads to move radially, as shown in Figure 3.12. To read or write on a specific position on the diskette, the drive moves the read/write head radially to the proper position. The drive then waits for the data to rotate under the read/write head. The radial positioning of the read/write head is called a **seek operation**. The rotation of the data under the read/write head is called a **search operation**. Both a seek and a search are required to read or to write to a diskette.

Some disk drives are capable of reading and writing on only one side of a diskette. Such drives are said to be **single-sided**. Most newer disk drives are **double-sided**, which means they are capable of reading and writing on both sides of a diskette and they have two read/write heads, one for each side of the diskette. The double-sided diskettes are, of course, preferable since they hold twice as much data.

A disk drive is managed by controller circuitry normally found on an adapter card plugged into one of the expansion slots. One controller card is usually sufficient to manage as many as four disk drives.

Most microcomputers have at least one disk drive. Even in systems using a hard disk (discussed later in this chapter), a disk drive reads programs that are purchased on floppy diskettes, and copies programs onto a hard disk. Many microcomputer systems have two or more disk drives, which allows the program to access data on more than one disk and to copy data from one disk to another without having to switch diskettes. (Switching diskettes back and forth with only one drive can be a genuine nuisance, especially if you must do it often.)

Disk drives, like most other microcomputer components, have improved rapidly in recent years. Early disk drives used 8-inch-diameter diskettes. Recent technology allows drives to record information more densely, so that now $5\frac{1}{4}$-inch and $3\frac{1}{2}$-inch diskettes can contain the same amount of (and even more) information. Smaller diskettes make more efficient use of storage space. Moreover,

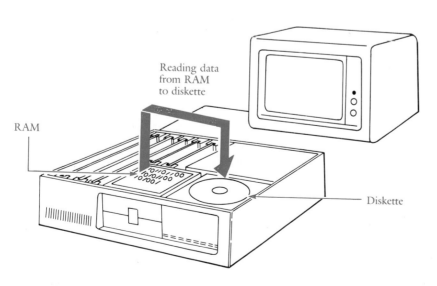

Reading data
from RAM
to diskette

RAM

Diskette

Figure 3.12 Reading and writing data on a diskette.

since they require the read/write heads to travel smaller distances, they generally allow for faster data access.

Disk drives cost about $500 in 1980. By 1985, their price dropped below $100. If a disk drive breaks, it is now cheaper to buy a new one and discard the old one, considering the high cost of repairs and technical labor.

About Diskettes

A diskette resembles a phonograph record. It consists of a circular piece of mylar plastic that rotates in a jacket. This mylar plastic is covered with a metal oxide that holds electromagnetic impulses, which are the data stored on the diskettes. The inside of the jacket contains a lubricant designed to smooth the rotation and a brush-like material designed to clean the surface of the disk as it rotates.

On both sides of the diskette jacket are elliptical cutouts, called the **read-write windows**, through which the read-write heads pass data to and from the diskette's mylar surface.

In the side of the diskette jacket is a notch, called the **write-protect notch.** If you cover this notch with a metallic tab (supplied with the diskette), the disk drive can read from but not write to the diskette, and thus the diskette is **write-protected**. If the write-protect notch is uncovered, then the disk drive can both read and write on the diskette.

Data is recorded on the diskette in circular rings called **tracks**. Each track is divided into sections called **sectors**. Figure 3.13 illustrates a floppy diskette and its tracks and sectors.

Some diskette manufacturers create tracks and sectors as part of the diskette manufacturing process. These are called **hard-sectored diskettes**. For microcomputer use, however, it is most common for diskettes to be manufactured without any tracks or sectors. These are called **soft-sectored diskettes**. You must add the track and sectors to the disk in a process called **formatting**. Chapter 4 will describe formatting in detail.

There are many common configurations of tracks and sectors. The variables include the number of sides on the diskette, the number of tracks per side, the number of sectors per track, and the number of bytes per sector. A common layout is the double-sided, double-density format (often abbreviated as DS/DD), which uses 40 tracks per side, each containing nine sectors of 512 bytes each. The capacity of such a diskette is determined by this formula:

(2 sides) × (40 tracks) × (9 sectors) × (512 bytes)

= 368,640 bytes

= 360K

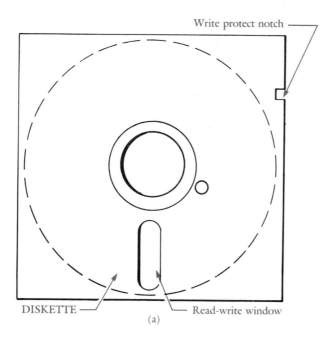

(a)

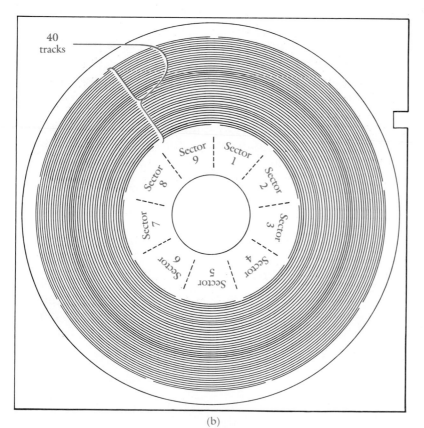

(b)

Figure 3.13   (a) A floppy diskette, and (b) a cutaway view showing a diskette's tracks and sectors.

Table 3.5 illustrates some sample diskette capacities and the amount of information they contain.

Precautions to Take in Using Diskettes

Don't fold, spindle, or mutilate your diskettes! Although floppies are hardy, you will get more mileage and dependability from them if you treat them with care.

You must be careful in using diskettes since they can be damaged by careless handling. Some diskette "don'ts" are pretty obvious:

1. Don't bend the diskette.
2. Don't handle the mylar media with your fingers.
3. Don't use a ballpoint pen or other sharp instrument to write on the diskette jacket.

Some other cautions are less obvious. They include the following:

4. Don't put diskettes near devices (like motors) that generate strong magnetic fields.
5. Don't put diskettes in strong heat (such as the trunk of your car).
6. Make backup copies of your diskettes so that if any of these accidents do occur you will not lose your data. (Backing up diskettes is discussed in Chapter 4.)
7. When you are not using a diskette, return it to its protective sleeve so that the read/write window is not exposed. Many manufacturers include reminders of good diskette handling procedures on the back of the sleeve.

If you avoid potential problems by following these guidelines, you will find that diskettes are remarkably sturdy. You can even send them through the mail (in rigid envelopes) and take them through airport x-ray security devices without mishap.

Table 3.5   Diskette Capacities

Description	Bytes
Single-sided, single-density, 5.25 inches	80K
Single-sided, double-density, 5.25 inches	160K
Double-sided, double-density, 5.25 inches	320K
Double-sided, double-density, 9 sector, 5.25 inches	360K
High-capacity, 5.25 inches	1.2M
Mini-diskette, 3.5 inches	720K

K = kilobyte = 1024 bytes
M = megabyte = 1024 × 1024 bytes

Section 3.3: Test Your Understanding

1. Explain the use of the word "floppy" in reference to diskettes.
2. Explain how a disk drive operates.
3. Why is more than one disk drive useful in a microcomputer system?
4. True or false: A microcomputer system needs only one form of long-term storage. If it is equipped with a hard disk, it does not need a disk drive. Explain your answer.
5. True or false: Disk drives are disposable.
6. What is a diskette track?
7. You have a diskette that is one-sided with 40 tracks, and each track has eight sectors of 512 bytes each. How many bytes can the diskette store?
8. What is the read/write window?
9. Explain the function of the write-protect notch.
10. Name three cautions in handling diskettes.

3.4 Secondary Storage—Hard Disks

If the history of computing has taught us one sure lesson, it is that no amount of secondary storage is ever enough. The original microcomputers used cassette tapes for storage. In no time at all, tapes were obsolete and replaced by disk drives. Even though the popularity of disk drives continues, the complexity of today's programs and the amount of data you must store has shifted attention to secondary storage devices that can store much more information than a diskette. The hard disk is the most common alternative secondary storage device used to store information.

What Is a Hard Disk?

A **hard disk** consists of a sealed enclosure containing one or more rigid metallic platters rotating at a very high speed. The enclosure houses a motor for rotating the platters and read/write heads for writing data to and reading data from the platters. The enclosure may be mounted in the same cabinet as the processing unit or in a separate cabinet. Figure 3.14 illustrates a hard disk. Some companies (in particular IBM) use the name **fixed disk** to refer to a hard disk.

(a)

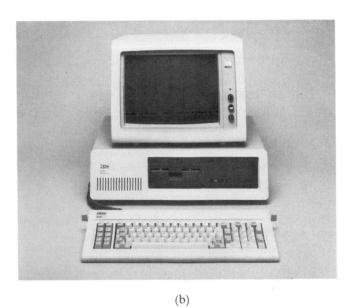

(b)

Figure 3.14 A hard disk, (a) interior and (b) exterior views.

In many ways, a hard disk works like a disk drive for floppy disks. Both types record data in tracks and sectors and the read/write head on both is positioned in two operations: a seek operation, in which the read/write head moves radially, and a search operation, in which the desired data rotates under the read/write head.

The first hard disks were developed by IBM and RCA in the 1960s. An early model by IBM used two platters, each capable of storing 30 megabytes. The number 30-30 reminded someone of the Winchester 30-30 rifle of Old West fame, so hard disks were dubbed **Winchester disks**. The nickname stuck, and today the term is used interchangeably with hard disk.

Hard disks for microcomputers were introduced in the late 1970s. The original hard disks provided five megabytes of storage and cost about $5,000. In 1982, IBM introduced the IBM PC XT, a microcomputer with a built-in 10-megabyte hard disk. IBM's entry did much to popularize the hard disk as a mass storage device for the microcomputer market.

Mass production, improvements in manufacturing technology, and intense competition in the computer hardware business have continually lowered the costs of hard disks. You can now purchase a 10-megabyte hard disk for under $500. As prices have dropped, hard disk capacities have soared. You can now purchase microcomputer-compatible hard disks capable of storing 20, 30, 50, 100, or even 1,000 megabytes. These hard disks accommodate storage needs for all but the very largest data processing tasks.

Hard disk size has become smaller as technological advances continue to allow for denser recording of information. Early microcomputer hard disks used 8-inch-diameter platters. Today, $5\frac{1}{4}$-inch- and $3\frac{1}{2}$-inch-diameter platters are the most common. The smaller diameter disks require the read/write heads to travel smaller distances and so allow for faster access times.

Advantages of the Hard Disk

You can use hard disks for large-scale storage needs. Indeed, a single 10-megabyte hard disk holds as much information as 28 double-sided, double-density diskettes. If a double-spaced typed page is estimated as 2,000 characters, a 10-megabyte hard disk has the capacity to store about 5,000 pages. Most users can store all of their programs and data on a single 10-megabyte hard disk, making it unnecessary ever to swap diskettes.

Hard disks also provide much faster access to data than do diskettes. As discussed earlier, a diskette spins at about 300 revolutions per minute; a hard disk spins at 3,000 revolutions per minute—10 times faster. The faster revolution means that it takes the read/write heads, on the average, less time to move to the correct spot on the disk to read or write data.

The hard disk originally supplied with the IBM PC XT had an average access time of about 80 milliseconds. Improved hard disk technology dropped this access time to about 38 milliseconds for the hard disk supplied with the IBM PC AT. It now appears that the next generation of hard disks will have an average access time of approximately 10 to 15 milliseconds.

The Need for Backup

In spite of all their advantages, hard disks do have a dark side. Hard disks are vulnerable to **head crashes,** malfunctions that can destroy data on the disk or even render an entire platter unreadable.

To understand how a head crash takes place, it is helpful to look at the way a hard disk functions. In a hard disk, the read/write head is supported on a cushion of air a few millionths of an inch from the platter surface. The cushion of air is created by the rotation of the platter. Any foreign matter on the platter looms like a boulder in the path of the read/write head, as Figure 3.15 illustrates. Imagine flying a Boeing 747 six feet above the surface of a choppy sea and unexpectedly encountering the tip of an iceberg—this will give you an idea of the impact on the hard disk's read/write head. For this reason, the platter must be kept absolutely free of any contaminants—a speck of dust, particles of cigarette smoke, or even the oil from a fingerprint. To prevent contamination at the factory, hard disks are manufactured in "clean rooms" where workers wear sterile garments and the air is filtered. To prevent contamination during use, platters are hermetically sealed inside their chambers.

Figure 3.15. Foreign matter on a hard disk platter.

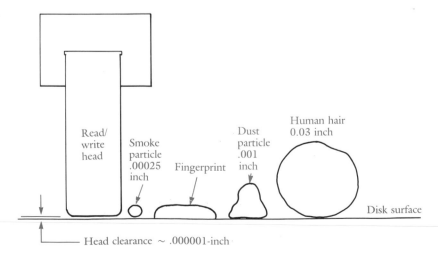

If the read/write head does contact a particle, a head crash occurs. The result can be damage to the platter surface with a consequent loss of data. Head crashes can also be caused by jolts to the hard disk chamber, say by someone bumping into the computer. A crash might also result from a sudden fluctuation in current that causes the platter to slow down and the read/write head to fall onto the surface of the platter.

After all these tales of potential grief, you might get the idea that storing your precious data on a hard disk drive is a risky proposition. Far from it. The chances of a hard disk crashing are minuscule.

Hard Disk Backup

The potential for disaster forces the hard disk user to take preventive steps—that is, to back up data regularly. With the older 5-megabyte and 10-megabyte hard disks, it was popular but tedious to make backups on diskettes. Without too much trouble, you could copy the contents of a 10-megabyte hard disk onto 24 diskettes, say once a day. Even though it was not always necessary to copy the contents of the entire hard disk—just those files that were changed since the last backup—it was still a time-consuming process.

As disk sizes have grown, it has become necessary to consider other means of backup. (Would you like to spend three hours each day backing up a 30-megabyte hard disk onto 72 diskettes?) One alternative, the **tape backup unit**, allows you to copy the contents of a hard disk onto a tape cartridge at the rate of 1 to 5 megabytes per minute. A typical backup unit is shown in Figure 3.16. The amount of data that can be stored on a tape varies with the tape backup system. Tape capacities of 10 to 60 megabytes are common.

Backup of hard disks is such an important issue that there is considerable experimentation to produce a backup systems that is simultaneously quick, inexpensive, and relatively trouble-free. Some systems utilize special high-density recording techniques on a floppy diskette. Others use a video recorder to store hard disk data on a VCR tape. Additional hard disk backup systems are sure to follow.

When using a hard disk, be sure to back up your data regularly to protect yourself in the event of a head crash.

Section 3.4: Test Your Understanding

1. How many double-sided, double density diskettes does it take to provide the same storage as a 30-megabyte hard disk?
2. A certain microcomputer has a 30-megabyte hard disk. Approximately how many double-spaced pages of text can be stored on the disk?

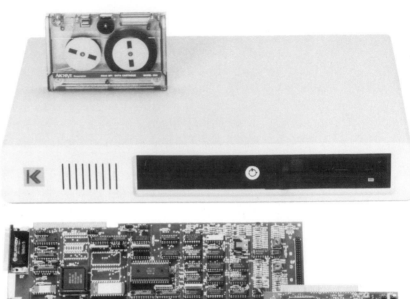

Figure 3.16 A tape backup system.

3. Assume that one page of a book contains 2,000 characters and that an average book contains 500 pages. How many average books can be stored in a 20-megabyte hard disk?

4. Explain the operation of a hard disk.

5. Why are hard disks sometimes called Winchester disks?

6. List two advantages of hard disks over diskettes.

7. What is a head crash and how does it occur?

8. How can you prevent the loss of data that might be caused by a hard disk head crash?

9. What is the function of a tape backup unit?

10. Can you scc any disadvantage in using a tape backup unit for secondary storage?

3.5 Other Forms of Secondary Storage

The widespread use of microcomputers has generated a near-insatiable demand for long-term storage devices. This demand has in turn sparked experimentation into alternative devices and improvements on existing devices. Two of the most promising long-term storage devices are the Bernoulli box and the optical disk.

The Bernoulli Box

The **Bernoulli box** is a disk-like storage device combining the convenience of a floppy diskette with the storage capacity of a hard disk. That is, it provides interchangeable storage media, each having the same capacity of a hard disk. In effect, it is a hard disk of unlimited capacity.

The Bernoulli box, illustrated in Figure 3.17, uses a mylar recording medium, similar to a diskette, encased in a hard plastic case. The mylar disk rotates at about 3,000 revolutions per minute. This speed of revolution causes an aerodynamic effect, described by the Bernoulli principle of physics: An object rotated at high speed is lifted by the air currents generated beneath it. In the case of a Bernoulli box, the mylar disk experiences a lift from the rotation and is lifted up toward the read/write head. If the speed of rotation is slowed or if a particle gets in the way, the disk falls away from the read/write head, so that a head crash does not occur.

Bernoulli boxes are available for a number of popular micro-computer systems and offer one or two 10-megabyte or 20-megabyte drives per system. A Bernoulli box offers data access times averaging about 38 milliseconds. Such speeds rival those of a high-performance hard disk. Moreover, since a Bernoulli box uses removable platters, it can provide potentially infinite storage capacity.

As with most optional devices, the Bernoulli box is controlled by an expansion card that is plugged into an expansion slot. The Bernoulli box is attached to a connector on the expansion card by a cable.

The Optical Disk

In recent years, microcomputer designers have done a great deal of experimentation with **optical disks** (also called **CD ROMs** or **laser disks**). These disks use a laser to write data onto a hard magnetic platter, which is the same technology used to record sound on a compact audio disk. Future optical disks will hold vast quantities of long-term storage, typically 1,000 megabytes per disk. Figure 3.18 shows an optical disk.

At the present time, optical disks can be written to only once. The process of writing makes a permanent recording on the disk. Therefore, optical disks can be used only for applications requiring access to a large prerecorded collection of data (say, an encylopedia on a disk). However, it seems likely that in the near future, technology will offer us optical disks that can be both read and written.

Section 3.5: Test Your Understanding

1. Explain the operation of a Bernoulli box.
2. What are two advantages of a Bernoulli box over a hard disk?
3. What is the current drawback of optical disks?

Figure 3.17 (a) The recording platter of a Bernoulli box, and (b) the drive.

(a)

(b)

Figure 3.18 An optical disk system.

3.6 Printers

Section 3.2 discussed how monitors provide you with output from programs. However, the disadvantages of this form of output were not presented. First, monitors are not the best medium for viewing and analyzing large volumes of output. A monitor can display only a limited amount of data and doesn't allow you to easily flip through output to get an overall picture. Also, the output from a monitor is not permanent. It is gone as soon as you turn the computer off. To remedy these difficulties, most microcomputer systems use a **printer**. This section surveys printer hardware suitable for a microcomputer system.

Modern printers can produce large quantities of high-quality output with amazing speed. In fact, some of today's desktop laser printers can produce several thousand pages of output per day with a quality that rivals a typeset book. It is ironic that computers promise us a "paperless office," yet they produce more paper than ever before, which means that we must continue to look for increasingly high-speed devices to print it.

Printers for microcomputer systems fall into six general categories:

Speed and print quality are two basic criteria for choosing a printer.

1. Dot-matrix printer
2. Daisy-wheel printer
3. Laser printer

(a)

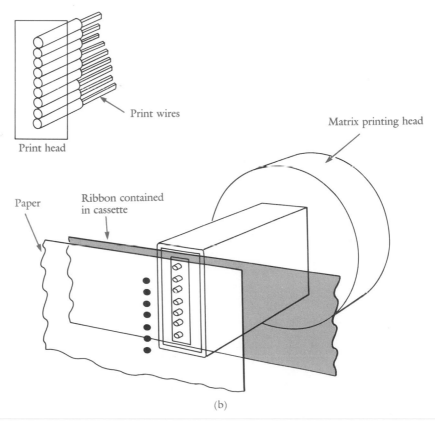

Print wires

Print head

Matrix printing head

Paper

Ribbon contained in cassette

(b)

Figure 3.19 (a) The popular Epson FX-185 dot-matrix printer, and (b) a diagram showing the operation of a typical dot-matrix printer.

4. Ink-jet printer
5. Thermal printer
6. Plotter

The Dot-Matrix Printer

Dot matrix printers are the least expensive of the microcomputer printers, ranging in price from $250 to $2,000. These printers are compact and rugged, and they can produce hard copy with quality ranging from barely legible to superb. Figure 3.19a shows a typical dot-matrix printer and how it works.

The device that does the printing on a dot-matrix printer is the **print head**. It is composed of a number of **print wires**. Under the control of a microprocessor within the printer, the wires push a ribbon against the paper to print a column of dots. Each letter is formed by printing columns of dots in consecutive horizontal positions. Figure 3.20 illustrates how the columns of dots correspond to a single letter.

The number of dots in a single column corresponds to the number of wires in the print head. This varies from 7 to 24 wires. Generally speaking, the greater the number of wires, the greater the density of dots and the higher the quality of printing. In Figure 3.21(a), the print samples were produced on a dot-matrix printer with a 9-wire print head; in Figure 3.21(b), the samples were produced on a printer with a 24-wire print head.

Figure 3.20. Forming a letter from columns of dots.

```
This is a test of the Epson
LQ-1500 in 9 pin draft mode.
```
(a)

```
This is a test of the Epson
LQ-1500 in 24 pin print mode.
```
(b)

Figure 3.21 Print samples from (a) a 9-wire dot-matrix printer, and (b) a 24-wire dot-matrix printer.

Figure 3.22 Assorted type fonts available on typical dot-matrix printers.

```
This is the standard type font.
This line is printed in italics.
This line is underlined.
This line is printed in boldface.
This  line  is  printed  double  width.
This line is printed in smaller type.
```

This is a Times Roman typeface.

Type fonts come in bold
and italics.

They also come in large sizes
and small ones.

This is a Sans Serif typeface.

This is a Classic typeface.

𝔗𝔥𝔦𝔰 𝔦𝔰 𝔞𝔫 𝔒𝔩𝔡𝔢 𝔈𝔫𝔤𝔩𝔦𝔰𝔥 𝔱𝔶𝔭𝔢𝔣𝔞𝔠𝔢.

(b)

Figure 3.23 (a) Type fonts produced by Fancy Word; (b) graphics produced by PC Paintbrush.

Printers with fewer print wires can produce high-quality print by making several passes over a single letter to "fill in the dots" more densely. Using this technique, they can often produce enhanced printing that rivals printers with more print wires, although at the price of slower printing.

The data used by the dot-matrix printers provide great versatility in the characters that can be produced. The typical dot-matrix printer offers a wide range of type fonts, some of which are shown in Figure 3.22.

Most dot-matrix printers may be programmed to print any specified dot pattern, which means they can print almost any character or even graphics. Figure 3.23(a) shows some type fonts produced on a dot-matrix printer using a program called Fancy Word; Figure 3.23(b) illustrates a graph printed on a dot-matrix printer using the program PC Paintbrush. Dot-matrix printers can print characters of foreign languages such as Russian or Japanese. Moreover, they can print Greek letters and symbols common in scientific and mathematical work.

The slowest dot-matrix printers take approximately a minute to print a page of text whereas the fastest can do the same task in as little as seven seconds.

The Daisy-Wheel Printer

The **daisy-wheel printer** uses a different printing concept than the dot-matrix printer: a print wheel rotates a series of spokes on the tip of which are embossed fully formed characters. These spokes resemble the petals of a daisy, hence the name "daisy-wheel." A magnetically-controlled hammer presses the spokes against a ribbon which, in turn, is pressed against the paper. Figure 3.24 illustrates this type of printer.

The advantages of a daisy-wheel printer are that it produces high-quality printing and a wide variety of type fonts, as illustrated in Figure 3.25. In fact, a daisy-wheel printer is often called a **letter-quality printer**, to distinguish it from the lower quality output of the dot-matrix printer. With the use of higher density dot configurations, manufacturers of dot-matrix printers speak of their output as being of "near letter quality." However, dot-matrix printing still does not equal the quality of the preformed letters of a daisy-wheel printer.

The two disadvantages of a daisy-wheel printer are speed and price. Daisy-wheel printers are very slow compared to dot-matrix printers. The typical daisy-wheel printer produces only 40 to 55 characters per second and takes about one minute to print a page.

A dot-matrix printer prints columns of dots with great rapidity. Manufacturers have offered models that are cheaper (in the $700 to $1,000 range) but slower (usually 10 to 25 characters per second).

Nevertheless, the speed of daisy-wheel printers should be kept in perspective. A 100-word-per-minute typist produces only about eight characters per second. So even the slowest of the daisy-wheel printers is fast compared to a typist using an electric typewriter.

Figure 3.24   (a) A daisy-wheel printer and (b) a diagram showing how the printer works.

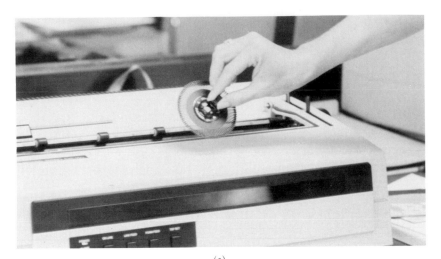

(a)

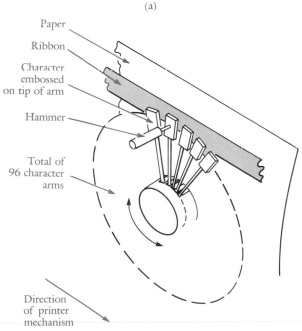

Paper

Ribbon

Character embossed on tip of arm

Hammer

Total of 96 character arms

Direction of printer mechanism

(b)

```
This is a print sample obtained
using the Diablo 630 ECS daisy
wheel printer.
```

(a)

APL-10	*ABCDEF* 012345 α⊥∩⌊ε_	**Manifold**	ABCDEF 012345 /\\&"_
Bold/Boldface	**ABCDEF abcdefgh ,?:";-./.**	**OCR-A**	ABCDEF abcdef */ȯ∅&ⁿ
Bold Italic	***ABCDEF abcdefgh ,?:";-./.***	**OCR-B**	ABCDEF abcdef /\\&"_
Courier	ABCDEF abcdef /\\&"_	**Pica**	ABCDEF abcdef ";-./.
Cubic PS	ABCDEF abcdefgh ,?:";-./.	**Prestige Elite**	ABCDEFGH abcdefg */_®&"_
Dual Gothic	ABCDEFG abcdefg */_®&"_	**Prestige Pica**	;µ§¢°® BLQ!K* wyucgs
Elite	ABCDEFG abcdefg */¦\\&"_	**Roman**	ABCDEF abcdefgh ,?:";-./.
Emphasis	ABCDEF ABCDEF °½¦¼↑↓	**Titan**	ABCDEF abcdef ";-./.
Forms Gothic	ABCDEF abcdef `{¦}~¬	**Titan/Italics**	*ABCDEFG abcdefg :";-./.*
General Scientific	∇∞Ψφ←<Λ 0123456 °⊙⊕™ˇ¶	**Tile 15**	ABCDEFGHI abcdefghi †_[]°!>@
Gothic	ABCDEF abcdefg ,?:";-./.	**Trend PS**	ABCDEF abcdefgh ,?:";-./.
Hebrew	ABCDEFG חזוהדגבא 0123456	**Trojan**	ABCDEF abcdef ";-./.
Letter Gothic	ABCDEFGH abcdefgh :";-./.	**Vintage**	ABCDEFG abcdefgh ?:";-./.

(b)

Figure 3.25   (a) Print sample and (b) type fonts from a daisy-wheel printer.

However, if you must print out a 500-page document, a daisy-wheel printer will give new meaning to the word *slowly*.

The Laser Printer

The **laser printer** combines high speed with impeccable print quality. A typical desktop laser printer, similar to the one shown in Figure 3.26(a), can produce eight pages per minute (which corresponds to about 400 characters per second) with a quality rivalling that of a typeset book.

The laser printer, like the dot-matrix printer, prints with dots. It uses a laser to position dots of magnetically charged ink-like toner on a rotating drum. In a process similar to photocopying, the drum deposits the toner on paper and fixes it by means of a heat process. The dots can be positioned with incredible accuracy because of the extreme precision of the laser. The typical laser printer uses a density of 300 × 300 dots per square inch. At this density, the individual dots merge to form smooth, continuous characters. Figure 3.27 shows print samples from a laser printer and the variety of type fonts available.

The only disadvantage to laser printers is their cost, currently starting at about $2,000. However, like most microcomputer

Figure 3.26 (a) A desktop laser printer, and (b) a diagram showing its operation.

(a)

Image to be printed is formed on drum by magnetized particles of toner

Image is transferred onto paper by xerographic process

(b)

The HP LaserJet is capable of handling type fonts whose
characters are formed of dots with a density of 300 x 300 to
the inch. What you are reading was printed using the Courier
10 pitch type font.

This paragraph is printed on the HP LaserJet using the Times Roman
proportionally spaced font cartridge.

The Times Roman cartridge includes boldface *and italic type*, as well as small type for
footnotes.

Figure 3.27   Type fonts available on the Hewlett-Packard LaserJet printer.

components, this cost will decline dramatically in the next few
years.

Other Printing Devices

There are several other types of printing devices that are used with
microcomputers, although they are less common than the printers
described above.

An **ink-jet printer** produces printed copy by spraying droplets
of ink onto the paper. Ink-jet printers are remarkably quiet and
produce print quality somewhere between a daisy-wheel printer
and a dot-matrix printer. Ink-jet printers are especially suitable for
multicolor printing.

A **thermal printer** uses a heat process to burn images onto
special thermal paper. Thermal printers are inexpensive to purchase
and quiet in operation, but they are expensive to operate because
of their need for special paper. Moreover, their print quality is at
the low end of the scale.

A **plotter** is a device used for producing graphics output. The
plotter draws images by means of one or more pens that move
over the paper surface. A plotter can produce multicolor output
and can be used to prepare large documents, such as blueprints or
posters.

Section 3.6: *Test Your Understanding*

1. Explain the operation of a dot-matrix printer.
2. What are the advantages of a dot-matrix printer?
3. What are the limitations of a dot-matrix printer?
4. Explain the operation of a daisy-wheel printer.

5. Explain how a daisy-wheel printer can print different type styles.
6. Compare the speeds of the dot-matrix, daisy-wheel, and laser printers.
7. Explain the operation of a laser printer.
8. What do a laser printer and a dot-matrix printer have in common?
9. As the price of laser printers falls, will the market for the dot-matrix printer or the daisy-wheel printer be most affected?

3.7 Customizing a Personal Computer System

From the discussion of hardware in this chapter, you can see that a personal computer system consists of a large number of components. To put together a system requires both homework and perseverance. Here are some questions for you to consider when putting a system together:

1. *How will I use my system?* Before you even begin to think about which components to buy, you must answer a fundamental question: What do you want to do with your system? That is, what application programs do you want to run? Answering this question is difficult for new users, since they probably don't even know all the possible application programs available, let alone which ones they want to buy.

   Even if you can't answer the question completely, it's important to make an attempt. You should begin by making a list of all the ways you think you would use your computer. Consult friends and colleagues, the salespeople at a computer store, the members of a computer club, and your teachers. Your colleagues are particularly important, since they have probably wrestled with the same problems that are confronting you and may have come up with some solutions in the way of application programs.

2. *What application programs do I want to run?* Once you have a general list of applications you would like to do with your computer, you must choose the actual application software you wish to run. Again, your colleagues will be your best source of advice, but also consult computer magazines for comparative reviews, professional journals, computer store salespeople, and user groups.

3. *What hardware do the application programs require?* Each application program specifies the hardware it needs to run. Of critical importance is the computer, the amount of RAM, the monitor type, and the printer. You can get these specifications from a computer magazine review or from your local computer store.

4. *What is the best way to design my system?* Choose system components based on your hardware requirements. You will have a wide choice of components of a particular type. It is critical that the components you choose be **compatible**—that is, that the components be able to work together. Your salesperson should be your guide here. Make sure that you can return any components in the event they prove incompatible. Finally, you should design your system so that it has some excess capacity. If your system can barely handle your current needs and cannot be easily expanded, you may find yourself needing a whole new system before very long. It is important to plan with the future in mind.

Section 3.7: Test Your Understanding

1. What is the first step in designing a system?
2. A microcomputer system must be used for word processing by a secretary in a law office. Speed and high quality of printing are essential. What type of printer would you recommend?
3. If you were looking for an inexpensive printer with reasonable print quality, what type of printer would be available to you?

KEY TERMS

processing unit	expansion board	address
circuit board	controller card	volatility
mother board	interface card	monitor
system board	binary number	monochrome monitor
central processing unit (CPU)	bit	color monitor
microprocessor	byte	display adapter card
bus	megabyte	pixel
system clock	ASCII system	screen resolution
expansion slot	ASCII code	high-resolution mode
	memory location	medium-resolution mode

display mode
text mode
graphics mode
keyboard
cursor motion key
function key
ENTER/RETURN key
BACKSPACE key
ESCAPE key
CONTROL and
   ALTERNATE keys
numeric keypad
NUMLOCK key
disk drive
floppy diskette
read/write head

seek operation
search operation
single-sided diskette
double-sided diskette
read-write window
write-protect notch
write-protected
track
sector
hard-sectored diskette
soft-sectored diskette
formatting
hard disk
fixed disk
Winchester disk
head crash

tape backup unit
Bernoulli box
optical disk
CD ROM
laser disk
printer
dot-matrix printer
print head
print wires
daisy-wheel printer
letter-quality printer
laser printer
ink-jet printer
thermal printer
plotter

CHAPTER REVIEW QUESTIONS

1. What is a display adapter?
2. Describe the attributes specified in a display mode.
3. What is the difference between a composite monitor and an RGB monitor?
4. Compare the relative speeds of the dot-matrix, daisy-wheel, and laser printers.
5. Compare the relative costs of the dot-matrix, daisy-wheel, and laser printers.
6. It has been said that the central processing unit is the brain of a computer system and the bus is the nervous system. Explain why.
7. What is a memory address?
8. What is a binary number?
9. Explain the use of binary numbers within a computer system. Why are binary numbers used?
10. Explain why it is necessary to back up data stored in secondary storage.
11. How can data in RAM be protected from erasure due to a power failure?
12. Explain the function of the ENTER/RETURN key.
13. Explain the function of the CONTROL key.
14. Explain the function of the ESCAPE key.
15. True or false: In designing a microcomputer system, the first step is to decide how much you can afford to spend. Explain your answer.
16. Explain the following statement: RAM is volatile.
17. How many bytes are in 64K? How many bits?

DISCUSSION QUESTIONS

1. Will we ever reach a stage where the quantity of information generated by microcomputers will be too much for us to comprehend and efficiently absorb?

2. Discuss the impact of being able to produce typeset quality documents in the average office. How will this affect meetings, customer presentations, advertising, sales promotions, and so forth?

3. The original Macintosh computer had no expansion slots. Discuss the implications of this design decision on the expandability of the system.

4. IBM has had a policy of publishing all of the design details of their microcomputers. Evaluate the effects of this "open architecture policy" on hardware developers, software developers, and microcomputer users.

4 The Operating System

A Smooth Operator

One problem with using a microcomputer is that there are often too many commands to learn and to remember—micros are still far from being completely user-friendly.

Today, many clever microcomputer products are being invented that do make the user's life a little easier. One such product is called Shuttle, a program that remembers many commands for you. Shuttle was invented by Bill Anderson, owner and president of Force One, Inc., a Stamford, Connecticut, microcomputer consulting firm.

Whenever you want to install a new program, or to format or copy a diskette, you've got to remember the exact commands to give to the operating system, the "traffic cop" of your micro system. The operating system, which issues commands to the monitor, keyboard, memory, and printer, prompts you to tell it what to do next but offers no hints as to *how* to proceed.

Shuttle neatly bypasses the operating system and always tells you what to do next. Jeanne Smith, an office coordinator for an orthodontists' practice in Westport, Connecticut, and an ardent fan of Shuttle, uses the program on an IBM PC AT. "Shuttle has made my life so easy. Uncomplicated, I should say," Smith says. Besides simplifying the command process, Shuttle also cuts down on all the diskette handling you must do to load new programs. "It's an organizer. I don't have to remember which disk goes in what drive. It's all organized for me," Smith says.

Smith never sees her operating system prompt anymore. When she turns on her PC AT every day, the first thing she encounters on screen is the message "Good morning. This is Shuttle." Then she sees a number of options listed, menu-style. Everything Smith needs to do in her job is on that menu: word processing, spreadsheeting, a memo writer and a calendar, administrative chores for the office, hard disk backup, and so on. All she has to do is press one key, and Shuttle takes over, automatically going right into the program of her choice.

As far as Smith is concerned, Shuttle is her best friend in the office. "It saves me time. In this office, with patients in and out and phones ringing all the time, that's what I need."

T HE SECOND COMPONENT of the problem-solving equation is **software**. Computer software performs an enormously wide range of tasks. However, for the purposes of this discussion, the software you will use in problem solving will be classified into two categories:

- Application software
- System software

Chapter 1 introduced you to application software and presented examples of the most popular types currently used in business. This chapter discusses system software, which is needed to control the operation of a computer system.

4.1 System Software Concepts

System software consists of the programs that control the operation of a microcomputer system. This software accepts and interprets user commands, manages the programs being run, and makes diagnostic checks on the operation of the hardware. In addition, system software provides application programs with access to the various system components. That is, there are system software programs that application programs can use in order to write data onto a diskette, to read data from the keyboard, and to write data to the monitor.

It is absolutely essential that you understand certain fundamentals about system software in order to use application software. This chapter provides the information you need to know.

Types of System Software

Managing a computer system is a complex task requiring many different programs. Accordingly, a number of different categories of system software exist, including the following:

- **Bootstrap loader**: This is the program that starts up the computer system when you turn on the power. This program is stored in ROM and the circuitry of the computer automatically runs this program whenever the computer is first turned on.
- **Diagnostic routines**: These are also stored in ROM and start up when you turn on the power. They test the operation of RAM, the CPU, and the various system components. The diagnostic routines give you some assurance that the computer is operating properly before you run any application programs.

Hardware + software + data + user = problem solution.

- **Service functions**: These are programs stored in ROM, which are used by application programs to perform "low level" hardware manipulation, such as writing characters onto a diskette, reading characters from the keyboard, and writing characters to the monitor. By using these functions, application programs can access and use the system's hardware. The service functions are collectively called the **BIOS**—Basic Input Output System.

- **Operating system**: This software manages the operation of the microcomputer system, coordinates the running of programs, allocates system resources, and manages communications with the user. From the viewpoint of the user of application software, the most important piece of system software is the operating system. The operating system interprets your commands to run programs, manages program execution, and provides the means for you to interact with the programs while they are running. Moreover, the operating system provides you with housekeeping programs for copying files, formatting disks, and determining the contents of diskettes and hard disks.

Starting Your Computer

The operating system is stored on a diskette or hard disk. As part of the system start-up, the bootstrap loader program reads the operating system into RAM and turns control of the computer over to the operating system.

The process of reading the operating system into RAM is called **booting the system**. The bootstrap loader programs of most microcomputer systems are designed to check the first disk drive (usually the one on the left or on the top) for the presence of a diskette. If one is there, the computer attempts to read the operating system from that diskette. If no diskette is in the drive, the bootstrap loader checks for the presence of a hard disk. If one is present, the computer attempts to read the operating system from there.

A diskette containing the operating system is called a **boot diskette**, or a **system diskette**. To boot the system, you insert the boot diskette into the first floppy disk drive and turn on the power to the computer. From then on, without further user intervention, the boot-up process proceeds with the following steps:

- The computer automatically runs the diagnostic routines stored in ROM. Normal start-up will proceed only if all systems pass the diagnostics. If any abnormalities (a bad memory chip, for example) are detected by the diagnostics, the computer displays an error message. The error message identifies the difficulty and usually prevents you from proceeding with the computer session.

- The bootstrap loader reads the operating system into RAM from either diskette or hard disk.
- The bootstrap loader then turns over control of the system to the **command processor**, the program that waits for and interprets commands to be typed on the keyboard.

This start-up procedure is summarized in Figure 4.1.

Figure 4.1   Booting the operating system. Insert (a) the boot diskette into the first diskette drive and turn on the power. The computer (b) automatically runs diagnostic routines and reads the operating system into RAM. When ready to receive your input, the computer (c) displays the prompt on its monitor.

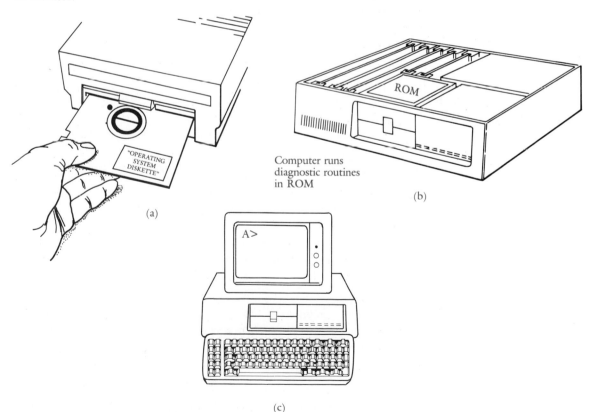

"OPERATING SYSTEM DISKETTE"

(a)

Computer runs
diagnostic routines
in ROM

(b)

A>

(c)

How an Operating System Is Organized

A boot diskette may contain the operating system alone or it may also contain application programs and data. Some diskettes of the latter sort include commands to start a particular applications program immediately after booting, which is called **self-booting**. For example, a particular boot diskette might allow you to start the operating system and immediately run your word-processing program. Many software packages contain instructions for setting up self-booting diskettes.

Actually, only a portion of the operating system is read into RAM at system start-up. The part read at this time consists of the command processor and certain critical routines. The rest of the operating system is kept in secondary storage and is read into RAM as it is needed. In the course of using your application software, you may either switch diskettes or change the default drive (the drive on which all the reading and writing will be done, explained in more detail in Section 4.2). When that happens, it may be necessary for you to periodically reinsert the boot diskette in the default drive. The computer will prompt you when this is required.

Often, the process of running a program will erase part of the operating system from memory. This can occur because either the program or data is very large and the only way it will fit in RAM is to use some of the space used by the operating system. If that happens, the computer needs to reread the operating system from secondary storage after the program has finished running. As described above, if the computer can't find the diskette containing the operating system, it will prompt you to insert the boot diskette.

The Role of the Operating System in Running Programs

Once the command processor program is running, you may request the operating system to run a program (either an application program or an operating system command). In response to such a request, the following will happen:

1. The operating system reads the program into RAM.
2. The operating system instructs the CPU to begin executing the program.
3. When program execution is done, control of the CPU is returned to the operating system.
4. The operating system awaits further instructions from you.

Figure 4.2 summarizes the sequence of operations that takes place in running a program.

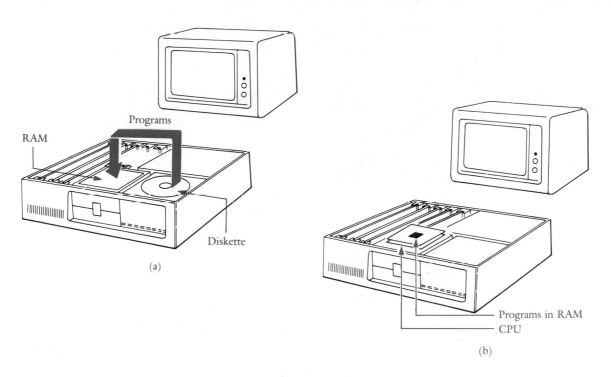

(a)

(b)

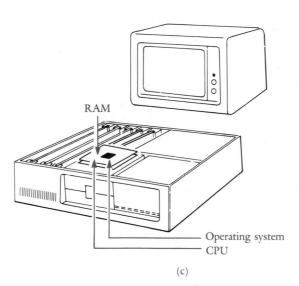

(c)

Figure 4.2 Running a program. Once your operating system is booted, you command the system to run a program. In response, the operating system (a) reads the program into RAM and (b) instructs the CPU to execute the program. (c) When the program has run, control of the CPU is returned to the operating system.

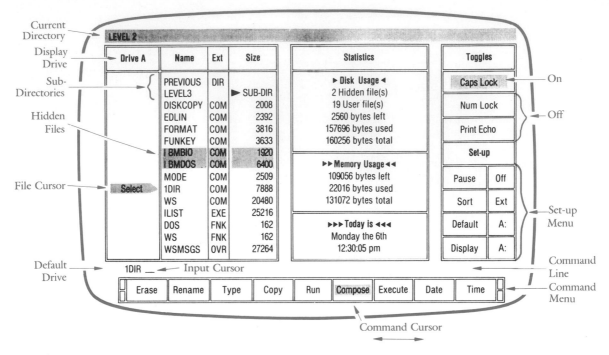

Figure 4.3   A menu-based interface.

The User Interface Provided by the Operating System

In order to use a microcomputer, you need to give the operating system various instructions: Run this program, carry out this command, report the status of the various system devices, and other similar instructions. Your interaction with the operating system is part of the **user interface** with the computer.

The most rudimentary user interface is one in which you type all commands directly from the keyboard. The disadvantage of such an interface is that you must remember the precise form of the commands in order to type them correctly.

An alternative user interface, called a **menu-based interface**, allows you to select commands from a displayed list called a **menu**. Having all possible options displayed in a menu relieves you from remembering what choices are available at each step in the program.

You select a command from a menu either by typing a letter or digit (as specified on the menu) or by pointing to the command with a pointing device. Figure 4.3 shows a menu with commands listed in a bar across the bottom of the screen. To choose a command, you use the arrow key to move the cursor to the command in the bar and press ⟨ENTER/RETURN⟩. In response, the program executes the command and redisplays the menu. If you press a keystroke other than one of the menu options, the program rejects it with a beep. The menu display continues until you enter an acceptable command.

Other user interfaces rely totally on a graphic representation of the commands. In a **graphics-based interface,** the commands are represented by **icons**, small pictures that appear on the monitor. Using a device called a **mouse**, you give a command to the operating system by pointing at the corresponding icon and then clicking a button on the mouse, as shown in Figure 4.4.

Graphics interfaces were introduced on an experimental computer, the Xerox Star, and popularized by Apple's Macintosh computer. Now programs such as IBM's Topview, Digital Research's Gem, and Microsoft's Windows can be used to create graphics interfaces on many different computers.

Graphic interfaces tend to be the most appealing to novice users, even though these interfaces usually react more slowly to user commands than simpler interfaces. This is due to the drain on CPU capability required to process the graphics.

Additional Operating System Features

Some operating systems incorporate features in addition to those we have already considered. Let's look at a few of them.

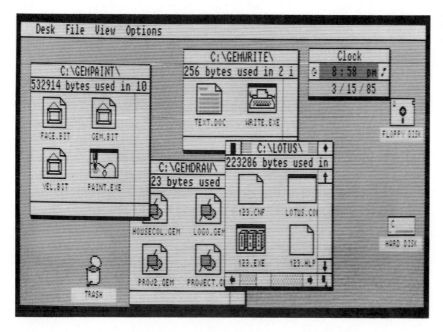

Figure 4.4 GEM Desktop, a graphics-based interface.

- *Housekeeping Functions.* The operating system performs various organizational and statistical functions for the computer system. The operating system automatically allocates space on diskettes and hard disks as required; it maintains on each diskette and hard disk a directory of the files and their respective locations. You may use operating system programs that include functions to display a directory, to format and copy diskettes, to copy files from one disk drive to another, to compare the contents of files, and to erase files.

- *Incorporating Additional System Devices.* Most operating systems can be reconfigured to match the specific hardware present in various systems. Using this capability, you can adapt the operating system to an expanding microcomputer system and can even incorporate devices that may not have been invented when you first set up the system.

- *Multi-User Capability.* In many operating systems, a number of different users must be able to access the same devices. This capability is called **multi-user**. For example, an office might have six assistants, all of whom must have access to the information stored in a single hard disk. To provide such access, we can configure six microcomputers in a **network**, with each microcomputer attached to the hard disk. Such a configuration is illustrated in Figure 4.5. The operating system in a network must have the ability to handle the competing demands for access to the hard disk.

- *Multi-Tasking Capability.* Some operating systems allow you to run several programs simultaneously. This capability, called **multi-tasking**, can be useful, for example, if you want to perform a financial analysis at the same time your word-processing program is printing out some correspondence. In this way, multi-tasking can make efficient use of all a microcomputer system's resources.

  Multi-tasking can also be helpful in situations where information must be interchanged between programs. Suppose you would like to insert information generated by a spreadsheet program into a report you are preparing on your word processor. Most multi-tasking systems are able to perform such an interchange of data between programs that are running concurrently.

  Most operating systems handle multi-tasking by running small portions of each program one after the other. Because of the great speed of the computer, it seems as if these tasks are being carried out simultaneously. In actuality, however, the

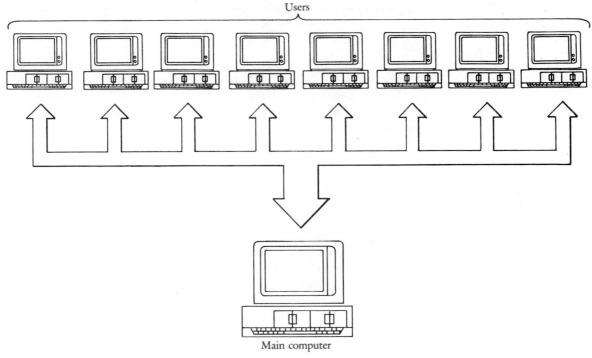

Figure 4.5   A multi-user configuration.

operating system is tending to only one at a time, in much the same fashion as a short order cook with many orders on the grill at once.

Some multi-tasking systems incorporate a system of **windows**, as shown in Figure 4.6. A window is a small opening or screen within the main screen. You can manipulate each window to run a separate program and to exchange data from one program to another.

Some Typical Operating Systems

The first microcomputer operating system was **CP/M** (control program for microcomputers), designed by Gary Kildall in the late 1970s. CP/M was a computer operating system using Intel's 8080 and Zilog's Z-80 microprocessors. A unique feature of CP/M was its incorporation of routines to control diskette drives. Accordingly, it was called a **disk operating system**, or **DOS** for short. The operating systems that have been developed since CP/M control many more devices besides disk drives, but they are still called disk operating systems.

Many of the features that originated in the design of CP/M are present in today's microcomputer operating systems. Most prominent was the idea to store the operating system on diskette (rather than in ROM). You might think that a program as important as the operating system should be stored in ROM, where it will be a permanent part of the computer. However, by storing the operating system on diskette, you can update it with very little trouble: Simply replace the boot diskette with an updated one.

Many microcomputer operating systems are in use today, including Apple DOS and Pro-DOS (both used in the Apple II family of computers), MS-DOS, (manufactured by Microsoft Corporation), PC-DOS (a variation of MS-DOS used on the IBM family of microcomputers), CP/M-86 (manufactured by Digital Research Corporation), and UNIX (designed by AT&T). Each of these operating systems has its advantages and disadvantages.

Note that each operating system is designed to work only with a particular microprocessor or family of microprocessors. For instance, MS-DOS is designed to run on Intel's 8088/8086/80286 microprocessors. Moreover, different operating systems are usually incompatible with one another. That is, programs written for use with one operating system will not work in another operating system.

Table 4.1 shows the microprocessors commonly used in microcomputers today and the operating systems available for them. Often there will be a choice of operating systems available for a

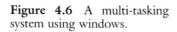

Figure 4.6 A multi-tasking system using windows.

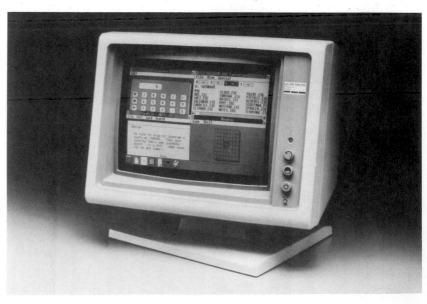

Table 4.1   Microprocessors and available operating systems

Manufacturer	Microprocessor	Operating Systems
Intel	8080	CP/M, TRSDOS, NEWDOS
Zilog	Z-80, Z-80A	CP/M, TRSDOS, NEWDOS
Motorola	6502	Apple DOS, Pro-DOS, Commodore 64, 128
Intel	8088, 8086, 80186, 80286	MS-DOS, CP/M-86, XENIX, UNIX
Motorola	68000	Macintosh, UNIX

particular microcomputer. For instance, MS-DOS, CP/M-86, and various versions of UNIX are all available for the IBM family of personal computers. You have a choice of systems to use, usually made on the basis of operating system features and software available to run with the operating system. However, because of the incompatability between operating systems, it is generally a bad idea to use more than one operating system on the same computer.

It is most important for you to note that a program is meant to run with a particular operating system. If you are using MS-DOS, then you can't run programs that run under Apple DOS, or vice versa. Moreover, many programs will run only with particular versions of an operating system. For instance, many MS-DOS application programs for the IBM PC require that you use version 2.0 or later. In deciding which programs to use, make sure that you select those that are compatible with the operating system and version you have.

Application software must be compatible with your operating system.

Section 4.1: Test Your Understanding

1. What is the function of a bootstrap loader?
2. True or false: The diagnostic routines of the operating system are stored in RAM. Explain your answer.
3. What is the command processor?
4. Give two examples of operating system commands.
5. Describe the service functions supplied by the operating system to application programs.
6. Why is the acronym DOS used as another name for an operating system?
7. What is meant by booting the operating system?

8. Explain the sequence of operations in running a program.
9. Describe three types of operating system user interfaces.
10. What is an icon and how is it used?
11. How do multi-tasking and multi-user capabilities differ?

4.2 The MS-DOS Operating System

The Microsoft disk operating system (**MS-DOS**) was chosen by IBM as the official operating system for its family of microcomputers. The application software discussed in this text is aimed primarily at business use, and because the IBM-compatible computers are a true standard for business, this text concentrates its discussion on MS-DOS rather than the other operating systems.

As you read, remember that this text will not attempt to be encyclopedic. Rather, it will cover just what you need to know to choose application programs and to keep them running smoothly.

Various versions of MS-DOS have been introduced over the years incorporate many changes and additional features. Each version is usually assigned a label number to distinguish it from other versions. As of this writing, the current version is 3.1; however, versions 4.0 and 5.0 have been planned for future release. The following discussion briefly introduces MS-DOS to novice microcomputer users. Remember that the descriptions of MS-DOS commands and procedures are currently applicable, but the commands and procedures may vary slightly in later versions. Consult your instructor or your operating system manual for any changes that may apply.

There is a customized version of MS-DOS, called **PC-DOS**, for use on IBM personal computers. Many other computer companies have adopted this version of MS-DOS for their machines in order to allow them to run the software written for IBM's computers. In this book, we shall refer loosely to MS-DOS instead of PC-DOS. However, you should understand that we are always referring to PC-DOS as our operating system.

Booting MS-DOS

Starting MS-DOS from a Diskette. The original boot diskette purchased with your computer system is used only for the original system start-up, at which time you should make additional copies for later use. (You will learn how to make copies of a diskette shortly.) The steps for starting up MS-DOS from a diskette are outlined below and illustrated in Figure 4.7.

1. Locate the diskette drive A of your system (the drive on the left if the drives are arranged side by side, and on top if the drives are arranged vertically).
2. Insert a copy of the boot diskette into the drive A and close the drive door.

Figure 4.7 Starting your computer. (a) Locate drive A: and (b) insert the DOS diskette. (c) Turn on the power, causing the computer to (d) run diagnostics and (e) read DOS. Enter (f) the date and (g) the time. (h) The screen displays the copyright message and the DOS prompt.

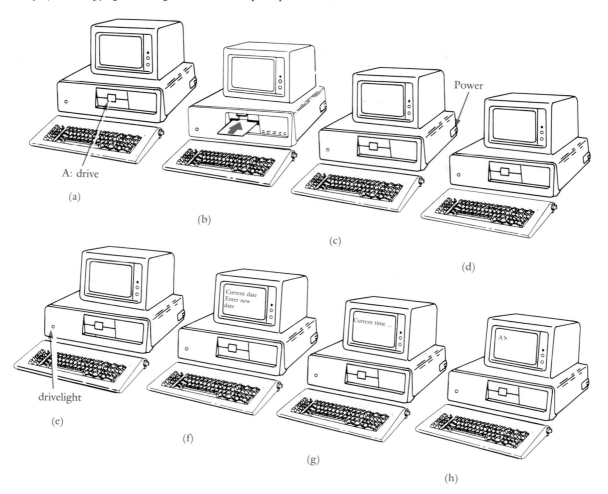

3. Turn on the power to the computer.

4. The computer will warm up and execute its diagnostic routines. Depending on the amount of memory in your computer, this may take as long as a minute.

5. The light on the drive will go on and the computer will make a whirring noise, indicating that the drive is in use. The computer is now reading MS-DOS from the diskette.

6. The computer will display a message that looks like this:

> Current date is Tue 1-01-1080
> Enter new date (mm-dd-yy):

Type in the current date (for example, 4-12-87 for April 12, 1987) and press the ENTER/RETURN key. As long as the computer is turned on, the operating system will use this date to mark directory entries, indicating the date on which files are created or changed. You'll also find this handy when you start using application programs. As a shortcut, you could respond to the above prompt simply by pressing ⟨ENTER/ RETURN⟩. However, in this case, the date will be set to Tuesday 1-01-1980. Even if it is a bother to type the correct date, you should persevere so that your files will be assigned the correct date in the directory.

7. The computer will next display a message like this:

> Current time is 0:00:50.36
> Enter new time (hh:mm:ss):

Type the current time (for example, 21:03:00 for 9:03 pm) and press ⟨ENTER/RETURN⟩. The time is used by the operating system to mark the time when a file was created or last changed. Again, you'll find this handy when using application programs. As with the date prompt, you can just press ⟨ENTER/RETURN⟩ without specifying the time. However, in the interest of keeping your directory accurate, you should put in the correct time.

8. The computer will display a copyright message similar to the one shown in Figure 4.7. Your message may differ somewhat from the one shown. The display will end with the **MS-DOS prompt**

> A⟩

A⟩ tells you the operating system is ready for a command.

This prompt indicates that MS-DOS is awaiting further commands and that, unless otherwise instructed, diskette reading and writing will take place on drive A:.

Starting MS-DOS from a Hard Disk. On most microcomputer systems with a hard disk, you may boot MS-DOS without a diskette. This procedure allows you to start the computer without having to insert any diskettes (which can be a nuisance, especially if you constantly misplace your boot diskette!). To boot the system from a hard disk, you must have previously stored the MS-DOS programs on the hard disk. Assuming that this has been done, booting is just a matter of turning on the computer. After the diagnostics, the hard disk light will go on and you can boot MS-DOS as described for diskettes. Note, however, that in most systems, the hard disk is called drive C: so the MS-DOS prompt is

> C⟩

Unless otherwise instructed, MS-DOS will thus do all reading and writing to drive C: (the hard disk).

At any given moment, one of the drives is designated as the **current drive** or the **default drive**. The default drive, the drive on which all reading and writing of data will be done, is identified in the MS-DOS prompt. For example, if the DOS prompt is A⟩, then A: is the default drive. Similarly, if the DOS prompt is C⟩, then C: is the default drive.

You may change the default drive by using a simple MS-DOS command. For example, to change the default drive to C:, simply type

> C: ⟨ENTER/RETURN⟩

(Here the ⟨ENTER/RETURN⟩ means "Press the ENTER/RETURN key." Recall that words and letters in brackets (⟨⟩) indicate keys you should press to execute a function.) Remember that an MS-DOS command may be given only when the MS-DOS prompt is displayed.

The MS-DOS prompt tells you the default drive.

Issuing Commands and Running Programs

When the MS-DOS prompt is displayed, you may give an MS-DOS command or run an application program. In either case, the procedure is similar: Type the command (or program name) and press ⟨ENTER/RETURN⟩. For example, to obtain the directory (the contents) of the diskette in drive A:, type

> DIR A: ⟨ENTER/RETURN⟩

The directory of the diskette in drive A: will be displayed on the screen followed by the MS-DOS prompt, indicating that MS-DOS is ready for the next command. Figure 4.8 illustrates a response to the command DIR A:.

```
Wed  6-04-1986
17:07:34.12 C>dir a:

 Volume in drive A has no label
 Directory of  A:\

MASM     EXE     77362  11-21-84    2:49p
LINK     EXE     41114  11-14-84    2:48p
SYMDEB   EXE     36538   6-07-85    4:26p
MAPSYM   EXE     51904   6-21-85   10:21a
CREF     EXE     10544  11-21-84    2:51p
LIB      EXE     24138  10-31-84    4:57p
MAKE     EXE     18675   8-13-84    1:24a
README   DOC     22986   6-21-85   10:03a
          8 File(s)      74752 bytes free


Wed  6-04-1986
17:07:40.36 C>
```

Figure 4.8   Response to the command DIR A:.

Another example can be illustrated by running the word-processing program WordStar. Suppose that the DOS prompt is showing on the monitor. Insert a diskette containing the WordStar program, which is stored in a file on the diskette called WS.COM. To initiate WordStar you ignore the extension .COM and enter the main filename WS. That is, you type the command:

WS ⟨ENTER/RETURN⟩

In response to this command, MS-DOS runs the program WS (that is, WordStar). This program first displays a copyright notice and then a menu of options from which you can choose, as shown in Figure 4.9. To end the program and return to MS-DOS, the menu tells you to type ⟨**X**⟩ for "Exit to System". The screen is erased and the MS-DOS prompt is displayed.

To MS-DOS, uppercase and lowercase letters mean the same thing.

MS-DOS does not distinguish between uppercase and lowercase letters. As far as MS-DOS is concerned, the following commands all mean the same:

DIR A:

dir a:

Dir A:

DiR a:

In typing MS-DOS commands, you may use the BACKSPACE key for editing. Each time you press ⟨BACKSPACE⟩, the cursor moves back one space and erases one character. Provided you have not yet pressed ⟨ENTER/RETURN⟩, you may erase all or part of a command using the backspace key. However, once you press ⟨ENTER/RETURN⟩, the command is sent to MS-DOS for processing and you can make no further corrections.

Some Tips for Novices

Correcting Command Lines. It won't be long before you give an incorrect command. For example, by mistyping a command, you may instruct MS-DOS to execute a nonexistent command. If MS-DOS cannot interpret your command, it responds with the message

Bad Command or File Name

followed by the MS-DOS prompt. In other words, unrecognized commands are ignored, and you then get another chance to type in the correct file name.

Interrupting a Command or a Program. You may type a valid command that is valid but that you did not mean to type. In this

Figure 4.9   Initial menu of WordStar.

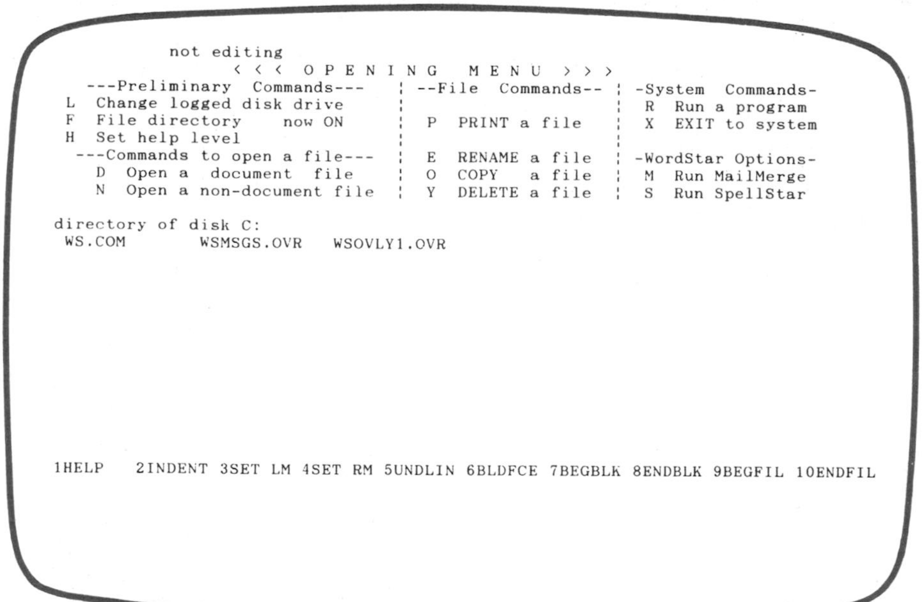

```
           not editing
                   < < <  O P E N I N G   M E N U  > > >
     ---Preliminary  Commands---  ¦  --File  Commands--  ¦  -System  Commands-
  L  Change logged disk drive     ¦                      ¦   R  Run a program
  F  File directory    now ON     ¦   P  PRINT a file    ¦   X  EXIT to system
  H  Set help level               ¦                      ¦
     ---Commands to open a file---  ¦  E  RENAME a file  ¦  -WordStar Options-
     D  Open a  document  file     ¦   O  COPY   a file  ¦   M  Run MailMerge
     N  Open a non-document file   ¦   Y  DELETE a file  ¦   S  Run SpellStar

directory of disk C:
 WS.COM        WSMSGS.OVR    WSOVLY1.OVR




1HELP    2INDENT 3SET LM 4SET RM 5UNDLIN 6BLDFCE 7BEGBLK 8ENDBLK 9BEGFIL 10ENDFIL
```

case, you have two choices: (1) wait until the command is executed, or (2) attempt to interrupt the command. In most cases, it is simplest to wait for MS-DOS to execute the command. Then you can give the correct command.

There are circumstances under which you will want to interrupt the command, however. If you just told MS-DOS to print 1,000 pages, it is better to interrupt the command. This may be done using the key combination

⟨CONTROL-BREAK⟩

To input this key combination, press and hold down the CON-TROL key (or ⟨CTRL⟩ on many keyboards) and then press ⟨BREAK⟩. This will interrupt the current command and return you to the MS-DOS prompt.

Changing Diskettes. In many applications, you will need to change diskettes while a program is running. For example, your data may be on a different diskette than your application program. In changing diskettes, there are several rules to follow:

Never remove a diskette when the drive light is on.

- Do not change diskettes when the drive light is on. This can damage your diskette and ruin its contents.
- Change diskettes when the MS-DOS prompt is displayed.
- While running a program, follow the particular rules of that program regarding when to change diskettes.

Error Messages

You will note that MS-DOS responds to unusual conditions with displayed messages, called **error messages**. As a beginner, you are most likely to see two messages besides the "Bad command or file name" message mentioned earlier. The first you might receive is the following:

Error accessing drive A:
Abort(A), Retry(R), or Ignore(I)

This message indicates that MS-DOS encountered an error either reading from or writing to the designated diskette. A common reason is that there is no diskette in the drive. Another reason is that the diskette may be damaged or you may have used an unformatted diskette. In any case, you can tell MS-DOS to abort the operation (type the letter A), retry the operation (type the letter R), or ignore the error and continue what it was doing (type the letter I).

The other common error message is

Not a system disk.

Insert disk with COMMAND.COM and press any key.

This message occurs after you have just run a program. At that time, the computer must access the boot diskette to read portions of MS-DOS, which were overwritten by the program. (If necessary, the current program is written over a portion of DOS in RAM.) If MS-DOS displays this message, just insert the boot diskette in the current drive and press any key. The MS-DOS prompt then returns to the screen. The above message can also occur if you try to boot a disk that is not self-booting.

Section 4.2: *Test Your Understanding*

1. What is a self-booting diskette?
2. Describe the procedure for starting MS-DOS from a diskette.
3. Describe the procedure for starting MS-DOS from a hard disk.
4. What is the disk drive light? What does it tell you about the drive?
5. What does the MS-DOS prompt signify?
6. Describe the procedures for correcting typing errors in a command line.
7. How may you interrupt a MS-DOS command or a program?
8. True or false: Change diskettes only when the diskette drive light is on. Explain your answer.
9. What is the significance of the error message

   Bad command or file name

4.3 Files and Devices

The third component of the problem-solving equation is data. When data are stored in a secondary storage device, they are organized into files. In this section, we discuss the file concept and the various facilities of the operating system for manipulating files.

The Concept of a File

A **file** is any collection of information stored in a secondary storage device. All manipulation of data involves manipulation of the files on which the data were entered. Files can be classified into two broad categories: program files and data files.

Program Files. A **program file** contains the instructions for a particular program. For example, the main part of the WordStar word-processing package is stored in the file named WS.COM. The main part of the dBASE III database management program is contained in the file DBASE.EXE. This data cannot be manipulated by the user.

Data Files. A **data file** contains data that can be manipulated by a program. Here are some examples of data files:

- The text of a document produced by a word processor.
- The payroll records of a business.
- A mailing list used by a catalog sales firm.
- The invoices corresponding to the current month's shipments by an office supply house.

The contents of typical data files is illustrated in Figure 4.10. Note how program files and data files are stored side-by-side in secondary storage.

File Manipulation

Much computer data manipulation can be defined in terms of file manipulations. Examples of file manipulation include the following:

- **Writing a file.** Data output from a program may be written into a file for later processing. For example, a program may allow a user to type in invoice information, which is then stored in a data file for later billing.
- **Reading a file.** The contents of a previously written file may later be read by a program for further processing. For example, the contents of the invoice file mentioned above may be read by a program for printing the invoices.
- **Appending a file.** Data may be added to an existing file. For example, a mailing list may be updated by adding new names.
- **Erasing a file.** A file that is no longer necessary may be deleted from storage.
- **Copying a file.** A copy of a file may be stored elsewhere in secondary storage. For example, a copy of a file may be stored on another diskette as a backup.

(a)

(b)

Figure 4.10   Just as you (a) keep information in files in your desk drawer, you can (b) store data files on diskette.

- **Editing a file.** The contents of a file may be altered. For instance, an inventory file may be updated to reflect the current amount of inventory.
- **File Concatenation.** Files may be combined. For example, two different address lists may be concatenated to produce one large list.

File Names

Each file is identified by a name that you, the operating system, and your programs must use when referring to the file. Some typical **file names** might be WS.COM, DBASE.EXE, IN-VOICE.JAN, APPLIC.010, or ANGSTROM.

In MS-DOS, a file name has two parts, a **base name** and an optional **extension**. The base name can consist of up to eight characters; the extension may have a maximum of only three characters. If you do use the extension, it must be separated from the base name by a period. For example, in the file name WS.COM, the base name is WS and the extension is COM. Some file names, such as ANGSTROM, have no extension.

Here are some important facts about file names:

- The characters in a filename can be any combination of letters or digits. Although some other characters are allowed, it is best for a beginner to stick to only letters and digits in file names.
- MS-DOS does not distinguish between uppercase and lower-case letters. For example, the file name EXAMPLE.TXT and example.txt are regarded by MS-DOS as the same.
- A file name should not include any spaces.
- Files containing programs in machine language always have the extensions COM or EXE. The extension COM stands for "COMmand" and EXE stands for "EXEcute." These extensions are reserved for program names and the operating system treats files with these extensions in special ways. Consequently, you should never use these extensions for data files or any other file types you use in connection with application programs.

Device Names

MS-DOS has special **device names** for the various system components. For example, MS-DOS identifies diskette drives and hard disks by letters followed by colons: A:, B:, C:, and so forth.

If a system has only one diskette drive, then MS-DOS considers this drive as both A: and B:. This is the case, for example, in a computer having a single diskette drive and a hard disk. In executing commands requiring two drives on such a computer, MS-DOS alternately considers the single drive as A: and B: and prompts you to exchange diskettes in this drive, as the command requires.

MS-DOS has specific names for other system devices as well. They are

LPT1: = printer #1
LPT2: = printer #2
KYBD: = keyboard
SCRN: = screen
COM1: = communications port #1
COM2: = communications port #2

These system device names can be used in connection with application programs. For instance, you may want a database-management program to send a report on sales activity to the printer instead of the screen. This may be accomplished by giving an operating system command to redirect the output from the screen (device SCRN:) to the printer (device LPT1:).

The operating system usually recognizes optional adapter cards as additional system devices. For instance, an asynchronous communications card or a modem is assigned one of the device names COM1: or COM2: (COM = communications).

File Specifications

To identify a file accurately, you need to enter both the file name and the device containing the file. The combination of a file name and a device name is called a **file specification**. For example, the file specification

A:EXAMPLE.TXT

identifies the file EXAMPLE.TXT, which is stored on the diskette in drive A:. Similarly, the file specification

C:WS.COM

identifies the file WS.COM on drive C:.

No device name is needed for files on the default drive. If you identify a file only by its file name (and not the device name), then the computer assumes that the file is on the current drive.

No device name is needed for files on the default drive.

```
Wed   4-16-1986
16:14:14.33 C>dir

 Volume in drive C has no label
 Directory of  C:\PROJECT

 .            <DIR>      11-27-85   11:09p
 ..           <DIR>      11-27-85   11:09p
 PROJ    COM    5617     10-09-84   12:00p
 PROJ    PGM   57856     10-09-84   12:00p
 PROJ    OVL   55296     10-09-84   12:00p
 PROJ    HLP   44905     10-09-84   12:00p
 LJG     CAL    1899      8-27-85   10:06p
 LJG     ACT    1728      8-27-85   10:06p
 LJG     RES     364      8-27-85   10:06p
 APPLIC  ACT    3072      1-01-80   11:15p
 APPLIC  RES     340      1-01-80   11:15p
 APPLIC  CAL    1898      1-01-80   11:15p
        12 File(s)  11554816 bytes free

Wed   4-16-1986
16:14:19.26 C>
```

Figure 4.11   The directory of a diskette.

Figure 4.12   An abbreviated directory display.

```
Wed   4-16-1986
16:16:06.08 C>dir /w

 Volume in drive C has no label
 Directory of  C:\C\LC

 .                    ..                    C                  L                     SOURCE
 MAKELC   BAT    LOADLC   BAT    LCS      BAT    LCL      BAT    LCD      BAT
 LCP      BAT    LINKS    BAT    LINKP    BAT    LINKD    BAT    LINKL    BAT
 LINKC    BAT    LINKMS   BAT    LINKMP   BAT    LINKMD   BAT    LINKML   BAT
 LINKMC   BAT    FXU      EXE    OMD      EXE    PLIB86   EXE    LC1      EXE
 LC2      EXE    LC       COM    STDIO    H      IOS1     H      CTYPE    H
 ERROR    H      MATH     H      SETJMP   H      LIMITS   H      DOS      H
 FCNTL    H      HDR      H      8087     MAC    TBLXN    C      CL       OBJ
 C        EXE    TBLXN    H      TBLXN    OBJ    LCM      LIB    LIBS
        45 File(s)  11554816 bytes free

Wed   4-16-1986
16:16:09.09 C>
```

The Directory

You may list the files on a particular drive by using the MS-DOS command DIR (for DIRECTORY). As you saw earlier in this chapter, to list the directory of the diskette in drive A:, you could use the MS-DOS command

DIR A: ⟨ENTER/RETURN⟩

In response, MS-DOS produces a display like the one in Figure 4.11. Note that the directory display contains a great deal of information about each file. At the extreme left is the file name and the extension. Next is the size of the file, in bytes, then the date and time that the file was last altered.

There are several useful variations on the DIR command. The command

DIR ⟨ENTER/RETURN⟩

gives the directory of the current drive.

Sometimes, the list of files in a directory is too large to fit on the screen. In this case, you can request an abbreviated directory display similar to the one in Figure 4.12. This display includes only the file name, but is arranged in columns across the screen so that many more directory entries fit onto a single screen. For example, to obtain an abbreviated directory of drive A:, use the following command (in which /W stands for "wide display"):

DIR A: /W

Section 4.3: *Test Your Understanding*

1. What is a file?
2. What are the two types of files?
3. List four file manipulations.
4. What is file editing?
5. What is file concatenation?
6. Identify which of the following file names are permissible in MS-DOS. If a file name is not permissible, explain why.
   a. ACCOUNTS.JAN
   b. ACCOUNTS.JANUARY
   c. SALESMEETING
   d. DIV BOOKS
7. What are the file name extensions used for machine language programs?
8. Write a file specification for the file PAYROLL.JAN located on the diskette in drive B:.

9. Write a command to change the current drive to B:.
10. What does MS-DOS command DIR do?
11. What is the directory of a disk?
12. Write a command to display the directory of drive C:.

4.4 Some Elementary MS-DOS Commands

To use application programs, you need to know only a few MS-DOS commands. We have already discussed the DIR command for reading the directory of a diskette. Now look at some other commands that are absolutely essential to using MS-DOS.

Formatting Diskettes

Before you can use a diskette for writing or reading, it must undergo a process known as **formatting**. To format a diskette using the MS-DOS **FORMAT** command, follow this procedure:

1. Place the boot diskette in the current drive and type
    FORMAT ⟨ENTER/RETURN⟩

2. MS-DOS will read the FORMAT program from the boot diskette. When the drive light goes out, remove the boot diskette and replace it with the diskette to be formatted.

3. You will see a message similar to this:
    A⟩ Insert new diskette for drive A:
    and strike ENTER when ready
    In response to the prompt, press ⟨ENTER/RETURN⟩.

4. The computer will now format the diskette. The process will take one or two minutes, depending on the type of diskette drive. When formatting is completed, MS-DOS will display a prompt asking whether you want to format another diskette. Answer the question with ⟨Y⟩ or ⟨N⟩ and press ⟨ENTER/RETURN⟩.

5. If you answer ⟨Y⟩, then you may insert another diskette to be formatted and press ⟨ENTER/RETURN⟩. In this way, you may format any number of diskettes in sequence.

6. If you answer ⟨N⟩ and press ⟨ENTER/RETURN⟩, the MS-DOS prompt will return to the screen.

The above procedure works on a system with one diskette drive. However, in systems with two or more drives, you can avoid the diskette swapping by using the command

FORMAT B: ⟨ENTER/RETURN⟩

Here we assume that A: is the current drive and that the boot diskette is in drive A:. The diskette to be formatted should be placed in drive B:. In response to this command, MS-DOS will format the diskette in drive B: without any diskette swapping.

You should plan to format in advance an adequate supply of diskettes to hold your data. There is nothing more annoying than to be in the middle of a project and not be able to find a formatted diskette to use.

Formatting a diskette will erase any data or programs already on the disk.

If your system has a hard disk, this also must be formatted before you can store data on it. The procedure is somewhat more complex than that for formatting a diskette. Moreover, since a hard disk holds so much more data, the formatting process for a hard disk can take as long an hour. We refer you to the MS-DOS manual for details of the process.

Be careful in formatting diskettes. If a diskette has already been formatted, then reformatting erases all data on the diskette. There is no way to retrieve the data on a reformatted diskette. The reformatting of a hard disk is even more of a disaster. Imagine losing thousands of pages of data because of an accidental FORMAT command!

Copying Files

The **COPY** command is a versatile command for making copies of files. It can make a copy of a file having either the same or a different file name. The general form of the command is

COPY (FILESPEC1) (FILESPEC2)

This command copies the file with specification FILESPEC1 (the original file) to the file with specification FILESPEC2 (the file in which a copy of the original is to be inserted). For example, the command

COPY A:ALPHA B:BETA

copies the file ALPHA on drive A: to the file BETA on drive B:. As another example, the command

COPY EXAMPLE.TXT C:EX1

makes a copy of the file EXAMPLE.TXT (from the current drive). The copy is named EX1 and is located on drive C:.

If you are not changing the file name on the copy, you may shorten the command. For example, the command

COPY A:EXAMPLE.TXT B:

copies the file EXAMPLE.TXT on A: to B:. The name of the copy is also EXAMPLE.TXT.

Copying Diskettes and Making Backups

We have already mentioned the importance of making backups. Diskettes are not that fragile, but accidents do happen. Your diskette might be run over by a bicycle, or, busily trying to make a deadline, you might spill coffee on it. To guard against mishaps, back up your diskettes. Make at least two copies of each of your diskettes. As you make changes in a diskette, back up those changes at least once each day. If you don't pursue a rigorous backup policy, **you will be sorry**.

The MS-DOS command **DISKCOPY** is used to back up diskettes while COPY will only copy individual files.

To use the DISKCOPY command on a system with two floppy disk drives, follow this procedure:

1. Place the boot diskette in the current drive.
2. Type
   DISKCOPY A: B:
3. You will see this display:
   Insert SOURCE diskette in drive A:
   and the TARGET diskette in drive B:
   Press any key when ready...

   In response to this prompt, remove the boot disk and replace it with the diskette from which you wish to copy (the **source diskette**). Place the diskette that will become the copy (the **target diskette**) in the diskette drive B: (the one on the right).
4. After you press any key, you will get a message similar to this:
   Copying 40 tracks
   9 Sectors/track, 2 side(s)

5. MS-DOS will copy the source diskette onto the target diskette.
6. If necessary, MS-DOS will format the diskette as it does the copying.
7. When the data has been copied you will see the message
   Copy another diskette (Y/N)?

If you do not wish to copy another diskette, press ⟨N⟩ and the MS-DOS prompt will reappear.

The above procedure may be used on systems having two diskette drives. For systems with only one drive, insert the boot diskette and type

DISKCOPY

MS-DOS will prompt you to swap diskettes, alternately inserting the source diskette and the target diskette into the drive.

The DISKCOPY command will format a new diskette as it copies to it.

Erasing Files

You may erase unneeded files by using the **ERASE** command. The format of the ERASE command is

ERASE (FILESPEC)

For example, to erase the file EXAMPLE.TXT on drive C:, use the command

ERASE C:EXAMPLE.TXT

Be extremely careful in using the ERASE command. It is easier than you think to accidentally erase files that you need.

Section 4.4: Test Your Undersatnding

1. What does formatting a diskette accomplish?
2. Can you guess what happens if you attempt to read from a diskette that has not been formatted?
3. Test your answer to question 2 by attempting to read the directory of an unformatted diskette.
4. Write a command to format the diskette in drive A:.
5. True or false: Formatting a diskette that has already been formatted erases all data contained on the diskette.
6. Write a command to copy the file PAYROLL.JAN from drive A: to drive B:.
7. Write a command to copy the file PAYROLL.JAN from drive B: to the file JAN on drive A:.
8. Make a backup copy of your boot diskette.
9. In a copying operation, what is the source diskette? The target diskette?
10. What is the difference between the MS-DOS commands COPY and DISKCOPY?
11. Write a command to erase the file MORTGAGE.001 on drive C: .

KEY TERMS

software	multi-user capability	appending a file
system software	network	erasing a file
bootstrap loader	multi-tasking capability	copying a file
diagnostic routines	windows	file concatenation
service functions	CP/M	file name
operating system	disk operating system	base name
booting the system	(DOS)	extension
boot diskette	MS-DOS	device name
system diskette	PC-DOS	file specification
command processor	MS-DOS prompt	formatting
self-booting	current drive	COPY command
user interface	default drive	DISKCOPY command
menu-based interface	file	source diskette
menu	program file	target diskette
graphics-based interface	data file	ERASE command
icons	writing a file	
mouse	reading a file	

CHAPTER REVIEW QUESTIONS

1. What are the three broad classifications of programs?
2. What is the the bootstrap loader? How does it function?
3. List the steps you must take in order to run a program.
4. What is a file?
5. Give three examples of data files.
6. Give three examples of manipulations that programs can perform on files.
7. Describe how to copy a file from drive B: to drive A:.

8. Which of the following are acceptable filenames?
   a) EXAMPLE TXT
   b) 123.COM
   c) A
   d) NEWPAYROLL
   e) RESEARCH.0001
9. What is multi-tasking?
10. Give an example where a multi-user system would be useful.

DISCUSSION QUESTIONS

1. Discuss the importance of making backups of all your diskettes.
2. Some people object to placing both their original and their backup diskette into the computer at the same time, since this can lead to mistakes and loss of data. Design a backup scheme to get around this limitation.

APPLICATION PROJECTS

1. Format a diskette.
2. Copy the file COMMAND.COM from the boot diskette onto your freshly formatted diskette.
3. Check that the copy of the file is on the formatted diskette by consulting the directory.
4. Erase the copy of the file COMMAND.COM that you just created.
5. Check that the copy has been erased by consulting the directory.

II
Application Software

5 Word Processing

Soup Is Good Food for Micros

If, as a child, you never spent a cold winter's lunchtime in front of a steaming bowl of Campbell's chicken noodle soup, you missed one of childhood's quintessential experiences. Though long since diversified into many other food product lines, Campbell Soup Company is most well-known for its soup in the famous red-and-white cans. With revenues of $4 billion, Campbell ranks within the top 100 companies of the Fortune 500.

Microcomputers have played a big role in the company's most recent growth. In particular, word processing is an important ingredient of micro use at headquarters in Camden, New Jersey. Hundreds of Campbell employees, from secretaries to professionals and managers, use micros and word processing software to write letters, memos, and reports.

Kathy Kilpatrick, a secretary at Campbell, remembers the days when she had no microcomputer and each successive draft had to be typed and retyped. Now she has a micro, and two programs: DisplayWrite 3 and Multi-Mate, which she uses to type documents for members of her work group. All her correspondence, memos, reports, and documentation are now done on the micro.

Creating a document on her micro is far simpler than rolling a sheet of paper into a typewriter—Kilpatrick just picks the command for creating a file out of a menu list. In a second, her new file opens up on screen. Once the document is keyed in, changes are simple to make and faster than when she retyped each document on a typewriter. "It's really fast to do revisions," Kilpatrick says.

The speed and ease of the micro are also a real advantage to her boss. In the past, a manager might have been reluctant to ask a secretary to retype something for the sixth time. "Bosses now feel freer to fine-tune their thoughts," Kilpatrick notes, because they know that revisions can just be typed right over the previous draft on screen. "It only takes minutes to change something," she says.

Kilpatrick gives her boss a printout of the letter or memo, which can be edited. She then enters all the changes from her boss's marked-up copy into her document. In a flash, all the edits are complete. As Kilpatrick says, the microcomputer "makes office work better for everybody."

A T THE BEGINNING of this book, you were introduced to the problem-solving equation:

Hardware + software + data + user = problem solution.

Chapters 5 through 11 of this text deal with the software element of this equation and introduce three primary types of application software: word processors, spreadsheets, and database management programs. Although this textbook will be generic in its approach, it will provide guidelines for hands-on experience with certain popular packages, including the GoldSoft package available with this text.

The first type of application software, word processing, has literally thousands of applications that can help you prepare almost any form of text material. Even a partial list, such as the following, that presents the types of documents a word processor can produce is impressive:

- Memos
- Reports
- Mailing lists
- Form letters
- Financial statements
- Letters
- Books
- Advertising brochures

The creation of this textbook makes an interesting case study in the use of word processing. I entered my manuscript using Word, a word processor from Microsoft Corporation. Completed chapters were transmitted via phone lines from my office in Maryland to the editors in Massachusetts, who edited the chapters on the same type of word processor and then sent printouts of the chapters to professors for review. The editors received the reviewers' comments, then entered them and final editorial changes into the electronic manuscript. These changes, which were set in boldface italic type so that they could be found at a glance, were then transmitted back to me via phone lines.

After acting upon the reviewers' comments and making my final alterations, I transmitted the manuscript back to Massachusetts via telephone lines. There the word processor again came into play, this time when a keyboarder entered control codes telling the phototypesetter the size and style of type to be used, the spacing between lines, the page layout, and so forth. The editors then transmitted the electronic manuscript to the compositor, who fed it into a phototypesetter and eventually generated the camera copy that would be sent to the printer.

By creating an electronic manuscript, we cut in half the amount of time it took to write and produce this book. This chapter and the next introduce you to the fundamentals and concepts of word processing so you can apply them to solve problems of your own.

5.1 Word Processors in the Office

A business runs on words. Some of the words are spoken, in oral instructions and discussions. Some of the words are printed or recorded, in the form of advertisements. Still others are written, in orderly business records, memos, reports, and letters. Some of this written material is for internal use. However, much of it is sent outside the business, to customers, suppliers, government regulators (such as the Internal Revenue Service), and many other individuals and organizations.

The typical business generates a large volume of work on paper each year. Even a small business can produce tens of thousands of pages. For the sake of both appearance and legibility, most of this material must be typed.

Until recently, the only way to produce printed material was to type it on a typewriter—an inefficient and costly approach. It has been estimated that it costs about $5 to produce a typical business letter, including labor costs involved. These costs quickly escalate when it becomes necessary to produce multiple drafts of a document, as is often the case. The typist must begin the typing task from scratch for each draft.

Enter the word processor, the application software that changed text-processing procedures in offices throughout the world. In only ten years, the word processor emerged as a standard part of almost every office and a cornerstone of the new, automated office concept.

> The word processor has enabled office workers to increase productivity and efficiency, thereby cutting costs and time involved in creating documents.

5.2 Word Processing Concepts

What Is a Word Processor?

A **word processor** is an application program for manipulating text. There are word processors for use on computers of all sizes. The following discussion focuses on word processing programs that run on microcomputers.

Using a word processor, you can enter text documents into RAM and save them, edit text (add, delete, or rearrange words), and print out documents on paper. Some word processors have additional features that can do the following:

- Correct the spelling in your document.
- Generate a table of contents or an index automatically.
- Use proportional spacing and varied type styles (e.g., bold and italic, as well as different type fonts) to enhance the look of your printed documents.
- Merge variable information, such as names and addresses from a mailing list, into a document.

Word processors were introduced in the early 1970s by corporations such as NBI, Wang, Lanier, and Lexitron. The first word processors were specialized microcomputers, not programs. These microcomputers used some of the first microprocessors, but they were not general-purpose computers. Called **stand-alone** or **dedicated word processors**, they were designed to run only a single program that allowed them to process text, not other application programs such as accounting or data management. These specialized word processors are still in common use today.

With the introduction of more flexible general-purpose micro-computers in the late 1970s came a number of accompanying word processing programs. Today these programs provide many (if not all) of the features found on the stand-alone word processors. However, they are independent programs that run the same way any other application program runs. Office workers can enhance their productivity by running not only a word-processing program but also spreadsheet and data management programs that could not run on a stand-alone word processor. Figure 5.1 illustrates the differences between a microcomputer and a dedicated word pro-cessor.

How Word Processing Works

A word processor allows you to create a document and store it in electronic form. Ultimately, the document conveys information to one or more recipients. To distribute the document, you may print it on paper (for example, a report to members of a project team) or you may transfer it to another microcomputer screen (perhaps via electronic mail, as detailed in Chapter 13).

Every word-processed document—from the time it is first conceived by its author until it reaches its audience—will pass through a number of phases:

1. *Input*. In this step, you type, or **enter**, the document just as you would on a typewriter; the result is called **input**. Your

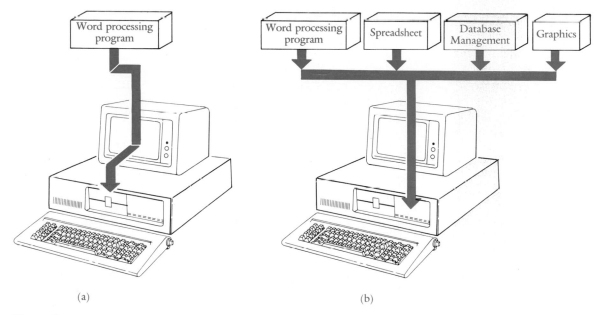

Figure 5.1 Word processors: (a) stand-alone word processor versus (b) micro-computer.

input appears on the monitor screen. Entering text is sometimes called **keyboarding**.

2. *Edit*. When you **edit**, you correct any errors in the document and make additions and alterations. You can edit as a separate step or you can incorporate editing as part of the keyboarding process.

3. *Save*. After you enter and edit the document, you can store or **save** it on diskette or hard disk.

4. *Recall*. You can retrieve or **recall** a document from storage on diskette or hard disk for editing or printing at any time.

5. *Print*. If you want to **print** a copy of a document on paper, you can ask for either a simple reproduction of the document as entered in RAM, a more complex formatting of the document if you want to create a particular "look." Printing may also include merging variable information in the document, such as names and addresses from a mailing list.

The steps involved in word processing are illustrated in Figure 5.2.

Section 5.2 Test Your Understanding

1. What is a word processor?

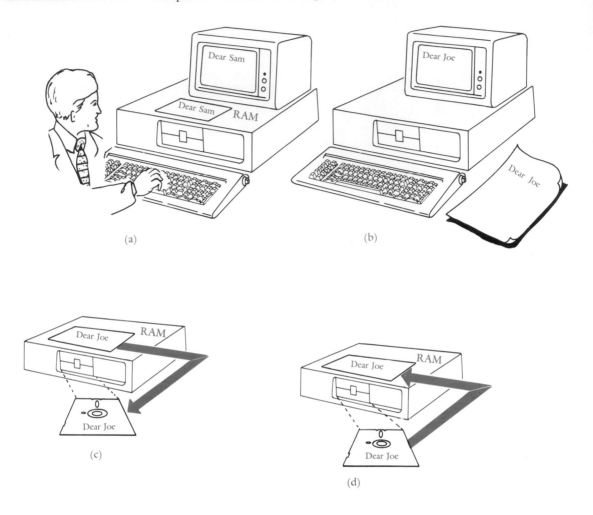

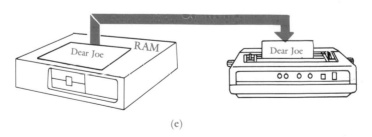

Figure 5.2   Steps in word processing. (a) Enter: type the document. (b) Edit: Correct your errors. (c) Save: Store your document on disk. (d) Recall: Recall your document from storage on disk. (e) Print: Print a hard copy of your document.

2. What is the difference between a stand-alone word processor and a word processing program?
3. List and describe the steps to follow in preparing a document on a word processor.
4. What is keyboarding?
5. List three applications of word processing.

5.3 Getting Started with a Word Processor

Installing Software

Before you can use a word processor (or any other piece of application software, for that matter), you need to install the software, so that it works with your particular configuration of disk drives, display adapter, and printer. The installation process includes the following steps:

1. *Make backup copies of the program diskette.* Note that some word processing programs are **copy-protected**, which means that you cannot make backup copies. (For a more detailed discussion of copy protection and software piracy issues, see Chapter 15.) With unprotected programs, you can make a limited number of backups. If backup copies are permitted, you should make copies of all diskettes supplied with the word processing package, as a safety precaution. You can copy them using the procedure described in Chapter 4.

   To protect your application program diskettes, make one or two backup copies.

2. *If you have a hard disk, write the word processing program onto the hard disk.* If your system has a hard disk, you will want to copy your word processing program onto this disk. You can usually do this by using the COPY command. By storing the program on your hard disk, you can save yourself the trouble of swapping diskettes between drives. Moreover, the program will perform better because a hard disk has faster access times than a diskette drive. Note, however, that some copy-protected programs may not allow copying onto a hard disk, while others allow copying onto a hard disk by using a special procedure.

3. *Specify the default data drive,* the drive that will, in the absence of further instructions, be used to save and retrieve documents. In MS-DOS systems, the program diskette goes in drive A: and the data diskette used for documents goes in drive B:. In hard disk systems, both the program and document locations default to the hard disk, which is usually drive C:.

4. *Specify your printer.* Different printers accept different control signals, so it is usually necessary to install your word processing program for a particular printer. Installation details vary from program to program, so consult your program manual for the details of installing your particular word processor. Many word processing programs lead you through the installation details using an installation program, typically called INSTALL.EXE or INSTALL.BAT on one of the diskettes supplied. Using such a program reduces the process of installation to answering a series of questions posed by the installation program.

You may, depending on the hardware available to you, want to make several working copies of the program, each one installed for a different hardware configuration, say one using a draft quality printer and another using a letter quality printer.

Hands-On: Some Particular Word Processors

This text utilizes the following three programs in the hands-on portions of the word-processing discussions:

WordStar from MicroPro Corporation
Word from Microsoft Corporation
GoldWord from Goldstein Software, Inc.

Each of these word processors is a so-called "full-featured word processor," meaning it includes most of the major functions available in modern word processing programs. These programs do exhibit some differences of design, but such differences will actually be helpful in pointing out the variety of design possibilities for today's application packages.

The text discussion provides the commands you can use with these particular word processors to implement word processing concepts and functions. If you are using one of these word processors, you can follow the discussion in a "hands-on" fashion.

Starting a Word Processor

To start a word-processing program, follow these steps:

1. Start the computer and boot up with your system disk to obtain the MS-DOS prompt.
2. If necessary, insert the program diskette in Drive A: and a formatted data diskette in Drive B: .
3. Make the drive containing the word processing program the default drive.
4. Give the command to execute the word processing program,

as shown in Command Table 5.1, for each of our sample word processors.

The program will display an identification screen telling you the name of the program along with the copyright information. The program then displays the opening menu, or **main menu**, from which you can choose your next action and communicate commands to the computer (change the default drive to store documents, edit a file, print a file, return to the operating system). Let's take a closer look at the main menus for our sample word processors.

The Main Menu

Figures 5.3, 5.4, and 5.5 show the main menus corresponding to our three sample word processors. The screens look different, but each serves the same function. Since the three programs illustrate different approaches to command structure, let's compare them by giving the command to edit a file for each of these word processors.

The main menu is a handy summary of your word processor's command structure.

WordStar. In WordStar, the main menu is called the No-File menu, since this menu is displayed when you are not manipulating a file. The No-File menu lists the possible commands you can give the word processor at that moment and the corresponding keystrokes to implement the commands. The No-File menu lists the command to edit a file as D (for "Open a document file"). Press the letter ⟨D⟩ (without pressing ⟨ENTER/RETURN⟩). The program requests the name of the file you want to edit. Note that the bottom of the screen shows the directory of the diskette in the default drive.

Now type in the name of the file to be edited. For example, to edit the file EXAMPLE.TXT, enter ⟨EXAMPLE.TXT⟩. Since

Command Table 5.1 Commands to start the word-processing programs WordStar, Word, and GoldWord.

Program	Command	Comments
WordStar	WS ⟨ENTER⟩	Start WordStar and go to main menu.
	WS filespec ⟨ENTER⟩	Start Wordstar and edit file.
Word	WORD ⟨ENTER⟩	Start Word and go to main menu.
	WORD filespec⟨ENTER⟩	Start Word and edit file.
GoldWord	GW ⟨ENTER⟩	Start GoldWord and go to main menu.
	GW filespec ⟨ENTER⟩	Start GoldWord and edit file.

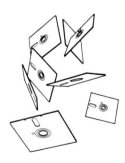

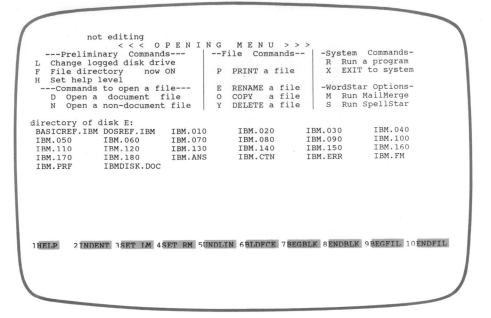

Figure 5.3   The WordStar No-File menu.

Figure 5.4   The Microsoft Word main menu.

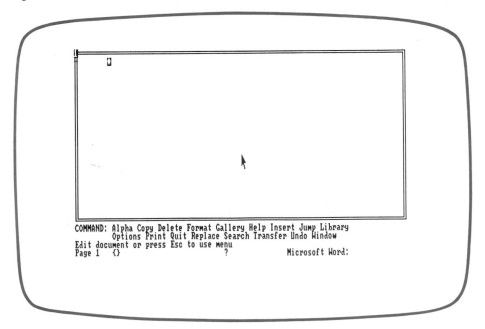

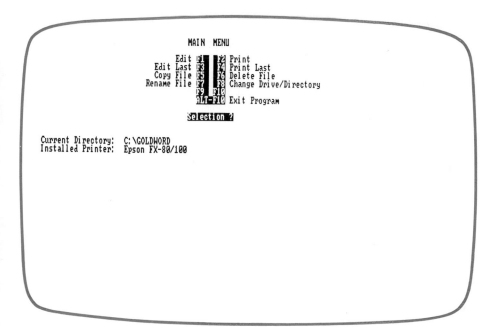

```
                    MAIN MENU
              Edit [F1]  [F2] Print
         Edit Last [F3]  [F4] Print Last
         Copy File [F5]  [F6] Delete File
       Rename File [F7]  [F8] Change Drive/Directory
                   [F9] [F10]
                   [ALT-F10] Exit Program
                   Selection ?

Current Directory:  C:\GOLDWORD
Installed Printer:  Epson FX-80/100
```

Figure 5.5 The GoldWord main menu.

you haven't specified a drive, WordStar assumes that the file is located on the diskette in the default drive. If the file exists, the program will retrieve it from the diskette and display the beginning of the file, ready for editing. If the file does not exist, the program assumes that it is a new file and creates an empty file to receive your document.

Word. Let's now perform the same sequence of operations using Word. Note that the main menu of Word does not contain the word EDIT or anything close to it. In Word, all file operations are called **transfers**. Note that TRANSFER is one of the entries on the menu. To execute a menu option, press the ESCAPE key, which causes the cursor to move from the top of the screen into the main menu options. Then enter the first letter of the command you want to execute. For example, to execute TRANSFER, press ⟨ESCAPE⟩, then ⟨T⟩. A new menu of choices replaces the main menu at the bottom of the screen. Figure 5.6 illustrates Word's TRANSFER menu.

In the jargon of Word, we wish to LOAD a file, so we press ⟨L⟩. The program now asks for the name of the file. Type ⟨EXAMPLE.TXT⟩ as you did with WordStar and press ⟨ENTER/

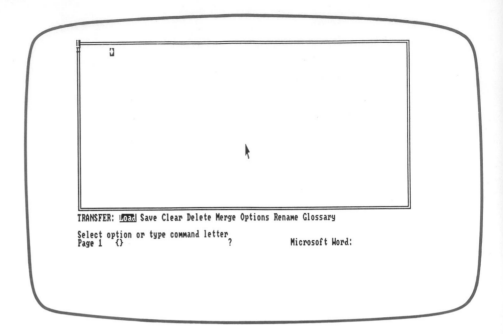

TRANSFER: Load Save Clear Delete Merge Options Rename Glossary

Select option or type command letter
Page 1   {}   ?   Microsoft Word:

Figure 5.6   Word's TRANSFER menu.

RETURN⟩. If the file exists, Word displays the beginning of the file, ready for editing. If the file does not exist, Word asks you for permission to create the file. If you answer ⟨Y⟩ (for YES), Word creates an empty file EXAMPLE.TXT and displays a blank screen ready for your document.

Word uses the ESCAPE key to indicate that the next keystroke or keystrokes are part of a command, not data to be entered into a file. If you want to cancel the current command, press ⟨ESCAPE⟩ repeatedly until the main menu is displayed. (Each time you press ⟨ESCAPE⟩, the menus go back one step.) To enter text, press ⟨A⟩ (for the ALPHA entry on the menu) followed by ⟨ENTER/ RETURN⟩. The cursor will return to the top of the screen, where you will enter your document.

This sequence of menus, called a **submenu approach**, has become a popular command structure in application software because, at any given moment, the user is presented with a list of the options available. You don't need to memorize a list of commands or to refer to an outside source, such as the program documentation, if you forget a command. Just select the command from the list shown.

Word also allows you to use a mouse to point to a menu choice rather than pressing ⟨ESCAPE⟩ and a letter. This option further enhances the user interface by simplifying the process of giving commands. However, since most schools don't have mice in their computer laboratories, we won't discuss their use here. If you are interested in using a mouse with Word, see the Word reference manual for details.

GoldWord. This word processor employs yet another command structure, which uses the function keys. Note that the main menu displays a replica of the ten function keys, F1 through F10. Beside each function key is a command description. The main menu also displays the directory of the default drive. Function key F1 activates the command EDIT. If you press ⟨F1⟩, the program asks you for a file name to edit. From here GoldWord proceeds very much like the other two sample word processors.

The main menu command structures of the three sample word processors are quite different, but they all accomplish the same thing: *they guide the user in choosing commands to execute particular functions*. You will see variations on each of these command structures repeated in many word processor packages.

Section 5.3: Test Your Understanding

1. Why must a word processor be installed?
2. What is the default data drive?
3. True or false: A word-processing program automatically works with any printer that is compatible with your computer. Explain your answer.
4. List the steps you must follow to start a word processor.
5. Describe your main menu and how it differs from the main menus of other word processors.

Hands-on Exercises

1. Install your word processor.
2. Start your word processor and obtain the main menu.
3. Find the command on your word processor's main menu that ends the word processing program. Execute this command and return to MS-DOS.

5.4 Creating and Editing Text

Now that you know how to start a word processor, you need to learn how to create and edit documents.

The Data Input Screen

When you give the command to edit a document, the program displays a **data input screen**. Think of this as a piece of electronic "paper" that you can type on with your keyboard. The layout of the data input screen varies with each word processor; a typical screen is shown in Figure 5.7. The bottom of the screen is the **typing area** where you enter your document. The cursor indicates the position at which the next typed characters will appear.

Just above the typing area is the **ruler line** (also called a **format line**), which serves as a reminder for the current line layout. The left end of the ruler line indicates the current left-hand margin; the right end of the ruler line indicates the current right-hand margin. The precise format of the ruler line depends on the particular word processor. The one shown in Figure 5.7 is the ruler line used by GoldWord. The dashes in the ruler line indicate character positions. In the ruler line shown, the lines are 65 characters wide. Each "v"

Figure 5.7   The WordStar screen, a typical data input screen.

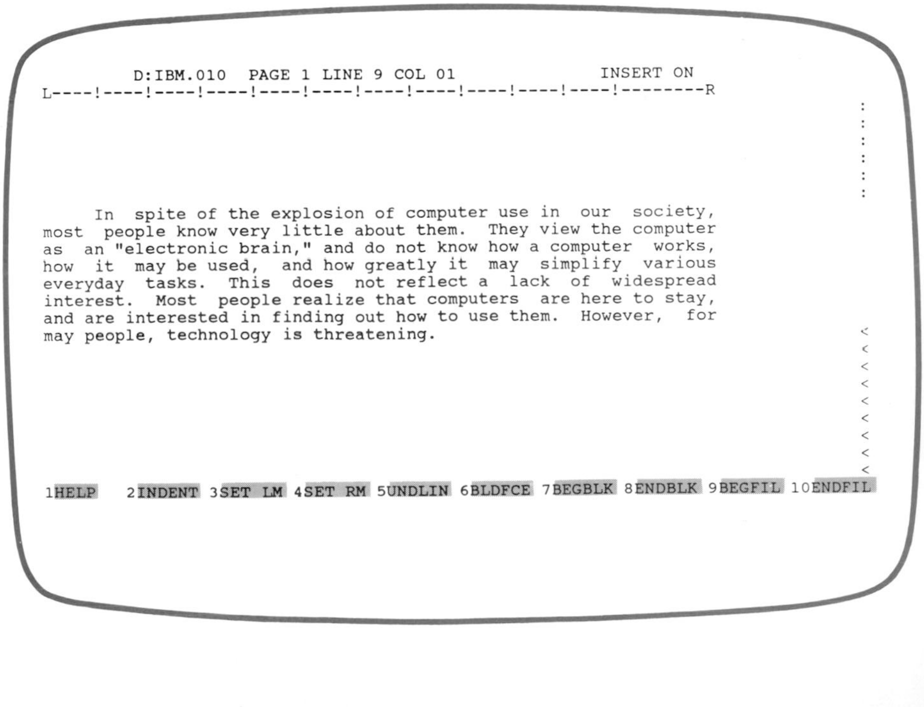

```
        D:IBM.010   PAGE 1 LINE 9 COL 01              INSERT ON
L----!----!----!----!----!----!----!----!----!----!----!-------R                :
                                                                                 :
                                                                                 :
                                                                                 :
       In  spite of the explosion of computer use in  our  society,
most  people know very little about them.  They view the computer
as  an "electronic brain," and do not know how a computer  works,
how  it  may be used,  and how greatly it  may  simplify  various
everyday  tasks.  This  does  not reflect  a  lack of widespread
interest.  Most  people realize that computers  are here to stay,
and are interested in finding out how to use them.  However,  for               <
may people, technology is threatening.                                          <
                                                                                 <
                                                                                 <
                                                                                 <
                                                                                 <
                                                                                 <
                                                                                 <

1HELP    2INDENT 3SET LM 4SET RM 5UNDLIN 6BLDFCE 7BEGBLK 8ENDBLK 9BEGFIL 10ENDFIL
```

indicates the position of a tab stop, every five character positions. You may reset these tab stops to align columns of data as needed. (The command for resetting tab stops is discussed in the next chapter.)

For the sake of comparison, we show the ruler lines for Word and WordStar in Figure 5.8. Note, however, that the ruler in Word is normally shown only while you assign a format to a paragraph.

The **status lines** give **status information**, including the name of the file being edited, the number of the line and the number of the column where the cursor is currently located on the page. The status lines can appear at the top or the bottom of the screen, depending on the word processor. In the example shown in Figure 5.7, the cursor is at the beginning of the document EXAMPLE.TXT, so the line number is 1 and the column number is 1. As you type, the line number and column number change according to the current cursor position.

Entering Text

In many ways, typing on a word processor is similar to typing on a typewriter, but there are some differences. Instead of recording the keystrokes on paper, the word processor stores keystrokes in RAM and displays them on the screen. Suppose you type the following sentence:

Here is an example of a sentence typed by a word processor.

The screen for one of our sample word processors, Goldword, will appear as shown in Figure 5.9.

The DELETE Key

When you make a mistake on a typewriter, you erase the erroneous characters and retype them. With a word processor, you use the **DELETE key** instead of an eraser. In most word processors, the DELETE key is the **BACKSPACE key** (often indicated with an arrow pointing left). There are some exceptions, such as WordStar, for which the DELETE key is the key combination ⟨CTRL-G⟩.

Here is how to use the DELETE key. Suppose that you have typed the following:

Please have this letter primted._

(The underscore (_) indicates the current position of the cursor.) To correct the typing mistake in the word *primt*, use the cursor-motion keys to reposition the cursor on the *m* in *primt*, and press ⟨DELETE⟩. The line now looks like this:

Please have this letter prited.

Use the DELETE key on your screen as you would use an eraser on paper.

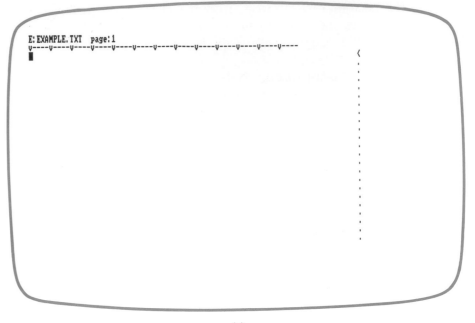

E: EXAMPLE.TXT   page: 1

(a)

```
1═[····|····1·········2·········3·········4·········5·········]·········7·····]
  manual calculations, they  were  able  to  devise  calendars
  which predicted the correct time to plant their  fields  and
  harvest their crops.

       For thousands of years, calculations and data  analysis
  was done by hand. One can only marvel  at  the  acheivements
  which were due as much to incredible  perseverance  as  they
  were to academic brilliance. For instance, Johannes  Keppler
  derived his laws which govern  the  motion  of  the  planets
  about  the  sun  from  forty  years  of  observations   and
  calculations. In  his  diary,  he  complains  of  individual
  calculations taking as long as 80 hours!

       In  the  last  decade,  microcomputers  have  become  a
  commonplace problem-solving tool for performing  calculation
  and data analysis tasks formerly done by  hand  or,  in  the
  last  few  decades,  by  large,  so-called  "mainframe",
```

FORMAT PARAGRAPH alignment: Left Centered Right Justified
       left indent: 0"   first line: 0.5"   right indent: 0"
       line spacing: 1 li   space before: 0 li   space after: 0 li
       keep together: Yes(No) keep follow: Yes(No) side by side: Yes(No)
Select option
P2 D2   ()   ?   Microsoft Word: APPLIC.010

(b)

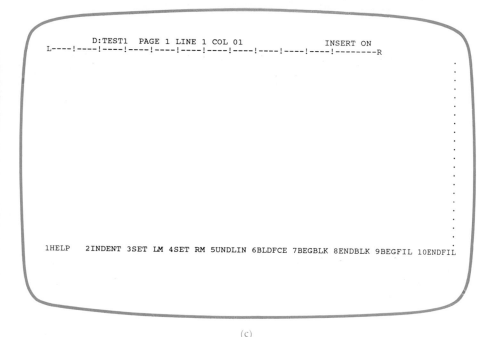

```
       D:TEST1  PAGE 1 LINE 1 COL 01              INSERT ON
L----!----!----!----!----!----!----!----!----!----!-------R
```

```
 1HELP    2INDENT 3SET LM 4SET RM 5UNDLIN 6BLDFCE 7BEGBLK 8ENDBLK 9BEGFIL 10ENDFIL
```

(c)

Figure 5.8 The ruler lines for (a) GoldWord, (b) Word, and (c) WordStar.

Now enter *n* to replace the deleted *m*; the *n* will be inserted after the *i*. The letters beginning with and to the right of the cursor are moved to the right, and the error is corrected. Use the cursor-motion keys to reposition the cursor to the end of the line and continue typing where you left off.

Word Wrap and Carriage Returns

When using a typewriter, you must manually advance lines by using the carriage return. In this respect, using a word processor is very different. Once you have set up the margins and line layout, the word processor automatically decides when to end a line. As soon as you type a word that will not fit on the current line, the word processor moves it to the next line. This feature is called **word wrap**—the word "wraps" around to the next line.

In some word processors, the word wrap feature includes automatic hyphenation. Among our sample word processors, only WordStar has this feature. When a word will not fit on a line, WordStar attempts to hyphenate it so that a portion of the word fits. The program presents you with the proposed hyphenation for you to approve. If you don't approve, the whole word is moved to the next line. You may turn the automatic hyphenation on or off.

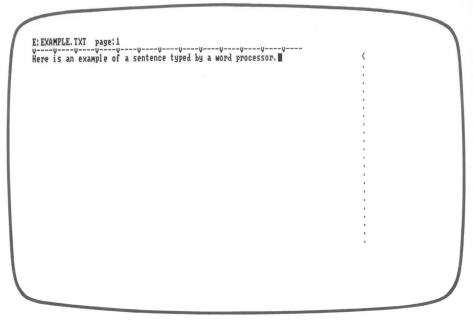

E: EXAMPLE.TXT   page: 1
ʋ----ʋ----ʋ----ʋ----ʋ----ʋ----ʋ----ʋ----ʋ----ʋ----ʋ----ʋ----ʋ---
Here is an example of a sentence typed by a word processor. █   ⟨

Figure 5.9   Entering part of a document using GoldWord.

Enter carriage returns only at the ends of paragraphs; the word processor will automatically enter them for you at the ends of lines.

You can force the word processor to go to the next line by pressing the **carriage return** key, the key labeled either ENTER or RETURN, or indicated by a bent arrow. Figure 5.10 shows several paragraphs of text entered on a word processor. The places where the carriage return key was pressed are indicated with the symbol "⟨". Note that the carriage return is used only to end paragraphs.

When a word processor displays a paragraph, it formats the paragraph into lines. The word processor places a carriage return, called a **soft carriage return**, at the end of each line, telling the display to move to the next line. Soft carriage returns are different from the ones you enter at the ends of paragraphs, which are called **hard carriage returns**. The difference is this: A soft carriage return is only present while the display has its present form. If editing requires the program to reform a paragraph, then the program can eliminate the original soft carriage returns and replace them with new ones, corresponding to the new line breaks. In contrast, hard carriage returns are unaffected by the program's efforts to reform paragraphs.

Novices are often tempted to use the ENTER/RETURN key just like the carriage return on a typewriter—that is, at the end of each line. Don't succumb to the temptation! If you enter carriage returns, you are circumventing the word processor's mechanism for automatically arranging lines. Your text may look fine on your monitor as you type it in. However, if you add or delete text later, the word processor won't be able to reform the lines for you, and your text will appear erratic and jagged. In this case, you will lose one of the most important advantages of a word processor.

Just as there are two types of carriage returns, a word processor also uses two types of spaces: hard spaces and soft spaces. A **hard space** is one that the user inserts by pressing the space bar. A **soft space** is one that the word processor inserts to correctly format the display. For instance, suppose that a word will not fit at the end of a line. The word processor moves the word to the next line and fills out the first line with soft spaces. In subsequent editing, these spaces may be removed as the document is reformatted.

If a word processing program incorporates an automatic hyphenation feature, it will use both hard and soft hyphens. A **hard hyphen** is one you insert by pressing the **HYPHEN key** (-). A **soft hyphen** is one the word processor inserts when it automatically hyphenates a word. A hyphen you insert will be included in the

Figure 5.10   How the carriage return key is used. The symbol "<" indicates the places where the carriage return key was pressed.

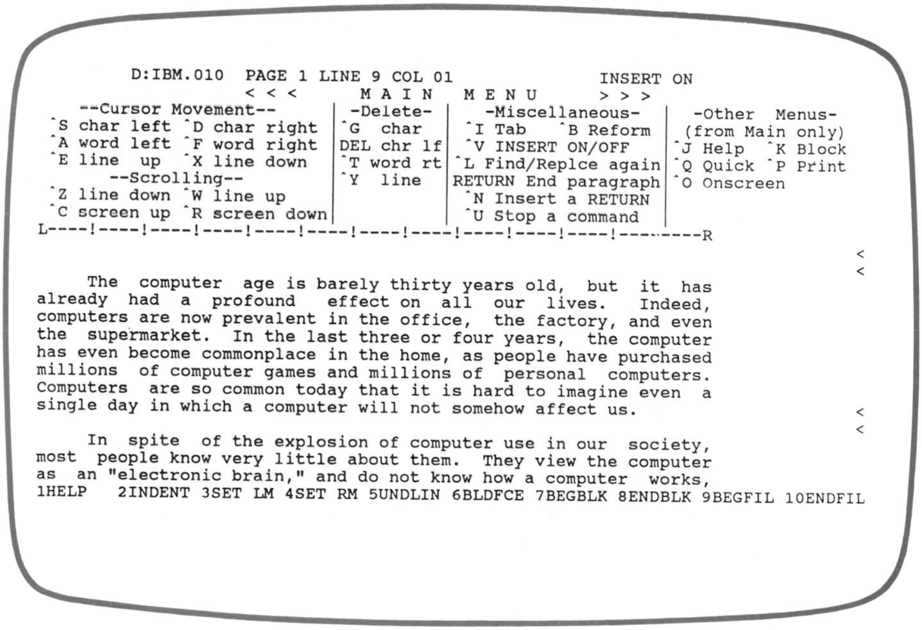

```
     D:IBM.010  PAGE 1 LINE 9 COL 01              INSERT ON
                 < < <      M A I N   M E N U      > > >
     --Cursor Movement--   |  -Delete-  |  -Miscellaneous-  |  -Other  Menus-
 ^S char left ^D char right | ^G  char  | ^I Tab   ^B Reform | (from Main only)
 ^A word left ^F word right |DEL chr lf | ^V INSERT ON/OFF   | ^J Help  ^K Block
 ^E line  up  ^X line down  | ^T word rt| ^L Find/Replce again| ^Q Quick ^P Print
     --Scrolling--         | ^Y  line   |RETURN End paragraph| ^O Onscreen
 ^Z line down ^W line up    |           | ^N Insert a RETURN |
 ^C screen up ^R screen down|           | ^U Stop a command  |
 L----!----!----!----!----!----!----!----!----!----!----!--------R
                                                                    <
                                                                    <
     The  computer  age is barely thirty years old,  but  it  has
 already  had  a  profound   effect  on  all  our  lives.  Indeed,
 computers are now prevalent in the office,  the factory,  and even
 the  supermarket.  In the last three or four years,  the computer
 has even become commonplace in the home, as people have purchased
 millions  of computer games and millions of  personal  computers.
 Computers  are so common today that it is hard to imagine even  a
 single day in which a computer will not somehow affect us.         <
                                                                    <
     In  spite  of the explosion of computer use in our  society,
 most  people know very little about them.  They view the computer
 as  an "electronic brain," and do not know how a computer  works,
 1HELP   2INDENT 3SET LM 4SET RM 5UNDLIN 6BLDFCE 7BEGBLK 8ENDBLK 9BEGFIL 10ENDFIL
```

document until you remove it. However, the program will remove a soft hyphen if future editing changes the location of hyphenation.

Behind the Scenes: The Document in RAM

While you type, your document is stored in RAM. You also see what you type on the monitor's screen. However, since the monitor has a limited amount of space, you can usually see only a small portion of the document at a time. In effect, the monitor provides you with a window into RAM, through which you can see a few lines of the document at any given moment, as is illustrated in Figure 5.11.

Some documents can fit completely into RAM, but very long ones might exceed RAM's capacity. The word processor keeps only a portion of such a document in RAM. Usually, the beginning and end of the document are stored on disk and the portion of the document currently being edited is stored in RAM, as shown in Figure 5.12. As you move to a different section of the document, the word processor changes the portion of the document kept in RAM. In making the change, any portions of the document moved out of RAM are saved on disk. This process of swapping sections of the document happens automatically, without any action by you.

Figure 5.11 The document in RAM.

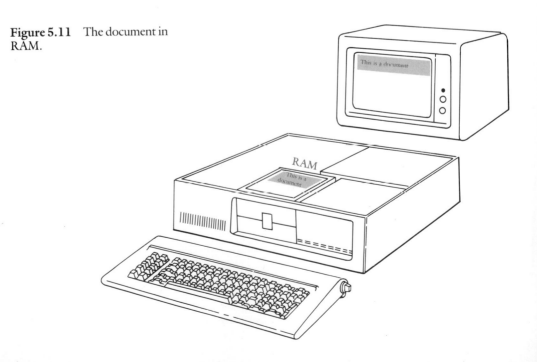

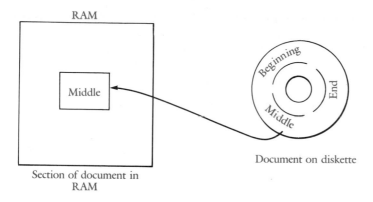

Figure 5.12 How the computer handles a document too large for RAM.

Saving the Document

You may save a copy of your document on disk by using the **SAVE command**, which stores your document as a file on disk with the file specification you assigned it. For example, if you assign your document the file specification B:EXAMPLE.TXT, the document is saved on the diskette in drive B: under the file name EXAMPLE.TXT.

Some word processors require that you assign a file specification to a document when you begin editing; others request the file specification as part of the SAVE command. If you do not specify a disk drive as part of the file specification, the word processor assumes that you mean the default disk drive. Command Table 5.2 shows the SAVE commands for the three sample word processors.

If you save a document that you have stored previously, most word processors retain the previous version by renaming it with the extension BAK. (BAK is short for "BACKUP".) For example, the previous version of the file EXAMPLE.TXT will be renamed EXAMPLE.BAK and will appear thus on the diskette directory. The BAK version is a safety precaution in case you mistakenly erase some vital data in the course of editing the EXAMPLE.TXT file, in which case you may refer to the BAK file for the data.

Save, Save, Save

The SAVE command—the most important word-processing command available to you—helps you avoid catastrophes. A power surge or a momentary blackout can erase the contents of RAM, and with it several hours of your hard work. It is tempting to postpone saving data, especially if the creative juices are flowing, but you shouldn't wait. When your document is in RAM, it can easily be destroyed. Practice defensive work habits and save your

As you work, save your data every 15 minutes!

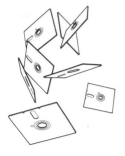

Command Table 5.2   The SAVE commands for WordStar, Word, and GoldWord.

Program	Command	Comments
WordStar	CTRL-KD	Save current file and go to main menu.
	CTRL-KS	Save current file and continue to edit it.
	CTRL-QP	Move cursor back to position just before SAVE (Ctrl-QS) command was issued.
	CTRL-KX	Save file and exit WordStar to DOS.
	CTRL-KQ	Abandon file and go to main menu.
Word	ESC Transfer Save ⟨file name⟩	Save current document under specified file name. Return to editing document. Position of cursor is unchanged.
GoldWord	CTRL-QS	Save current document and return to main menu.
	CTRL-QQ	Abandon current document and return to main menu.

work approximately every 15 minutes. It will save you hours of lost time later on.

Section 5.4: *Test Your Understanding*

1. What is the data input screen?
2. How does the cursor function in a word-processing program?
3. What is the ruler line?
4. Describe how you would correct typing errors with the DELETE key.
5. When do you use a hard carriage return?
6. What is word wrap?
7. Describe how a word processor handles a document that is too large to fit into RAM.
8. What does the file name extension BAK mean?
9. How often should you save data that you are working on?

Hands-on Exercises

1. Perform the following steps in the order in which they appear.

   a. Start your word processor.

   b. Give the command to edit the file EXAMPLE1.

   c. Enter the following data into the file. (Your lines don't have to look exactly like the lines below. Let the word processor form the lines.)

   > This is my first word processing document. It contains a few sentences and gives me a chance to test my skill at entering text.
   > This is the second paragraph of my document.

   d. Add the word "Mistake" at the end of the second paragraph. Erase this word.

   e. Save the file EXAMPLE1.

   f. Reload the file EXAMPLE1. Compare the document on the screen with the one you saved. Check that the document was saved correctly.

   g. Save the file EXAMPLE1 again. You will also use this file in the hands-on exercises in Sections 5.5 and 5.6.

   h. End the word-processing program and return to MS-DOS.

   i. Check the directory of your data disk to see how your word processor created a BAK copy of EXAMPLE1.

5.5 Editing a File

When you create a document, or at some later date, you may wish to add to, delete, or rearrange the text. The process of making these changes is called **editing**. This section discusses how you may use word processing commands to easily make editing changes that perfect your documents.

Moving Around a Document: The Cursor-Motion Keys

As you learned in the last section, the cursor indicates the position of the next typed character. To edit a document, you may need to enter and delete text in a number of places in the document. To do so, you must be able to position the cursor freely at any place within a document. This movement is accomplished with the **cursor-motion commands**.

The simplest cursor-motion commands use the **cursor-motion keys**, which are shown in Figure 5.13. These keys, labeled with

You may feel awkward when you first use the cursor-motion keys, but once you are comfortable with them, they will facilitate efficient motion within your document.

Figure 5.13 Cursor-motion keys.

arrows, are used to move the cursor up, down, right, or left. They correspond, respectively, to the 8, 2, 6, and 4 keys of the numeric keypad. You may use the cursor-motion keys to move the cursor to any character position within the document. Note, however, that you cannot move the cursor before the beginning or after the end of a document.

The CURSOR-RIGHT and CURSOR-LEFT keys operate in a manner that may be somewhat disconcerting to beginners. Suppose you position the cursor at the beginning of a line, as we have done in Figure 5.14. Pressing ⟨CURSOR-LEFT⟩ will move

Figure 5.14 How the (a) CURSOR-LEFT and (b) CURSOR-RIGHT keys operate.

The sales report for the month of
——— ⟨cursor-LEFT⟩ ———
August shows a healthy increase in
the cosmetic division

The sales report for the month of
——— ⟨cursor-RIGHT⟩ ———
August shows a healthy increase in
the cosmetic division

(a)   (b)

the cursor to the last character of the preceding line. Similarly, if you position the cursor at the end of a line, pressing ⟨CURSOR-RIGHT⟩ then moves the cursor to the beginning of the next line. In other words, the CURSOR-RIGHT and CURSOR-LEFT keys act as though the entire document is a horizontal, continuous flow of text, printed on a thin streamer of paper, one character wide. The CURSOR-RIGHT and CURSOR-LEFT keys move the cursor one character in either direction along the streamer.

The cursor-motion keys allow for relatively minor motions of the cursor. It is very clumsy to try using these keys to move a large distance, more than a paragraph or two, within a document. For this purpose, word processors provide a variety of other motion commands. The commands vary with each word processor, but here are some typical functions:

WORD LEFT—Move the cursor to the beginning of the next word on the left.

WORD RIGHT—Move the cursor to the beginning of the next word on the right.

PAGE UP—Scroll the document up one screenful.

PAGE DOWN—Scroll the document down one screenful.

END OF DOCUMENT—Go to the end of the document.

START OF DOCUMENT—Go to the beginning of the document.

START OF SCREEN—Go to the beginning of the screen.

END OF SCREEN—Go to the end of the screen.

START OF LINE—Go to the beginning of the line.

END OF LINE—Go to the end of the line.

GO TO PAGE—Go to the beginning of a designated page.

Command Table 5.3 summarizes how these motion commands are implemented in each of our three sample word processors.

Insert Mode versus Overtype Mode

Word processors operate on two modes of input: insert mode and overtype mode. In the **insert mode**, the word processor inserts keystrokes at the current cursor position and moves existing text to the right to accommodate the insertions. In the **overtype mode**, the word processor uses the current keystroke to replace the character at the cursor position. The overtype mode resembles typing on a typewriter, where typing at a position currently occupied by a character results in one character being typed over another. On a word processor, however, the original character is replaced

Command Table 5.3 Cursor-motion commands for Wordstar, Word, and GoldWord.

Program	Command	Comments
WordStar	CTRL-D or CURSOR-RIGHT	Move right one character.
	CTRL-F	Move right one word.
	CTRL-QD	Move to right end of line.
	CTRL-S or CURSOR-LEFT	Move left one character.
	CTRL-A	Move left one word.
	CTRL-QS	Move to left end of line.
	CTRL-E or CURSOR-UP	Move up one line.
	CTRL-W	Scroll screen down one line.
	CTRL-X or CURSOR-DOWN	Move down one line.
	CTRL-Z	Scroll screen up one line.
	CTRL-R	Scroll up one screen.
	CTRL-C	Scroll down one screen.
	CTRL-QE	Move to top of screen.
	CTRL-QX	Move to bottom of screen.
	CTRL-QR	Move to beginning of file.
	CTRL-QC	Move to end of file.
Word	CURSOR-RIGHT	Move right one character.
	CURSOR-LEFT	Move left one character.
	CURSOR-UP	Move up one line.
	CURSOR-DOWN	Move down one line.
	PGUP	Move up one screen.
	PGDN	Move down one screen.
	CTRL-PGUP	Move to beginning of document.
	CTRL-PGDN	Move to end of document.
	HOME	Move to left end of line.
	END	Move to right end of line.
	CTRL-HOME	Move to beginning of screen.
	CTRL-END	Move to end of screen.
GoldWord	CURSOR-RIGHT	Move right one character.
	CURSOR-LEFT	Move left one character.
	CURSOR-UP	Move up one line.
	CURSOR-DOWN	Move down one line.
	PGUP	Move up one screen.
	PGDN	Move down one screen.
	CTRL-PGUP	Move to beginning of document.
	CTRL-PGDN	Move to end of document.
	HOME	Move to left end of line.
	END	Move to right end of line.
	CTRL-HOME	Move to beginning of screen.
	CTRL-END	Move to end of screen.

rather than overtyped. Figure 5.15 compares the two input modes.

The standard (or default) mode for most word processors is the insert mode. This is the mode activated when you first start the word processor. A command is used to switch between the two input modes. Command Table 5.4 summarizes the commands particular to our sample word processors.

It takes a while to feel comfortable using the insert mode. For a skilled typist, the insert mode can be frustrating at first, because things don't work the way they do on a typewriter. However, the insert mode will soon seem quite natural. In fact, the overtype mode will feel strange by comparison.

From here on, let's assume that the word processor is in the insert mode. If you accidentally shift your word processor into the overtype mode, use the commands in Command Table 5.4 to shift back into the insert mode.

Inserting Text

To insert text, simply position the cursor on the character that is to appear just after the insertion and type the insert. For example, suppose that you wish to add the word *only* before the word *five* in the following sentence:

This dress costs five hundred dollars. __

To do so, use the cursor-motion commands to position the cursor (indicated with the underscore) on the *f* in *five*:

This dress costs f̲ive hundred dollars.

Now type the word *only* followed by a space. The display will show

This dress costs only f̲ive hundred dollars.

Command Table 5.4   How to change input modes with WordStar, Word, and GoldWord

Program	Command	Comments
WordStar	CTRL-V or INS	Toggles between insert and overtype mode. Default equals insert. Mode displayed on status line.
Word	F5 (function key)	Toggles between insert and overtype mode. Default equals insert. Mode displayed on status line in overtype mode only.
GoldWord	INS	Toggles between insert and overtype mode. Default equals insert.

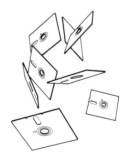

```
T: TEST        page: 1
U----U----U----U----U----U----U----U----U----U----U----U----U---
Here is a sentence in which to insert ords at the cursor
position.                                                              -
                                                                      <
```

(a)

```
T: TEST        page: 1
U----U----U----U----U----U----U----U----U----U----U----U----U---
Here is a sentence in which to insert a few ords at the cursor
position.                                                              -
                                                                      <
```

(b)

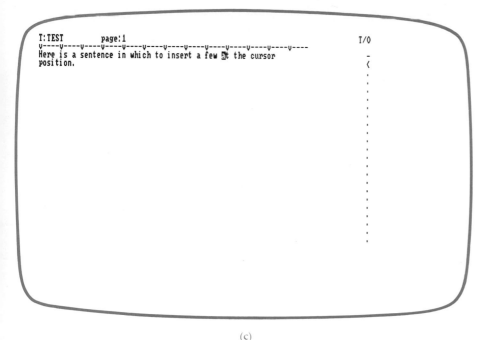

```
T:TEST        page:1                                          I/O
V----V----V----V----V----V----V----V----V----V----V----
Here is a sentence in which to insert a few at the cursor    -
position.                                                    <
                                                             :
                                                             :
                                                             :
                                                             :
                                                             :
                                                             :
                                                             :
                                                             :
```

(c)

Figure 5.15 Insert mode versus overtype mode. (a) Original text. (b) Typing "a few" in insert mode. (b) Typing "a few" in overtype mode.

Deleting Text

You may delete characters using the DELETE key. Just position the cursor on the characters or words you want to delete and press ⟨DELETE⟩. For example, to delete the word *only* that you just inserted, position the cursor on the letter *o*:

This dress costs only five hundred dollars.

Now press ⟨DELETE⟩ five times, once for each letter in *only* and once for the space following. Five characters will be deleted and the sentence will be restored to its original form:

This dress costs five hundred dollars.

Command Table 5.5 lists the DELETE key assignments for each of our sample word processors.

The DELETE key is practical in deleting a few characters, but for larger amounts of text (such as a paragraph), it is more convenient to use one of the various **DELETE commands**. Here are some typical commands:

DELETE WORD—Delete the word in which the cursor is positioned.

DELETE LINE—Delete the line in which the cursor is positioned.

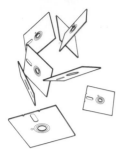

Command Table 5.5   DELETE key assignments for WordStar, Word, and GoldWord.

Program	Command	Comments
WordStar	CTRL-G	Delete character at cursor position.
Word	DEL	Delete selected text (character at cursor position if no text selected).
GoldWord	DEL	Delete selected text (character at cursor position if no text selected).

DELETE SENTENCE—Delete the sentence in which the cursor is positioned.

DELETE PARAGRAPH—Delete the paragraph in which the cursor is positioned.

DELETE TO END OF LINE—Delete from the cursor position to the end of the line.

DELETE TO END OF DOCUMENT—Delete from the cursor position to the end of the document.

Command Table 5.6 summarizes the implementation of these commands in our sample word processors.

Reforming Paragraphs

The process of inserting and deleting text generally destroys the arrangement of text lines and paragraphs. For example, Figure 5.16 shows a paragraph on which extensive editing has been performed using WordStar. Note how some lines are now too short and some are too long. The program now needs to undergo **paragraph reform**. If the paragraph in Figure 5.16(a) is reformed, it will appear as shown in Figure 5.16(b). In reforming the paragraph, WordStar redistributes the text on the lines, taking into account the specified margins. On the screen, the old lines are overwritten by the reformed lines. If you watch closely when you edit your own document, you can see this overwriting taking place.

Some word processors automatically reform paragraphs as you edit; others require a command to reform. Command Table 5.7 describes how to accomplish paragraph reforming for each of our sample word processors.

Breaking Paragraphs

While editing your document, you may want to break one paragraph into two. With a word processor, nothing could be easier. Just position the cursor on or before the first character of the word that will begin the new paragraph and press ⟨ENTER/RETURN⟩, as is shown in Figure 5.17. This procedure places a carriage return at the end of the first paragraph, splitting off a new second paragraph, which the word processor automatically reforms.

Joining Paragraphs

To a word processor, a carriage return is simply another character, namely the character corresponding to ASCII code 13. This means

Command Table 5.6 The DELETE commands for WordStar, Word, and Goldword.

Program	Command	Comments
WordStar	CTRL-G	Delete character at cursor position.
	DEL	Delete character to the left of cursor.
	CTRL-T	Delete word from cursor position to the right.
	CTRL-Y	Delete current line.
	CTRL-QY	Delete from cursor position to end of line.
	CTRL-QDEL	Delete from cursor position to beginning of line.
Word	DEL	Delete selected text. (See block marking commands for selecting text.)
GoldWord	DEL	Delete character at cursor.
	CTRL-DH	Delete head of word beginning at cursor.
	CTRL-DT	Delete tail of word beginning at cursor.
	CTRL-DW	Delete entire word at cursor.
	CTRL-DB	Delete to beginning of line.
	CTRL-DE	Delete to end of line.
	CTRL-DL	Delete line.
	CTRL-DP	Delete paragraph.

Command Table 5.7 Paragraph reforming commands for WordStar, Word, and GoldWord.

Program	Command	Comments
WordStar	CTRL-B	Reform from cursor position to end of paragraph.
Word	- (hyphen)	Automatic reform.
GoldWord	- (hyphen)	Automatic reform

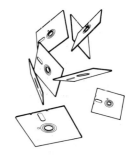

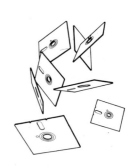

```
            D:IBM.010  PAGE 1 LINE 9 COL 13              INSERT ON
L----!----!----!----!----!----!----!----!----!----!----!-------R
                                                                    :
                                                                    :
                                                                    :
                                                                    :

        In  spite  of the explosion of computer use in  our  society,
most  people know very little about them.  They view the computer
as  an "electronic brain," and do not know how a computer  works,
how  it  may be used,  and how greatly it  may  simplify  various
everyday tasks.
This  does  not reflect a lack of widespread interest.  Most people  realize
that computers  are here to stay,  and are interested in  finding
out  how  to use them.  However,  for may people,  technology  is
threatening.
                                                                   <
                                                                   <
                                                                   <
                                                                   <
                                                                   <
                                                                   <
                                                                   <
1HELP    2INDENT 3SET LM 4SET RM 5UNDLIN 6BLDFCE 7BEGBLK 8ENDBLK 9BEGFIL 10ENDFIL
```

(a)

```
            D:IBM.010  PAGE 1 LINE 9 COL 01              INSERT ON
L----!----!----!----!----!----!----!----!----!----!----!-------R
                                                                    :
                                                                    :
                                                                    :
                                                                    :
                                                                    :

        In  spite of the explosion of computer use in  our  society,
most  people know very little about them.  They view the computer
as  an "electronic brain," and do not know how a computer  works,
how  it  may be used,  and how greatly it  may  simplify  various
everyday  tasks.  This  does  not reflect a  lack  of  widespread
interest.  Most  people realize that computers  are here to stay,
and are interested in finding out how to use them.  However,  for
may people, technology is threatening.
                                                                   <
                                                                   <
                                                                   <
                                                                   <
                                                                   <
                                                                   <
                                                                   <
                                                                   <
1HELP    2INDENT 3SET LM 4SET RM 5UNDLIN 6BLDFCE 7BEGBLK 8ENDBLK 9BEGFIL 10ENDFIL
```

(b)

Figure 5.16 A paragraph (a) before and (b) after reforming using WordStar's REFORMAT command.

```
E: EXAMPLE.TXT   page:1
ʊ----ʊ----ʊ----ʊ----ʊ----ʊ----ʊ----ʊ----ʊ----ʊ----ʊ----ʊ----
Dear Mr. Smith:

      Thank you very much for your letter of March 11, in which     <
you expressed an interest in a dealership for our products. We      -
will be expanding our list of authorized dealers in the near        -
future. If you would be so kind as to fill out the enclosed         -
dealer application, we will be happy to consider it within the      -
next 60 days.                                                       <
      We look forward to receiving you application and to working    -
with you in the near future to our mutual benefit.                  <
                                                                    <
                  Sincerely yours,                                  <
                                                                    <
                  Dr. Larry Joel Goldstein                          <
                  President                                         <
                  Goldstein Software, Inc.                          <
                                                                    -
                                                                    ·
                                                                    ·
                                                                    ·
```

(a)

```
E: EXAMPLE.TXT   page:1
ʊ----ʊ----ʊ----ʊ----ʊ----ʊ----ʊ----ʊ----ʊ----ʊ----ʊ----ʊ----
Dear Mr. Smith:

      Thank you very much for your letter of March 11, in which     <
you expressed an interest in a dealership for our products. We      <
will be expanding our list of authorized dealers in the near        -
future.                                                             <
If you would be so kind as to fill out the enclosed dealer          -
application, we will be happy to consider it within the next 60     -
days.                                                               <
      We look forward to receiving you application and to working    <
with you in the near future to our mutual benefit.                  <
                                                                    <
                  Sincerely yours,                                  <
                                                                    <
                  Dr. Larry Joel Goldstein                          <
                  President                                         <
                  Goldstein Software, Inc.                          <
                                                                    ·
                                                                    ·
                                                                    ·
```

(b)

Figure 5.17 Breaking a paragraph into two. (a) Place the cursor on the first letter of the word that will begin the new paragraph, and press <ENTER/RETURN>. (b) The program inserts a return between sentences, forming a new paragraph.

that you may position the cursor at a carriage return by using the cursor-motion keys or the commands that allow you to position the cursor at the end of a line.

By deleting the carriage return at the end of a paragraph, you may join two paragraphs. For example, suppose the cursor is positioned as shown in Figure 5.18(a). By pressing the DELETE key, you delete the carriage return at the end of the first paragraph. After the paragraph reforms, the document will appear as shown in Figure 5.18(b).

Section 5.5: Test Your Understanding

1. What is editing?
2. Explain the function of the cursor-motion keys.
3. Give three examples of cursor-motion commands other than those given by pressing the cursor-motion keys.
4. What is the difference between insert mode and overtype mode?
5. Which input mode should you use as your normal text input mode? Why?
6. Explain a method for inserting text in a document.
7. Explain a method for deleting text from a document.
8. List three DELETE commands commonly found in word processors.
9. What is paragraph reforming? Why is it necessary?
10. How do you break a paragraph in two?
11. How do you join two paragraphs to make one paragraph?

Hands-on Exercises

These exercises involve editing operations on the file EXAMPLE1 that you created and saved in the Hands-on Exercises in Section 5.4. Boot your word processor and load that file.

1. Position the cursor on the first letter of the word *sentences*.
2. Insert the word *choice*. If your word processor does not reform paragraphs automatically, reform the paragraph.
3. Move the cursor to the end of the document.
4. Add the following paragraph:

    A word processor is an extremely useful tool. I can think of many applications for it in my own work.

5. Indent each of the paragraphs five spaces.

```
E: EXAMPLE.TXT   page:1
U----U----U----U----U----U----U----U----U----U----U----
Dear Mr. Smith:

     Thank you very much for your letter of March 11, in which    <
you expressed an interest in a dealership for our products. We     -
will be expanding our list of authorized dealers in the near       -
future.                                                            <
     If you would be so kind as to fill out the enclosed dealer    -
application, we will be happy to consider it within the next 60    <
days.█ We look forward to receiving your application and to working <
with you in the near future to our mutual benefit.                 <
                                                                   <
                                                                   <
                         Sincerely yours,                          <
                                                                   <
                         Dr. Larry Joel Goldstein                  <
                         President                                 <
                         Goldstein Software, Inc.                  <
                                                                   :
                                                                   :
                                                                   :
```

(a)

```
E: EXAMPLE.TXT   page:1
U----U----U----U----U----U----U----U----U----U----U----U----U----
Dear Mr. Smith:

     Thank you very much for your letter of March 11, in which    <
you expressed an interest in a dealership for our products. We     -
will be expanding our list of authorized dealers in the near       -
future.                                                            <
     If you would be so kind as to fill out the enclosed dealer    -
application, we will be happy to consider it within the next 60    -
days.█    We look forward to receiving your application and to      -
working with you in the near future to our mutual benefit.         <
                                                                   <
                                                                   <
                         Sincerely yours,                          <
                                                                   <
                         Dr. Larry Joel Goldstein                  <
                         President                                 <
                         Goldstein Software, Inc.                  <
                                                                   :
                                                                   :
                                                                   :
```

(b)

Figure 5.18   Joining paragraphs. (a) Place the cursor on the carriage return at the end of the first paragraph and press <DELETE>. The new paragraph (b) will automatically reform.

6. Break the first paragraph into two, with each paragraph consisting of one sentence.
7. Join the last two paragraphs into one.
8. Delete the second paragraph.
9. Save the file.

5.6 Printing a Document

After entering and editing your memo, letter, or report, you will probably want to print it on paper for distribution or filing. You can create a paper copy ("hard copy") by using the **PRINT command**.

As you will recall from Section 5.3, you must first install the word processor so that it works with your particular printer. Once this is done, you may print a document by following this procedure:

- Turn on the printer.
- Give the PRINT command.

With most word processors, the PRINT command has a number of options associated with it. These options allow you to do the following:

- Print multiple copies of a document.
- Start printing at a particular page.
- Stop printing at a particular page.
- Stop after printing each page to allow for single sheet insertion. (In printing, you may use either continuous form stationery or single sheets. If you choose the latter, you'll need to specify that the printer stop while you insert single sheets.)

Command Table 5.8 gives a summary of the PRINT commands and the print options for each of our sample word processors.

Section 5.6: Test Your Understanding

1. Describe the steps to install a printer.
2. Describe some of the options available to you when printing a document.

Command Table 5.8   The PRINT commands and options for Wordstar, Word, and GoldWord.

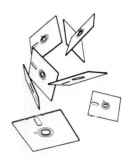

Program	Command	Comments
WordStar	CTRL-KP file name	Print file from within edit mode. It is dangerous to print the file you are currently editing.
	P file name	Print file from main menu.
Word	ESC Print Options	Set print options by filling in a menu that includes the following fields: *Printer*—printer type to be used. *Draft*—print draft copy (formatting omitted) or final draft. *Queued*—make a list of documents to be printed. *Copies*—number of copies to print *Range*—range of page numbers to print *Feed*—cut-sheet, continuous, or multi-bin paper feed arrangement *Setup*—DOS device name assigned to printer
	ESC Print Printer	Print current document according to the current option settings. Document is automatically repaginated.
	ESC Print Repaginate	Repaginate current document.
GoldWord	F2 file name F4	Print file from main menu. Print last file edited from main menu.

Hands-on Exercises

1. Load continuous form paper into your printer.
2. Consult your printer manual and determine the command to perform a printer diagnostic test. Perform the test.
3. Print out the document EXAMPLE1 that you created in the Hands-on Exercises in Section 5.4.

KEY TERMS

| word processor | dedicated word processor | enter |
| stand-alone word processor | input | keyboarding |

edit	format line	HYPHEN key
save	status lines	soft hyphen
recall	status information	SAVE command
print	DELETE key	BAK
install	BACKSPACE key	editing
copy-protected	word wrap	cursor-motion commands
main menu	carriage return key	cursor-motion keys
transfers	soft carriage return	insert mode
submenu approach	hard carriage return	overtype mode
data input screen	hard space	DELETE commands
typing area	soft space	paragraph reform
ruler line	hard hyphen	PRINT command

CHAPTER REVIEW QUESTIONS

1. Where should the ENTER/RETURN key be used when entering text on a word processor? Why?
2. Describe the options commonly available in the PRINT command of a word processor.
3. What is insert mode?
4. Explain how to make an addition to a document.
5. Explain how to make a deletion from a document.
6. Why is it necessary to install a word processor for a particular printer?
7. In what ways is preparing a document on a word processor similar to preparing a document on a typewriter? In what ways is it different?
8. Why is backing up a file so crucial?
9. Describe the procedure for backing up a file.
10. Why is it necessary to back up files?
11. Describe the procedure for joining two paragraphs together.
12. Suppose that you want to start your word processor. Describe how you do the following:

a) Obtain the MS-DOS prompt.
b) Insert the proper diskettes.
c) Tell the computer to execute the word-processor program.
d) Select your first option.

13. Suppose that you have the main menu of your word processor on your screen.

a) Describe the main menu and how it may differ from the main menus of other word processors.
b) Describe how to give the command to create a file for your word processor.

14. Suppose that you have created a file one page long.

a) How would you delete a paragraph of your file?
b) How would you correct a one-letter typographical error in the first paragraph of your file?

15. How does RAM handle your document while you work with it?
16. What is the SAVE command for your particular word processor?
17. How does a word-processing program provide a safety precaution in the event you inadvertently erase a portion of a file?

18. Describe how to use the cursor-motion keys to move the cursor within a document.

19. What command would you use to move from the beginning of a document to the end?

20. Describe each step needed to delete the last paragraph of your document.

DISCUSSION QUESTIONS

1. Some people prefer to use a printed copy of a document for proofreading and editing, while others prefer to edit directly from the image on screen. Discuss the advantages and disadvantages of each approach.

2. Word processing allows documents to be stored electronically rather than on paper. What are the advantages of such an approach to document storage? The disadvantages?

3. Electronic copies of documents are subject to a number of new hazards that paper documents are not subject to. List some of these hazards. If you were in charge of a word-processing department in a large company, what security measures would you institute to safeguard documents against these hazards?

4. Does word processing make all text processing tasks more efficient? Defend your answer with examples.

APPLICATION PROJECTS

1. Type a letter to a friend using your word processor. *Do n't hand in to me by Fri begin*

2. Input, edit, and print the first page of this chapter using your word processor. *print, class Sep 16,88*

3. CircleStair, Inc., is a manufacturer of circular stairways. Most of the firm's customers are do-it-yourselfers who are fixing up a basement, attic, or second-story porch. CircleStair sells directly to its customers through space advertising in home magazines such as *Good Housekeeping, Better Homes and Gardens, and Sunset.* Because each stairway must be custom-fitted to the customer's specifications, it takes CircleStair almost four weeks to fill an order.

    Alvin Smith, CircleStair's Marketing Manager, knows that the longer it takes to fill an order, the more likely the customer is to cancel that order. To discourage cancellations, Alvin wants to send each customer an acknowledgement letter upon receipt of an order.

    Write a form letter Alvin could use to acknowledge CircleStair's orders. This letter should say the following:

    a) Thank the customer for the order;

    b) Explain that custom-fitting will require time; ask the customer for patience while the order is being filled.

    c) Assure the customer that he or she has made the correct decision in ordering from CircleStair.

4. A service provided by a certified public accountant (CPA) is the independent audit—the examination of a company's financial statements. Upon completion of the audit, the CPA issues an opinion as to the fairness of the financial statements. An example of an auditor's opinion letter is shown in Figure 5.19.

Board of Directors
MM & C, Incorporated
15 Big Bucks Avenue
Boston, Massachusetts 00030

Dear   :
We have examined the Consolidated Balance Sheets of MM & C, Incorporated, and subsidiaries, as of December 31, 1986 and 1985, and the
related Consolidated Statements of Income, Retained Earnings, and
Changes in Financial Position for the years then ended. Our examinations
were made in accordance with generally accepted auditing standards and,
accordingly, included such tests of the accounting records and such other
auditing procedures as we considered necessary in the circumstances. In
our opinion, the consolidated financial position of MM & C, Incorporated, and subsidiaries, as of December 31, 1986 and 1985, and the
results of their operations and changes in financial position for the years
then ended, in conformity with generally accepted accounting principles
applied on a consistent basis.

Yours sincerely,

Kamnikar & Kamnikar
Certified Public Accountants

Figure 5.19. An auditor's opinion letter.

a) Using your word processor, create a file for the auditor's opinion letter and enter the letter as it appears here.

b) In reviewing the draft of the letter, the audit partner notes that the opinion letter should be composed of two paragraphs instead of one. The second paragraph should begin with the sentence "In our opinion. . . ." Split the letter into two paragraphs as directed by the audit partner.

5. You have heard that an Individual Retirement Account (IRA) at a local bank can be used to lower your federal taxes. Compose a letter on your word processor to your local bank in which you request information about their IRA plans. Be sure to ask about the following:

a) The interest rates they offer.

b) Maturity of the various securities.

c) Penalties for early withdrawal of the money.

d) Why an IRA saves taxes and increases the earning power of your investment.

Now mail the letter. You might as well also learn about investing your money in this course!

6 Advanced Word Processing

Don't Discount the Power of Word Processing

The most sophisticated features of a word-processing program, such as the ability to move a block of words anywhere in a document with one keystroke, are lifesavers for people who must rework reports and memos many times under deadline pressure.

Countless revisions are an inescapable fact of life in writing advertising copy. Bill Fergusson, an advertising copywriter for Charles Schwab and Company, Inc., in San Francisco, says he has to change his ad copy an average of three to seven times per piece. And there's a *lot* of copy to be written.

Schwab is one of the nation's largest discount brokerages, with more than one million customers and an annual volume of $7 billion in securities transactions. Schwab advertises its services throughout the country in major magazines and newspapers, including *The Wall Street Journal*, and sends out volumes of direct mail brochures as well. To keep readers from getting bored and to prevent them from labelling pieces "junk mail," Schwab's copywriters must constantly think up new and catchy ideas for ads.

Fergusson may find himself writing 12 pages of text for one piece of direct mail. "We have to write every word that appears," he says. That includes the brochure, cover letter, envelope, and any special incentive discount certificates. He uses the word-processing program MultiMate and a microcomputer for all his writing and editing. According to Fergusson, if every change had to be typed and retyped on a conventional typewriter, it would take four to five times as long. "The computer allows us to make editing changes very rapidly," he asserts.

Fergusson says there is no way he would want to do his job without a micro. "The biggest advantage is that you can make a correction very quickly. If you have to move copy around, you can do it instantly. If we had to go in and do that all over again, it would be an incredible waste of time, very unproductive."

CHAPTER 5 INTRODUCED the basic concepts of word processing: document entry, editing, saving, and printing. However, this subject encompasses much more. In Chapter 6, you'll learn about the more advanced features of word processors.

6.1 The SEARCH Command and the FIND AND REPLACE Command

Two of the most powerful commands in a word processor are SEARCH and FIND AND REPLACE. Let's take a look at these commands and the reasons they are so powerful.

The SEARCH Command

Use the SEARCH command to quickly locate a word or phrase in your document.

The **SEARCH command** tells the computer to scan a document for a particular **string**, of characters; that is, a particular sequence of characters. Here are some examples of strings:

John Jones

$500.00

200   300

The first string contains ten characters (the space between the words counts as a character), the second string seven characters, and the third string 12 characters (there are six spaces between 200 and 300).

The SEARCH command is useful if you need to locate a particular place within a document that is identified by the use of a certain word or phrase. Using the SEARCH command to locate the place can be far more efficient than searching the document by a visual scan.

An Application of the SEARCH Command. The process of writing a term paper provides a good example of a SEARCH command application. Suppose you are editing the paper and want each section to begin on a separate page. To accomplish this, you tell the computer to break the page at the end of each section. This is easy enough to do once you locate the end of each section. But if the paper is 35 pages long, you can spend a lot of time scrolling through it, scanning it visually for the ends of sections.

A simpler approach is to use the SEARCH command. Suppose that each section begins with the word *Section*. You can tell the word processor to search for each instance of the word *Section*. The program will read through the document, pausing at each instance of the word for which you are searching. If the word appears within text material, you can ignore it because you are searching for the occurrences of the word *Section* that denote the beginning of a section. When you locate these occurrences, you can insert the desired page breaks.

Operating the SEARCH Command. The following steps execute the SEARCH command in most word-processing programs:

1. Position the cursor to indicate the initial point of the search. (See below for a more detailed explanation.)
2. Give the SEARCH command for your word processor.
3. The logic of the SEARCH command asks you to specify the sequence of characters for which to search. This sequence of characters is called the **search string**.
4. The SEARCH command logic now initiates the search for the search string.
5. The SEARCH command logic indicates the first instance of the search string by displaying the surrounding text and highlighting the search string, as is shown in Figure 6.1. Your word processor will tell you if it cannot find the search string.
6. The SEARCH command logic returns control to you with the cursor positioned at the found search string. In the event that the search string is not found, the program will inform you via a written message and will position the cursor at its last location.

This sequence of steps may seem to be quite straightforward, yet there are a number of subtleties in the SEARCH command, some of which are summarized below.

The Direction of Search. The search normally proceeds from the current cursor position toward the end of the document. However, some word processors allow options for searching from the beginning of the document, or from the current position of the cursor back to the beginning of the document. The possible directions of search are illustrated in Figure 6.2.

Case-Sensitive Searches. Most search functions on word processors allow you to specify whether capitalization (also called **case**) should be included in the search. For example, suppose that the search string is *Algebra*. If you specify **a case-sensitive search**, then the strings *algebra* and *Algebra* will be passed over in the search. On the other hand, if you specify that capitalization can be ignored, then the latter strings will be found as matches for the search string.

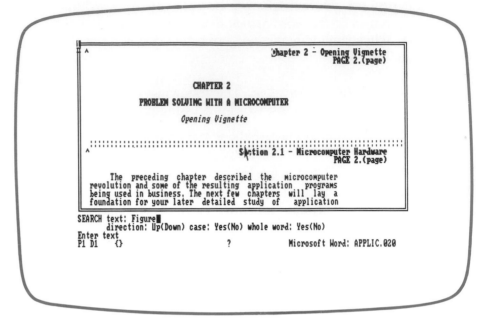

(a)

(b)

Figure 6.1   How Word indicates that a search string has been found. (a) Specifying the search. (b) Finding the search string.

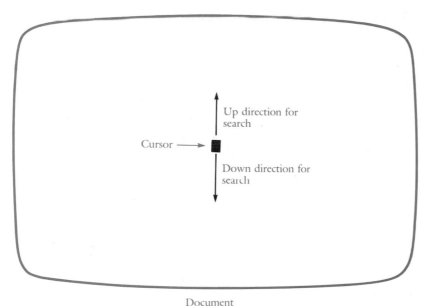

Document

Figure 6.2   The possible directions of search.

Most word processors assume that capitalization does not matter unless you specify a case-sensitive search. However, you should determine what your word processor assumes in the way of a default.

Repeated Searches. Most word processors allow you to search repeatedly for the same search string without retyping the string. Each search begins at the cursor position reached at the end of the previous search. In some word processors, you may be able to specify the number of times to repeat the search, or that the search should be repeated until the program reaches the end of the document.

Wild Card Searches. Many word processors allow you to perform **wild card searches**. In MS-DOS, you can, in effect, leave the file name blank by replacing it with question marks. For instance, the file name ????.TXT stands for a file with a main name consisting of four characters and an extension TXT. Similarly, the character * stands for an arbitrary sequence of chaacters in a file name. For instance, the file name JAN.* refers to any file with the main name JAN combined with any extension.

The characters ? and * are called **wild card characters**. In many word processors, you can use wild card characters in a search string. In such searches, the search string is only partially specified.

For example, in some word processors, you may specify a search string *.TXT. This specifies any string followed by a period and the characters TXT. A wild card search for such a string will find strings such as EXAMPLE.TXT, EXAM.TXT, BOOK.TXT, and HISTORY.TXT.

Spaces and Whole Word Searches. A search string may be contained within a word. If it is, we refer to it as an **embedded string**. If you are searching for the string *the*, for example, the search will accept as matches the following strings:

> the
>
> their
>
> theater
>
> bathe

The search string *the* is embedded in the last three strings. You can avoid matches with inappropriate strings such as *their, theater*, and *bathe* in two ways:

- As far as a word processor is concerned, a space is a character like any other. In particular, spaces may be included within a search string. You must type your search string exactly as you mean it to be, including spaces. If you type the search string *the* ⟨SPACEBAR⟩, then only the first and last of the strings listed above provide a match. If you type the search string ⟨SPACEBAR⟩*the*⟨SPACEBAR⟩, then only the first string provides a match.

- Some word processors provide a function called the **whole word search**, which allows you to specify that the search string must match only whole words. That is, the found string must have a space before and after it. If you specify a whole word search for the string *the*, then only the first string in the above list qualifies. Command Table 6.1 summarizes the operation of the SEARCH command in each of our sample word processors.

The FIND AND REPLACE Command

Use FIND AND REPLACE to scan a document for a word or phrase you want to replace.

Another useful editing command in a word processor is **FIND AND REPLACE**, which allows you not only to search for particular strings but to replace one text string with another throughout a document.

Applications of the FIND AND REPLACE Command. Applications of FIND AND REPLACE are limited only by your own imagi-

Command Table 6.1   The SEARCH command in Wordstar, Word, and GoldWord.

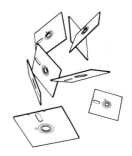

Program	Command	Comments
WordStar	CTRL-QF ( ) (Type ⟨search string⟩ in response to FIND? prompt) ( ) ⟨ENTER⟩ (Type in ⟨Option String⟩ in response to OPTIONS?) ⟨ENTER⟩	⟨Search string⟩ can consist of up to 30 characters. ⟨Options string⟩ can consist of a string formed from the following characters: *n* Repeat the search *n* times. *B* Perform the search from the current cursor position backward. *W* Look for whole words only. *U* Ignore uppercase/lowercase distinction. *G* perform a global replacement, that is, throughout the document.
	CTRL-L CTRL-QV	Repeat last search operation. Return to the previous point in the text after a search operation.
Word	ESC Search ⟨menu entries⟩ ⟨ENTER⟩	Pop-up menu. Entries to fill in: *Text* (search string), *direction* (direction of search—up, down) *Case* (case sensitive—yes, no) *Whole word* (select only whole words—yes, no) Use TAB key to move between menu entries. To cancel SEARCH command, press ESC.
GoldWord	CTRL-F (Fill in ⟨search string⟩ in ⟨ENTER⟩ response to prompt.)	Search for a designated string.

nation. Of the dozens of possible applications, some typical ones are as follows:

- *Produce a new document by replacing one name with another throughout the document.* Suppose that you have written a proposal for IBM and you would like to submit the same proposal to Hewlett-Packard. You may use the FIND AND REPLACE command to find all instances of the string *IBM* in the original document and replace them with the string *Hewlett-Packard*.

- *Update chronology of material.* Suppose that you need to update a table of contents by adding a new chapter 3. The old chapter 3 becomes chapter 4, chapter 4 becomes chapter 5, and so on. You may easily make these numbering changes by using the FIND AND REPLACE command. For example, you can give a command to change all 3s to 4s, all 4s to 5s, and so forth. Of course, there will be some instances where no change is warranted—for example, if your search locates section 1.3. In that case, the 3 should not be changed to a 4. Most FIND AND REPLACE commands give you the option of individually approving replacements, which is necessary in this instance. If you use this option, the word processor displays the word to be replaced in context and asks you if you want to replace it.

- *Change document format.* Suppose that you have indented by five spaces the first word of all paragraphs in a two-page letter and you would like to change to a "box" style with no indentations. Simply use the FIND AND REPLACE command to replace all instances of paragraph indentation (that is, five consecutive blank spaces) with nothing. This command will remove the indentations at the beginning of each paragraph. As with the preceding example, it's a good idea to approve each replacement individually.

Operating FIND AND REPLACE. The operation of the FIND AND REPLACE command varies with each word processor. Generally, you can operate it this way:

1. Give the FIND AND REPLACE command.
2. The word processor asks for the string you want to find. You type in the string just as you did with the SEARCH command.
3. The word processor now requests that you type in the replacement string.
4. You also specify any options applicable to the FIND AND REPLACE operation, which you will see in more detail later.
5. The word processor now searches the document for the specified search string. When an instance of the string is found, it is replaced by the specified replacement string. As one of the options, you may request that the word processor allow you to individually approve or disapprove each replacement.
6. The search and replacement continues until the entire document is searched.

FIND AND REPLACE Command Options. The FIND AND RE-PLACE command has many options, some of which vary with the word processor. Here is a summary.

- *Search String Specification.* Specifying the FIND AND RE-PLACE search string is similar to specifying the search string in the SEARCH command. You may specify a case-sensitive search, or a whole word search.
- *Scope of the Command.* Many word processors allow you to specify the scope of the FIND AND REPLACE operation. Among the many variations exhibited are those that specify the following:
    1. *Direction of Search.* Specifies the direction of search, either forward to the end of the document or backward to the beginning.
    2. *Portion of Document.* Specifies that only a portion of the document is to be sought.
    3. *Number of Replacements.* Specifies the maximum number of replacements that are to be carried out.

Automatic versus User-Controlled Replacements. You may specify whether the replacements are to be made automatically or only with your approval. Automatic replacements can save a great deal of time, but in using them you give up a certain measure of control. Until you are accustomed to using FIND AND REPLACE, don't use the automatic option. If you do, you risk some strange alterations to your document. Remember, the word processor will slavishly replace the search string with the replacement string, and it may find some instances of the search string that you would not think of and would never intend to replace.

Until you are accustomed to using FIND AND REPLACE, do not use the automatic option.

Embedded Search Strings. Be very careful in specifying search strings without the whole word option. Your word processor will often locate the search string embedded within a word. Automatically replacing the string will often lead to crazy results.

Reforming Paragraphs. After you perform a FIND AND RE-PLACE, your paragraphs may lose their structure because the replacement resulted in a new line either shorter or longer than the original line. Your word processor may provide automatic paragraph reform after a FIND AND REPLACE operation. In the event that your word processor does not automatically reformat, you will need to do so manually.

Command Table 6.2 summarizes the operation of the FIND AND REPLACE command in our sample word processors.

Section 6.1: Test Your Understanding

1. What is the purpose of the SEARCH command?
2. What is a search string?
3. Describe the various directions of search that are involved in the SEARCH command.
4. Suppose that you specify a case-sensitive search for the word *the*. Which of the following words will trigger a match?

> The
>
> THE
>
> the
>
> There
>
> THERE

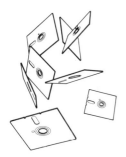

Command Table 6.2 The FIND AND REPLACE command in WordStar, Word, and GoldWord.

Program	Command	Comments
WordStar	CTRL-QA (Type ⟨search string⟩ in response to FIND? prompt.) ⟨ENTER⟩ (Type ⟨replacement string⟩ in response to REPLACE WITH? prompt.) ⟨ENTER⟩ (Type ⟨option string⟩ in response to OPTIONS? prompt.) ⟨ENTER⟩	Both ⟨search string⟩ and ⟨replacement string⟩ can be up to 30 characters long. The ⟨options string⟩ can contain the same characters as the SEARCH command. In addition, you may use: N– Not necessary to ask for approval to make replacement.
Word	ESC Replace ⟨menu entries⟩ ⟨ENTER⟩	Pop-up menu. Entries to fill in: *Replace text* (text to search for) *With text* (substitute text) *confirm* (Yes, No) *Case* (Yes, No) *Whole word* (Yes, No) Use TAB key to move between menu entries. To cancel SEARCH command, press ESC.
GoldWord	CTRL-R (Specify replace string in response to prompt.) ⟨ENTER⟩ CTRL-N ⟨ENTER⟩	Find and replace string. Perform the preceding FIND AND REPLACE command again.

Thank you very much for your interest in our product line and your invitation to bid on the injection molding machinery for Acme Plastics.

The price for the deluxe model of our machine is $158,000 FOB our plant. The price includes delivery and set up by our personnel; training for your staff is also included. Delivery can be made within 90 days.

We look forward to working with Acme Plastics in installing and maintaining our innovative new machinery. If you have any questions, please call at 555-6666. My secretary can reach me if I am out of the office.

Figure 6.3 A document on which to practice the SEARCH command and the FIND AND REPLACE command.

5. What is a wild card search? Give an example in which a wild car search might be useful.

6. What is an embedded search string? Give an example.

7. Describe the operation of the FIND AND REPLACE command.

8. Give an example of an application of the FIND AND REPLACE command.

9. Explain how a FIND AND REPLACE operation can destroy paragraph layouts.

Hands-on Exercises

The following questions refer to the document shown in Figure 6.3, which you should type into your own document on your word processor.

1. Find all instances of the string *the* in the document.

2. Find all instances of the string *the*⟨SPACEBAR⟩ in the document.

3. Find all instances of the string ⟨SPACEBAR⟩*the*⟨SPACEBAR⟩.

4. Change all instances of the word *Acme* to *ACME*.

5. Change all occurrences of *Acme Plastics* to *Continental Ceramics*.

6.2 Block Operations

Few of us are able to write perfect prose on the first draft. After rereading what we have written, most of us want to do some editing and reorganizing. As a part of this rewriting, it is often necessary to move some words, sentences, or paragraphs, and to delete others.

In Chapter 5 you discovered some of the more elementary editing operations that you can accomplish on a word processor. Let's now look at the operations that allow you to perform more advanced editing.

What Is a Block?

A **block** is any sequence of consecutive characters in a document. A block may consist of as little as a single character or it may consist of an entire document; it may contain any number of words, sentences, or paragraphs. It may begin at any character in a document (even in the middle of a word) and may end at any character. Figure 6.4 shows a block highlighted within a document.

You must define blocks within a document as a prelude to certain editing procedures. A document can have only one block defined at a time. The procedure for defining a block varies with the word processor, but it generally goes like this:

1. Place the cursor at the first character of the block.
2. Give the command to specify the beginning of the block.
3. Place the cursor at the last character of the block.
4. Give the command to specify the end of the block.

Figure 6.4   A block of text.

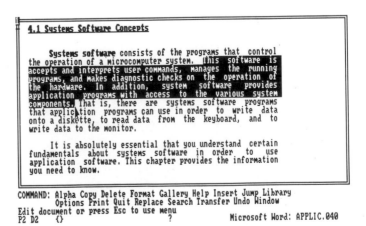

Command Table 6.3   The Wordstar, Word, and GoldWord commands to define a block.

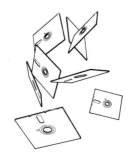

Program	Command	Comments
WordStar	CTRL-KB	Mark block beginning at current cursor position.
	CTRL-KK	Mark block ending at current cursor position.
	CTRL-KH	Unmark the block.
Word	F8	Select word at current cursor position.
	F9	Select sentence at current cursor position.
	F10	Select paragraph at current cursor position.
	SHIFT-F9	Select line at current cursor position.
	SHIFT-F10	Select entire document.
	F6	Extend current selected text. Any cursor movement beyond the selected text will add to the selection.
GoldWord	CTRL-BB	Mark block boundary at current cursor position.
	CTRL-BL	Mark current line.
	CTRL-BP	Mark current paragraph.
	CTRL-BW	Mark current word.

5. The block will be identified on the screen by highlighting or brackets.

A block remains defined until you define another block, change something within the block, or cancel the block definition. The commands for defining a block on our sample word processors are summarized in Command Table 6.3.

Block Manipulations

Once you define a block, you can manipulate it through the use of a number of **block operations**—the text movements involved in editing your document. Presented here is a summary of these operations.

Defining a block of text is the first step toward editing your document.

Block Move. You may move the block to another location in the document. Just define the block to be moved, then place the cursor at the position where you wish to insert the block and give the

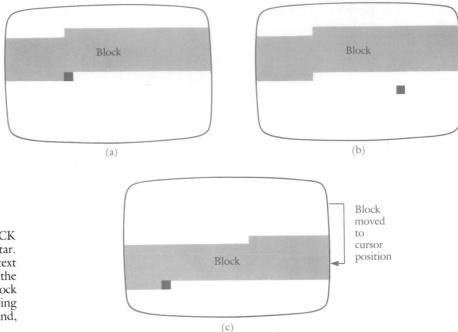

Figure 6.5 Using the BLOCK MOVE command in WordStar. (a) Highlight the block of text to be moved, and (b) place the cursor where you want the block to be located. (c) After giving the BLOCK MOVE command, the document is revised.

BLOCK MOVE command. Figure 6.5 shows a paragraph in which a block to be moved is highlighted; the cursor is then placed at the desired new location of the block. After the BLOCK MOVE command is given, the program moves the block to the new location. Command Table 6.4 describes the BLOCK MOVE commands for each of the sample word processors.

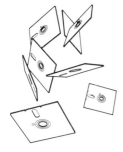

Command Table 6.4 The BLOCK MOVE commands for WordStar, Word, and GoldWord

Program	Command	Comments
WordStar	CTRL-KV	Move marked block to current cursor position.
Word	ESC Delete ⟨ENTER⟩ (Move cursor to desired insert position) ESC Insert ⟨ENTER⟩	Delete the selected block to the scrap heap, move the cursor to the desired insert position, then insert the block from the scrap heap.
GoldWord	CTRL-BD (Move cursor to insert position) CTRL-BI	Delete marked block to the scrap heap; move cursor to desired insert position; insert block from scrap heap.

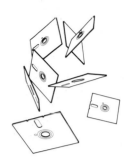

Command Table 6.5   The BLOCK DELETE commands for WordStar, Word, and GoldWord.

Program	Command	Comments
WordStar	CTRL-KY	Delete marked block. Deleted material cannot be retrieved.
Word	ESC Delete ⟨ENTER⟩	Delete the selected block to the scrap heap.
GoldWord	CTRL-BD	Delete the marked block to the scrap heap. Any text in the scrap heap is lost.

Block Delete. You may erase a block by giving the **BLOCK DELETE command**. In some word processors (WordStar, for example), the erased block is simply deleted. In other word processors (Word and GoldWord), the block is deleted from the document but is stored in a **scrap heap** from which it can later be recovered.

Figure 6.6 shows a paragraph in Word with a block highlighted. After the BLOCK DELETE operation, the paragraph is deleted. Note that the contents of the scrap heap are indicated in abbreviated form at the bottom of the screen. Command Table 6.5 shows the BLOCK DELETE commands for our sample word processors.

Block Copy. You may insert a duplicate of the block anywhere in a document. Just position the cursor at the point where you wish to insert a copy of the block and give the **BLOCK COPY command**. For example, Figure 6.7 shows a highlighted block of text, in

Figure 6.6   Using the BLOCK DELETE command in Word. (a) Highlight the block to be deleted, and (b) give the BLOCK DELETE command.

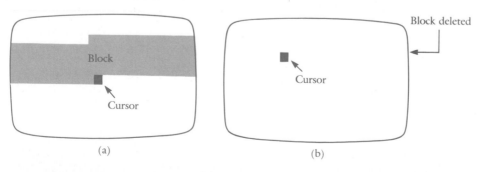

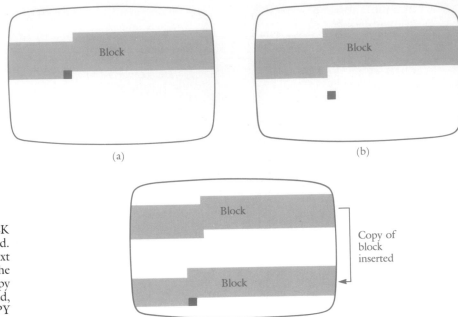

(a)

(b)

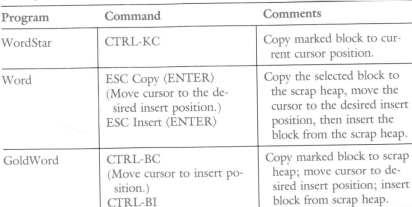

Copy of
block
inserted

(c)

Figure 6.7 Using the BLOCK COPY command in GoldWord. (a) Highlight the block of text to be copied, (b) position the cursor at the point where a copy of the block is to be inserted, and (c) give the BLOCK COPY command. A copy of the block appears at the new location.

which the cursor is positioned at the point where a copy of the block is to be inserted. After the BLOCK COPY command is given, the block will occur twice in the document. Command Table 6.6 gives the details of the BLOCK COPY commands for our sample word processors.

Block Write. You may also store a block of text in a file for later use. To store a block for later use, you execute the **BLOCK**

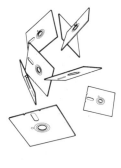

Command Table 6.6 The BLOCK COPY commands for WordStar, Word, Goldword.

Program	Command	Comments
WordStar	CTRL-KC	Copy marked block to current cursor position.
Word	ESC Copy ⟨ENTER⟩ (Move cursor to the desired insert position.) ESC Insert ⟨ENTER⟩	Copy the selected block to the scrap heap, move the cursor to the desired insert position, then insert the block from the scrap heap.
GoldWord	CTRL-BC (Move cursor to insert position.) CTRL-BI	Copy marked block to scrap heap; move cursor to desired insert position; insert block from scrap heap.

Command Table 6.7 The BLOCK WRITE commands for WordStar, Word, and GoldWord.

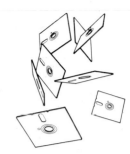

Program	Command	Comments
WordStar	CTRL-KW ⟨file name⟩	Copy marked block to a file.
Word	ESC Copy ⟨glossary name⟩	Copy the selected block to a glossary entry with the specified name. To save the block when you exit Word, you must save the glossary in response to the prompt provided by the QUIT command.
GoldWord	CTRL-BS ⟨file name⟩	Save the marked block in a file.

WRITE command. The word processor will ask for the name of the file in which to store the block. After you specify the name, the word processor writes the contents of the block to the file. In Figure 6.8, a block of text is highlighted in GoldWord. After the BLOCK WRITE command has been given, the word processor asks for the name of the file to which the block should be written. Once the block has been written to the file, the document remains unchanged. Command Table 6.7 gives the details of the BLOCK WRITE commands for our sample word processors.

Figure 6.8 Using the BLOCK WRITE command in GoldWord. (a) Highlight the block of text to be stored for later use, and (b) give the BLOCK WRITE command. The document is unchanged, but the block is stored in a file on diskette.

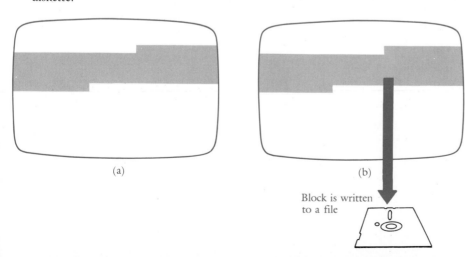

(a)

(b)

Block is written to a file

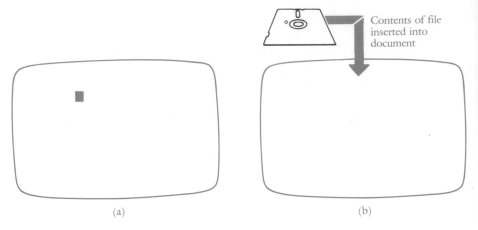

Figure 6.9   The BLOCK READ command in GoldWord. When you want to insert stored material from a file into your document, (a) position the cursor at the insert point and (b) give the BLOCK READ command.

Block Read. You may insert the contents of a file or of a **glossary** entry at any point in the document. Just position the cursor at the insert point and give the **BLOCK READ command**, as shown in Figure 6.9.

A block read is a **non-destructive read**—that is, reading the block does not erase the file or the glossary entry. You may use a single file or glossary entry for an unlimited number of block read operations. Command Table 6.8 summarizes the BLOCK READ commands for our sample word processors.

Command Table 6.8   The BLOCK READ commands for Wordstar, Word, and GoldWord.

Program	Command	Comments
WordStar	CTRL-KR ⟨file name⟩	Read contents of file and insert them at the current cursor position.
Word	ESC Insert ⟨glossary name⟩	Insert block of text stored in the glossary under the specified name.
GoldWord	CTRL-BR ⟨file name⟩	Read the contents of the file and insert them at the current cursor position.

Using Block Operations

The BLOCK MOVE, COPY, and DELETE operations are extremely handy in editing a document. The BLOCK MOVE command lets you rearrange text quite simply. The BLOCK DELETE command allows you to delete text much more quickly than you would be able to with the delete key. With the BLOCK COPY command, you can quickly duplicate paragraphs of text. If you want to duplicate paragraphs that are similar (but not identical), you can use the BLOCK COPY command to create several copies of the paragraph and then alter each one as required.

The BLOCK READ and BLOCK WRITE commands are valuable time-savers. You can use them to store any text that you use regularly, such as your address or the signature lines of a letter, in files that have been created by using BLOCK WRITE operations. Whenever you need these pieces of text, you can retrieve them from their files through the use of a BLOCK READ operation.

You can avoid the time-consuming retyping of your name, address, and telephone number each time you write a letter. The BLOCK READ command allows you to simply type the letter head once on your word processor and then store it in a file. Whenever you need to include the letterhead, use the BLOCK READ command to insert the letterhead at the desired position in the document.

You can also use the BLOCK READ operation to include "boilerplate" text within your documents. Boilerplate is standard-ized data such as the resumes of key employees, price lists, company profiles, and project descriptions. Again, it's easy to see the value of separately storing these bits of information for use in many kinds of documents, rather than recreating them each time you need them.

Section 6.2: Test Your Understanding

1. What is a block?
2. Describe the operation to define a block.
3. Give an application of a BLOCK COPY operation.
4. Give an application of a BLOCK MOVE operation.
5. What is a scrap heap and how is it used?
6. What is the difference between writing a block to a file and to a glossary entry?
7. Describe an application of the BLOCK READ command.

XYZ Software is pleased to announce the release of version 5.0 of its popular accounting software, HOLD ACCOUNT. This new version of HOLD ACCOUNT, which can be used with a majority of personal computers, corrects all known bugs and incorporates the many suggestions made by users. (Although the menu and command structures are identical to the previous version, 5.0 is not file compatible with previous versions.)

For a demonstration of version 5.0 of HOLD ACCOUNT, contact your local XYZ Software sales representative.

XYZ Software offers an attractive update package at a considerable discount from the list price. Call for a list of the computers and printers on which the new version will run.

Figure 6.10 A document on which to practice block operations.

Hands-on Exercises

1. Use the BLOCK WRITE command to create a file, named TIMELIM, containing the following text:

   ALL BIDS ARE VALID FOR A PERIOD OF 30 DAYS
   FROM THE DATE OF THIS LETTER.

2. Create a file named BID containing the document in Figure 6.10.

   a) Edit a new file called BID2. Use the BLOCK READ command to insert the contents of BID into BID2.

   b) Interchange the first two paragraphs of the resulting document.

   c) Delete the second sentence of the third paragraph.

   d) Insert a copy of the third paragraph at the end of the document and change all instances of *XYZ Software* to *Accountability Software* in the copy.

   e) Use the BLOCK READ command to insert the file TIMELIM created in Exercise 1. It should appear at the end of the document, with three lines of space added before the insert.

6.3 Text Formatting

In preparing documents, typing and editing the words correctly is only the first step. The next step involves **text formatting**, the process of arranging the text on the page. Formatting can give your document a certain "look," which can help convey your ideas and make the document easy to read and to refer to. The many format elements include the following:

- Margins (top, bottom, right, left)
- Pagination (style and position)
- Headings
- Indentation
- Character attributes (boldface, italics, underline)
- Line spacing
- Number of lines per page

Most word processors have extensive sets of commands for document formatting. This section surveys some of the more common formatting elements and how they may be used with our sample word processors.

Some General Comments

Formatting in WordStar and GoldWord. To define formatting, WordStar and GoldWord both use **dot commands**. Inserted into the document at print time, a dot command is a command line that is included within the text but does not correspond to printed text. Instead, a dot command communicates control information to the word processor. The word processor identifies a dot command as a line beginning with a period. For example, the code for the document's top margin is MT, and the top margin is measured in terms of lines. So, the dot command to set a top margin of 4 lines is .MT 4.

Dot commands are used to set formatting characteristics that the user controls when the document is printed. The same is true with the top and bottom margins: You don't see them in the document as you edit. The margins are added to the document only at print time.

In addition to dot commands, both WordStar and GoldWord use **embedded format commands** to control various formatting elements. These commands use control characters embedded directly within the document. For example, the format command to turn on boldfacing is CTRL-PB in both programs. A second CTRL-PB turns off boldfacing. For instance, to enter the sentence

*This is an example of **boldface**.*

you type

This is an example of ⟨CTRL-PB⟩boldface⟨CTRL-PB⟩.

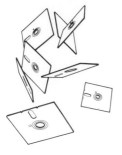

Command Table 6.9 Formatting commands for WordStar.*

Command	Comments
.PL *n*	Set *n* lines per page.
.LH *n*	Set line height of *n* 48ths of an inch.
.MT *n*	Set *n* lines from top of page to beginning of text.
.MB *n*	Set *n* lines from bottom of page to beginning of text.
.HM *n*	Set *n* lines between header and first line of text.
.FM *n*	Set *n* lines between end of text and footer.
.HE ⟨text⟩	Set header to ⟨text⟩. A # in ⟨text⟩ is interpreted as current page number.
.FO ⟨text⟩	Set footer to ⟨text⟩. A # in ⟨text⟩ is interpreted as current page number.
.PA	Forced page break.
.CP *n*	Conditional page break, provided that there are at least *n* lines per page.
.OP	Omit page numbering.
.PN	Start page numbering.
.PN *n*	Start page numbering with the number *n*.
.PC *n*	Place the page numbers beginning in column *n*.
.SR *n*	Set subscript or superscript roll to *n* 48ths of an inch.
.BP OFF	Turn off bidirectional printing.
.BP ON	Turn on bidirectional printing.
.PO *n*	Offset printing *n* columns to the right.
.. or .IG	Ignore remainder of line.
.CW *n*	Set carriage width to *n* 120ths of an inch.
.UJ OFF	Turn microjustification off.
.UJ ON	Turn microjustification on.

* Formatting in WordStar is achieved by using dot commands, which consist of a line beginning with a period followed by a command. A dot command affects the text following its position in the document.

In WordStar, CTRL-PB is displayed as ^B. So on the screen you see

> *This is an example of* ^Bboldface ^B.

Note that control characters don't count when line lengths are computed. For this reason, lines containing control characters will appear onscreen as though they are spilling beyond the set margins. However, the document will print correctly.

In GoldWord, boldface is displayed on the screen, so you see

> *This is an example of **boldface**.*

Command Table 6.9 summarizes the formatting commands for use with WordStar. Command Table 6.10 summarizes the formatting commands for GoldWord.

Formatting in Word. Word uses a completely different formatting philosophy. In Word, you assign a format to a document entity (character, word, sentence, paragraph, division, whole document). Formats are classified into character attributes (boldface, underline, italics), paragraph attributes (right and left margins, line spacing), and division attributes (page numbering, top and bottom margins). To assign a format in Word, you must do the following:

1. Select the entity to be formatted, and position the cursor within that entity. Press the appropriate function key, as summarized in Command Table 6.11.

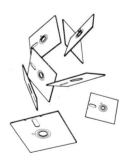

Command Table 6.10   Formatting commands for GoldWord.*

Command	Comments
ALT-FLH *n*	Set line height to *n* units. The unit size will vary from printer to printer. Better to use ALT-LP command.
ALT-FLP *n*	Print *n* lines per 11-inch page.
ALT-FMT *n*	Set top margin to *n* lines.
ALT-FMB *n*	Set bottom margin to *n* lines.
ALT-FMH *n*	Set margin heading to *n* lines.
ALT-FMF *n*	Set footing margin to *n* lines.
ALT-FPA	Forced page break.
ALT-FCP *n*	Conditional page break if at least *n* lines already exist on the page.
ALT-FPO *n*	Move text offset to the right *n* columns.
ALT-FBP *0*	Turn off bidirectional printing.
ALT-FBP *1*	Turn on bidirectional printing.
ALT-FIG ⟨text⟩	Ignore ⟨text⟩ when printing.

* Each format command must be placed on a line by itself, with no blank spaces before the first format character.

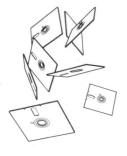

Command Table 6.11   Formatting commands for Word.

Type of Command	Command	Comments
Select text to format	F8	Select current word.
	F9	Select current sentence.
	F10	Select current paragraph.
	CTRL-F9	Select current line.
	CTRL-F10	Select entire document.
	F6	Allow cursor movements to extend selected text.
	ESC Format Character	Set character attributes for selected text.
Set format parameters	ESC Format Paragraph	Set paragraph attributes for selected text.
	ESC Format Division	Set division attributes for selected text.

2. Execute the appropriate format command, also summarized in Command Table 6.11.

Command Table 6.12 on pages 192–193 shows the character, paragraph, and division formatting menus for Word. You can set right and left margins by using the paragraph menu, and top and bottom margins by using the division menu.

Now that you understand formatting commands and the methods for executing them, let's look in more detail at the different formatting features used by word processors.

Margins

The simplest format elements on a printed page are the margins at top, bottom, right and left, as illustrated in Figure 6.11. You can set these margins by using word processor commands. (See the Command Table related to the formatting commands for your word processor.)

During editing or after, you may reset the margins anywhere within a document to achieve a particular layout. For example, you may want to indent a paragraph or display a portion of your text in a narrow column (which is useful in laying out newsletters) by making a temporary change in margins.

Tabs and Tables

You may use the TAB key (indicated by two arrows, one pointing left and one pointing right) on your word processor just as you use it on a typewriter. Once set, the tab stops enable you to move to a specific column by pressing the TAB key. For example, if there are tab stops at columns 5, 10, and 15, and the cursor is currently positioned in column 1, you simply press the TAB key once to position the cursor in column 5; pressing the TAB key a second time positions the cursor in column 10; pressing it a third time positions the cursor in column 15.

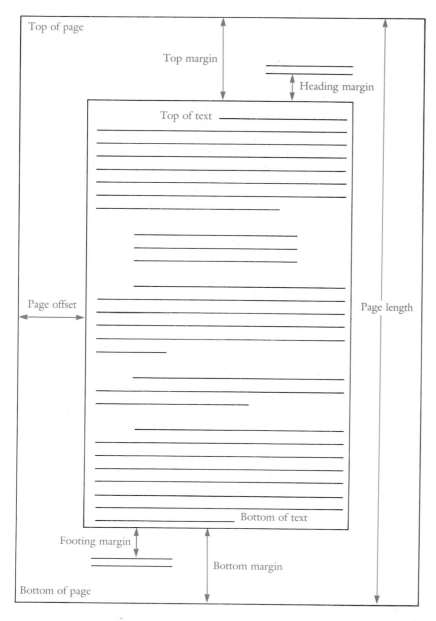

Figure 6.11 The margins on a printed page.

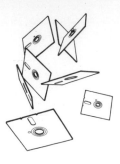

Command Table 6.12 The character, paragraph, and division formatting menus for Word.*

Menu	Field	Comments
Character	Bold	Set selected text to bold.
	Italic	Italicize selected text.
	Underline	Underline selected text.
	Strikethrough	Strike through selected text.
	Uppercase	Display selected text in uppercase.
	Small caps	Display selected case in small capital letters.
	Double underline	Double underline selected text.
	Position (Normal, Subscript, Superscript)	Specify the vertical position of selected text.
	Font name	Specify the font in which selected text is to be printed. Font selections are determined by printer specified in PRINT OPTIONS command. Fonts do not show on the screen.
	Character size	Size of character to be printed. Available sizes depend on printer selected. Character sizes are expressed in printer's points. One point equals 1/72nd of an inch.
Paragraph	Alignment (Left, Right, Centered, Justified)	Select alignment of paragraph.
	Left indent	Specify indent for paragraph, in inches, from left side of page.
	First line	Specify indent of first line relative to specified left indent of paragraph. This parameter may be positive or negative and is expressed in inches.
	Right indent	Specify indent of paragraph, in inches, from right side of the page.
	Line spacing	Specify spacing between lines. 1 = single-spacing, 2 = double-spacing, and so forth. Fractional lines are permitted.
	Space before	Number of lines of space preceding paragraph.
	Space after	Number of lines of space after paragraph.
	Keep together	Can paragraph be broken across pages?

Menu	Field	Comments
	Keep follow	Should paragraph and the one that follows be kept on the same page?
	Side by side	Should paragraph and the one that precedes be placed side by side?
Division		
	Margins:	
	Left	Specify left margin in inches.
	Right	Specify right margin in inches.
	Top	Specify top margin in inches.
	Bottom	Specify bottom margin in inches.
	Page length	Specify page length in inches.
	Width	Specify page width in inches.
	Gutter margin	Specify space, in inches, that page is to be offset from edge of page.
	Running head from top	Specify number of inches from top of page to running head.
	Running head (footer) from bottom	Specify number of inches from footer to bottom of page.
	Page Numbers:	
	Use page numbers	Number pages?
	Page number position from left	In inches.
	Page number position from right	In inches.
	Page number style	Arabic, uppercase, or lowercase Roman numerals; uppercase or lowercase letters.
	Page number sequence	Continuous with preceding division, begin a new sequence starting with given page number.
	Layout:	
	Footnote position	At bottom of each page or at end of document.
	Number of columns	A given division can print several columns across a page.
	Space between columns	In inches.
	Division break	A division can end at the end of a column, or a page, and at the end of an even page or an odd page.

* Each menu consists of a number of fields that the user can fill in. To move between fields, use the TAB key. To accept the settings of the menu, press ⟨ENTER⟩. To cancel any settings you have just entered, press ⟨ESCAPE⟩.

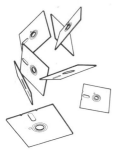

Command Table 6.13   Using TAB keys with WordStar, Word, and GoldWord.

Program	Command	Comments
WordStar	CTRL-OI-*n*	Set tab stop at column *n*. To set tab in current cursor column, use ESC for *n*.
	CTRL-ON	Clear tab stop at column *n*. To clear tab in current cursor column, use ESC for *n*.
Word	ESC Format Tabs Set ESC Format Tabs Clear	
GoldWord	CTRL-TS *n*	Set tab stop at column *n*. To set tab in current cursor column, use ESC for *n*.
	CTRL-TC *n*	Clear tab stop at column *n*. To clear tab in current cursor column, use ESC for *n*.

    With careful planning, you can use the TAB key to create neat columns and tables. Command Table 6.13 summarizes how to set the tab stops and determine the current tab stops in each of our sample word processors.

Centering

All word processors have a **CENTERING command**. To center a line, position the cursor anywhere within the line and give the CENTERING command. Command Table 6.14 summarizes the CENTERING commands for our sample word processors.

Line Spacing

A document is usually single-spaced or double-spaced; some word processors even allow fractional line spacing, such as $1\frac{1}{4}$ line spacing. However, for drafts that require written comments directly on the document, double-spacing is preferred.

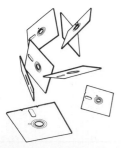

Command Table 6.14   The CENTERING commands for WordStar, Word, and GoldWord.

Program	Command	Comments
WordStar	CTRL-OC	Center current line.
Word	ALT-XC	Center selected text.
GoldWord	CTRL-C	Center current line.

Command Table 6.15   The commands to set line spacing for WordStar, Word, and GoldWord.

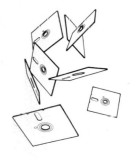

Program	Command	Comments
WordStar	.LH *n*	Dot command. Sets line spacing to *n* 48ths of an inch.
Word	ESC Format Paragraph (Set *line spacing* field.)	A setting of 1 gives single-spacing, 2 gives double-spacing, 3 triple-spacing, and so forth. Word also allows for fractional line spacing, such as .75 or 1.38 lines. Fractional lines are rounded to the nearest 72nd of an inch, which equals one printer's point.
GoldWord	ALT-FLH *n* ALT-LHP *n*	Set line spacing of *n* 72nds of an inch. Set line spacing to *n* lines per 11-inch-long page.

You can control the spacing between lines and the number of lines printed on a page. Command Table 6.15 summarizes the commands for setting line spacing and the number of lines per page in our sample word processors. Bear in mind that a document's line spacing may not appear onscreen as it appears on the printed page.

Justification

In most printed texts, the characters along the right margin line up under each other; in other words, the text is justified. You can achieve this effect through **justification**, which means that the empty spaces on a line are distributed evenly between the words so that the last character on every line will align. More sophisticated justification schemes even distribute fractional character spaces between the individual characters of a word.

Text that is not justified is often called **ragged right**, since the right margin has a ragged appearance. This format is usually preferred for business letters. Figure 6.12 illustrates both justified and ragged right text. Command Table 6.16 tells you how to turn justification on and off in our sample word processors.

Proportional Spacing

Some word processors support **proportional spacing**, in which different letters take up different amounts of horizontal space. For

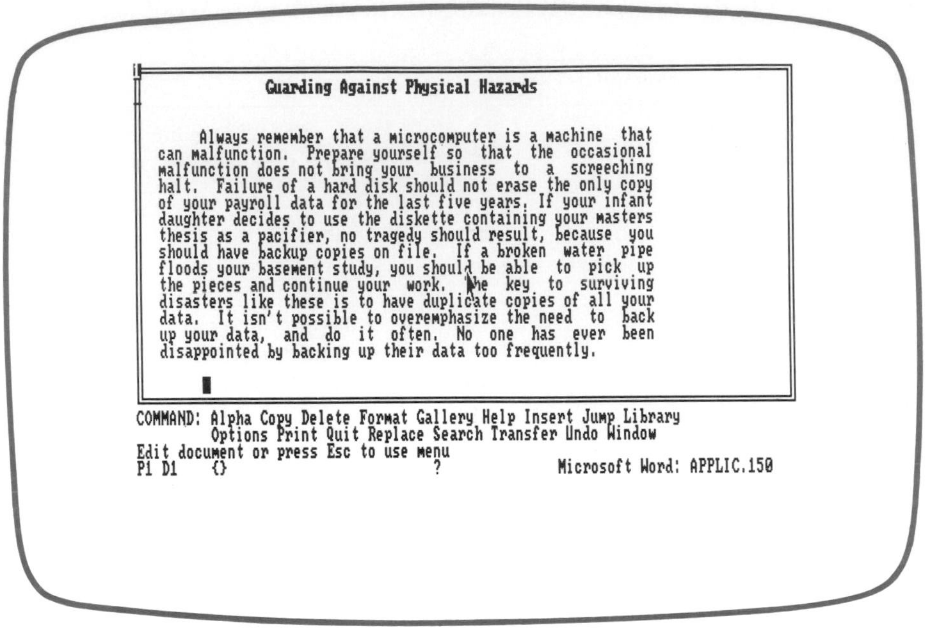

(a)

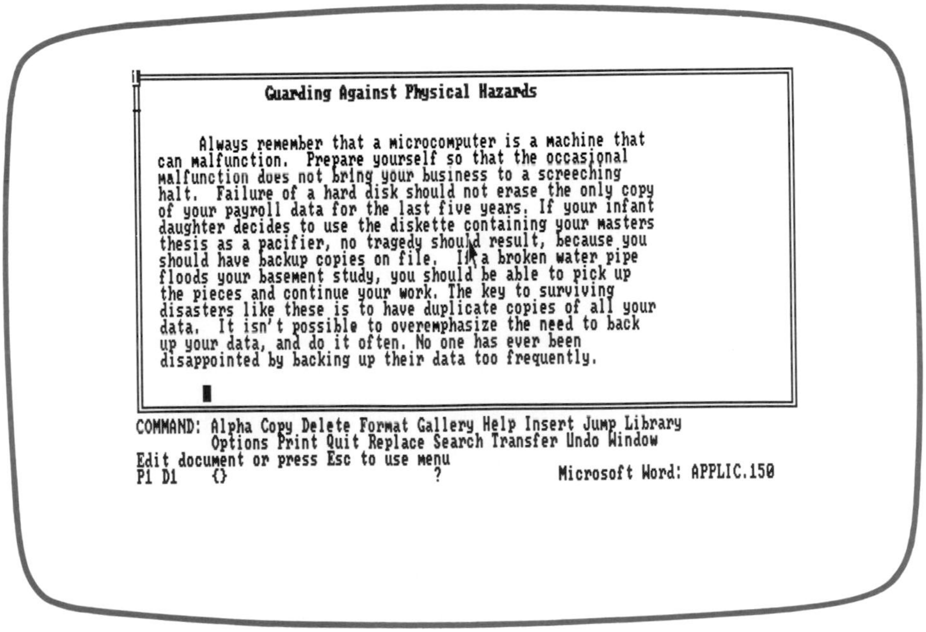

(b)

Figure 6.12   Samples of (a) justified and (b) ragged right text.

```
This  is  an  example  of  monospaced  text.
It  is  printed  in  Courier  10-point  type.
```

This is an example of proportionally-spaced text. It is
printed in Times-Roman 10-point type.

Figure 6.13   Proportional
versus monospaced text.

example, "w" takes up more horizontal space than "l." Proportional
spacing gives a document a very polished appearance. In contrast
to proportional spacing is **monospacing**, in which each character
takes up the same amount of horizontal space. Figure 6.13 contrasts
proportional and monospaced text.

Many word processors support only monospaced text, or
support proportional spacing on only selected printers. Neither
WordStar nor GoldWord support proportional spacing. However,
Word supports proportional spacing on selected printers.

Pagination

The process of breaking a document into pages is called **pagination**.
Some word processors (like WordStar) perform pagination dynam-
ically. That is, the word processor computes **page breaks** as you
edit your document and displays the current page breaks on the
screen. This feature is illustrated in Figure 6.14.

The page breaks are determined by the page layout currently
in effect (number of lines per page, number of lines for top and

Command Table 6.16   The commands to turn justification on and off
with WordStar, Word, and GoldWord.

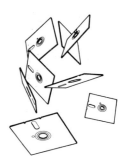

Program	Command	Comments
WordStar	CTRL-OJ	First CTRL-OJ turns justifi-cation on. The second turns it off.
Word	ESC Format Paragraph (Set *alignment* field to Justified.)	Justify selected paragraphs.
	ESC Format Paragraph (Set *alignment* field to Right, Left, or Centered.)	Select a non-justified align-ment (aligned on right margin, aligned on left margin, or centered) for se-lected paragraphs.
GoldWord	Justification not supported.	

bottom margins). The page breaks are inserted into the document after the last text line of a page. In a word processor with dynamic pagination, editing changes that result in addition or deletion of lines on a page result in immediate changes in the pagination. In such a scheme, the screen and document always reflect the current pagination in effect.

Other word processors (like GoldWord and Word) compute the page breaks only in response to a user request or by printing the document. In such word processors, there is a **PAGINATE command**, which instructs the word processor to divide the current document into pages. The pagination shown on the screen is determined in response to the last PAGINATE command, or the last time the document was printed. This sort of pagination scheme is helpful if you want to transfer corrections or comments from hard copy, since the pagination doesn't change while you enter the changes and you can then easily compare the hard copy to the document on screen.

You may insert a **forced page break** to end a page where the word processor's automatic pagination might not otherwise break the page. For example, you can force a page break to end one section in a paper and start a new section on a new page.

Regardless of how page breaks are handled during editing, all word processors paginate a document during the printing process.

Figure 6.14   A page break in WordStar.

```
        D:IBM.040  PAGE 4 LINE 10 COL 01              INSERT ON
L----!----!----!----!----!----!----!----!----!----!--------R
program  while  it  is running.  This is done by  ^Bsimultaneously^B
pressing the Ctrl and Break keys. It's a two-handed operation and
with  good  reason.  The  keys are arranged  so  that  you  won't
interrupt  programs  accidentally.  To  illustrate  how  you  may
interrupt a program,  run MUSIC and play a song. In the middle of
the  song,  simultaneously hit Ctrl and Break.  The  program  will
stop. The screen will display a message of the sort:              <
                                                                  <
      Break in line xxxx                                          <
      Ok                                                          <
-------------------------------------------------------------------P
      -                                                           <
                                                                  <
The line xxxx gives the place in the program at which you stopped
the  computer.  (We'll  learn  about  line numbers  in  the  next
section.)  The BASIC prompt Ok indicates that BASIC  is  awaiting
another  command.  Interrupting a program does not erase it  from
RAM. To run the program again, just type RUN and press ENTER.     <
                                                                  <
      Well, enough music for now! Let's end the program. According
to the instructions on the screen,  you may "EXIT" the program by
pressing  Esc,  a key which is located on the upper left side  of
1HELP   2INDENT 3SET LM 4SET RM 5UNDLIN 6BLDFCE 7BEGBLK 8ENDBLK 9BEGFIL 10ENDFIL
```

Command Table 6.17   PAGE BREAK commands for WordStar, Word, and GoldWord.

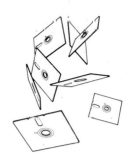

Program	Command	Comments
WordStar	.PA	Dot command. Forced page break.
	.PC n	Dot command. Conditional page break if the current page has at least n lines.
Word	⟨SHIFT⟩-⟨ENTER⟩	Insert a forced page break at the current cursor position. Shown on the screen as a dotted line.
GoldWord	ALT-FPA	Forced page break.
	ALT-FPC n	Conditional page break. Occurs if the current page has at least n lines on it.

Command Table 6.17 summarizes how page breaks are handled during editing in each of our sample word processors.

Most word processors automatically number pages for you. Some word processors can even use various numbering schemes, such as

1, 2, 3, . . .

i, ii, iii, . . .

I, II, III, . . .

a, b, c, . . .

You can control page numbering through the use of formatting commands. Moreover, there are commands to control the position of the page numbers on the page. Command Table 6.18 summarizes the PAGINATE commands for each of our sample word processors.

Text Attributes

Most word processors allow you to assign **attributes**—such as boldface, italics, underline, double underline, strikethrough, subscript, and superscript—to text. Figure 6.15 illustrates some of

Figure 6.15   Text attributes.

This line is printed without any text attributes.
This line is printed in italics.
This line is printed in boldface.
<u>This line is printed underlined.</u>
<u>This line is printed double underlined.</u>
~~This line is printed with a strikethrough.~~

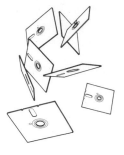

Command Table 6.18   PAGINATION commands for WordStar, Word, and GoldWord.

Program	Command	Comments
WordStar	.OP .PN *n* .PC *n*	Omit page numbering. Set page numbering to ON and begin numbering with page *n*. Set the page number column to column *n*.
Word	ESC Format Division (Insert menu entries. For versions 2.1 or earlier.) ESC-FDPN (Insert menu entries. For versions 3.0 or later.)	Set page numbering, position, and format by filling in the fields: *Page numbers* (Yes, No) *From top* (position of page number from top of page, in inches) *From left* (position of page number from left margin of page) *Continuous start* (continue page numbering from preceding division or begin new numbering sequence) *At* (if starting new sequence, beginning page number) *Number format 1 I i A a* (format for page numbers—Arabic numbers, uppercase Roman numerals, lowercase Roman numerals, capital letters, lowercase letters In versions 2.1 and earlier, the menu has a number of entries which have nothing to do with page numbering.
GoldWord	ALT-FPC *n* ALT-FOP ALT-FPN	Set page number column to column *n*. Omit page numbering. Turn page numbering on. ALT-FPN *n*

these attributes. Depending on the word processor, the attributes may or may not be displayed on the screen. Moreover, the characteristics of your printer will determine how the various attributes are printed, if at all. Command Table 6.19 summarizes the available text attributes and the formatting commands for invoking them on our sample word processors.

Predefined Paragraph Formats

Some word processors allow you to define certain paragraph formats and store them on disk. You may then assign a format to a particular paragraph within a document by using only a few keystrokes. For example, you can define a paragraph format in which the first line is indented $\frac{1}{2}$ inch, the left margin indented $1\frac{1}{2}$ inches, the right margin indented 1 inch, and the characters of the paragraph set in boldface type. Figure 6.16 on page 204 shows a paragraph having such a format.

You can use an extensive set of predefined formats, including formats for lists, exercise sets, titles, and others to suit your needs. For example, consider the second paragraph shown in Figure 6.16(a). It is indented one inch from the left-hand margin. The first line is outdented three characters, and includes a subheading set in italics. The collection of all these characteristics make up a particular paragraph format.

Word allows you to store predefined formats of characters, words, and divisions. You assign identifying keystrokes to formats and store them in a file called a **style sheet**. For example, the style of the second paragraph shown in Figure 6.16 might be assigned the keystrokes IP (indented paragraph). To give a paragraph this style, you merely position the cursor anywhere in the paragraph and type the keystrokes ⟨ALT-IP⟩. The paragraph is then automatically formatted according to the style specified.

A style sheet may contain many different formats. You may attach a style sheet to a document, thereby making available to the document all of the predefined styles in the style sheet. You can change the format of the document merely by redefining the styles in the style sheet. The document is then automatically reformatted in accordance with the new specifications.

Section 6.3: Test Your Understanding

1. What is document formatting?
2. What is a dot command?
3. What is an embedded format command?
4. What is justification?
5. In some documents, individual characters can take up different amounts of horizontal space. What is this type of printing called?
6. What is monospaced text?
7. List three text attributes.

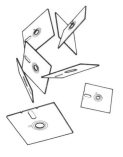

Command Table 6.19   Text attributes and their formatting commands for WordStar, Word, and GoldWord.

Program	Command	Comments
WordStar	CTRL-PB	Attribute is turned on by a FORMAT command of the form CTRL-P ⟨character⟩. Attribute is turned off by second occurrence of same command. The CTRL-P portion of an attribute command is shown on screen as the symbol ^. Display of attribute commands can be suppressed by giving the command CTRL-QP. They can be turned back on by repeating command. Boldface.
	CTRL-PS	Underline
	CTRL-PD	Doublestrike
	CTRL-PH	Overstrike next character.
	CTRL-P ⟨ENTER⟩	Overprint next line on top of this one.
	CTRL-PY	Change ribbon color (depends on printer).
	CTRL-PT	Superscript
	CTRL-PV	Subscript
	CTRL-PA	Pica print (10 characters per inch)
	CTRL PN	Elite print (12 characters per inch)
	CTRL-PO	Insert a hard space, one which is ignored by word wrap or paragraph reform.

Hands-on Exercises

These exercises refer to the latest version of the file EXAMPLE1. Turn on your word processor and load EXAMPLE1.

1. Format the first paragraph so that it is in boldface.
2. Add the title MY FIRST DOCUMENT and center it before the first paragraph, with two blank lines of space before the title. Boldface and underline the title.

Program	Command	Comments
Word		Attribute commands apply to selected text.
	ALT-B	Boldface
	ALT-I	Italics
	ALT-+	Superscript
	ALT−	Subscript
	ALT-U	Underlined
	ALT-D	Double underlined
GoldWord		An attribute is turned on by the first occurrence of a command and turned off by the second. The screen shows the attributes so that the commands are not displayed.
	ALT-M	Cancel all currently active attributes.
	ALT-B	Boldface
	ALT-C	Condensed print (depends on printer)
	ALT-R	Correspondence mode (depends on printer)
	ALT-D	Doublestrike
	ALT-L	Elite (depends on printer)
	ALT-E	Enlarged (depends on printer)
	ALT-N	Inverse (depends on printer)
	ALT-I	Italics
	ALT-P	Proportional spacing (depends on printer)
	ALT-U	Underscore
	ALT-V	Subscript
	ALT-A	Superscript

3. Repaginate the document with one paragraph on each page.
4. Underline the first word of the second paragraph.
5. Set the line spacing for double-spaced text.
6. Justify one paragraph of the document, then unjustify it.
7. Set the page numbering so that the first page starts at page number 10.
8. Print out the formatted document and save the document.

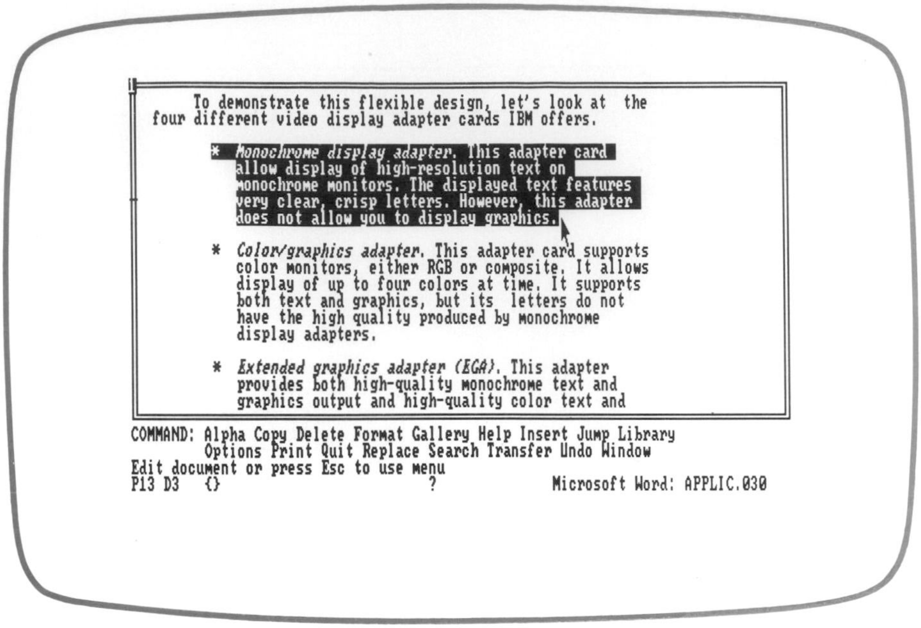

(a)

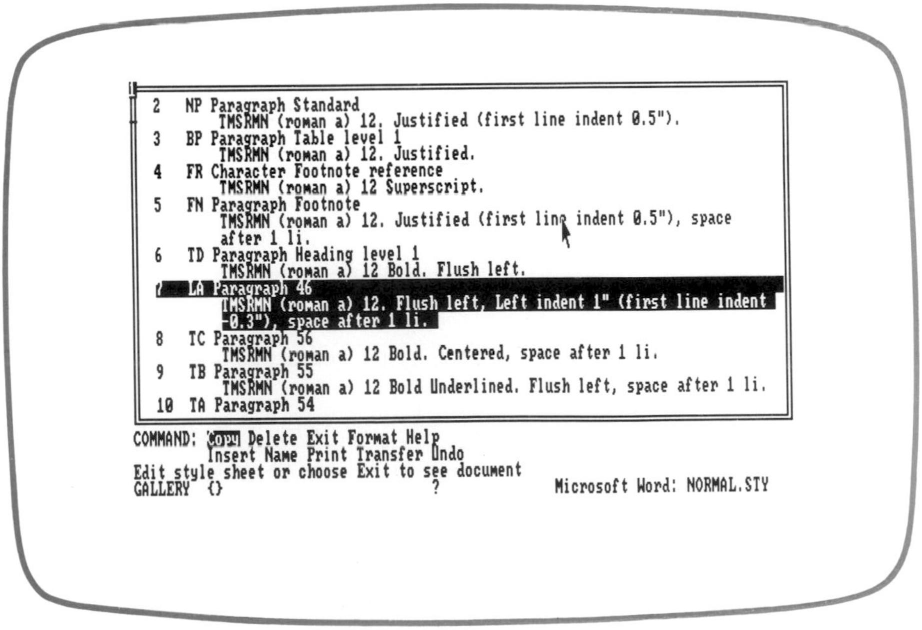

(b)

Figure 6.16   A paragraph formatted according to a predefined format in Word.
(a) A paragraph formatted with FORMAT LA. (b) Definition of the format LA.

6.4 Word-Processing Enhancements

Up to this point, you have read about what may be called a word processor's "basic" features—the features that are common to most word processors. In addition, a number of other features are present in some word processors and not in others. Given the significance of word processing in today's offices, it is likely that the options described here will become standard features in the word processors of tomorrow.

Spelling Checkers

A **spelling checker** is exactly what its name implies—a program for checking the spelling of the words in a document. Spelling checkers are incorporated in some word processors, or exist as stand-alone programs that can be used with files produced on a word processor.

If your spelling or typing skills aren't perfect, a spelling checker can catch your errors for you.

A spelling checker employs a dictionary stored in RAM while the checker is operating. This dictionary contains 25,000 to 125,000 of the most commonly used words. When implemented, the spelling checker consults the dictionary for every word in the document. (It may seem inefficient for the spelling checker to look up every word, but a computer's high speed allows it to accomplish the task in a short time.)

If the checker cannot locate a word in the dictionary, it is flagged as a possible spelling error and is presented to you, along with some surrounding text for context. You are then given the option of correcting the word or leaving it as it is. After the spelling checker runs through the list of all potential misspellings, it modifies the document accordingly. The sequence of operations of a spelling checker are summarized in Figure 6.17.

Some spelling checkers even assist you in correcting misspelled words by providing suggestions for the word you might have intended. You can then choose a word from the suggested list or you can enter your own spelling.

You can't always gauge the quality of a spelling checker by the size of its dictionary. Some excellent spelling checkers employ small dictionaries of "root" words and then use various spelling rules to build words from these roots. Most spelling checkers allow you to add new words to the dictionaries. Some checkers also allow you to add one or more additional dictionaries of specialized words, such as a dictionary of medical or engineering terms. If you use certain words often, it is far more efficient to add them to the dictionary than to let the spelling checker flag them each time they appear.

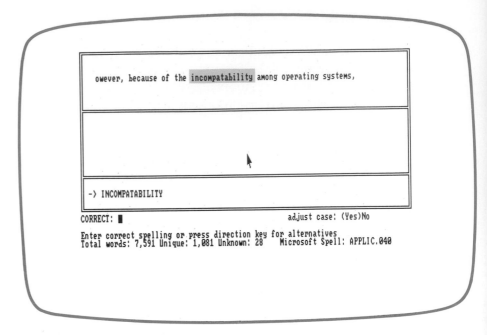

owever, because of the incompatability among operating systems,

-> INCOMPATABILITY

CORRECT: ▮   adjust case: (Yes)No

Enter correct spelling or press direction key for alternatives
Total words: 7,591 Unique: 1,081 Unknown: 28   Microsoft Spell: APPLIC.040

Figure 6.17   How a spelling checker works.

Like any software tool, a spelling checker has strengths and weaknesses. One strength is efficiency in spotting some typographical errors. For example, if you type *hte* instead of *the* or *porcessor* instead of *processor*, a spelling checker will surely spot the errors. However, a spelling checker's weakness becomes apparent if your mistyped word happens to be a valid word, in which case the spelling checker will pass it by. For example, if you want to type *wear* and type *ware* instead, the error will not be caught. A spelling checker has no way of judging the appropriateness of a word from its context.

Some spelling checkers will question more words than others, depending on the analysis process programmed into the checker. Ideally, a spelling checker should question only words that are incorrectly spelled. However, in practice, it questions many legitimate words, including the following:

- Words not in the spelling checker's dictionary
- Technical terms and jargon
- Numbers
- Abbreviations

By appropriately expanding the dictionary, you can use a spelling checker to proofread documents without being bothered by too many false alarms.

Grammar Checkers

A number of **grammar checkers** have recently appeared on the market. At this time, no available word processors have a built-in grammar checker; all of the checkers on the market are stand-alone programs. A grammar checker checks the grammar of a document in much the same way that a spelling checker checks the spelling.

Style Analyzers

Software designers are now designing **style analyzers**—programs that analyze the style of a document and can be used to improve your writing style. The program points out sentences that are too long and constructions that are too complex. A style analyzer could adversely affect individual style, however, as evidenced when Thomas Jefferson's Declaration of Independence was fed into one style analyzer. The program suggested that "When in the course of human events" be shortened to "When." A style analyzer is unlikely to improve great writing, but it can make poor writing acceptable.

Outliners

Some word processors have an **outline mode** (also called an **auto-indent mode**). In this mode, each line is automatically indented the same number of spaces as the line above it. Of course, you may move the beginning of a line right or left manually, by using either the SPACEBAR or BACKSPACE key. However, the automatic indentation produces a convenient paragraph format for creating outlines, such as the one shown in Figure 6.18.

Indexing

An **index** is used to locate information in a text. It makes a document easier to use as a reference by providing an alphabetical list of topics discussed in the document and their accompanying page numbers, as is shown in Figure 6.19. Unfortunately, indexes are time-consuming to create. Moreover, they must be updated to reflect changing pagination as the document is altered.

For longer documents, an index program is ideal. It saves you the tedium of preparing a list of reference points within the document.

A number of programs that can create an index for a document are now on the market. To use an index program, you flag the terms you wish to include in the index using a control character that the word processor has been programmed to ignore for purposes of editing and printing. Some programs even allow you to specify index subentries—for example, *Computers, personal* and *Computers, history of.*

When you run the index program, it reads the document, picks out the indexed terms, combines multiple entries, and deter-

Menu Outline

Following is an outline of Gold/Sheet's menu system and a brief desciption of its command functions. Sub-menus are indented under their parent menus.

/Print -
    Printer - Print to printer
        Align - Resets top of page on printer
        Clear - Clear print settings
            All - Clear all print settings
            Borders - Clear border settings
            Format - Clear margin, setup string and page length to defaults
        Go - Start printing
        Line - Move printer to start of new line
        Page - Advance to top of new page
        Options -
            Borders - Specify range to print as border
                Columns - Specify vertical border
                Rows - Specify horizontal border
            Footer - Specify footer text
            Header - Specify header text
            Margins - Specify page margins
                Bottom -
                Left -
                Right -
                Top -
            Other -
                As-Displayed - Print range as it appears on the screen
                Cell-Formulas - Print cells as displayed in the control panel
                Formatted - Print using specified formatting
                Unformatted - Print without using specified formatting
        Quit - Return to Main Menu
        Range - Specify range to print
    File - Print to file (see **Printer**)
/Quit - Leave the spreadsheet
/Graph -
    A-F - Select data ranges A through F
    Name - Specify or delete named graph settings

Figure 6.18   A page of a document produced by using outline mode.

mines the page number for each entry. The program then formats the index and stores it as a document accessible to your word processor, either to edit or print out. Once the indexed terms have been marked, simply rerun the program to get an updated index reflecting document editing and changed pagination.

Internal Numbering in a Document

A document may use many different sequences of numbers to keep track of its contents. The simplest and most common of these is

page break 68, 69
page break, conditional 68, 69, 157
   function & remarks 157
page break, forced 68, 69, 158
   function & remarks 158
page down through document 159
   function & remarks 159
page layout 63
page length 58, 61, 160
   function & remarks 160
page number 68
page number, column 69, 161
   function & remarks 161
page number, set column of 68
page number, starting value 68, 165
   function & remarks 165
page number, turn off 68, 162
   function & remarks 162
page number, turn on 68, 164
   function & remarks 164
page offset 67, 166
   function & remarks 166
page up through document 167
   function & remarks 167
Panasonic KX-P1091 60, 204
paragraph 9
   changing margins 34
   close 32, 168
     function & remarks 168
   delete 45, 46, 116
   formation 32
   marking a 47
   splitting 35
preface to tutorial 23
previous word 169
print:
   bidirectional off 74, 90
     function & remarks 90
   bidirectional on 74, 91
     function & remarks 91
   document 27, 75-77
   file 11, 27, 75-77
   interrupt 77
   last used file 75
   most recent file 12
printer, install 75
printers supported 1, 2
   list of 199-207
proportional mode 41, 170
   function & remarks 170

quick start 25

quit file 40, 171
   function & quit GOLD/WORD, 12, 26, 27
remarks 171

read in another file 47, 49, 50
recall files 26, 27
remove help screen 16
remove help window 29, 30
rename file 12, 79, 82
replace 55, 172
   function & remarks 172
replace, instructions for 56
replace, next 174
   function & remarks 174
replace, options for 55
retrieve and edit most recent file 12
return to MAIN MENU 13
revising text 45
running feet 71-72
running foot text 71, 73
   justification 71, 73
running head 71
running head text 71
   justification 71, 73

save block as separate file 47, 50
   instructions 50
save file 26 27 40, 175
   function & remarks 175
scrap heap 47, 48, 49
   how to clear 47, 50, 105
screen:
   drive/directory selection menu 14
   edit 15
   file selection menu 13
   help 16, 28
   main menu 11, 12
   margin 35
   TAB control 37
scroll, file directory 13
search 53-56
search and replace, instructions for 56
set top margin 21
setting margins 34
setting tab stops 37
setting up, first time 5
single space 58-61
space and a half 58-61
spacing, vertical line 58
split a paragraph 35
Star Micronics Gemini 10X,15X 60, 204

Figure 6.19 A sample page from the index of an application software package manual.

the sequence of page numbers. A long document is usually divided into chapters and sections. The sequence of chapters and sections within a chapter are usually numbered, employing one of many possible numbering schemes. For example, section 3 of Chapter 8 may be denoted as 8.3, VIII.3, or 8.iii.

The section numbers may change as you create the document. If you decide to add a section between sections 8.2 and 8.3, the program will renumber all sections from section 8.3 to the end of Chapter 8.

Some word-processing programs allow for automatic numbering of chapters and sections, and they even allow for numbering of subsections. Similarly, some word-processing programs automatically number figures and tables. Using this information on sections and figures, such word-processing programs can prepare a table of contents and a figure list for a document.

Footnotes

A **footnote** is a piece of text that provides additional information, clarification, or support for a statement made in the main text of a document. A footnote is usually indicated by a **footnote reference**, a symbol (such as * or **) or a superscript number (such as [1] or [2]). The text of a footnote may be placed on the same page as the footnote (usually at the bottom), or listed with all other footnotes and placed at the end of the document. A typical arrangement of footnotes is shown in Figure 6.20.

Some word processors can automatically generate footnote references in sequence as the footnotes are entered into the document. If you delete a footnote, this type of word processor automatically renumbers all the remaining footnotes.

Some word processors, including Word, can automatically format pages (usually at print time) to place the footnotes on the same page as the reference. In word processors without this feature, it is very difficult and time-consuming to correctly place footnotes on the page where they are referenced. Even if you do this, the placement is usually destroyed as soon as the document is edited further.

Headers and Footers

Headings containing a chapter title, section title, page number, version number, revision date, or some other data describing the contents of the page can further reference and organize a lengthy document. A **header** is a heading placed at the top of a page; a **footer** is one placed at the bottom of a page. A document may use

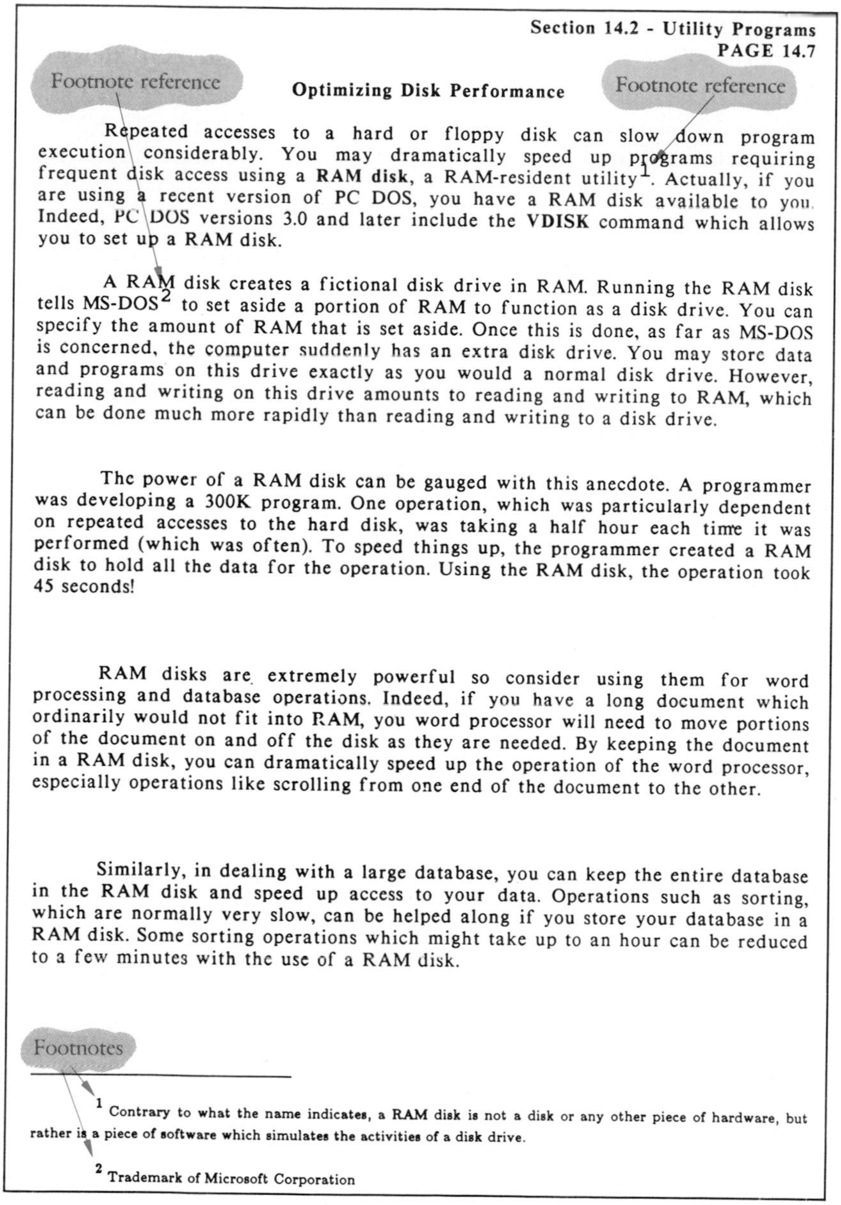

Section 14.2 - Utility Programs
PAGE 14.7

Footnote reference   **Optimizing Disk Performance**   Footnote reference

Repeated accesses to a hard or floppy disk can slow down program execution considerably. You may dramatically speed up programs requiring frequent disk access using a **RAM disk**, a RAM-resident utility[1]. Actually, if you are using a recent version of PC DOS, you have a RAM disk available to you. Indeed, PC DOS versions 3.0 and later include the **VDISK** command which allows you to set up a RAM disk.

A RAM disk creates a fictional disk drive in RAM. Running the RAM disk tells MS-DOS[2] to set aside a portion of RAM to function as a disk drive. You can specify the amount of RAM that is set aside. Once this is done, as far as MS-DOS is concerned, the computer suddenly has an extra disk drive. You may store data and programs on this drive exactly as you would a normal disk drive. However, reading and writing on this drive amounts to reading and writing to RAM, which can be done much more rapidly than reading and writing to a disk drive.

The power of a RAM disk can be gauged with this anecdote. A programmer was developing a 300K program. One operation, which was particularly dependent on repeated accesses to the hard disk, was taking a half hour each time it was performed (which was often). To speed things up, the programmer created a RAM disk to hold all the data for the operation. Using the RAM disk, the operation took 45 seconds!

RAM disks are extremely powerful so consider using them for word processing and database operations. Indeed, if you have a long document which ordinarily would not fit into RAM, you word processor will need to move portions of the document on and off the disk as they are needed. By keeping the document in a RAM disk, you can dramatically speed up the operation of the word processor, especially operations like scrolling from one end of the document to the other.

Similarly, in dealing with a large database, you can keep the entire database in the RAM disk and speed up access to your data. Operations such as sorting, which are normally very slow, can be helped along if you store your database in a RAM disk. Some sorting operations which might take up to an hour can be reduced to a few minutes with the use of a RAM disk.

Footnotes

---

[1] Contrary to what the name indicates, a RAM disk is not a disk or any other piece of hardware, but rather is a piece of software which simulates the activities of a disk drive.

[2] Trademark of Microsoft Corporation

Figure 6.20 A document page with several footnotes.

both headers and footers in its page design, as illustrated in Figure 6.21.

Headers and footers consist of a single line or multiple lines, depending on the limitations of the word processor. A header or footer can be placed in the center of its line, at the extreme left of the margin (**flush left**), or at the extreme right of the margin (**flush right**). A common arrangement uses one set of headers or footers on odd-numbered pages and another set on even-numbered pages.

For example, in one common header design, even-numbered pages display the chapter title and odd-numbered pages display the section title.

To incorporate headers and footers in your documents, specify either a dot command or a special formatting command, which

Figure 6.21   A document page with a header and footer.

Section 14.1 - Integrated Software

Header

The preceding chapters introduced a number of different types of applications software packages. These are not the only packages available for microcomputer applications. The field of microcomputing is still very young, and the applications discussed so far are those that have come to the fore as the most important up to this point in the microcomputer revolution. However, there are many other types of applications software available, and many more will be created in the near future. Here we take a look at some of the other categories of applications software.

14.1 Integrated Software

The most commonly used business applications packages are the ones described in this text: word processors, spreadsheets, database management systems, graphics packages, and communications programs. **Integrated software** is designed to perform the functions of two or more of these packages. In recent years, integrated software has become quite popular as is evident by the enormous success of packages such as Lotus 1-2-3, which integrates in a single package spreadsheet, data management and graphics.

The applications included in an integrated package vary with the package. For instance, 1-2-3 includes a spreadsheet, data manager, and graphics capability. Packages such as Symphony, Jazz and Framework include these functions and add word processing and communications.

There are many advantages to using integrated software instead of individual applications packages. For one, an integrated package allows you to learn a single, consistent set of commands that perform a wide variety of functions. As you have seen by performing the exercises and applications projects in this text, it takes time and effort to master any software package. If you need to use more than one applications package, having to learn a separate command set for each can be very confusing and can lead to time-consuming mistakes. It is much more convenient to have a uniform approach for saving and retrieving files, whether they be worksheet files, word processing files or graphics. Similarly, it is convenient to learn only one set of error messages and the proper responses to each. Integrated software offers such a uniform approach.

A second compelling advantage of integrated software over individual applications packages is that the integrated package allows the interchange of data between different applications in the package. Spreadsheet data can be incorporated into word processing documents. Graphics can easily be prepared from spreadsheet data. Database reports can be prepared from spreadsheet data and included in word processed reports.

Footer

PAGE 14.2

formats from that point on. A header or footer remains in effect until you specify another header or footer. You can turn off the specified header or footer by specifying a blank header or footer. Command Table 6.20 describes how to use headers and footers in each of our sample word processors.

Additional Type Styles and Fonts

Varied type styles and sizes can help you convey your ideas to a reader. Headings can be in a large, bold typeface. Italics can be used for emphasis. Footnotes can be in a smaller type size. Some word processors allow you a choice of type styles in printing out your document.

Dress up your document by employing different type fonts and styles for emphasis and a distinctive look.

In most cases, your choice of type style is limited by those that your printer will support. A daisy-wheel printer, for example, is limited by the print wheel that is installed for a particular print run. Some dot-matrix printers have a number of available type styles that can be used within a single print run. If you are willing to settle for very slow print speeds, a dot-matrix printer can be used to draw letters from dots. This graphics approach allows an almost unlimited selection of type styles. A number of commercial packages allow you to print documents in a large selection of type styles and sizes. (Chapter 3 discusses printer capabilities in more detail.)

Note that even when a word processor allows you to use various type styles, you may not be able to see on the screen what will be printed on paper. Some word processors display control codes on screen rather than showing the document as it will actually print. For example, WordStar displays the superscript 1 as

^V1^V

Displaying type styles and sizes exactly as they will appear in print depends on the capabilities of your video display adapter and your word processor. A word processor that displays exactly what will be printed is called a **WYSIWYG** ("What you see is what you get") **word processor**.

In addition to varying type styles, many documents require special symbols, such as mathematical or scientific terms. These can pose a considerable problem: The ability to display special symbols depends both on the hardware of the video display adapter and on the way the word processor is programmed to display characters. On the other hand, the ability to print special characters depends on the printer hardware and the way the word processor is programmed to print characters.

To get some idea of the problems involved in handling documents with additional symbols, look at Figure 6.22, which

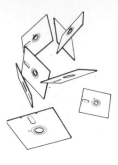

Command Table 6.20 The commands to specify headers and footers for WordStar, Word, and GoldWord.

Word Processor	Command	Comments
WordStar	.HE⟨heading text⟩	Dot command placed at beginning of line. Command takes effect starting with the beginning of the page following. (A page does not begin until it includes at least one character.) Number within heading text is replaced by the page number at print time.
	.FO⟨footer text⟩	Dot command placed at beginning of line. Command takes effect starting with the beginning of the page following. (A page does not begin until it includes at least one character.) Number within footer text is replaced by the page number at print time.
Word	ESC Format Running head (Fill in menu entries)	The menu entries are: *Position (top, bottom—*top for running head, bottom for running foot.) *Even pages (yes, no)* Include heading on even numbered pages? *Odd pages (yes, no)* Include heading on odd numbered pages? *First page (yes, no)* Include heading on first page possible after the running head position in document?
GoldWord	ALT-FO ⟨ENTER⟩	Set footing to default (page number centered).
	ALT-FFO ⟨text⟩ ⟨ENTER⟩	Set footing to ⟨text⟩.
	ALT-FFJ ⟨text⟩ ⟨ENTER⟩	Use justified footing of ⟨text⟩ aligned on one margin of page. Choice of right or left side in response to prompt.
	ALT-FHE ⟨text⟩⟨ENTER⟩	Set heading to ⟨text⟩.
	ALT-FHJ ⟨text⟩ ⟨ENTER⟩	Use justified heading of ⟨text⟩ aligned on one margin of page. (Choice of right or left side in response to prompt.)

Display and print up to 960 distinct characters:

a b c α β γ ▒ ▓ █ ü é â ≐ ⊇ ⌿ ↓ ↑ ⇥ ↤ ∂ ∀ ⊗

Display and print any number of modes with all characters:

boldface   doublestrike
italics   `inverse`   <u>underscore</u>
inline ^{super}script   inline $_{sub}$script
half-roll ^{super}script   half-roll $_{sub}$script

With a single keystroke, access common mathematical constructs:

fraction: $\dfrac{x+1}{7}$ *square root*: $\sqrt{x^2-1}$

matrix: $\begin{bmatrix} a_{11} & a_{12} \\ a_{21} & a_{22} \end{bmatrix}$ *double levels*: $\lim_{\varepsilon \to 0}$ *triple levels*: $\displaystyle\int_{x=0}^{\infty}$

A n d   m u c h   m u c h   m o r e !   Some examples:

$\alpha x^2 + \beta x + \gamma = 0$ implies $\boxed{x = \dfrac{-\beta \pm \sqrt{\beta^2 - 4\alpha\gamma}}{2\alpha}}$

$$\sum_{n=0}^{\infty} \frac{1}{n!} = e \qquad\qquad \oint \frac{1}{z}\, dz = 2\pi i$$

$$\int_{x=0}^{\rho} \frac{-1}{\sqrt{1-x^2}}\, dx = \cos^{-1}(x) \Big|_{x=0}^{x=\rho}$$

$$\begin{vmatrix} 1 & 2 & 3 \\ 8 & 9 & 4 \\ 7 & 6 & 5 \end{vmatrix} = 1 * \begin{vmatrix} 9 & 4 \\ 6 & 5 \end{vmatrix} - 2 * \begin{vmatrix} 8 & 4 \\ 7 & 5 \end{vmatrix} + 3 * \begin{vmatrix} 8 & 9 \\ 7 & 6 \end{vmatrix} = -48$$

$$\|w\|^2 = \int_{D} \left[\left(\frac{\partial w}{\partial x_1}\right)^2 + \ldots + \left(\frac{\partial w}{\partial x_n}\right)^2 + Pw^2 \right] dx$$

Figure 6.22   A page of scientific text produced with the word processor TECH/WORD.

shows a page of text generated from the scientific word processor TECH/WORD. Note the large number of symbols, their unusual positioning, and varying sizes. This word processor was designed to meet the needs of mathematicians and other scientists who must deal with technical symbols and equations within their text.

Section 6.4:   Test Your Understanding

1. Explain how a spelling checker operates.
2. Give examples of the type of errors that a spelling checker can catch.
3. Give examples of the type of errors that a spelling checker can't catch.
4. Explain how the outline mode functions.
5. What functions are peformed by an index program?
6. Explain the difficulties involved in placing footnotes on the same page as the footnote reference.
7. What is a header? A footer?
8. What is a WYSIWYG word processor?

6.5 Merging Variable Information

Until now you have worked only with documents that were completed prior to printing. In many applications, however, you will need to add **variable information** to a document. This is information that is added to the document at the time it is printed, and that usually changes from document to document. For example, in preparing form letters, names and addresses from a data file can be added to the letters as variable information.

We have all seen form letters prepared using variable information. Here is an example:

Mr. Anthony Jones
2111 Main St. Apt. 201
College Park, MD 20742
Dear Mr. Jones:

   As you are aware, during the week of April 15 you must preregister for the Fall semester. Please start thinking of the courses you would like to take and make an appointment to see your adviser during that week. Plan to make your appointment well in advance since most advisers are quite busy during this period. Best wishes for the rest of the semester.

John Armbruster
Undergraduate Dean

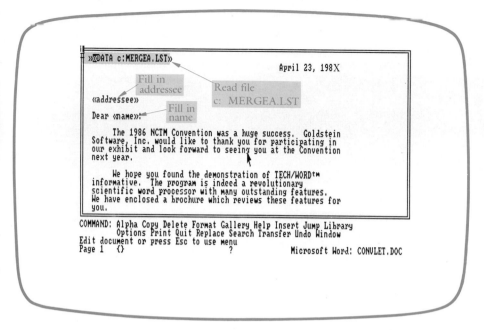

Figure 6.23   A letter to be printed with the mailmerge feature of WordStar.

A form letter of this type incorporates variable information, in this case the name and address of the addressee. The sender prepares the text of the letter at print time and inserts the variable information from a data file containing a mailing list.

The ability to merge variable information into a document is called **mailmerge**. This feature, found in a number of word processors, allows preparation of form letters. Word has a built-in mailmerge feature and WordStar has mailmerge as an option.

Your word processor can prepare a mailmerge document in much the same way that it can prepare any other document. However, special symbols will be used to indicate any variable information that must be inserted into the document. Figure 6.23 shows a sample form letter prepared with WordStar's optional mailmerge feature. Note that the address portion of the letter has several lines that look different from the rest of the letter. These lines are the ones to be filled in with variable information at print time. The special symbols that begin and end each line indicate to the print program the beginning and end of the variable information. For example, the print program reads the first variable information line and determines that it must fill in a piece of variable information called *NAME*. The second line requires a piece of variable information called *ADDRESS*, and so forth.

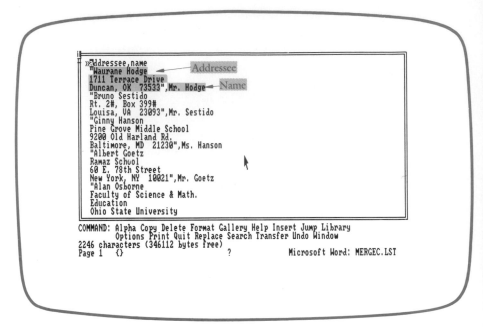

Figure 6.24   A data file for use with the mailmerge feature of WordStar.

Where does the variable information come from? There are two possibilities:

1. *Interactive entry of variable information.* The print program pauses and prompts you to enter the variable information.
2. *Reading variable information from a data file.* The variable information is prepared in advance and entered into a data file on your word processor. During the print process, the print program reads the variable information directly from the data file.

You must prepare a data file to store variable information in a format that the print program can read. The format differs for each word-processing program. Figure 6.24 shows you the format of a data file to be used with the mailmerge feature of Word.

Each line of the data file provides the information for a single address. The items in each line are separated by commas. Each data item can be used separately within the document. For example, the name can be used by itself in the above salutation of a letter.

When using a data file, you can have the word-processing program prepare any number of form letters in sequence without your intervention. The print program reads the items from the data file one by one and uses them to prepare the corresponding form letter. Then the program reads the next set of data items. The process of preparing a sequence of form letters is described by the diagram in Figure 6.25.

Some mailmerge facilities are sophisticated enough to do **conditional merging**. That is, the print program can be instructed to include certain data in some letters and not in others. For example, you can send letters to people beginning with the zip code 20002 and have the merge skip zip code 20715.

It takes time and effort to prepare a data file. Indeed, the data must be assembled, keyboarded, and checked for accuracy. However, once the file is prepared, it may be used an unlimited number of times. For example, you may use it to prepare a set of mailing labels, a customer list, and a variety of form letters.

Section 6.5: Test Your Understanding

1. What is variable information?
2. Give two examples in which it is convenient to insert variable information into a document.
3. What are the two methods for entering variable information into a document? Explain how the methods function.
4. What are the relative advantages and disadvantages of the two methods for entering variable information into a document?
5. How is a data file created?
6. What is conditional merging of variable information?

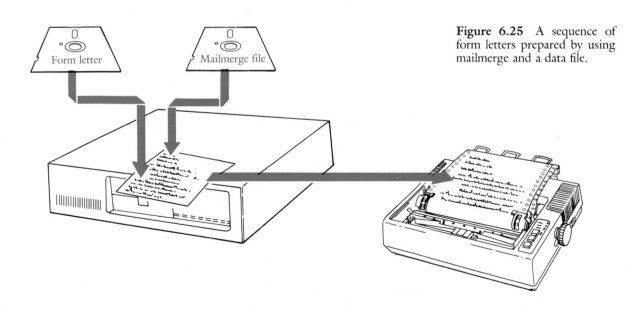

Figure 6.25 A sequence of form letters prepared by using mailmerge and a data file.

Form letter

Mailmerge file

6.6 Desktop Publishing

Most of the printed material we read, including books, magazines, and newspapers, is set in type by a typesetting machine and printed by a printing press. In many businesses, some of the written material produced by word processors needs to be reproduced in typeset form. From this need a link has emerged between the office word processor and the phototypesetter, the machine that produces the typeset copy from which printing plates are made.

It is relatively easy to modify a document in a file produced by a word processor so that the document can serve as input to a phototypesetter. Using the word processor itself, you need only add to the file certain control codes that specify type styles and sizes, along with spacing requirements. The resulting coded file is then fed into the typesetter, which then produces typeset copy. Starting from the word processor output, the process of typesetting can be reduced from weeks (for a book-length document) to a day or two.

A phototypesetter is really a glorified printer capable of printing a large selection of type styles and sizes of very high quality. In the last year or two, relatively cheap ($2,000 to $6,000) laser printers have become widely available. These printers rival phototypesetters in their high-quality output. The sample page in Figure 6.26 will give you an idea of the laser printer's capabilities.

The widespread availability of inexpensive laser printers has prompted the emergence of **desktop publishing**, a field in which laser printers are used to produce typeset-quality copy for reproduction. This new field promises to bring the previously arcane art of typesetting directly into the office.

Documents produced by a publisher differ from standard microcomputer output (that is, documents produced on a dot-matrix printer) in a number of respects. As part of the publishing process, a document is designed to have a certain look and format. This is achieved through the use of varied type styles, type sizes, typefaces (standard, italic, bold), page layout, paragraph design, and line spacing. In addition, published documents often are printed in several columns and intermingle text and graphics, as is seen in a newspaper or magazine.

In order to achieve the look of a published document, laser printers must have the capacity to print documents according to complex designs. Moreover, there must be software to communicate the design to the printer.

A recent development in this area has been **page description languages**. These can be used by word processors to communicate page makeup to a laser printer. Usually, the page-makeup language is stored in ROM within the laser printer and the type fonts are stored within either ROM or RAM. To print a document, a word processor communicates the document and the format to the printer. The task of document formatting is done within the printer. In effect, the laser printer becomes a specialized computer in its own right, dedicated to the task of reducing a printed page to a sequence of dots.

Apple was the first company to introduce a laser printer with a page description language. If you use this printer along with the Macintosh computer, you can produce newsletters for clubs, advertising pieces, or even annual reports for small businesses.

The first generation of inexpensive laser printers has produced dots at a density of 300×300 per inch. This density produces letters that are very near typeset quality. Perfect typeset quality, probably achievable in the near future, requires densities of about 500×500 to 1000×1000 dots per inch.

A L I G N   F O R M

Keys:

Ctrl - A

Command: Control

Function: To align the text within a paragraph to new margins.

Remarks: Alignment begins with the line on which the cursor lies. After each alignment operation, the cursor is left at the first character of the next paragraph. Thus repeated entry of [Ctrl - A] will align successive paragraphs.

Open modes remain open after an alignment. Thus, by setting an open mode at the beginning of a paragraph and entering [Ctrl - A], it is possible to advance to the end of the paragraph and alter all the text within the paragraph.

Figure 6.26 A page from a manual "typeset" by a laser printer.

To appreciate the magnitude of the task faced by a laser printer, note that an $8\frac{1}{2}$-by-11-inch page printed with a density of 300×300 dots per inch requires approximately one megabyte of RAM to store a single page. This represents not only a large amount of memory, but an incredible amount of processing to print each page. You can see why printers are equipped with their own microprocessors and data-processing capability.

Producing type fonts for a laser printer is a complex, time-consuming, and specialized task. A compositor using traditional typesetting technology offers a choice of thousands of type styles. At the present time, the choice of fonts for laser printers is considerably more limited and is confined to a list of a dozen or so of the most popularly used fonts. However, designers are now giving considerable attention to the task of generating fonts and specialized graphics programs that allow developers to design fonts.

A character to be printed in a high-density mode (say 500×500) requires a large amount of memory if it is described in terms of dots. In order to overcome these large memory requirements designers are experimenting with methods of describing characters in terms of the length, direction, position, and weight of the keystrokes necessary to generate a character, in much the same way the character would be written by hand. A character described in terms of keystrokes is then translated into dots by a program stored in the ROM of the printer.

With the increasing sophistication and user-friendliness of desktop publishing hardware and software, it seems likely that many routine publishing tasks will soon become microcomputer applications. Reports, newsletters, advertisements, and brochures will be prepared in typeset form within the office that generated the data. Laser-generated output will be used increasingly to directly prepare printing plates, bypassing the traditional typesetting process entirely.

Section 6.6: Test Your Understanding

1. What is a phototypesetter?
2. What is desktop publishing?
3. At what dot density does laser print output equal typeset quality?
4. Describe two methods for describing characters to a laser printer.

KEY TERMS

SEARCH command	BLOCK READ command	style analyzer
string	non-destructive read	outline mode
search string	text formatting	auto-indent mode
case-sensitive search	dot command	index
wild card search	embedded format command	footnote
wild card character	CENTERING command	footnote reference
embedded search string	justification	header
whole word search	ragged right	footer
FIND AND REPLACE	proportional spacing	flush left
command	monospacing	flush right
block	pagination	WYSIWYG word processor
block operation	page break	variable information
BLOCK MOVE command	PAGINATE command	mailmerge
BLOCK DELETE command	forced page break	conditional merging
scrap heap	attributes	desktop publishing
BLOCK COPY command	style sheet	page description language
BLOCK WRITE command	spelling checker	
glossary	grammar checker	

CHAPTER REVIEW QUESTIONS

1. Explain the functions of the BLOCK WRITE and BLOCK READ operations. Give an example to show how each operation may be applied.

2. What is a whole word search? Can you think of an example in which a whole word search is not desired?

3. An engineer preparing a 50-page report has consistently referred to a company as *GSX Corp.* instead of *GXS Incorporated.* Describe the procedure she can use to correct the error.

4. Describe three elements used in formatting a document.

5. Describe two approaches to pagination employed by word processors. Discuss the advantages and disadvantages of each.

6. List three text attributes used by word processors.

7. Describe the process of printing a series of form letters that utilize variable information contained in a data file.

8. What is desktop publishing?

9. Explain why inexpensive laser printers make desktop publishing possible.

10. What is a style analyzer? Discuss its advantages and disadvantages.

DISCUSSION QUESTIONS

1. You are given the task of handling customer relations for a farm equipment company. Part of your job is to communicate regularly with your firm's customers and inform them of new products, updates, and recalls. How can you use a word processor to generate the required correspondence?

2. Your local church has just purchased a microcomputer system. Describe three word-processing applications that could be used by church committees. What applications of desktop publishing would be possible?

3. Explain the strengths and weaknesses of a spelling checker used with a word-processing program.

APPLICATION PROJECTS

1. Learn to operate the text-formatting features of your word processor. Use the concepts discussed in this chapter and consult your word-processing manual for details.

2. If your word processor comes with a spelling checker, learn to operate it and check the spelling of a sample document. Use the concepts discussed in this chapter and consult your word-processing manual for details.

3. John Gapper is the Sales Manager for Schmitt & Sons, a manufacturer of industrial microscopes. Among the many different markets in which Schmitt sells its microscopes are three main customer groups: schools and colleges, hospitals and medical laboratories, and industrial research facilities.

    Schools buy microscopes primarily for teaching purposes and are concerned with price and durability. Hospitals buy microscopes to analyze medical samples and care more about ease and speed of use. Industrial labs buy microscopes for new product research and quality-control analysis and are primarily concerned with accuracy. There are additional customers who seek other features: a variety of lenses and other optional optical accessories, or simply the standard basic unit.

    John generates sales leads by sending potential customers a promotion letter and a response postcard. Returned postcards are turned over to the sales force for personal contact to discuss the products.

    John believes that by customizing the original promotion letter, Schmitt & Sons will be able to improve the postcard response rate. Of course, it would be too expensive to write individual promotion letters, but John would like to use a form letter with interchangeable paragraphs. Each potential customer would then receive a letter containing those paragraphs most appropriate for the market situation.

    a) Using your word processor, prepare a form letter that John could use. The opening and closing paragraphs might be the same for each customer group; you'll then need to prepare separate paragraphs for each product feature.

    b) Explain how John should select the paragraphs to use.

4. Sandra Lockheed, a CPA, needs to prepare income tax returns for several hundred individuals. She sends a letter with similar instructions to all her clients. The variable

information in each letter includes the address, client name, the amount of tax due with the return (or the refund receivable from the Internal Revenue Service), and the estimated tax payments due for the following year. An example of a form letter that Sandra can use when filing IRS Form 1040 is shown in Figure 6.27.

a) Using your word processor, create a file for Sandra's tax instruction letter and enter the letter.

April 1, 1987

Dear   :

Enclosed are two copies of your income tax return Form 1040 for 1986. The copy marked "Client's Copy" is for your records. The other copy should be signed by you and mailed no later than April 15, 1987 to the Internal Revenue Service, Atlanta, Georgia, 31101. It should be accompanied by a check for $_____ made payable to the Internal Revenue Service.

The following estimated payments should be made for the year 1987. Each estimate voucher should be accompanied by a check made payable to the Internal Revenue Service. Your social security number should be written on each check. The vouchers should be mailed to the Internal Revenue Service, Atlanta, Georgia, 31101.

Estimate Number	Due Date	Amount
1	4/15/87	$
2	6/15/87	
3	9/15/87	
4	1/15/87	_____
	Total estimate $	

Please review your return carefully before you mail it. Call us if you have any questions.

Very truly yours,

Golden & Golden, CPAs

Figure 6.27   A form letter to accompany IRS Form 1040.

b) Modify the letter to reflect the following information:

Client: Ms. Bernice Lee
Address: 101 Green Street, Auburn, Alabama 36830
Tax due with the return: $3,515
Estimated tax payments: $1,250 each ($5,000 total)

Turn in this part
A2

c) Now assume that Ms. Lee is due to receive an income tax refund of $1,216 and that no estimated tax payments should be made for 1986. Modify the letter to reflect these circumstances.

5. You are applying for a bank loan to purchase a new car. Using your word processor, compose a letter to several banks based on the following information:

a) Request a loan for the car of your choice, and indicate the price, years for repayment you desire, and amount of down payment you will make. Also request the interest rate that the bank will charge and the terms of the loan.

b) Include a statement of net worth. Net worth is the value of everything you own (assets) less your liabilities (what you owe). Your assets include

Cash	$ 800.37
Securities	1500.50
Personal property	1250.85
Car	500.00
Total assets	$4051.72
Your liabilities in-clude	
Credit card balance	300.00
Student loan	2000.00
Bank loan	1000.00
Total liabilities	$3300.00
Net worth	$ 751.72

c) Indicate the names and addresses of two people who could serve as character references for you.

d) Send the letter to

Mr. Sam Spade, Vice President
Second National Bank
One Crest Falcon Plaza
San Francisco, CA 92804

and

Ms. Juliet Montague, Vice President
Commerce Bank and Trust
Ten Romeo Drive
Verona, OH 69472

and

Mr. Bruce Spinnaker, Vice President
Smooth Sailing Security Trust
55 Windjammer Way
Beachfront, MA 00400

If your word processor has a mailmerge feature, use it to produce the three letters. If not, use the block move commands to reproduce the letters and use the edit features to change the addressees.

Hint: Most word processors have a special tab character that can be used for entering numbers in a table. For example, in WordStar, setting a decimal tab in column 45 is accomplished by pressing ⟨CTRL-O-I⟩, then ⟨45⟩. All decimal points will then be aligned in column 45.

7 Spreadsheets

Micros Pour It on at Ocean Spray

Through a combination of innovative product and packaging designs and perceptive marketing strategies since the 1930s, Ocean Spray Cranberries, Inc., has made cranberry blended drinks and sauces popular throughout the year, not just at Thanksgiving and Christmas. The company's strength in the market has paid off in other ways as well. In 1985, the Plymouth, Massachusetts, cooperative won membership in the Fortune 500.

Today, microcomputers play a big role in Ocean Spray's plans for future growth. In finance and marketing at headquarters, and at plants and warehouses across the country, microcomputers are used for numerous and diverse applications.

To help plant managers determine how their bottling and canning equipment should best be used, Gail Tuominen, an industrial engineer for Ocean Spray, turns to a Lotus 1-2-3 spreadsheet model of Ocean Spray's design. Her model contains the production rates for each machine in a particular line of equipment. One line may have as many as 25 operations, and each one affects how many cases of juice or sauce the line can produce.

Using the model, Tuominen can isolate the slowest pieces of equipment that may cause production delays. Then she can calculate how many cases of bottles an hour that line could produce if the slowest piece of equipment were replaced with a faster one.

Quickly and easily, she can plug any number of variables into her spreadsheet and calculate how fast each production line could work with any number of equipment alterations. Creating these "what if" scenarios is critical to setting production goals, which in turn are closely tied to sales and marketing goals. "This information can be used in so many areas," Tuominen points out. For example, the accounting department can take the data from Tuominen's spreadsheet and use it to calculate the return on investment of buying new equipment for each production line.

Before she got her micro, Tuominen sat endlessly with her calculator and "lots of pieces of paper" to get the same answers, taking at least an hour to do one set. On her microcomputer, it takes three minutes.

THE PRECEDING TWO CHAPTERS introduced word processing, our first broad category of application software. In this chapter and the next, you will learn the general principles of spreadsheets, our second category of application software.

Since the introduction of VisiCalc in 1979, electronic spreadsheets have become indispensable business tools for planning and analysis at all levels. Both businesses and individuals use spreadsheets to plan budgets, set up project schedules, analyze financial data, and track stock portfolios.

As with word processing, there are many spreadsheet programs on the market. This book not only will help you grasp the concepts common to all spreadsheets, but will give you some hands-on experience and provide specific commands for three software packages:

- *1-2-3 from Lotus Development Corporation.* Unquestionably the most popular spreadsheet on the market today, 1-2-3 is used by hundreds of thousands of businesses throughout the world. As of this writing, there are two versions of 1-2-3, numbered 1.1A and 2.0. Our discussion describes the more recent version, 2.0.
- *SuperCalc 3 from SORCIM, Inc.* Another very popular spreadsheet, this package traces its roots to the earliest days of spreadsheet programs. Like 1-2-3, it has several different versions. Our discussion will describe Release 2.
- *GoldSpread.* This is the spreadsheet available with this text. The commands for GoldSpread are identical to those of 1-2-3. Moreover, GoldSpread is file-compatible with 1-2-3. That is, GoldSpread can use the spreadsheets prepared with 1-2-3, and 1-2-3 can use the spreadsheets prepared with GoldSpread.

7.1 Spreadsheet Concepts

What Is a Spreadsheet Program?

Consider the budget of the Jones family shown in Figure 7.1. This budget is arranged in the form of a **worksheet**, which consists of arrays of numeric data and titles in a tabular format.

The first column of the budget consists of various **titles**. The first title, *EXPENSES*, is followed by specific categories of expenses in the Jones budget. The second title, *INCOME*, is followed by specific categories of income. In the first column, there are also three special categories: *TOTAL EXPENSES, TOTAL INCOME,*

Spreadsheet titles describe the data within a worksheet.

Budget

	Jan.	Feb.	March	April	May
Expenses					
RENT	$ 795.00	795.00	795.00	795.00	795.00
FOOD	400.00	400.00	400.00	400.00	400.00
CAR LOAN	297.80	297.80	297.80	297.80	297.80
CAR OPERATION	135.00	135.00	135.00	135.00	135.00
CLOTHES	125.00		350.00		
ENTERTAINMENT	200.00	200.00	200.00	200.00	200.00
TAXES	1272.49	1272.49	1272.49	1272.49	1272.49
MEDICAL	200.00	200.00	200.00	200.00	200.00
TUITION	3000.00				
PERSONAL	200.00	200.00	200.00	200.00	200.00
DECORATING			800.00	800.00	1000.00
Total Expenses	$ 6625.29	3500.29	4650.29	4300.29	4500.29
Income					
Jim's Salary	2450.00	2450.00	2450.00	2450.00	2450.00
Betty's Salary	1950.00	1950.00	1950.00	1950.00	1950.00
Bank Interest	300.00			300.00	
Total Income	4700.00	4400.00	4400.00	4700.00	4400.00
Net	(1925.29)	899.71	($250.29)	399.71	(100.29)

Figure 7.1 Worksheet for the Jones family budget.

and *NET*. Next to the first column are 12 columns representing the months of the year and one column for the year.

In addition to titles, the worksheet contains numeric information. Across from the title *RENT*, for instance, are the amounts the Jones family budgets each month for rent. The last column shows the total rent budget for the year—that is, the total of all the monthly rent figures.

If you read the worksheet down the columns, you can determine the budget for a particular month. For example, the column for January lists the budget figures for that month. The row labeled *TOTAL EXPENSES* contains the total budget expenses for a

June	July	Aug	Sept	Oct	Nov			
795^{00}	795^{00}	795^{00}	795^{00}	795^{00}	795^{00}			
400^{00}	400^{00}	400^{00}	400^{00}	400^{00}	400^{00}			
297^{80}	297^{80}	297^{80}	297^{80}	297^{80}	297^{80}			
135^{00}	135^{00}	135^{00}	135^{00}	135^{00}	135^{00}			
100^{00}			300^{00}		350^{00}			
1500^{00}	200^{00}	200^{00}	200^{00}	200^{00}	200^{00}			
1272^{49}	1272^{49}	1272^{49}	1272^{49}	1272^{49}	1272^{49}			
200^{00}	200^{00}	200^{00}	200^{00}	200^{00}	200^{00}			
		3000^{00}						
200^{00}	200^{00}	200^{00}	200^{00}	200^{00}	200^{00}			
4900^{29}	3500^{29}	6500^{29}	3800^{29}	3500^{29}	3850^{29}			
2450^{00}	2450^{00}	2450^{00}	2450^{00}	2450^{00}	2450^{00}			
1950^{00}	1950^{00}	1950^{00}	1950^{00}	1950^{00}	1950^{00}			
	300^{00}			300^{00}				
4400^{00}	4700^{00}	4400^{00}	4400^{00}	4700^{00}	4400^{00}			
(500^{29})	1199^{71}	(2100^{29})	599^{71}	1199^{71}	549^{21}			

particular month or the entire year, depending on the column. Similarly, the row labeled *TOTAL INCOME* contains the total income for a particular month or the entire year. Finally, the row labeled *NET* contains the difference between income and expenses, again, for a particular month or the entire year.

A **spreadsheet program** is a computer program that allows you to set up and manipulate worksheets like the Joneses'. Let's transfer the Jones worksheet to a spreadsheet program. (See Figure 7.2.) Note that only a portion of the worksheet is visible because of the limited size of the screen. However, you can scroll the worksheet both horizontally and vertically to view all entries.

```
A1: [W15]                                                              READY

            A            B          C          D          E          F
                       JAN        FEB        MAR        APR        MAY
1
2   EXPENSES
3   Rent             $795.00    $795.00    $795.00    $795.00    $795.00
4   Food             $400.00    $400.00    $400.00    $400.00    $400.00
5   Car Loan         $297.80    $297.80    $297.80    $297.80    $297.80
6   Car Operation    $135.00    $135.00    $135.00    $135.00    $135.00
7   Clothes          $125.00               $350.00
8   Entertainment    $200.00    $200.00    $200.00    $200.00    $200.00
9   Taxes          $1,272.49  $1,272.49  $1,272.49  $1,272.49  $1,272.49
10  Medical          $200.00    $200.00    $200.00    $200.00    $200.00
11  Tuition        $3,000.00
12  Personal         $200.00    $200.00    $200.00    $200.00    $200.00
13  Decorating                             $800.00    $800.00  $1,000.00
14  TOTAL EXPENSES $6,625.29  $3,500.29  $4,650.29  $4,300.29  $4,500.29
15  INCOME
16  Jim's Salary   $2,450.00  $2,450.00  $2,450.00  $2,450.00  $2,450.00
17  Betty's Salary $1,950.00  $1,950.00  $1,950.00  $1,950.00  $1,950.00
18  Bank Interest    $300.00                          $300.00
19  TOTAL INCOME   $4,700.00  $4,400.00  $4,400.00  $4,700.00  $4,400.00
20  NET          ($1,925.29)   $899.71  ($250.29)    $399.71  ($100.29)
03-Jun-86  03:47 PM
```

Figure 7.2 The Jones family budget as it would be set up using a spreadsheet program.

What Does a Spreadsheet Program Do?

A spreadsheet program allows you to enter data into an electronic worksheet, just as you do on paper. The advantage of using a microcomputer instead of paper is that you may enter relationships between data items as formulas which express the relationships, rather than perform the necessary calculations in your head. In the Jones worksheet, the spreadsheet program uses a formula to add up the expenses in each column to obtain the figures for *TOTAL EXPENSES*. Similarly, the data in the *YEAR* column is obtained by using a formula.

A spreadsheet program also allows you to change data entries easily. Using the specified formulas, the spreadsheet program automatically recalculates all data items. Suppose that the Joneses increase their May entertainment budget to allow for a vacation. This single change affects a number of other figures on the worksheet. The spreadsheet program automatically changes the worksheet and updates the display for the following data items:

- Total expenses for May
- Total expenses for the year
- Total entertainment expenses for the year

- Net for May
- Net for the year

Updating a worksheet could require recalculating hundreds or even thousands of data items—a job that could take several hours if done manually but only a few seconds if done on a spreadsheet.

Applications of Spreadsheet Programs

You can probably think of many situations in which you might want to arrange data in a worksheet format and compute changes in the data easily and quickly. The versatility provided by spreadsheet programs has made them an indispensable tool. Compiling a comprehensive list of such applications is virtually impossible, but a list of sample applications like the ones below will give you an idea of the range of possibilities.

- *Business planning.* You can plan business expenses and project future business income with a spreadsheet program. The projection spreadsheet program details all expected expenses and sources of income on a monthly basis. Summary figures are computed, which allows you to analyze the amounts spent in a number of categories, such as labor or taxes. The most important role of the spreadsheet is to allow the user to do "what-if" analyses. By varying the data entries in the worksheet, you can, for example, analyze the effect on expenses of hiring an extra worker or the effect on profits of increasing prices.

A spreadsheet program helps solve business planning problems and allows the user to perform "what-if" analyses.

- *Project planning.* In making a proposal for a contract, you can use a spreadsheet program to detail the resources you need to complete the job and to plan when the resources will be required. The spreadsheet program also computes the cost of the resources and the amount you can afford to bid for the job.

- *Investment analysis.* A spreadsheet can monitor your personal investment fund by keeping track of the individual investments, dividends, and additions or withdrawals to the fund, as well as gains and losses. A spreadsheet can also help you to analyze "what-if" questions: What if stock A were to double? What if stock B went down by 30 percent? What if the interest rate on certificates of deposit went up by 2 percent?

A Short History of the Electronic Spreadsheet

The electronic spreadsheet, a brainchild of the microcomputer revolution, was one of the first programs developed expressly for microcomputers. In fact, many people purchased early microcomputers just to use a spreadsheet program.

The first electronic spreadsheet was VisiCalc, designed in the 1970s by Harvard graduate student Daniel Bricklin for use on the Apple II computer. Bricklin shared his ideas with a finance professor who was dubious about the spreadsheet's chances for success because financial forecasting software was readily available on mainframes and minicomputers. The professor also felt that there was no market for microcomputer software in general and advised Bricklin not to waste his time.

For confirmation of his viewpoint, the professor pointed Bricklin in the direction of Daniel Fylstra, a graduate student who was an associate editor of *Byte* magazine and an expert on the market for microcomputer software. Contrary to expectations, Fylstra was enthusiastic about the project and teamed Bricklin with a friend, Bob Frankston, another pioneer in microcomputing, to carry out VisiCalc programming for the Apple II. By early 1979, the spreadsheet was ready for marketing by Fylstra. The program caught on like wildfire and by 1981, sales had risen from 500 to 12,000 copies per month. At a retail price of $150 per copy, VisiCalc established Bricklin's business, Software Arts, and Fylstra's Personal Computing (later VisiCorp) as two early business successes in the microcomputer revolution.

After their rapid success, Bricklin and Fylstra had a falling out and their companies ended up fighting in court. While they fought, the market passed them by and VisiCalc retreated into history. However, business computer users were quick to see the importance of spreadsheets and used them in ever-increasing numbers. VisiCalc's success spawned a number of imitators who introduced many new spreadsheet features. Moreover, as users wrestled with increasingly complex problems, they demanded more powerful spreadsheet programs. In 1982, software designers responded to user demands with the production of **integrated software**, which combined several functions within a single program. Today, the typical integrated program can offer the user a spreadsheet, database management, and graphics—and even word processing and telecommunications.

The advantage of integrated software is that information can be readily interchanged between portions of the program. It is thus simple to create graphs that use data from a spreadsheet, to produce management summaries of spreadsheet data, and so forth. Without question, the most popular integrated software to date is Lotus 1-2-3. This program has set the standard in spreadsheets and has sold more than 500,000 copies to date, making it one of the all time best-sellers in computer software.

Section 7.1: Test Your Understanding

1. What is a spreadsheet program?
2. Give an example of a spreadsheet formula.
3. Explain the operation of a spreadsheet program.
4. List possible applications of spreadsheet programs that an accountant, a financial analyst, and a payroll manager would find useful.
5. What was the name of the first spreadsheet package?
6. Explain how spreadsheet programs helped foster the micro-computer revolution.

7.2 Getting Started with a Spreadsheet Program

Now that you understand the concepts and applications of a spreadsheet program, let's discuss the specifics and learn how to use one.

Installation

As with any piece of software, you need to install the spreadsheet program before you can use it. This installation procedure, often referred to as **configuration** or **configuring the system**, varies with each spreadsheet program and is detailed in the documentation for the program. Usually, the installation procedure consists of the following steps:

1. Make backup copies of the original diskettes (if they are not copy-protected).
2. If your system has a hard disk, copy the spreadsheet program files onto the hard disk.
3. Specify the display adapter and the type of monitor attached. This step is usually necessary only if you have an integrated program that can display graphics as well as text.
4. Specify the printer. This step is usually necessary only if you have an integrated program that will be used to print graphics. For printing text, most printers are interchangeable.

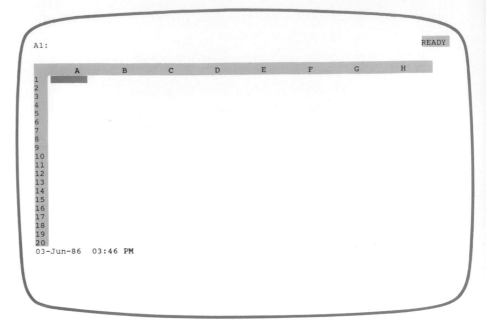

Figure 7.3 The initial worksheet screen for Lotus 1-2-3.

Starting a Worksheet

To create a worksheet with your spreadsheet program, follow these steps:

1. After you boot your system and obtain the A⟩ prompt, insert the program diskette in drive A:.

2. Give the command to start the program. To start Lotus 1-2-3, type the command
   ⟨LOTUS⟩⟨ENTER/RETURN⟩

   To start SuperCalc 3, type the command
   ⟨SC3⟩⟨ENTER/RETURN⟩

   To start GoldSpread, type the command
   ⟨GS⟩⟨ENTER/RETURN⟩

3. Most programs start by displaying copyright information followed by a blank worksheet, such as the one shown in Figure 7.3.

Cells and Addresses

Looking once again at Figure 7.3, let's explore the anatomy of a worksheet. The worksheet consists of a rectangular grid into which you can insert data. The grid is divided into **cells**, which are identified by row and column position. The row-column labelling of a cell is called its **address.** The information that the cell contains is called its **contents**. The conventions for numbering rows and columns vary, but the most common method is to label rows with integers beginning with 1 and columns with letters beginning with A. Since this is the labelling used by all of our sample spreadsheets, we will use it throughout our discussion. (Note, however, that some spreadsheets use numbers to label both rows and columns.) In Figure 7.4, for example, the cell at the tenth row, fourth column has an address of D10, and its contents is the number 155.

Spreadsheets usually allow a large number of rows and columns, the precise number depending on the particular spreadsheet and, usually, the version of that spreadsheet. (The number of allowable rows and columns tends to increase with each new version.)

In larger worksheets, the first 26 columns are labelled A through Z, the next 26 columns are labelled AA through AZ, the next 26, BA through BZ, and so forth. Here are some typical cell addresses:

AB11 (row 11, column 28)
AC15 (row 15, column 29)
BE110 (row 110, column 57)

Figure 7.4 Identifying a position on the worksheet.

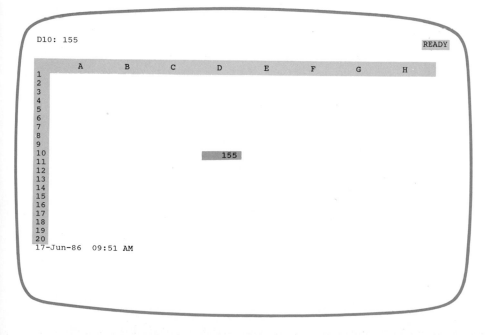

```
D9: 1272.49                                                          READY

              A            B          C          D          E          F
                          JAN        FEB        MAR        APR        MAY
 1
 2  EXPENSES
 3  Rent                $795.00    $795.00    $795.00    $795.00    $795.00
 4  Food                $400.00    $400.00    $400.00    $400.00    $400.00
 5  Car Loan            $297.80    $297.80    $297.80    $297.80    $297.80
 6  Car Operation       $135.00    $135.00    $135.00    $135.00    $135.00
 7  Clothes             $125.00               $350.00
 8  Entertainment       $200.00    $200.00    $200.00    $200.00    $200.00
 9  Taxes             $1,272.49  $1,272.49  $1,272.49  $1,272.49  $1,272.49
10  Medical             $200.00    $200.00    $200.00    $200.00    $200.00
11  Tuition           $3,000.00
12  Personal            $200.00    $200.00    $200.00    $200.00    $200.00
13  Decorating                               $800.00    $800.00  $1,000.00
14  TOTAL EXPENSES    $6,625.29  $3,500.29  $4,650.29  $4,300.29  $4,500.29
15  INCOME
16  Jim's Salary      $2,450.00  $2,450.00  $2,450.00  $2,450.00  $2,450.00
17  Betty's Salary    $1,950.00  $1,950.00  $1,950.00  $1,950.00  $1,950.00
18  Bank Interest       $300.00                         $300.00
19  TOTAL INCOME      $4,700.00  $4,400.00  $4,400.00  $4,700.00  $4,400.00
20  NET             ($1,925.29)   $899.71   ($250.29)   $399.71   ($100.29)
17-Jun-86  09:52 AM
```

Figure 7.5   The cursor indicates the position of the current cell.

Moving Around a Spreadsheet

At any given moment, one of the cells is designated as the **current cell**, the cell into which typed input will be placed. The position of the current cell may be indicated visually by a cursor as illustrated in Figure 7.5, or depending on your video adapter and spreadsheet, it may be indicated differently. (The most common method is to highlight the current cell, but some spreadsheets use brackets or boldface.) In any case, once you look at the worksheet, the current cell is easy to pick out: it's the cell that has a different visual treatment.

When you begin a worksheet, the current cell is A1, also called the **home position**. You may move the cursor around the screen and change the current cell by using the cursor-motion keys. For example, to change the current cell from A1 to B5, press the CURSOR-RIGHT key once to move the cursor to the B column and then press the CURSOR-DOWN key four times to move the cursor to row five.

The screen provides a "window" on a portion of the worksheet. You may change the portion of the worksheet visible in the window by using the cursor-motion keys to move the cursor off the screen, which causes the worksheet to scroll. (See Figure 7.6.) For example, if the cursor is at the right edge of the screen, moving the cursor to the right will cause the worksheet to scroll to the left by one column. Note that as the worksheet scrolls, the vertical and horizontal cell addresses just to the top and side of the worksheet change to reflect the portion of the worksheet that is currently visible.

It can be quite tedious to move the cursor long distances (say, from A1 to BB200). To speed up cursor movements, you may use the GOTO command, which in Lotus 1-2-3 and GoldSpread is implemented by using the function key F5. When you press this key, the program asks you which cell you want to go to. You then type in the cell address (in this example, BB200) and press ⟨ENTER/RETURN⟩. The cursor will then be positioned at the specified location.

← F5 GOTO

The **PGUP** (page up) and **PGDN** (page down) **keys** on the numeric keypad allow you to scroll the worksheet vertically a screen at a time. When these keys are used, the cursor remains in the same physical position on the screen, but the worksheet scrolls under it.

As the cursor moves, its current position is shown in the **status line**. This line also shows the contents of the current cell. The **data input line** shows the data currently being typed into the

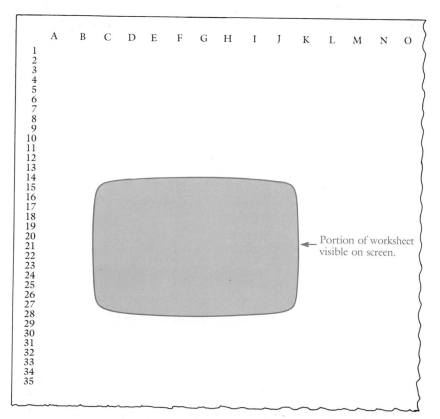

Portion of worksheet visible on screen.

Figure 7.6 The screen provides a window on a portion of a worksheet. Moving the cursor to the right will cause the worksheet to scroll to the left by one column.

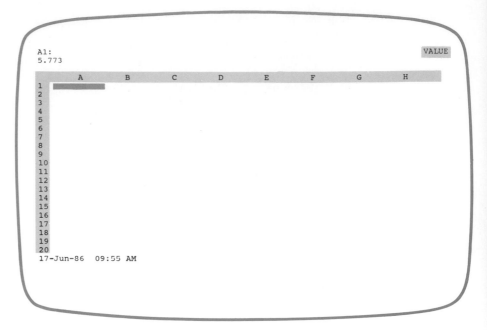

A1:
5.773

VALUE

	A	B	C	D	E	F	G	H
1								
2								
3								
4								
5								
6								
7								
8								
9								
10								
11								
12								
13								
14								
15								
16								
17								
18								
19								
20								

17-Jun-86   09:55 AM

Figure 7.7   The status and data input lines for Lotus 1-2-3. The status line shows the current cell and its contents. The data input line shows the data currently being typed into the worksheet.

worksheet. The data shown on this line is entered into the current cell, but only after you press ⟨ENTER/RETURN⟩ or move the cursor to a different cell. Figure 7.7 shows the status and data input lines for Lotus 1-2-3. Note, however, that the positions of these two lines may be different on your particular spreadsheet.

Contents of a Cell

Each cell holds a single data item. A spreadsheet program recognizes three types of data: label, numeric, and formula.

- *Label.* A **label** is a sequence of characters (letters, digits, or punctuation marks) used to add verbal descriptions to a worksheet. The Jones budget that was discussed earlier used labels for titles such as *EXPENSES* and *INCOME*. Most spreadsheets allow for some text formatting, such as centering text within a cell, which will be discussed in Chapter 9.

- *Numeric.* A **numeric** cell entry is a number, such as 5, 124582, or −5.3. Numeric data can be displayed in many different formats. For example, the number 5000 can be displayed as 5000, 5000.00, $5000, or 5,000. Later in this chapter we'll discuss how a spreadsheet allows you to control the format (scientific or currency format, number of decimal points and their alignment, insertion of commas, etc.) of numeric data.

- *Formula.* A **formula** determines a value from the contents of worksheet cells. For example, the formula +A1+A2 computes the sum of the values in cells A1 and A2. If A1 contains the number 5, A2 the number 3, and A3 the formula +A1+A2, then A3 has the value 8. As another example, consider the formula 100*A1. Assuming that A1 still contains the number 5, this formula has the value 100*5 or 500. A formula can be stored in a cell, exactly like text or a numeric data item. If a cell contains a formula, the worksheet displays the current value of the formula. If the contents of any of the cells mentioned in the formula are changed, then the value of the formula is automatically recalculated and redisplayed. We'll discuss formulas extensively later in this chapter and in the next two chapters.

Input Mode versus Command Mode

A spreadsheet program operates in one of two modes—input mode or command mode. In **input mode**, the spreadsheet accepts cursor-motion instructions or cell data input. The spreadsheet displays cell data entries in the current cell position and recalculates formula values based on the new cell value. In **command mode**, the operator can give the spreadsheet commands to perform various manipulations, such as erasing a worksheet or saving it on disk, or recalling a worksheet that has been saved.

You cannot enter command mode if you are in the middle of a data input operation. That is, the data input line must be blank. To enter the command mode, press the **slash** (/) **key**. This key choice was made for the original VisiCalc program and has become almost universal. The spreadsheet displays a command menu consisting of a list of the available commands. A typical command menu is illustrated in Figure 7.8.

/ key

If you want to enter command mode, you cannot be in the process of entering data; your data input line must be blank.

Many of today's spreadsheets use a **nested menu structure** in which each command contains a number of subcommands. For example, look at the main command menu for Lotus 1-2-3 shown in Figure 7.8. Within that menu, the **WORKSHEET command** contains these subcommands: GLOBAL, INSERT, DELETE, COLUMN, ERASE, TITLES, WINDOW, STATUS, PAGE. Note that the command menu has a **command cursor** that highlights one of the commands. The subcommands for the highlighted command are shown on the line below the command menu. You may move the command cursor by using the cursor-right and cursor-left keys. The list of subcommands also changes to reflect

```
A1: [W15]                                                           MENU
Worksheet Range  Copy  Move  File  Print  Graph  Data  System  Quit
Global, Insert, Delete, Column, Erase, Titles, Window, Status, Page
          A            B          C          D          E          F
1                      JAN        FEB        MAR        APR        MAY
2     EXPENSES
3     Rent         $795.00    $795.00    $795.00    $795.00    $795.00
4     Food         $400.00    $400.00    $400.00    $400.00    $400.00
5     Car Loan     $297.80    $297.80    $297.80    $297.80    $297.80
6     Car Operation $135.00   $135.00    $135.00    $135.00    $135.00
7     Clothes      $125.00               $350.00
8     Entertainment $200.00   $200.00    $200.00    $200.00    $200.00
9     Taxes       $1,272.49  $1,272.49  $1,272.49  $1,272.49  $1,272.49
10    Medical      $200.00    $200.00    $200.00    $200.00    $200.00
11    Tuition    $3,000.00
12    Personal     $200.00    $200.00    $200.00    $200.00    $200.00
13    Decorating                         $800.00    $800.00  $1,000.00
14    TOTAL EXPENSES $6,625.29 $3,500.29 $4,650.29 $4,300.29 $4,500.29
15    INCOME
16    Jim's Salary $2,450.00  $2,450.00  $2,450.00  $2,450.00  $2,450.00
17    Betty's Salary $1,950.00 $1,950.00 $1,950.00 $1,950.00 $1,950.00
18    Bank Interest $300.00                          $300.00
19    TOTAL INCOME $4,700.00  $4,400.00  $4,400.00  $4,700.00  $4,400.00
20    NET        ($1,925.29)   $899.71   ($250.29)   $399.71   ($100.29)
03-Jun-86   03:54 PM
```

Figure 7.8   A Lotus 1-2-3 command menu.

Figure 7.9   Moving the command cursor.

```
A1: [W15]                                                           MENU
Worksheet Range  Copy  Move  File  Print  Graph  Data  System  Quit
Format, Label, Erase, Name, Justify, Protect, Unprotect, Input, Value, Transpose
          A            B          C          D          E          F
1                      JAN        FEB        MAR        APR        MAY
2     EXPENSES
3     Rent         $795.00    $795.00    $795.00    $795.00    $795.00
4     Food         $400.00    $400.00    $400.00    $400.00    $400.00
5     Car Loan     $297.80    $297.80    $297.80    $297.80    $297.80
6     Car Operation $135.00   $135.00    $135.00    $135.00    $135.00
7     Clothes      $125.00               $350.00
8     Entertainment $200.00   $200.00    $200.00    $200.00    $200.00
9     Taxes       $1,272.49  $1,272.49  $1,272.49  $1,272.49  $1,272.49
10    Medical      $200.00    $200.00    $200.00    $200.00    $200.00
11    Tuition    $3,000.00
12    Personal     $200.00    $200.00    $200.00    $200.00    $200.00
13    Decorating                         $800.00    $800.00  $1,000.00
14    TOTAL EXPENSES $6,625.29 $3,500.29 $4,650.29 $4,300.29 $4,500.29
15    INCOME
16    Jim's Salary $2,450.00  $2,450.00  $2,450.00  $2,450.00  $2,450.00
17    Betty's Salary $1,950.00 $1,950.00 $1,950.00 $1,950.00 $1,950.00
18    Bank Interest $300.00                          $300.00
19    TOTAL INCOME $4,700.00  $4,400.00  $4,400.00  $4,700.00  $4,400.00
20    NET        ($1,925.29)   $899.71   ($250.29)   $399.71   ($100.29)
03-Jun-86   03:55 PM
```

the currently chosen command. Figure 7.9 shows how the command cursor is moved.

To execute a command, either type the first letter of the command name or select the command with the command cursor and press ⟨ENTER/RETURN⟩. For example, if you are using Lotus 1-2-3, you may execute the command WORKSHEET by typing the letter ⟨W⟩.

In response to the command, the list of subcommands becomes the new command menu, like the one shown in Figure 7.10. You may select a subcommand by moving the command cursor and pressing ⟨ENTER/RETURN⟩, or by pressing the first letter of the command name. For some commands, you will need to go through four, five, or even six sets of menus, each one called up by a subcommand in a previous menu. This method of nested menus is a neat way of implementing a complicated set of commands in an application program. The original VisiCalc program used only a single level of menus. However, as spreadsheets incorporated more functions, the multiple-level command scheme was introduced.

Pull-down menus are an alternative to the nested menu command structure. In this command scheme, you point to a command, either by typing the command letter or by clicking a button on a mouse. In response, the program displays a pull-down menu of subcommands. You can then select one of the subcom-

Figure 7.10   Selecting from a list of subcommands.

```
A1: [W15]                                                              MENU
Global  Insert  Delete  Column  Erase  Titles  Window  Status  Page
Set worksheet settings
           A           B           C           D           E           F
                       JAN         FEB         MAR         APR         MAY
 1  ▬▬▬▬▬▬▬▬▬▬▬▬
 2  EXPENSES
 3  Rent              $795.00     $795.00     $795.00     $795.00     $795.00
 4  Food              $400.00     $400.00     $400.00     $400.00     $400.00
 5  Car Loan          $297.80     $297.80     $297.80     $297.80     $297.80
 6  Car Operation     $135.00     $135.00     $135.00     $135.00     $135.00
 7  Clothes           $125.00                 $350.00
 8  Entertainment     $200.00     $200.00     $200.00     $200.00     $200.00
 9  Taxes           $1,272.49   $1,272.49   $1,272.49   $1,272.49   $1,272.49
10  Medical           $200.00     $200.00     $200.00     $200.00     $200.00
11  Tuition         $3,000.00
12  Personal          $200.00     $200.00     $200.00     $200.00     $200.00
13  Decorating                                $800.00     $800.00   $1,000.00
14  TOTAL EXPENSES  $6,625.29   $3,500.29   $4,650.29   $4,300.29   $4,500.29
15  INCOME
16  Jim's Salary    $2,450.00   $2,450.00   $2,450.00   $2,450.00   $2,450.00
17  Betty's Salary  $1,950.00   $1,950.00   $1,950.00   $1,950.00   $1,950.00
18  Bank Interest     $300.00                             $300.00
19  TOTAL INCOME    $4,700.00   $4,400.00   $4,400.00   $4,700.00   $4,400.00
20  NET            ($1,925.29)    $899.71    ($250.29)    $399.71    ($100.29)
03-Jun-86   03:55 PM
```

mands from the menu, either by typing the command letter or by pointing to the command with a mouse. The main difference between the nested command structure and the pull-down menu structure is that the pull-down menus temporarily overwrite part of the worksheet. After the menu is used, the overwritten portion of the worksheet is restored to the screen. None of our sample spreadsheets use the pull-down menu structure.

Using the ESCAPE Key in Command Mode. The ESCAPE key (usually labelled ESC) serves as a general cancellation command. By pressing ⟨ESCAPE⟩ in command mode, you cancel the operation just performed and return to the previous step. For instance, if you enter command mode by pressing ⟨/⟩, you may cancel the operation by pressing ⟨ESCAPE⟩ and return to data input mode. If you enter data in response to a command prompt, then you can use the ESCAPE key to clear the data entry. If you are viewing a subcommand menu, you may move to the preceding menu by pressing ⟨ESCAPE⟩. For example, if you are viewing the Lotus 1-2-3 command menu containing the GLOBAL command, you can return to the command menu containing the WORKSHEET command by pressing ⟨ESCAPE⟩.

Saving and Recalling Worksheets

As with a word-processing program, the two most fundamental spreadsheet commands are the **SAVE command** and the **RECALL command**. You may save the contents of a worksheet in a diskette or hard disk file. The file-naming rules are the same as those already described in our discussion of MS-DOS. Namely, a file name can consist of a main name having up to eight characters followed by an optional extension consisting of a period and up to three characters. Unless you assign an extension of your own, most spreadsheet programs assign a default extension name to a worksheet file. This extension varies, but WKS or WK1 are commonly used. For example, if you specify a file name PAYROLL, Lotus 1-2-3 (version 2.0) assigns the file the name PAYROLL.WK1.

Command Table 7.1 summarizes the commands for saving a worksheet in our sample programs. Command Table 7.2 summarizes the commands for recalling the worksheet.

Exiting from a Worksheet

To exit from a worksheet and return to the A⟩ prompt, you must execute an **exit sequence**. With most spreadsheet programs, you begin this sequence by issuing the **QUIT command**. Most spreadsheets will then ask you whether you are sure. If you answer by

If you want to exit your worksheet, be sure you have saved the data before executing the QUIT command.

Command Table 7.1 The Lotus 1-2-3, GoldSpread, and SuperCalc 3. commands to save a worksheet in a file.

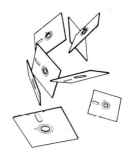

Program	Command	Comments
Lotus 1-2-3 and GoldSpread	/ File Save {Choose file name from menu or type in file name.} ⟨ENTER⟩	Select file name from menu by using SPACEBAR. Edit file name by using BACK-SPACE key. Erase file name be pressing ESC. If file of specified file name exists, program asks if you wish to replace existing file. If you answer yes, file replaces existing one. In 1-2-3, original file is overwritten. In GoldSpread, original file is retained under original file name but with extension .BAK.
SuperCalc 3	/ Save ⟨file name⟩	In an existing file, you may use one of the following options: *Change name:* Change name of file. *Backup:* Save old version of file. *Overwrite:* Destroy current version of file.

pressing ⟨Y⟩ (for yes), some spreadsheets will ask you if you want to save the current worksheet before quitting. However, note that some spreadsheets will not ask this question; you'll need to remember to save your worksheet before quitting, or you might accidentally quit the program and lose several hours of work in the process. Be careful in exiting the program. Command Table 7.3 shows the exit sequences for each of our sample spreadsheets.

Section 7.2: Test Your Understanding

1. How do you install a worksheet program?
2. What is a worksheet cell?
3. Where is cell B16 located on a worksheet?
4. Where is cell AC130 located on a worksheet?
5. What is the designation of the cell in the fourth column and eighty-ninth row?

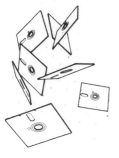

Command Table 7.2 The Lotus 1-2-3, GoldSpread, and SuperCalc 3 commands to recall a worksheet from a file.

Program	Command	Comments
Lotus 1-2-3 and GoldSpread	/ File Retrieve {select file name from menu or type in file name.} ⟨ENTER⟩	Select file name from menu by using the SPACEBAR. Edit file name by using the backspace key. Erase file name by pressing ESC.
SuperCalc 3	/ Load ⟨file name⟩	Load worksheet from file. After entering file name, select one of the options: (a) All (b) Part (c) Consolidate. All loads entire file. Part loads only a rectangular section of file, which the program prompts you to specify. Consolidate inserts all or part of file into current spreadsheet at current cursor location.
	/ Load ⟨ENTER⟩	Obtain directory information.

6. How can you determine the current cell by looking at a worksheet?
7. Describe the contents of the status line of a worksheet.
8. Identify the following data items by type:
   a) PROFIT
   b) 1.075

Command Table 7.3 The exit sequences for Lotus 1-2-3, GoldSpread, and SuperCalc 3.

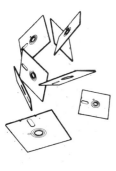

Program	Command	Comments
Lotus 1-2-3 and GoldSpread	/ Quit ⟨ENTER⟩ Verify exit of program by answering Yes to prompt.	This sequence will exit from GoldSpread to DOS prompt and from 1-2-3 to Lotus Access System. To exit from latter to DOS prompt, choose menu entry EXIT.
SuperCalc 3	Same as 1-2-3	

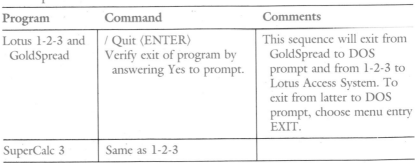

   c) 15%
   d) $45.38
   e) $+A1 - 3*A3$
   f) 1,302,408

9. Explain the function of input mode.
10. Explain the function of command mode.
11. What is the command cursor?
12. Explain how a nested menu command structure works.
13. Explain the function of the ESCAPE key in a spreadsheet program.

Hands-on Exercises

1. Install your spreadsheet program.
2. Start your spreadsheet program.
3. Move the cursor to the following cells:
   a) A2
   b) B3
   c) H17
   d) HOME
   e) BB80
4. Scroll to the bottom of your worksheet.
5. Move the cursor to the column farthest right on your worksheet.
6. Enter command mode.
7. Save the current worksheet (it has no entries) under the file name TEST0.
8. Exit from the spreadsheet program.

7.3 Entering and Editing Data

Section 7.2 gave you some general information about how spreadsheet programs work. Now let's get specific and look more closely at worksheet construction. As a concrete example, this section will help you construct a worksheet corresponding to the Jones budget, introduced in Section 7.1.

Entering Data in a Cell

Here is the procedure for placing data into a cell:

1. Position the cursor to make the desired cell the current cell.
2. Type the desired data (text, numeric or formula). As you type, the data is displayed on the data input line, which is either above or below the worksheet display. The data input line acts like a "scratch pad" on which you can compose an entry before actually inserting it on the worksheet. You may correct or erase the contents of the data entry line, as discussed below.
3. When the data input lines reads correctly, press ⟨ENTER/ RETURN⟩.

Note that you may replace the contents of a cell simply by entering new data. In doing so, the old contents of the cell are permanently lost.

For example, to enter the number 1.58 in cell A1, position the cursor at A1 and type ⟨1.58⟩.

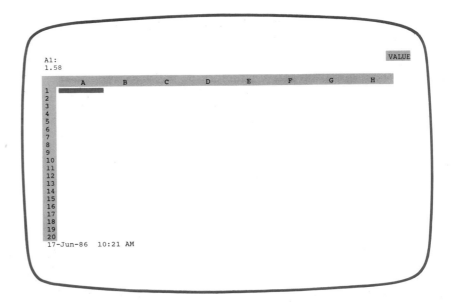

Then press ⟨ENTER/RETURN⟩.

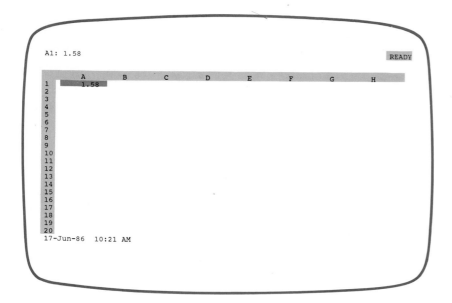

To enter the text *JAN* in the cell to the right (cell B1), press the CURSOR-RIGHT key and type ⟨JAN⟩.

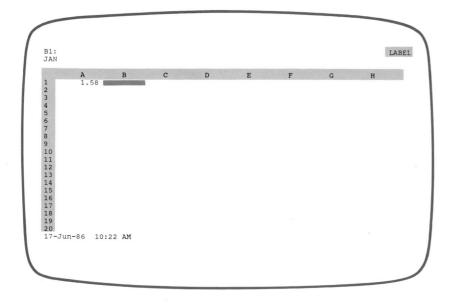

Then press ⟨ENTER/RETURN⟩.

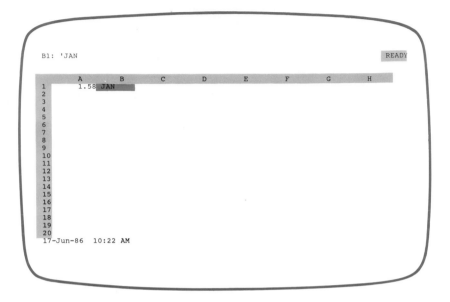

To enter the formula 2*A1 (2 times the value of the number in cell A1, which is 1.58 in our example) in cell A3, position the cursor on the cell C1 and type ⟨2*A1⟩.

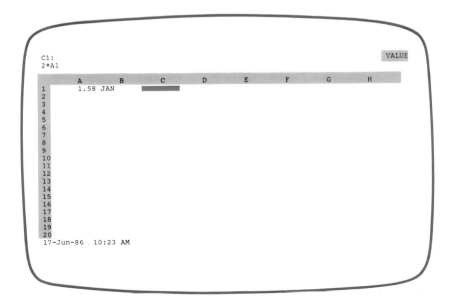

Then press ⟨ENTER/RETURN⟩.

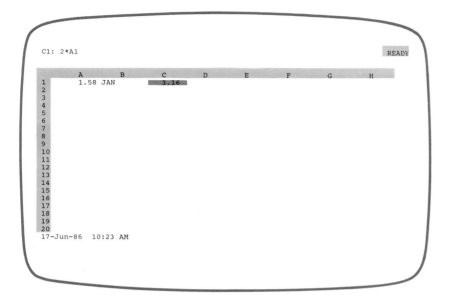

In this case, the formula is displayed on the data input line, but cell A3 displays the value 3.16 (which is 2 times the value in A1).

If the data item is a formula, the spreadsheet evaluates it by substituting current values for any cell references. In this case, the spreadsheet saves both the formula and the current value, and displays that value on the worksheet. The status line displays the contents of the current cell. If the cell contains a formula, the status line displays the formula rather than the current value. The figure the cell displays is the result of the formula.

After determining the value of the current cell, the spreadsheet formats the value according to the format you specified and displays it in the current cell. (We'll talk about the possible formats later.) The spreadsheet then goes through a **recalculation**, a process in which the spreadsheet uses the new value of the current cell to recalculate the values of all formulas. For instance, suppose that you change the value in cell A1 above to 4. The discussion below will explain how to do this.

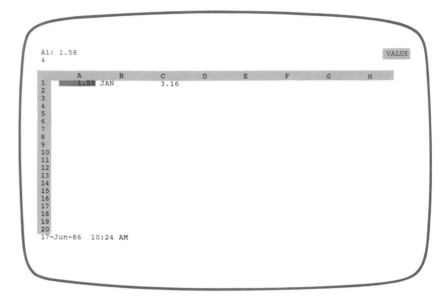

The spreadsheet automatically recalculates the value in cell A3 to be 8, that is, 2 times A1.

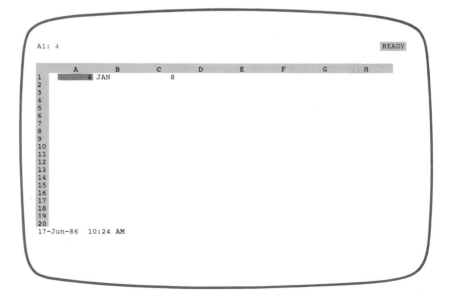

Through constant recalculation, the various cells maintain the relationships specified in the formulas.

You can, if you wish, give a command to the spreadsheet to omit this recalculation until further notice. This can save a great deal of time if you want to make a large number of changes in the spreadsheet but don't want to wait while the spreadsheet does the recalculation after each data entry. In such a circumstance, you could turn off the recalculation option until you were done entering the changes. All formula recalculations would thus be done only once when you turn on recalculation again.

Editing Worksheet Entries

As with a word processor, you can use editing functions to perfect your worksheet entries.

Correcting Input. You may make corrections while typing data on the data input line. The simplest method (and the only one we will discuss) is to use the BACKSPACE key. As with a word processor, the BACKSPACE key erases any characters it backs over.

For example, suppose you position the cursor on cell A4 and type *FRB*. To change this entry to *FEB*, press the BACKSPACE key twice (this erases the *B* and the *R*) and type *E* followed by *B*, as shown in Figure 7.11. You may now insert the corrected entry into the worksheet by pressing ⟨ENTER/RETURN⟩ or by moving the cursor.

Replacing Entries. You may replace the contents of a cell by positioning the cursor on the cell and typing a new entry. The spreadsheet automatically recalculates all formulas to reflect this changed entry. For instance, in the above example, you may replace the entry in cell A1 with the number 8.1. Just position the cursor on cell A1 and type

⟨8.1⟩⟨ENTER/RETURN⟩

As shown in Figure 7.12, on page 256, the value in cell A3 is automatically recalculated to be 16.2 (which is 2 times the value in cell A1).

Cancelling an Incomplete Entry. You may cancel an incomplete entry by pressing the ESCAPE key, an action that erases the data input line. The program then ignores any data on this line and no recalculation takes place. For instance, position the cursor on cell A1 and type ⟨JAN⟩. You may cancel the input by pressing ⟨ESCAPE⟩. The data entry line is erased and the worksheet is unchanged. Note, however, that you may cancel only input that has not yet been inserted into the worksheet.

Press ⟨ESCAPE⟩ to cancel entries on the data input line. Remember, you can cancel only input not yet inserted into the worksheet.

Erasing Worksheet Entries. You may erase data that has been inserted into the worksheet by using the **RANGE ERASE command**,

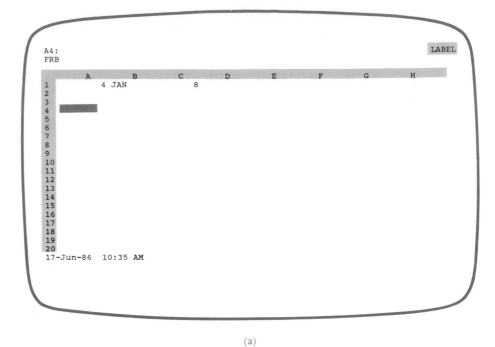

(a)

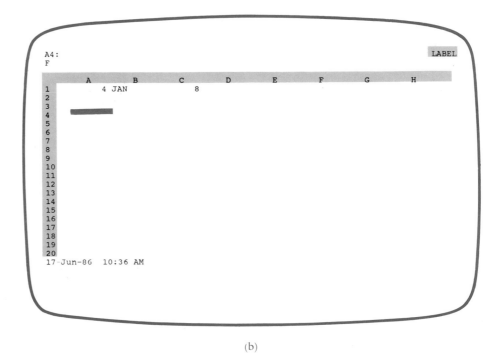

(b)

Figure 7.11 Correcting input by using the BACKSPACE key. (a) Position the cursor at cell A4; type *FRB*. (b) Press ⟨BACKSPACE⟩ twice, erasing the *B* and *R*. (c) Type *EB*. (d) Press ⟨ENTER/RETURN⟩ to insert the corrected entry into the worksheet.

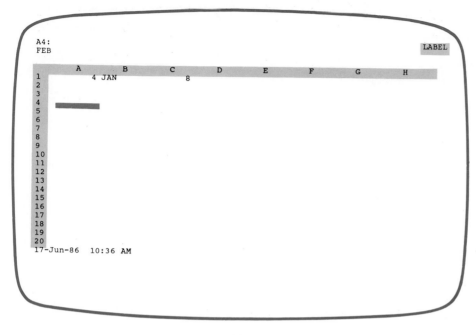

(c)

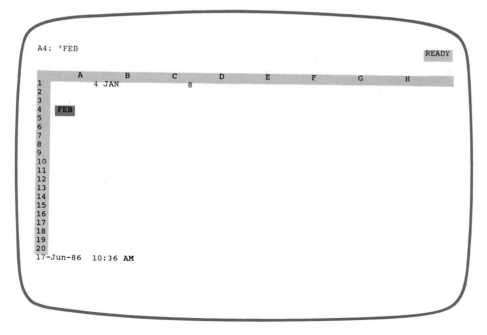

(d)

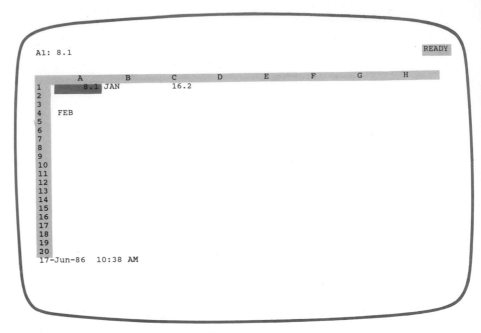

Figure 7.12 Replacing a worksheet entry.

which is available within command mode. The RANGE ERASE command allows you to erase the contents of a single worksheet cell or a range of cells. (We will discuss ranges later in this chapter.) Command Table 7.4 summarizes the operation of the RANGE ERASE command for our sample spreadsheets.

If you are using your spreadsheet software to follow this discussion, you should now erase the contents of cell A4.

Erasing the Worksheet. You may erase the contents of all worksheet cells by using the **ERASE WORKSHEET command,** available

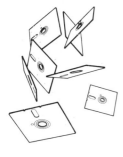

Command Table 7.4 The RANGE ERASE commands for Lotus 1-2-3, GoldSpread, and SuperCalc 3.

Program	Command	Comments
Lotus 1-2-3 and GoldSpread	/ Range Erase ⟨ENTER⟩	Erase a designated range of cells.
SuperCalc 3	/ Blank {Range} ⟨ENTER⟩	Erases contents of a designated range of cells.
	{Position cursor to cell} / Blank ⟨ENTER⟩	Erases contents of current cell.

Command Table 7.5 The ERASE WORKSHEET commands for Lotus 1-2-3, GoldSpread, and SuperCalc 3.

Program	Command	Comments
Lotus 1-2-3 and GoldSpread	/ Worksheet Erase ⟨ENTER⟩	Erases entire worksheet from memory (not from disk).
SuperCalc 3	/ Zap ⟨ENTER⟩	Erases worksheet from memory (not from disk).

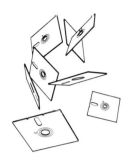

in command mode. Depending on your particular spreadsheet, this command may have a different name. However, all spreadsheets always have a command to erase the worksheet. Command Table 7.5 summarizes the operation of the ERASE WORKSHEET command for our sample spreadsheets.

If you are using your spreadsheet software to follow this discussion, you should now erase your worksheet in preparation for entering the Jones budget.

Entering the Jones Budget

As an example of worksheet construction, let's enter some of the data from the Jones budget into a worksheet. For our examples, we'll use Lotus 1-2-3.

To begin, enter the titles across the top of the worksheet. Since the first title is located in cell B1, position the cursor there. Type ⟨JAN⟩⟨ENTER/RETURN⟩ and press the CURSOR-RIGHT key. Then type ⟨FEB⟩⟨ENTER/RETURN⟩ and press ⟨CURSOR-RIGHT⟩. Follow this procedure until all of the titles in the top row are inserted, and your worksheet looks like the one shown in Figure 7.13. If you make a typing error, use the editing techniques described above to correct it.

Next, insert the row titles. The first row title is in cell A2. The quickest way to position the cursor there is to first press the HOME key on the numeric keypad, which positions the cursor at cell A1, and then to press the CURSOR-DOWN key. Now type in the row titles one by one. After each title, press ⟨ENTER/RETURN⟩ followed by the CURSOR-DOWN key to position the cursor for the next entry. After all the row titles are entered, press ⟨HOME⟩ to position the cursor at cell A1. The screen now appears as shown in Figure 7.14.

The numeric data corresponding to the various monthly income and expenditure amounts can now be entered across the rows, beginning with row 3 (the first row of expenses). Before you enter

When entering data into your worksheet, be sure to omit commas and dollar signs, and don't try to align decimal points.

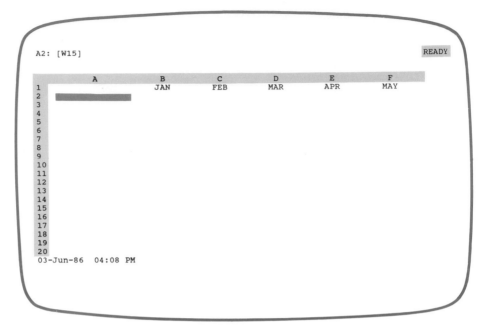

Figure 7.13 Inserting the column titles in the Jones budget, using Lotus 1-2-3.

Figure 7.14 The Jones budget with the titles in place, using Lotus 1-2-3.

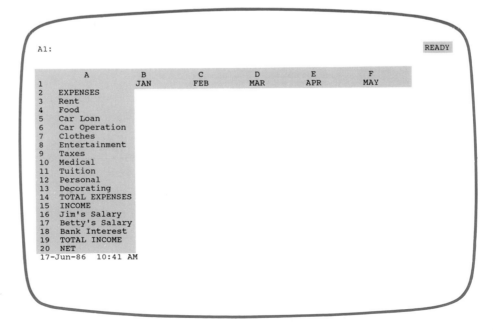

the data, note the following rules:

1. Do not include commas. For example, enter 5000 rather than 5,000.
2. Do not include dollar signs in currency amounts. Enter 3.23 rather than $3.23.
3. Do not include spaces in an attempt to line up decimal points. For example, in entering 14.3 and 1.7, you might be tempted to put a space before the second number to align the decimal points. Don't do this.

Commas, dollar signs, and aligned decimal points can all be taken care of during the later stage of formatting. Your data as entered should not include any of these formatting elements.

Now enter the first row of numeric data, corresponding to the months January through December. Don't enter the row total yet; in the next section of this chapter, you will find out how to make the spreadsheet calculate this total. Part of the first row of the Jones budget as entered is shown in Figure 7.15.

Setting the Column Width

You can set the width of worksheet columns to suit your particular application by using the **COLUMN WIDTH command**. To set

Figure 7.15 Entering the first row of numeric data into the Jones budget, using Lotus 1-2-3.

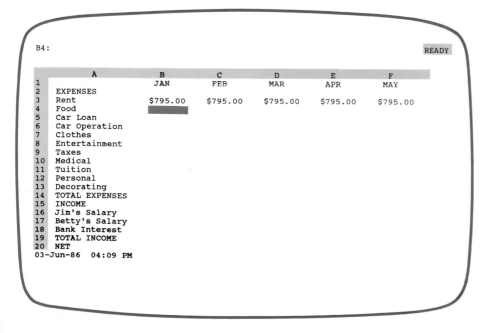

```
B4:                                                                READY

          A              B          C          D          E          F
 1                      JAN        FEB        MAR        APR        MAY
 2    EXPENSES
 3    Rent           $795.00    $795.00    $795.00    $795.00    $795.00
 4    Food
 5    Car Loan
 6    Car Operation
 7    Clothes
 8    Entertainment
 9    Taxes
10    Medical
11    Tuition
12    Personal
13    Decorating
14    TOTAL EXPENSES
15    INCOME
16    Jim's Salary
17    Betty's Salary
18    Bank Interest
19    TOTAL INCOME
20    NET
03-Jun-86  04:09 PM
```

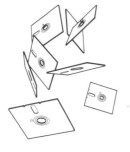

Command Table 7.6   The COLUMN WIDTH commands for Lotus 1-2-3, GoldSpread, and SuperCalc 3.

Program	Command	Comments
Lotus 1-2-3 and GoldSpread	/ Worksheet Column-width *n* ⟨ENTER⟩	Set width of current column to *n* characters. *n* is in range 1 to 72, inclusive.
SuperCalc 3	/ Format Global *n* ⟨ENTER⟩	Set global column width to *n* characters.
	/ Format Column ⟨column range⟩ *n* ⟨ENTER⟩	Set width of a range of columns to *n* characters.

equal widths for all your worksheet columns, use the **GLOBAL COLUMN WIDTH command**. Setting the column width is necessary, for example, if some of the numeric data to be displayed contain too many characters for the set column width. When a spreadsheet encounters such a data item, it displays a row of asterisks (*****) in the cell. No data is lost, however. By setting a wider column width, the asterisks are erased and the correct cell contents will automatically be displayed. Command Tables 7.6 and 7.7 summarize the operation of the COLUMN WIDTH and GLOBAL COLUMN WIDTH commands for each of our sample spreadsheets.

To illustrate the column width commands, let's improve the appearance of the Jones budget worksheet by setting the column width for the vertical titles row to 15 characters and the width of the remaining columns to 10 characters. This is most easily done by first using the GLOBAL COLUMN WIDTH command to set the width of all columns to 10 characters, then using the COLUMN WIDTH command to set the width of the first column to 15 characters. The resulting worksheet is shown in Figure 7.16.

Command Table 7.7   The GLOBAL COLUMN WIDTH commands for Lotus 1-2-3, GoldSpread, and SuperCalc 3.

Program	Command	Comments
Lotus 1-2-3 and GoldSpread	/ Worksheet Global Column-width *n* ⟨ENTER⟩	Set global column width to *n* characters. *n* is in range from 1 to 72, inclusive.
SuperCalc 3	/ Format Global *n* ⟨ENTER⟩	Set global column width to *n* characters. *n* is in range from 1 to 72, inclusive.

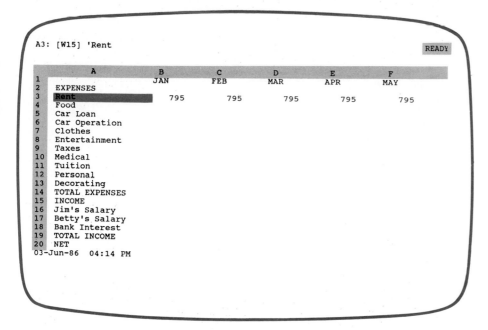

```
A3: [W15] 'Rent                                                    READY

              A            B          C          D          E          F
                          JAN        FEB        MAR        APR        MAY
 1
 2    EXPENSES
 3    Rent               795        795        795        795        795
 4    Food
 5    Car Loan
 6    Car Operation
 7    Clothes
 8    Entertainment
 9    Taxes
10    Medical
11    Tuition
12    Personal
13    Decorating
14    TOTAL EXPENSES
15    INCOME
16    Jim's Salary
17    Betty's Salary
18    Bank Interest
19    TOTAL INCOME
20    NET
03-Jun-86   04:14 PM
```

Figure 7.16   Varying the column widths in the Jones budget worksheet, using Lotus 1-2-3.

Column width is specified in terms of characters. The standard (or default) column width varies with the spreadsheet, but nine characters is a common value.

A spreadsheet program retains data whether or not the current column width allows it to be displayed on the screen. The maximum number of characters of text data that can be accommodated by the column width are displayed. Numeric data that does not fit is not displayed at all. Instead, the spreadsheet displays a message (usually a row of asterisks) to indicate that the data is too wide to display. The data is not lost, however. You may view the data by increasing the column width.

Titles

Entering the numeric data into the Jones budget is fairly simple. However, after making the first few entries, the vertical titles scroll off the screen and it is no longer possible to see the row title where you are entering data. Similarly, to place data on a row past the bottom of the screen causes the column titles to scroll off the screen. When you don't see the titles, it is easy to place data in the wrong cell. To combat this problem, spreadsheets allow you to hold the titles in place as the rest of the worksheet scrolls.

The **TITLES command** lets you fix the vertical titles, the horizontal titles, or both. If you fix the vertical titles, then the

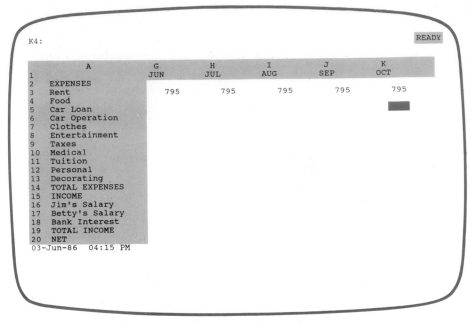

Figure 7.17 Fixing the horizontal and vertical titles, using Lotus 1-2-3.

column of titles always remains on the screen as the worksheet scrolls, as illustrated in Figure 7.17. If you fix the horizontal titles, then the row of titles always remains on the screen as the worksheet scrolls.

The TITLES command also lets you release any titles previously fixed. To release a title, position the cursor in the topmost left cell that is not part of the title border, then give the TITLES command. The details of the TITLES command for each of our sample spreadsheets are shown in Command Table 7.8.

Returning to the Jones budget, fix both the horizontal and vertical titles and fill in the remainder of the expenditures and income items. Don't fill in the totals yet (the items in the last row and last column). The spreadsheet for the Jones budget now appears as shown in Figure 7.18.

Data Formats

The Jones budget deals with money. However, this is not immediately apparent from looking at the worksheet because there are no dollar signs. The worksheet format is sloppy in other respects: the number of decimal points is inconsistent, and the decimal points don't line up. All of these matters can be adjusted by using special formatting commands.

The **FORMAT command** allows you to choose a format for a particular cell. The **GLOBAL FORMAT** command lets you specify a format for all the cells of a worksheet. The precise formats allowed vary with the spreadsheet. Here are some of the typical formats for numeric data with some examples:

- **General format**: Free-form decimals rounded to a varying number of places. Examples:

5.88

-5511.2

12.53

Command Table 7.8 The TITLES command for Lotus 1-2-3, GoldSpread, and SuperCalc 3.

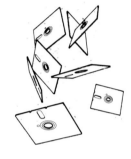

Program	Command	Comments
Lotus 1-2-3 and GoldSpread	/ Worksheet Titles Both	Set both horizontal and vertical titles. Use horizontal and vertical bands determined by current cursor position. Horizontal titles include current cursor row up to the first row; vertical titles include the current cursor column left to the first column.
	/ Worksheet Titles Clear	Release any titles currently set.
	/ Worksheet Titles Horizontal	Set horizontal titles. Use horizontal band determined by current cursor position.
	/ Worksheet Titles Vertical	Set vertical titles. Use vertical band determined by current cursor position.
SuperCalc 3	/ Titles Both	Set both horizontal and vertical titles. Use horizontal and vertical bands determined by current cursor position. Horizontal titles include current cursor row up to first row; vertical titles include current cursor column left to first column.
	/ Titles Clear	Release any titles currently set.
	/ Titles Horizontal	Set horizontal titles. Use horizontal band determined by current cursor position.
	/ Titles Vertical	Set vertical titles. Use vertical band determined by current cursor position.

```
J2:                                                                      READY

            A            F         G         H         I         J
  1                     MAY       JUN       JUL       AUG       SEP
  2  EXPENSES
  3  Rent               795       795       795       795       795
  4  Food               400       400       400       400       400
  5  Car Loan         297.8     297.8     297.8     297.8     297.8
  6  Car Operation      135       135       135       135       135
  7  Clothes                      100                           300
  8  Entertainment      200      1500       200       200       200
  9  Taxes          1272.49   1272.49   1272.49   1272.49   1272.49
 10  Medical            200       200       200       200       200
 11  Tuition                                        3000
 12  Personal           200       200       200       200       200
 13  Decorating        1000
 14  TOTAL EXPENSES 4500.29   4900.29   3500.29   6500.29   3800.29
 15  INCOME
 16  Jim's Salary      2450      2450      2450      2450      2450
 17  Betty's Salary    1950      1950      1950      1950      1950
 18  Bank Interest                         300
 19  TOTAL INCOME      4400      4400      4700      4400      4400
 20  NET
 03-Jun-86   04:18 PM
```

Figure 7.18   Entering all expenditures and income items on the Jones budget, using Lotus 1-2-3.

- **Fixed format**: Decimals rounded to a fixed number of places that you specify. Decimal points are vertically aligned. Some examples of numbers in two-place fixed format:

    5.88

  − 5511.20

    12.53

- **Currency format**: Include dollar signs and commas. You specify the number of decimal places (usually two). The decimal points are aligned. Negative amounts are in parentheses. Some examples of currency format:

    $5.88

  ($5,511.20)

    $12.53

- **Percentage format**: Convert numbers to a percentage. Some examples:

  588%

  551120%

  1253%

- **Scientific format**: Numbers expressed as a decimal times a power of 10. Some examples:

$5.88E+0$

$5.51120E+3$

$1.253E+1$

The operation of the FORMAT and GLOBAL FORMAT commands for our sample spreadsheets are summarized in Command Tables 7.9 and 7.10.

Since all numeric data in the Jones budget represent dollar amounts, use the GLOBAL FORMAT command to specify the currency format for all cells. Your worksheet should now look something like the one in Figure 7.19.

Section 7.3: *Test Your Understanding*

1. Describe the procedure for entering a data item into a cell.
2. What is the data entry line? What is its function?
3. What is recalculation?
4. Explain how to change the contents of a worksheet cell.
5. How do you cancel an incomplete data entry?

Figure 7.19 Formatting numeric data in the Jones budget, using Lotus 1-2-3.

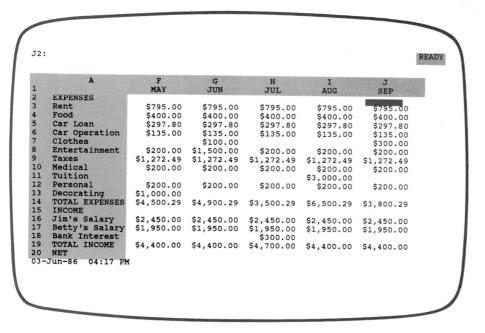

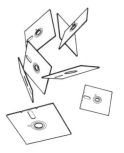

Command Table 7.9 The FORMAT command for Lotus 1-2-3, GoldSpread, and SuperCalc 3.

Program	Command	Comments
Lotus 1-2-3 and GoldSpread	/ Range Format ⟨ENTER⟩ Choose format from menu.	Set format for current cell. The menu choices for format are as follows: *Fixed:* Fixed number of decimal places (x.xx) *Scientific:* Exponential format (x.xxE + xx) *Currency:* ($x,xxx.xx) *Comma:* Comma inserted; negative values in parenthesis (x,xxx.xx) *General:* Standard format (x,xx or x.xxExx) *Plus or Minus:* Horizontal bar graph format (+ + + or − − −) *Percent:* Percent format (x.xx%) *Date:* Date format *Text:* Display formula instead of value *Hidden:* Omit cell display
SuperCalc 3	/ Format ⟨level⟩ Choose format from menu. ⟨ENTER⟩	Set format for current cell. The ⟨level⟩ indicates cells to which format command should apply. The choice for level are as follows: *Global:* Applies to all cells *Column range:* Applies to a range of columns *Row range:* Applies to a range of rows *Entry:* A single cell or any range The choices for the format are: I: Integer (no decimals) G: General (standard representation) E: Exponential (scientific) notation $: Two decimal places R: Right numeric justification L: Left numeric justification TR: Text right justification TL: Text left justification TC: Text centered *: For bar chart display U: User-defined format H: Hide values D: Default settings (G, R, TL, 9) (0–127) Column width

Command Table 7.10 The GLOBAL FORMAT command for Lotus
1-2-3, GoldSpread, and SuperCalc 3.

Program	Command	Comments
Lotus 1-2-3 and GoldSpread	/ Worksheet Global Format {Choose format from menu.}	Set format for all numeric and formula entries whose format is not individually specified. Menu choices for format are same as those available for formatting individual cells. (See Command Table 7.9.)
SuperCalc 3	/ Format Global {list}	List gives formats as shown in Command Table 7.9.

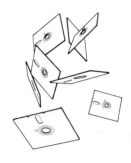

6. How do you correct an incomplete data entry?
7. How do you insert the contents of the data entry line into the current cell?
8. What is the appropriate format you should request to have numeric displays of the following types?
   a) 175.1
   b) $200.38
   c) $2.17E - 3$
   d) 2.5, 7.81, 3.875, with the decimal points aligned
9. What is the minimum column width necessary to display the following numeric data items?
   a) 58.354
   b) 100,358,000
   c) $5.731E + 01$

Hands-On Exercises

The following steps lead you through the initial phases of constructing the worksheet for the Jones budget.
1. Insert the row titles.
2. Insert the column titles.
3. Insert the monthly expense and income data.
4. Set the width of all the columns to 10 characters.
5. Set the width of the first column equal to 15 characters.

6. Set the format of all cell entries to currency.

7. Save the worksheet under the file name JONES.

8. Increase the amount for rent by $10 per month. Adjust the appropriate worksheet entries.

9. Mr. Jones receives a pay increase in April that brings his pay to $3700 per month. Adjust the appropriate worksheet entries.

10. In July, the Jones family takes a vacation costing $2,000. Add this figure to July. Add this cost into their budget.

7.4 Formulas

You have learned to enter text and numeric entries into worksheet cells. Now turn your attention to understanding and entering formulas. Recall that a formula is a "recipe" for calculating the contents of a cell in terms of the contents of other cells.

Arithmetic Operations

Spreadsheets allow you to write formulas involving the usual arithmetic operations. Addition and subtraction are written with the standard symbols—the plus sign ($+$) and the minus sign ($-$). Multiplication is indicated by an asterisk (*). For example, 5 times 8 is written as 5*8. Division is indicated by a slash (/). So, 12.5 divided by 11 is written as 12.5/11. Raising a number to a power is indicated by a caret (^). Thus, 2 to the fifth power is written as 2^5.

You may input cell entries by specifying a sequence of arithmetic operations. Suppose a cell is to contain the sum of the three numbers 85.8, 12.1, and 455.32. Type the entry for the cell in this form:

⟨85.8 + 12.1 + 455.32⟩

The spreadsheet program processes this input by computing the sum and inserting its value into the current cell.

A spreadsheet evaluates a formula according to the following rules:

1. Any cell references in the formula are replaced with their current numeric values. This reduces the formula evaluation to arithmetic operations.

2. All power operations (^) are performed, proceeding from left to right.

3. All multiplications are performed, proceeding from left to right.

4. Additions and subtractions are performed, proceeding from left to right.

5. If parentheses are present, they are evaluated according to the above rules, with the innermost parentheses evaluated first.

For example, the formula 1*2 + 3*5 is evaluated by performing the multiplications first (since there are no power operations present) to obtain

2 + 15

Next, the addition is performed, to obtain the value

17

As another example, consider the formula 6*3/2 + 3^2. First the power operation is performed to obtain

6*3/2 + 9

Next, the multiplication and division are performed, proceeding from left to right:

18/2 + 9

9 + 9

18

Don't feel insecure about the above rules for evaluating an algebraic expression. You have seen them before in elementary algebra. The Hands-on Exercises at the end of this section provide you with some practice in using these rules in case you are a bit rusty on their application.

By all means, let the spreadsheet do any required calculations in computing entries. By entering formulas such as those shown above, you can use the spreadsheet's data input line as a scratchpad to perform any calculations you want to do yourself.

Entering Formulas

As stated earlier, a formula is an arithmetic expression that references the contents of one or more cells. You may enter a formula into a cell by typing the formula exactly as you wish it to be calculated, assuming that the cell names are replaced by their current values. For example, the formula

1.05*B17

stands for 1.05 times the contents of the cell B17. The formula

(A1 + A2 + A3 + A4)/4

stands for the sum of the contents of cells A1, A2, A3, and A4

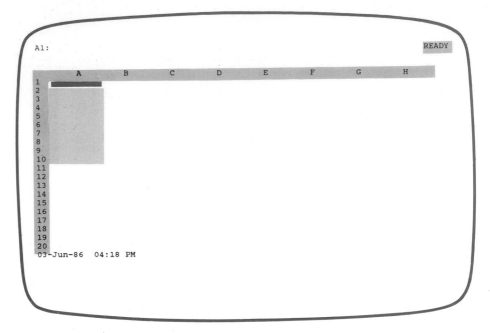

Figure 7.20   The range A2..A1O.

Figure 7.21   The range C3..E6.

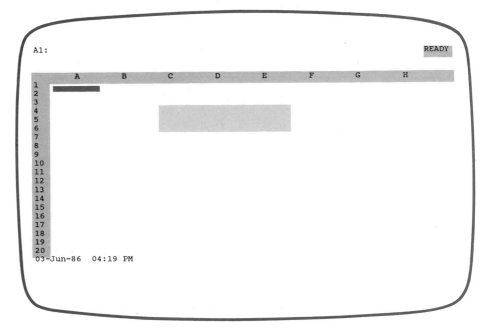

divided by 4. Similarly,

+A1+A2

stands for the sum of the contents of the cells A1 and A2. (The leading plus sign must be included for Lotus 1-2-3 but may be omitted in SuperCalc 3. In our discussion, we will always include the leading plus sign so that our formulas will work with all our sample spreadsheets.)

Functions

A **function** is a formula that has been built into the spreadsheet. A spreadsheet program has a number of such functions that you can use either by themselves or within your own formulas. For example, the function @ SUM is used to add the values of a collection of spreadsheet cells. The initial character @ is used by Lotus 1-2-3 and GoldSpread to tell the spreadsheet that the entry is a formula. (Note: No such introductory character is required in SuperCalc 3 functions.) To add the values of cells B1, B2, and B7 in Lotus 1-2-3 or GoldSpread, use the formula

@SUM(B1,B2,B7)

This formula has the same effect as the formula

+B1+B2+B7

The advantage of using the function @SUM becomes apparent when dealing with ranges of cells. A **range of cells** is a group of cells in a rectangular section of a worksheet. For instance, all the cells from A2 through A10 constitute a range, which is denoted in shorthand terms as A2 . . A10. (See Figure 7.20.) Similarly, the collection of cells in the rectangle C3 (upper-left corner) to E6 (lower-right corner) constitute a range that is denoted as C3 . . E6. (See Figure 7.21.)

You may use the function @SUM to add the values of all cells within a range. For example, the formula

@SUM(A2 . . A10)

computes the sum of all the cells in the range A2 . . A10. This formula has the same effect as the formula

+A2+A3+A4+A5+A6+A7+A8+A9+A10

This example should clearly illustrate why the @ SUM function is preferred to the longer form.

You may also combine ranges with individual cells when using a function. For example, the function

@SUM(A2 . . A10,B11,C3 . . E6)

computes the sum of the values of the cells A2 . . A10, B11, and C3 . . E6.

```
N3: @SUM(B3..M3)                                                      READY

         I           J           K           L           M           N
 1      AUG         SEP         OCT         NOV         DEC         YEAR
 2
 3      $795.00     $795.00     $795.00     $795.00     $795.00    $9,540.00
 4      $400.00     $400.00     $400.00     $400.00     $400.00
 5      $297.80     $297.80     $297.80     $297.80     $297.80
 6      $135.00     $135.00     $135.00     $135.00     $135.00
 7                  $300.00                 $350.00
 8      $200.00     $200.00     $200.00     $200.00     $200.00
 9    $1,272.49   $1,272.49   $1,272.49   $1,272.49   $1,272.49
10      $200.00     $200.00     $200.00     $200.00     $200.00
11    $3,000.00
12      $200.00     $200.00     $200.00     $200.00     $200.00
13
14    $6,500.29   $3,800.29   $3,500.29   $3,850.29   $3,500.29
15
16    $2,450.00   $2,450.00   $2,450.00   $2,450.00   $2,450.00
17    $1,950.00   $1,950.00   $1,950.00   $1,950.00   $1,950.00
18                              $300.00
19    $4,400.00   $4,400.00   $4,700.00   $4,400.00   $4,400.00
20
03-Jun-86   04:21 PM
```

Figure 7.22 Using @SUM to compute the row sums with Lotus 1-2-3.

Function expressions may be used as part of a formula, just as they are in algebra. For example, the formula

.05*@SUM(A2 . . A10) + B1

computes the product of .05 and @ SUM(A2 . . A10) and adds it to B1.

We'll survey the variety of functions available in typical spreadsheets in the next chapter. For now, let's get some practice in using functions by applying the single function @SUM.

Back to the Jones Budget

Let's return to the worksheet for the Jones budget and insert the entries for the row and column sums. Starting with the row sums, the first entry you should make is N3, which should contain the sum of the cells B3, C3, D3, . . . , M3. This group of cells forms the range B3 . . M3. The formula for the desired sum is

@SUM(B3 . . M3)

Enter this formula into cell N3. The spreadsheet program automatically calculates and displays the value of the desired sum, as shown in Figure 7.22.

You can compute other row sums by using similar formulas. For example, you can compute the sum for entry N4 by using the formula

@SUM(B4 . . M4)

Enter the various row formulas into your worksheet. If you find that the job is rather tedious, take heart; you will learn a shortcut for entering these formulas in the next section of this chapter.

Let's now proceed to the column sums. For each monthly column, you need to compute two sums: one for expenses and one for income. As a specific example, consider January. The expenses are listed in cells B3 through B13. You must add these and insert the sum into cell B14 by using the function

@SUM(B3 . . B14)

The income items for January are contained in cells B15 through B18. You must add these and insert the sum into cell B19 by using the function:

@SUM(B15 . . B18)

To compute the monthly surplus (or deficit), you must compute the income (B19) minus expenses (B14). In cell B20 you should thus insert the formula

+B19−B15

(Note the leading plus sign.)

Insert the formulas for the other column sums into the worksheet. This is a tedious job, but by completing the job once, you will appreciate the shortcut presented in the next section. Now your worksheet should look like the one shown in Figure 7.23.

Figure 7.23 Using @SUM to compute the column sums with Lotus 1-2-3.

A1: [W15]   READY

	A	B JAN	C FEB	D MAR	E APR	F MAY
1						
2	EXPENSES					
3	Rent	$795.00	$795.00	$795.00	$795.00	$795.00
4	Food	$400.00	$400.00	$400.00	$400.00	$400.00
5	Car Loan	$297.80	$297.80	$297.80	$297.80	$297.80
6	Car Operation	$135.00	$135.00	$135.00	$135.00	$135.00
7	Clothes	$125.00		$350.00		
8	Entertainment	$200.00	$200.00	$200.00	$200.00	$200.00
9	Taxes	$1,272.49	$1,272.49	$1,272.49	$1,272.49	$1,272.49
10	Medical	$200.00	$200.00	$200.00	$200.00	$200.00
11	Tuition	$3,000.00				
12	Personal	$200.00	$200.00	$200.00	$200.00	$200.00
13	Decorating			$800.00	$800.00	$1,000.00
14	TOTAL EXPENSES	$6,625.29	$3,500.29	$4,650.29	$4,300.29	$4,500.29
15	INCOME					
16	Jim's Salary	$2,450.00	$2,450.00	$2,450.00	$2,450.00	$2,450.00
17	Betty's Salary	$1,950.00	$1,950.00	$1,950.00	$1,950.00	$1,950.00
18	Bank Interest	$300.00			$300.00	
19	TOTAL INCOME	$4,700.00	$4,400.00	$4,400.00	$4,700.00	$4,400.00
20	NET	($1,925.29)	$899.71	($250.29)	$399.71	($100.29)

03-Jun-86   04:27 PM

Some Other Functions

Spreadsheets come equipped with a wide range of functions to perform various calculations. The precise set of built-in functions varies with the spreadsheet—and it would take us well beyond the scope of this book to describe the wide range of functions offered by various spreadsheets. However, let's look at three functions that you will use to construct sample worksheets in Chapter 8.

@MAX—This function determines the largest value in the listed cells. For example, the function

@MAX(C1,C2,C5)

determines the largest value in cells C1, C2, and C5.

@MIN—This function determines the smallest value in the listed cells. For example, the function

@MIN(A1 . . A50)

determines the smallest value in the range of 50 cells, A1 . . A50.

@AVG—This function determines the average of the values in the listed cells. For example, the function

@AVG(B1,A1 . . A10)

determines the average of the values in 11 cells, B1, A1 . . A10.

Common Difficulties in Using Functions

Built-in functions are a tremendous help in computing worksheet entries. However, as with any powerful tool, their use can create problems. The two most common difficulties concern circular formulas and the treatment of cells containing text.

A formula that refers to its own cell is called a **circular formula**. For example, consider the formula $+A1+A2$ placed in cell A1. In order to calculate the value of this function, the spreadsheet must use the value of A1. As a novice, you should refrain from using circular formulas in your worksheets. If you do define a circular function, most spreadsheets display a warning message.

Another difficulty can occur if you include either a blank cell or a cell containing text within a function that requires a number. For example, suppose you use the function

@SUM(A1 . . A10)

This function sums up the entries in the cells A1 . . A10, which is fine as long as all of the entries are numbers. But what if blanks or text are included? Most spreadsheets evaluate these entries as having a value of 0. However, some spreadsheets may refuse to evaluate such a formula. Before using such functions, you need to see how your spreadsheet handles them.

Section 7.4: Test Your Understanding

1. Write the following formulas as they would be entered into a worksheet cell.
   a) 2 plus the product of 5 times the contents of A1.
   b) The contents of A15 divided by 2.
   c) The contents of B10 raised to the power 3.
   d) 7.18 divided by the sum of the contents of A1 and A2.
   e) The sum of the contents of A1 and A5.
   f) The sum of A1 and 5.1.
   g) Fifteen percent of the value of A4.
   h) The difference between B1 and B17.
   i) Increase B19 by 1 percent of the value of C2.
   j) The sum of A1, A2, A3, A4, and A5.
   k) The sum of the range B5 . . B12.
   l) The largest of the numbers in the range A1 . . B10.
   m) Half the average of the numbers in the range A1 . . A10.

Hands-on Exercises

1. Recall the Jones budget worksheet saved in the Hands-on Exercises of Section 7.3.
2. Insert all of the monthly expense sums into the worksheet.
3. Insert all of the monthly income sums into the worksheet.
4. Insert the formulas that compute the monthly surplus amounts.
5. Insert the formulas that compute the annual totals for each income and expense item.
6. Save the worksheet under the file name JONES.
7. Decrease Mr. Jones's income for January by $50. What effect does this have on Mr. Jones's annual income and on the total income for January?
8. Add to the entertainment budget the cost of a $2,000 vacation taken in July. What effect does this have on the total expenses for July? For the year? On the amount of surplus for July?
9. Insert into column O formulas that compute the percentages represented by the corresponding annual totals for each category of expense and income.

10. Insert into column P formulas that compute the average monthly amounts for each of the categories of expense and income.

7.5 Ranges and Copying

The typical worksheet can consist of hundreds of rows and dozens of columns. You might think you will never encounter such a complex worksheet, but you almost certainly will. Even relatively innocent business problems involve hundreds of pieces of data and require large worksheets. As you saw in the preceding sections, inserting the data into a large worksheet can be a tedious, time-consuming affair. Yet, by using labor saving spreadsheet commands, you can significantly decrease the amount of drudgery. The most significant of these labor saving commands is the **COPY command**.

How the COPY Command Operates

The COPY command allows you to copy one range of cells onto another. Implementing the COPY command varies slightly among the spreadsheets, but here is a general description of how the command functions:

1. Give the COPY command.
2. The spreadsheet asks you for the range from which to copy from, sometimes called the **source range**. Type in the range. For example, to copy the range A1 through N1, type

   ⟨A1 . . N1⟩⟨ENTER/RETURN⟩

3. The spreadsheet now asks for the range to which to copy, sometimes called the **target range**. Type in this range. For

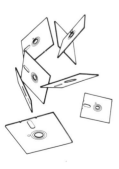

Command Table 7.11 The COPY commands for Lotus 1-2-3, GoldSpread, and SuperCalc 3.

Program	Command	Comments
Lotus 1-2-3 and GoldSpread	/ Copy {Range to copy from.} {First cell of range to copy to.} ⟨ENTER⟩	Copy range of cells from one location to another.
SuperCalc 3	/ Replicate {Range to copy from} {First cell of range to copy to} ⟨ENTER⟩	Copy range of cells from one location to another.

```
L16: 2450                                                          READY

         A              L        M         N          O          P
1                      NOV      DEC       YEAR        JAN        FEB
2    EXPENSES
3    Rent            $795.00   $795.00   $9,540.00    $834.75    $834.75
4    Food            $400.00   $400.00   $4,800.00    $420.00    $420.00
5    Car Loan        $297.80   $297.80   $3,573.60    $312.69    $312.69
6    Car Operation   $135.00   $135.00   $1,620.00    $141.75    $141.75
7    Clothes         $350.00             $1,225.00    $131.25      $0.00
8    Entertainment   $200.00   $200.00   $3,700.00    $210.00    $210.00
9    Taxes         $1,272.49 $1,272.49 $15,269.88  $1,336.11  $1,336.11
10   Medical         $200.00   $200.00   $2,400.00    $210.00    $210.00
11   Tuition                            $6,000.00  $3,150.00      $0.00
12   Personal        $200.00   $200.00   $2,400.00    $210.00    $210.00
13   Decorating                          $2,600.00      $0.00      $0.00
14   TOTAL EXPENSES $3,850.29 $3,500.29 $53,128.48  $6,956.55  $3,675.30
15   INCOME
16   Jim's Salary  $2,450.00 $2,450.00 $29,400.00  $2,646.00  $2,646.00
17   Betty's Salary $1,950.00 $1,950.00 $23,400.00  $2,106.00  $2,106.00
18   Bank Interest                       $1,200.00    $324.00      $0.00
19   TOTAL INCOME  $4,400.00 $4,400.00 $54,000.00  $5,076.00  $4,752.00
20   NET             $549.71   $899.71   $871.52 ($1,880.55) $1,076.70
17-Jun-86   11:13 AM
```

Figure 7.24   Adding a second year to the Jones budget, using Lotus 1-2-3.

example, to copy to the range O1 through AA1, type

⟨O1 . . AA1⟩⟨ENTER/RETURN⟩

4. The spreadsheet copies the contents of the source range onto the target range.

The details of the COPY commands for our sample spreadsheets are summarized in Command Table 7.11.

To put the COPY command to work, let's return to the Jones budget and add a new section to the worksheet to describe next year's budget. This new section will be situated beside the columns currently used, as shown in Figure 7.24. The column headings for the second year are the same as those for the first year. Instead of retyping them, use the COPY command to copy the original headings, which occupy the range B1 . . N1. The second-year column headings will occupy the range O1 . . AA1. When you copy the first range onto the second, your worksheet will appear as shown in Figure 7.25.

Suppose that expenses and income for January of the second year are to remain the same as they were in the previous year. You can reflect this in the worksheet by copying the January column for year 1 to the corresponding column for year 2, as illustrated in Figure 7.26. Note that the program copies numeric data items unchanged from column to column. Moreover, the program adjusts

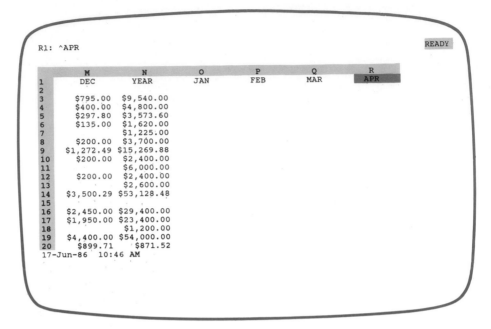

Figure 7.25   Copying the column headings onto the second-year worksheet, using Lotus 1-2-3.

Figure 7.26   Copying data for January, using Lotus 1-2-3.

```
R2:                                                                    READY

          M            N            O         P        Q        R
  1      DEC         YEAR         JAN        FEB      MAR      APR
  2
  3     $795.00    $9,540.00     $795.00
  4     $400.00    $4,800.00     $400.00
  5     $297.80    $3,573.60     $297.80
  6     $135.00    $1,620.00     $135.00
  7                $1,225.00     $125.00
  8     $200.00    $3,700.00     $200.00
  9   $1,272.49   $15,269.88   $1,272.49
 10     $200.00    $2,400.00     $200.00
 11                $6,000.00   $3,000.00
 12     $200.00    $2,400.00     $200.00
 13                $2,600.00
 14   $3,500.29   $53,128.48   $6,625.29
 15
 16   $2,450.00   $29,400.00   $2,450.00
 17   $1,950.00   $23,400.00   $1,950.00
 18                $1,200.00     $300.00
 19   $4,400.00   $54,000.00   $4,700.00
 20     $899.71      $871.52  ($1,925.29)
 17-Jun-86   10:49 AM
```

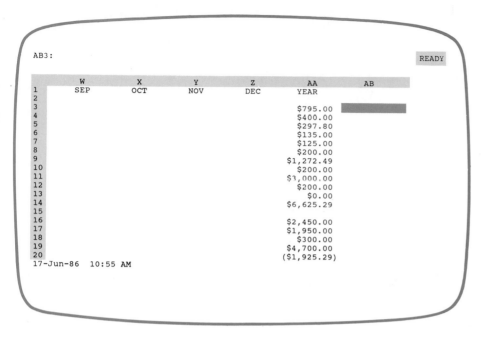

Figure 7.27 Copying the row total formulas from the first year to the second year, using Lotus 1-2-3.

the formulas that compute the total income, total expenses, and surplus to reflect the new column, O rather than B. For example, the formula

@SUM(B3 . . B13)

in cell B15 is replaced by the formula

@SUM(O3 . . O13)

in cell O15. This is correct. The entry in cell O15 should be the sum of the entries above it, namely N3 . . N13.

You can use a similar command to copy the row total formulas for the first year (source range N3 . . N20) to row total formulas for the second year (target range AA3 . . AA20). The program automatically adjusts the formulas to reflect the new positions of the columns. (See Figure 7.27.) The ability to copy formulas from one place to another on a worksheet is one of the most significant features of the COPY command.

More Applications of the COPY Command

You can use a single COPY command to create many duplicate copies of a single row or column. Suppose that you want to repeat the data for January of the first year in every month of the second year. To accomplish this, specify the source range as the first-year

S3: 795   READY

	N	O	P	Q	R	S
	YEAR	JAN	FEB	MAR	APR	MAY
1	YEAR	JAN	FEB	MAR	APR	MAY
2						
3	$9,540.00	$795.00	$795.00	$795.00	$795.00	$795.00
4	$4,800.00	$400.00	$400.00	$400.00	$400.00	$400.00
5	$3,573.60	$297.80	$297.80	$297.80	$297.80	$297.80
6	$1,620.00	$135.00	$135.00	$135.00	$135.00	$135.00
7	$1,225.00	$125.00	$125.00	$125.00	$125.00	$125.00
8	$3,700.00	$200.00	$200.00	$200.00	$200.00	$200.00
9	$15,269.88	$1,272.49	$1,272.49	$1,272.49	$1,272.49	$1,272.49
10	$2,400.00	$200.00	$200.00	$200.00	$200.00	$200.00
11	$6,000.00	$3,000.00	$3,000.00	$3,000.00	$3,000.00	$3,000.00
12	$2,400.00	$200.00	$200.00	$200.00	$200.00	$200.00
13	$2,600.00					
14	$53,128.48	$6,625.29	$6,625.29	$6,625.29	$6,625.29	$6,625.29
15						
16	$29,400.00	$2,450.00	$2,450.00	$2,450.00	$2,450.00	$2,450.00
17	$23,400.00	$1,950.00	$1,950.00	$1,950.00	$1,950.00	$1,950.00
18	$1,200.00	$300.00	$300.00	$300.00	$300.00	$300.00
19	$54,000.00	$4,700.00	$4,700.00	$4,700.00	$4,700.00	$4,700.00
20	$871.52	($1,925.29)	($1,925.29)	($1,925.29)	($1,925.29)	($1,925.29)

17-Jun-86   11:05 AM

Figure 7.28   Duplicating the first-year January data for each month of the second year, using Lotus 1-2-3.

Figure 7.29   Creating second-year worksheet without data, using Lotus 1-2-3.

O16:   READY

	A	O	P	Q	R	S
1		JAN	FEB	MAR	APR	MAY
2	EXPENSES					
3	Rent					
4	Food					
5	Car Loan					
6	Car Operation					
7	Clothes					
8	Entertainment					
9	Taxes					
10	Medical					
11	Tuition					
12	Personal					
13	Decorating					
14	TOTAL EXPENSES	$0.00	$0.00	$0.00	$0.00	$0.00
15	INCOME					
16	Jim's Salary					
17	Betty's Salary					
18	Bank Interest					
19	TOTAL INCOME	$0.00	$0.00	$0.00	$0.00	$0.00
20	NET	$0.00	$0.00	$0.00	$0.00	$0.00

17-Jun-86   11:08 AM

January column (B3 . . B20), then specify the target range as all second-year columns (O3 . . AA20). The COPY command will make copies of the first-year January data for each month of the second year, as shown in Figure 7.28.

As an exercise, use the ERASE command to erase the second year data. Leave the row titles and the formulas in rows 14, 18, 20 and column AA). You will then have a blank worksheet for the second year, which includes all the built-in numeric relationships for row and column. (See Figure 7.29.)

To further illustrate the power of the COPY command, construct a budget for the second year in which all expense items are increased by 5 percent and all income items are increased by 8 percent. This process may sound complicated, but using the COPY command makes it easy. To begin, enter in cell O3 the first expense item for the second year, which must be the corresponding expense item for the first year (cell B3), increased by 5 percent. Compute this via the formula

$1.05*B3$

The spreadsheet now computes the correct value for this expense item. (See Figure 7.30.) You could enter corresponding formulas for each of the other expense items. However, it is simpler to use

Figure 7.30 Inserting the formula for the first expense item of the second year, using Lotus 1-2-3.

```
O3: 1.05*B3                                                    READY

        A           O        P        Q        R        S
                    JAN      FEB      MAR      APR      MAY
1
2    EXPENSES
3    Rent           $834.75
4    Food
5    Car Loan
6    Car Operation
7    Clothes
8    Entertainment
9    Taxes
10   Medical
11   Tuition
12   Personal
13   Decorating
14   TOTAL EXPENSES $834.75   $0.00    $0.00    $0.00    $0.00
15   INCOME
16   Jim's Salary
17   Betty's Salary
18   Bank Interest
19   TOTAL INCOME    $0.00    $0.00    $0.00    $0.00    $0.00
20   NET           ($834.75)  $0.00    $0.00    $0.00    $0.00
17-Jun-86   11:09 AM
```

```
O3: 1.05*B3                                                              POINT
Enter range to copy FROM: O3..O3

              A            O          P          Q          R          S
1                         JAN        FEB        MAR        APR        MAY
2       EXPENSES
3       Rent           $834.75
4       Food
5       Car Loan
6       Car Operation
7       Clothes
8       Entertainment
9       Taxes
10      Medical
11      Tuition
12      Personal
13      Decorating
14      TOTAL EXPENSES   $834.75      $0.00      $0.00      $0.00      $0.00
15      INCOME
16      Jim's Salary
17      Betty's Salary
18      Bank Interest
19      TOTAL INCOME       $0.00      $0.00      $0.00      $0.00      $0.00
20      NET            ($834.75)      $0.00      $0.00      $0.00      $0.00
17-Jun-86   11:10 AM
```

(a)

```
Z13:                                                                     POINT
Enter range to copy TO: O3..Z13

              A            V          W          X          Y          Z
1                         AUG        SEP        OCT        NOV        DEC
2       EXPENSES
3       Rent
4       Food
5       Car Loan
6       Car Operation
7       Clothes
8       Entertainment
9       Taxes
10      Medical
11      Tuition
12      Personal
13      Decorating
14      TOTAL EXPENSES     $0.00      $0.00      $0.00      $0.00      $0.00
15      INCOME
16      Jim's Salary
17      Betty's Salary
18      Bank Interest
19      TOTAL INCOME       $0.00      $0.00      $0.00      $0.00      $0.00
20      NET                $0.00      $0.00      $0.00      $0.00      $0.00
17-Jun-86   11:10 AM
```

(b)

```
O3:  1.05*B3                                                    READY

            A          O          P          Q          R          S
                      JAN        FEB        MAR        APR        MAY
1
2    EXPENSES
3    Rent          $834.75    $834.75    $834.75    $834.75    $834.75
4    Food          $420.00    $420.00    $420.00    $420.00    $420.00
5    Car Loan      $312.69    $312.69    $312.69    $312.69    $312.69
6    Car Operation $141.75    $141.75    $141.75    $141.75    $141.75
7    Clothes       $131.25      $0.00    $367.50      $0.00      $0.00
8    Entertainment $210.00    $210.00    $210.00    $210.00    $210.00
9    Taxes       $1,336.11  $1,336.11  $1,336.11  $1,336.11  $1,336.11
10   Medical       $210.00    $210.00    $210.00    $210.00    $210.00
11   Tuition     $3,150.00      $0.00      $0.00      $0.00      $0.00
12   Personal      $210.00    $210.00    $210.00    $210.00    $210.00
13   Decorating      $0.00      $0.00    $840.00    $840.00  $1,050.00
14   TOTAL EXPENSES $6,956.55 $3,675.30  $4,882.80  $4,515.30  $4,725.30
15   INCOME
16   Jim's Salary
17   Betty's Salary
18   Bank Interest
19   TOTAL INCOME   $0.00      $0.00      $0.00      $0.00      $0.00
20   NET        ($6,956.55)($3,675.30)($4,882.80)($4,515.30)($4,725.30)
17-Jun-86   11:10 AM
```

(c)

Figure 7.31   Increasing all expenses by 5 percent for the second year, using Lotus 1-2-3. (a) Specify the source range O3 . . O13 to be copied onto (b) the target range O3 . . Z13. (c) A formula that is 1.05 times greater than the corresponding first-year cell is placed in each expense cell.

the COPY command. Merely copy the source range O3 . . O13 onto the target range O3 . . Z13. This places in each expense cell a formula that is 1.05 times greater than the corresponding expense cell for the first year. (The contents of cell O3 is copied onto itself, but this does no harm.) The spreadsheet automatically computes the values for all these formulas. Moreover, the row and column totals, which are already specified by formulas, are also computed. (See Figure 7.31.)

To increase all income items by 8 percent, proceed in a similar fashion. The first income item for year 2 is in cell O16. In this cell insert the formula

    1.08*B16

That is, increase the first income item of year 1 by 8 percent. Then copy this formula to all year 2 income cells. The spreadsheet then calculates all the new income amounts, as well as all row and column totals. (See Figure 7.32.)

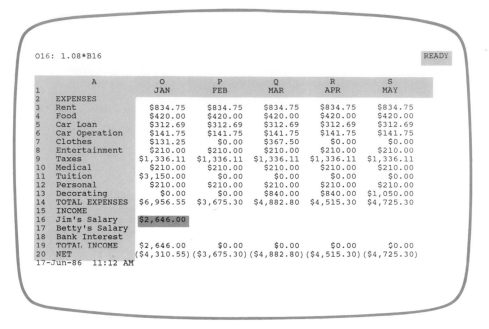

(a)

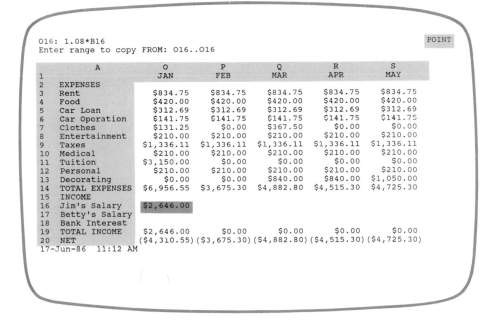

(b)

Figure 7.32 Completing the worksheet for the second year of the Jones budget, using Lotus 1-2-3. (a) Insert 1.08*B.16 in cell O16. Copy formula from (b) cell O16 to (c) all year 2 income cells (O16 . . Z18). (d) The spreadsheet recalculates the new income amounts, as well as all row and column totals.

```
Z18:                                                                    POINT
Enter range to copy TO: O16..Z18

              A         V          W          X          Y          Z
1                      AUG        SEP        OCT        NOV        DEC
2     EXPENSES
3     Rent           $834.75    $834.75    $834.75    $834.75    $834.75
4     Food           $420.00    $420.00    $420.00    $420.00    $420.00
5     Car Loan       $312.69    $312.69    $312.69    $312.69    $312.69
6     Car Operation  $141.75    $141.75    $141.75    $141.75    $141.75
7     Clothes          $0.00    $315.00      $0.00    $367.50      $0.00
8     Entertainment  $210.00    $210.00    $210.00    $210.00    $210.00
9     Taxes        $1,336.11  $1,336.11  $1,336.11  $1,336.11  $1,336.11
10    Medical        $210.00    $210.00    $210.00    $210.00    $210.00
11    Tuition      $3,150.00      $0.00      $0.00      $0.00      $0.00
12    Personal       $210.00    $210.00    $210.00    $210.00    $210.00
13    Decorating       $0.00      $0.00      $0.00      $0.00      $0.00
14    TOTAL EXPENSES$6,825.30  $3,990.30  $3,675.30  $4,042.80  $3,675.30
15    INCOME
16    Jim's Salary
17    Betty's Salary
18    Bank Interest
19    TOTAL INCOME     $0.00      $0.00      $0.00      $0.00      $0.00
20    NET          ($6,825.30)($3,990.30)($3,675.30)($4,042.80)($3,675.30)
17-Jun-86   11:18 AM
```

(c)

```
O16: 1.08*B16                                                           READY

              A         O          P          Q          R          S
1                      JAN        FEB        MAR        APR        MAY
2     EXPENSES
3     Rent           $834.75    $834.75    $834.75    $834.75    $834.75
4     Food           $420.00    $420.00    $420.00    $420.00    $420.00
5     Car Loan       $312.69    $312.69    $312.69    $312.69    $312.69
6     Car Operation  $141.75    $141.75    $141.75    $141.75    $141.75
7     Clothes        $131.25      $0.00    $367.50      $0.00      $0.00
8     Entertainment  $210.00    $210.00    $210.00    $210.00    $210.00
9     Taxes        $1,336.11  $1,336.11  $1,336.11  $1,336.11  $1,336.11
10    Medical        $210.00    $210.00    $210.00    $210.00    $210.00
11    Tuition      $3,150.00      $0.00      $0.00      $0.00      $0.00
12    Personal       $210.00    $210.00    $210.00    $210.00    $210.00
13    Decorating       $0.00      $0.00    $840.00    $840.00  $1,050.00
14    TOTAL EXPENSES$6,956.55  $3,675.30  $4,882.80  $4,515.30  $4,725.30
15    INCOME
16    Jim's Salary $2,646.00  $2,646.00  $2,646.00  $2,646.00  $2,646.00
17    Betty's Salary$2,106.00  $2,106.00  $2,106.00  $2,106.00  $2,106.00
18    Bank Interest  $324.00      $0.00      $0.00    $324.00      $0.00
19    TOTAL INCOME $5,076.00  $4,752.00  $4,752.00  $5,076.00  $4,752.00
20    NET         ($1,880.55) $1,076.70  ($130.80)   $560.70     $26.70
17-Jun-86   11:12 AM
```

(d)

More About Copying Formulas

In all of the above examples showing the copying formulas, the cell references were automatically adjusted to reflect their new positions in the worksheet. Actually, there are two approaches to copying cell references used in formulas: You may automatically adjust a cell reference when it is copied or you may interpret the cell reference literally.

Automatically adjusted cell references are called **relative references**. These are the cell references that we have been using up to this point. Cell references that are not automatically adjusted are called **absolute references**. In Lotus 1-2-3 and GoldSpread, you may indicate an absolute reference to a row or column by preceding it by a dollar sign. As an example, consider the formula

5.8*$A$1

This formula is evaluated as 5.8 times A1. The dollar signs indicate that the reference to A1 is absolute. That is, if you copy the formula, it will still be evaluated as 5.8 times A1.

SuperCalc 3 does not allow you to declare individual references absolute. However, as part of the COPY command, it allows you to specify whether all the cell references in a formula to be copied should be treated as absolute or relative.

Absolute references are used to refer to cells that contain data referenced throughout the worksheet. For example, an economist might use a worksheet to analyze the effects of inflation on a particular industry. The percentage of inflation can be stored in cell A1 and used in formulas throughout the worksheet. Such formulas should use A1 as an absolute reference—allowing the formulas to be copied, yet still referring to the percentage of inflation in the same cell. The formula

5.8*A1

is also evaluated as 5.8 times A1. However, the reference to A1 in this formula is relative. That is, if you copy the formula to another cell, the spreadsheet adjusts the reference to reflect the new position.

To completely understand how relative references work, let's look in detail at the way relative references are adjusted. Suppose that you are copying the above formula to a cell that is three cells to the right and four cells down from the source. The spreadsheet will increase the column reference by three units (to D) and the row reference by 4 units (to 5). The adjusted reference is then D5 and the formula is copied as

5.8*D5

In deciding whether a cell reference should be absolute or relative, ask yourself this question: If I copy the formula, should the cell reference be adjusted? If so, then you should use a relative reference. If the cell reference should stay the same, use an absolute reference.

You can have the column reference be absolute and the row reference be relative. For example, in the cell reference A$1, the column reference A is absolute and the row reference is relative. Such references are called **mixed references**.

Section 7.5: Test Your Understanding

1. Explain the operation of the COPY command.
2. Describe how to insert the value 1.5 into each cell of the range A5 . . B10.
3. Suppose that cell A1 contains the formula $+A2-A3$. What is the result if this formula is copied into
   a) cell B8
   b) cell C1
   c) cell C5
   d) range B1 . . B8
4. Suppose that A12 contains the formula $15*\$A\$5+1$. What is the result if this formula is copied into cell B1?
5. Explain the difference between relative and absolute cell references.

Hands-on Exercises

1. Recall the worksheet saved in the file JONES in the Hands-on Exercises of Section 7.4.
2. Use the COPY command (several times) to erase all formulas on this worksheet.
3. Insert the first formula for annual expenses into cell N2. Copy this formula into the range N3 . . N18.
4. Insert the formula for January expenses into cell B11. Use the COPY command to construct all other monthly expense formulas.
5. Use the COPY command to insert the monthly income formulas into the worksheet.
6. Insert the formulas for monthly surplus into the worksheet.
7. Use the COPY command to duplicate the column titles for the second year (in columns O through AA).

8. Insert formulas for the second year that increase expenses by 5 percent.

9. Insert formulas for the second year that increase income by 8 percent.

10. Suppose that we allow expenses in the second year to increase by a variable amount that is stored in cell A19. In the case of Exercise 8, A19 would contain the value .05. Insert formulas to calculate the expense amounts for the second year.

11. Suppose that we allow income in the second year to increase by a variable amount that is stored in cell A20. In the case of Exercise 9, A20 would contain the value .08. Insert formulas to calculate the income amounts for the second year.

KEY TERMS

spreadsheet
worksheet
title
spreadsheet program
integrated software
configuration
configuring the system
cell
address
contents
current cell
home position
PGUP and PGDN keys
status line
data input line
label
numeric
formula

input mode
command mode
slash (/) key
nested menu structure
WORKSHEET command
command cursor
pull-down menu
SAVE command
RECALL command
exit sequence
QUIT command
recalculation
RANGE ERASE command
ERASEWORKSHEET command
COLUMN WIDTH command
GLOBAL COLUMN WIDTH command

TITLES command
FORMAT command
GLOBAL FORMAT command
general format
fixed format
currency format
percentage format
scientific format
function
range of cells
circular formula
COPY command
source range
target range
relative reference
absolute reference
mixed reference

CHAPTER REVIEW QUESTIONS

1. Describe three applications of spreadsheets. For each one cite at least one formula used.

2. Explain the role of formulas in spreadsheet development.

3. Give an example of a formula containing

a relative cell reference.

4. Give an example of a formula containing an absolute cell reference.

5. What is a built-in function? Give an example.

6. What is a range?

7. Give an example of a function that references both individual cells and ranges.

8. Suppose that A1 has the value 5, A2 the value 5, A3 the value 9 and A4 the value 7. Suppose that A5 contains each of the following formulas. What value is displayed for cell A5?

a) +A2 – A3

b) 3*A4

c) @AVG($A$1 . . $A$4)

d) @MIN(A1,A3,A4)

e) 2*@SUM($A$1,A4)

9. What is the result if the formula in Question 8(a) is copied to cell D5?

10. What is the result if the formula in Question 8(b) is copied to cell D5?

11. What is the result if the formula in Question 8(c) is copied to cell D5?

12. What is the result if the formula in Question 8(d) is copied to cell D5?

13. What is the result if the formula in Question 8(e) is copied to cell D5?

DISCUSSION QUESTIONS

1. A spreadsheet might be called a word processor for numeric data. Explain this statement.

2. For what types of numeric problems would a spreadsheet be most useful? Least useful?

3. How would you go about checking that the formulas of a spreadsheet correctly express the relationships you intend? (The techniques for such checking have recently undergone quite a rapid development and have formed the field of spreadsheet auditing.)

APPLICATION PROJECTS

1. A software developer assembles a product consisting of a number of different components. Table 7.1 lists the various components and their unit costs.

a) Construct a spreadsheet that lists the various unit costs, the number of each units required for the package, the cost of each category of component, and the total cost for the package.

b) Expand the spreadsheet to show the effect of increasing each of the costs by 10 percent, 20 percent, and 50 percent.

c) Add to the spreadsheet to show the effect of decreasing each cost by 10 percent, 20 percent, and 50 percent.

d) Add columns to show the percentages of the costs accounted for by each category of component. (There should be seven such columns, one for each set of costs.)

2. Flora Norris, an advertising manager, wants to use a spreadsheet to keep track of her advertising budget of $2,000,000. Every month she wants to enter the money that was spent in each medium and in each vehicle. She will then be able to see at a glance how much money has been spent to date in each medium and region of the country. Her budget for media would cover the following:

Table 7.1   The costs of manufacturing a software package.

Component	Unit Cost
Binder	$3.00
Index Tabs	$1.00
Documentation	$3.00
Diskettes	$3.50
Command Cards	$0.85
Slip Case	$2.00
Packaging	$0.50
Diskette Duplication	$0.75
Assembly	$0.50

Television
Radio
Magazines
Newspapers
Direct mail
Outdoor (billboards, etc.)

The number of vehicles Flora will use will depend on the medium. She may want to track ads in only six different magazines but in 50 different newspapers.

The spreadsheet should provide totals for each medium and vehicle by month and year. Design the spreadsheet Flora could use for this purpose. Explain the types of what-if analyses she might be able to do with that spreadsheet.

8 Spreadsheet Formulas

Micros Are Working on the Railroad

When a freight train rolls by, the first thing you see is a powerful locomotive chugging away, pulling the train. Because locomotives are extremely expensive items, railroad organizations spend billions each year buying and repairing them.

Now microcomputers are helping railroads improve cost planning and management. In Washington, D.C. at the Association of American Railroads (AAR), a trade group that supports commercial freight railroads, analysts have developed a spreadsheet model for this very purpose.

Greg Stephens, assistant manager of the AAR freight equipment management program, says their customized spreadsheet model uses Lotus 1-2-3 or Symphony on an IBM PC/XT. The model can be used by any member railroad to plan for expenditures when replacing or repairing worn-out locomotives.

With appropriate formulas already programmed into the model, any railroad can quickly discern the financial picture in managing its locomotive fleet, or experimenting with different financial scenarios. "To recalculate each spreadsheet takes less than a minute. But even that is several hundred thousand calculations, which is pretty awesome to do by hand," Stephens says.

In the past, railroads were forced to figure costs with pencil and paper. Because that took so long, analysts could consider only a very few spending plans. Now that planning can be done on a microcomputer, planners have many more viable alternatives to consider, which makes managing budgets a much smoother process.

"It would be virtually impossible to be thorough about developing strategies without a computer model to help you do it. There are too many variables," Stephens asserts. For the railroad industry, such variables include fuel efficiency, crew and maintenance costs, and the most practical location of locomotives to meet traffic requirements. The AAR model helps railroads devise their strategies at the least possible cost—which results in savings for manufacturers and consumers as well.

FORMULAS ARE A KEY INGREDIENT in building worksheets. A formula describes the value of a particular cell, which must be calculated from the values of other cells—and a worksheet describes the relationships implicit in such calculations. Because of the importance of formulas in spreadsheets, this chapter is devoted to presenting, in detail, the procedures for designing formulas that will solve typical, real-world problems.

8.1 Built-in Functions

Writing formulas can be easier if you utilize your program's built-in functions.

Using the usual operations of arithmetic, you can write your own formulas, as described in Chapter 7. However, the task of writing formulas is made much easier if you use the built-in functions of your spreadsheet program. Accordingly, this chapter begins with a survey of the functions typically included in spreadsheet software.

Functions can be grouped into four categories:

1. Statistical functions
2. Financial functions
3. Scientific functions
4. Conditional functions

In addition, there are a number of miscellaneous functions that don't fall into any of these categories and tend to vary with the spreadsheet program.

Some Comments on Functions in General

In order to better understand the ensuing discussion of functions, a few preliminary remarks are in order. Recall that a function responds to data you specify by producing a **value**. Think of a function as a machine that produces an output value in response to one or more input values you provide. This conceptualization of a function is illustrated in Figure 8.1.

Figure 8.1   The operation of a function.

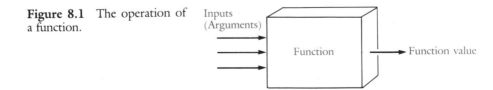

Function Names

Every function has a name. In most spreadsheets, this name is preceded by the symbol @. Some typical function names are @SUM, @COUNT, @INT, @AVG. For the most part, function names are standardized within all spreadsheets. In our discussion, we shall list function names applicable to our sample spreadsheets. However, you should check for name variations if you use a different spreadsheet.

Be careful to check for function name variations in different spreadsheet packages.

Function Arguments

The input values for a function are called **arguments**. For instance, consider the function @SUM(A1,B1,3). This function has three arguments, namely A1, B1, and 3. Note that two of the arguments are cell addresses and one is a number. The value of the function is the sum

[Value in A1] + [Value in A2] + 3

Of course, the value of the function depends on the values stored in cells A1 and A2. For instance, if A1 contains the value 2.3 and A2 the value 4.9, then the value of the function is

2.3 + 4.9 + 3 = 10.2

Most of the functions we shall consider have a numeric value. However, some spreadsheets permit functions with text values. We'll see some examples of such functions later in the chapter.

Functions usually have a numeric value; occasionally, however, a function has a text value.

The function arguments are listed within parentheses after the function name, as in the following examples:

@SUM(A1,A2,3) (This represents three arguments:
   A1, A2, 3)

@INT(B10) (This represents one argument: B10)

@AVG(A1..A10) (This represents one argument: the range
   A1 . . A10)

Many functions allow you to include any number of arguments. An example of such a function is @SUM, which allows you to list any number of cell references, numbers, or ranges to sum up. Other functions allow only a fixed number of arguments, such as @INT(X), which calculates the largest integer less than or equal to the single argument X.

A function argument can be specified in any one of the following ways:

- A numeric data item, such as 12.83.
- A cell reference, such as C18.
- An expression, such as $12*3 + 3/2$.

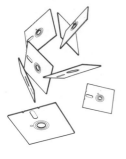

Command Table 8.1 RANGE NAME commands for Lotus 1-2-3, GoldSpread, and SuperCalc 3.

Program	Command	Comments
Lotus 1-2-3 and GoldSpread	/Range Name Enter ⟨range name⟩ in response to prompt. Enter ⟨range⟩ in response to prompt.	Assign name to range of cells. The name may be used in place of formal range designation in functions, such as @SUM and @AVG, which require range arguments.
SuperCalc 3		

- A combination of the above, such as: 3*A1 + 5/A2.
- An expression involving other functions, such as 3*@SUM(A1 . . A10). Functions used within arguments of other functions are said to be **nested**.

In making a function easier to understand, it is often advantageous to use a **named range**, which is simply a range of cells to which you have assigned a name. For example, you might assign to the range A1 . . A10 the name SALES. Using such a name, you can create descriptive functions, such as @SUM(SALES), which is the same as the function @SUM(A1 . . A10). That is, the function value is the sum

[Value of A1] + [Value of A2] + · · · + [Value of A10]

Many spreadsheets provide a NAME RANGE command to assign names to ranges. This is the case with all of our sample spreadsheets, for which the relevant commands are summarized in Command Table 8.1. Note that range names are stored as part of the spreadsheet so that they are available to you in consecutive sessions with the spreadsheet.

Statistical Functions

Statistical functions allow you to calculate some of the most elementary statistical data involving cell contents, namely sums, counts, and averages. Here are some examples of these functions at work:

@AVG(SALES)—Calculates the average of cell values specified in the range named SALES.

@COUNT(A1,A2,A3)—Calculates the number of non-zero numbers among the values in A1, A2, and A3.

@MAX(A1 . . A10)—Calculates the largest among the values in the range A1 . . A10.

@MIN(B1,B2,B3)—Calculates the smallest among the values in B1, B2, B3.

The most common statistical functions are listed in Command Table 8.2.

Financial Functions

Financial functions allow you to calculate numbers associated with financial transactions, especially those dealing with compound interest. These functions are especially useful in designing work-

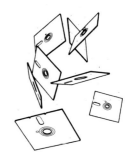

Command Table 8.2 Statistical functions available in Lotus 1-2-3, GoldSpread, and SuperCalc 3.

Program	Command	Comments
Lotus 1-2-3 and GoldSpread	@COUNT(list)	Count number of non-blank, non-label values in cells in list.
	@SUM(list)	Compute sum of cells in list.
	@AVG(list)	Compute average of values in cells of list.
	@MIN(list)	Compute minimum of values in cells of list.
	@MAX(list)	Compute maximum of values in cells of list.
	@STD(list)	Compute standard deviation of set of values given by cells of list. (Use "N" method.)
	@VAR(list)	Compute variance of set of values given by cells of list. (Use "N" method.)
SuperCalc 3	@COUNT(list)	Count number of non-blank, non-label values in cells of list.
	@SUM(list)	Compute number of non-blank, non-label values in cells of list.
	@SUM(list)	Compute sum of cells in list.
	@AVERAGE(list)	Compute average of values in cells of list.
	@MIN(list)	Compute minimum of values in cells of list.
	@MAX(list)	Compute maximum of values in cells of list.

sheets to solve business problems. For instance, the function @PMT allows you to compute the payment for a loan for which you specify the principal, the number of payments, and the interest rate per payment. When this function is used, the value

@PMT(100000, .10/12, 360)

equals the monthly payment on a $100,000 mortgage with an annual interest rate of 10 percent (monthly rate equals .10/12) and lasting 30 years (equals 360 months).

Spreadsheets also include a variety of other financial functions. Some of the most popular functions and their implementations are shown in Command Table 8.3.

Scientific Functions

Scientific functions compute the values of mathematical functions, such as sine, cosine, tangent, exponential, and logarithm. By implementing these functions, you may use spreadsheet programs to solve engineering and other scientific problems. For instance, the value of the trigonometric function SIN(.55) may be calculated as the function value @SIN(.55). The scientific functions available with our sample spreadsheets are listed in Command Table 8.4.

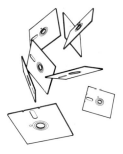

Command Table 8.3 Financial functions available in Lotus 1-2-3, GoldSpread, and SuperCalc 3.

Program	Command	Comments
Lotus 1-2-3 and GoldSpread	@IRR(guess, range)	Internal rate of return.
	@NPV(x, range)	Net present value.
	@FV(pmt, int, term)	Future value of an income stream of payment (*pmt*) with interest rate (*int*) after a period (*term*).
	@PV(pmt, int, term)	Present value of an income stream of payments (*pmt*) with interest rate (*int*) and a period (*term*).
	@PMT(prn, int, term)	The payment on a loan of amount (*prn*) at interest rate (*int*) for a period (*term*).
SuperCalc 3	Same as 1-2-3, except that function names are not preceded by @.	

Command Table 8.4 Scientific functions available in Lotus 1-2-3, GoldSpread and SuperCalc 3.

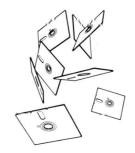

Program	Command	Comments
Lotus 1-2-3 and GoldSpread	@ABS(x)	Compute absolute value of x.
	@ACOS(x)	Compute inverse cosine of x.
	@ASIN(x)	Compute inverse sine of x.
	@ATAN(x)	Compute 2-quadrant arctangent of x.
	@ATAN2(x)	Compute 4-quadrant arctangent of x.
	@COS(x)	Compute cosine of x.
	@EXP(x)	Compute exponential of x.
	@INT(x)	Compute largest integer less than or equal to x
	@LN(X)	Compute natural logarithm of x.
	@LOG(x)	Compute logarithm base 10 of x.
	@MOD(x,y)	Compute remainder when integer x is divided by non-zero integer y.
	@PI	Give value of pi (3.1415926535)
	@RAND	Give random number lying between 0 and 1.
	@ROUND(x,n)	Round x to n decimal places.
	@SIN(x)	Compute sine of x.
	@SQRT(x)	Compute square root of x.
	@TAN(x)	Compute tangent of x.
SuperCalc 3	Same as 1-2-3 except that: 1. @ATAN2 is not supported. 2. The function names must not be preceded by @.	

Section 8.1: Test Your Understanding

1. Explain the calculation performed in response to each of the following functions:

   a) @SUM(A1,A10,A11)

   b) @SUM(4,5,8)

   c) @AVG(3,A1,A1 . . A12)

   d) @COUNT(A1,A2,A3 . . A10)

   e) @MAX(3*A1,15)

  f) @PMT(100 . . 01, 30)

  g) @TAN(A1)

2. Write a formula to calculate the following:

  a) The sum of 100, 105, 107, and 115.

  b) The sum of 3 times A1, 4 times A2, and 7 times A3.

  c) The average of the range SALES.

  d) The monthly payment on a $100,000 mortgage for 30 years at 12% annual interest.

  e) The sum of 5, the contents of B2, and the range PAYMENT.

Hands-on Exercises

1. Make a table of all the functions offered by your spreadsheet program. Test the operation of each function by using it in a formula.

2. Insert the following cell values into your worksheet: A1 = 1, A2 = 2, A3 = 3, . . . , A10 = 10. Now do the following.

  a) Assign the range A1 . . A10 the name NUMBERS.

  b) Insert into B1 a formula to calculate the sum of the range NUMBERS. What value is displayed in B1?

  c) Insert into B2 a formula to calculate the average of the range NUMBERS. What value is displayed in B2?

  d) Insert into B3 a formula to calculate the largest of the numbers in the range NUMBERS. What value is displayed in B3?

  e) Insert into B4 a formula to calculate the smallest of the numbers in the range NUMBERS. What value is displayed in B4?

3. In cell A1, store the amount deposited into a bank account on January 1, 1987. In cell A2, store the interest rate paid on the account (as a decimal). In cell A3, use a function to calculate the amount in the account after five years.

4. Use the same cell contents of A1 and A2 as described in Exercise 3. Make a table of the amounts in the account at the end of years 1, 2, 3, . . . , 10.

5. You are considering buying furniture for your apartment. The interest rate charged on an installment loan is 21 percent. Use a spreadsheet to calculate the amount of furniture you can afford to buy if you can distribute payments over 36 months and you can afford to pay $300 per month on the loan. (Hint:

Set up a table that determines the monthly payments for various loan amounts and choose the largest loan amount that yields payments of less than $300 per month.)

_____

8.2 Conditional Functions

A **conditional function** is a function with a value determined by evaluating a logical expression, such as determining whether two values are equal to each other (say A1 and A2). A variety of conditional functions are included in most spreadsheet programs. This section describes these functions and how they may be applied.

Relational Expressions

In many applications, you see quantities that are compared with one another. For example, in analyzing two mortgage payments, you might make the comparison

838.48 > 649.39

That is, the first quantity is greater than the second. (The symbol > is read "greater than.") Or you might compare the return on an investment, stored in cell A1, to determine if the return is at least 10 percent. This requires the comparison

A1 >= .10

That is, is the contents of cell A1 greater than or equal to .10? (The symbol >= is read "greater than or equal to.") Or you might ask if the inventory of a certain quantity, as stored in cell B11, is 0. This requires the comparison

B11 = 0

That is, is the contents of cell B11 equal to 0?

Each of the three comparisons is stated in terms of a **relational expression**, in which the two quantities being compared are connected by a **relational operator**: >, >=, or =. A relational expression is assigned a value of true or false according to whether the stated comparison is valid or not. For instance, the comparison

838.48 > 649.39

is valid, so the relational expression has the value "true." On the other hand, the comparison

A1 >= .10

is valid for some values of A1 and not for others. If A1 contains 1, then the comparison is valid and the relational expression is true. On the other hand, if A1 contains .005, then the comparison is not valid and the relational expression is false.

You can use a number of relational operators to make comparisons. Here is a list of them:

=	Equal to
>	Greater than
<	Less than
>=	Greater than or equal to
<=	Less than or equal to
<>	Not equal to

Conditional Functions

Conditional functions help you perform "what if" analyses, a critical spreadsheet function.

A conditional function is one that asks a question. For example, many spreadsheets support the function @IF, which asks the question, "What if?" Here is a worksheet entry using @IF:

@IF(A3 > 5, 500, 300)

There are three items within the parentheses. First, the question A3 > 5, which asks whether or not the contents of cell A3 is greater than 5. The second and third items are, respectively, the numbers 500 and 300. In response to such an entry, the spreadsheet program examines the contents of cell A3. If the value is larger than 5, then the value of the formula is set equal to 500. If not, the value of the formula is set equal to 300.

An @IF function possesses three arguments. The first argument is a relational expression, such as A3 > 5 in the above example. The second and third arguments (500 and 300, respectively) are expressions whose values are numeric. If the relational expression is true, then the function value is set equal to the value of the first expression; if the relational expression is false, then the function value is set equal to the value of the second expression.

Here are some other examples of @IF functions:

@IF(3*A1 > B1, 5*A1-11, 3*A1)

A spreadsheet would evaluate this function as follows: If 3*A1 is greater than B1, then the value is 5*A1-11. If 3*A1 is not greater than B1, then the value is 3*A1. So, for example, if A1 is equal to 5 and B1 is equal to 3, then 3 multiplied by 5 equals 15, which is greater than 5. Thus the function has the value

$$5*A1-11 = 5*5-11 = 14$$

If the above function is entered into cell C1, and if A1 and B1 have the values indicated, then the value of C1 displayed is 14.

Using the function @IF, you can describe many of the conditional calculations that arise in applications. For example, consider the calculation of the service fee charged by a bank for the operation of a checking account. A typical fee arrangement is that no fee is charged provided the monthly balance is at least $1,000. Otherwise, the fee is $.20 per check. Suppose you want to calculate the fee charged and store it in cell A1. To do that, you need to provide two relevant pieces of information: the number of checks written (store in cell B1) and the minimum monthly balance (cell C1). The amount of the fee is 0 if

  C1 >= 1000

Otherwise it is

  .20*B1

That is, the amount of the fee is given by the formula

  @IF(C1>=1000, 0, .20*B1)

This is the formula that should be entered into A1 in order to calculate the amount of the fee.

  In addition to @IF, there are a number of other conditional functions that ask questions of various sorts. A summary of some of the most popular conditional functions and how they are implemented on the sample spreadsheets appears in Command Table 8.5.

Section 8.2: Test Your Understanding

1. Suppose that A1 has the value 5 and A2 has the value 1. Determine whether the following relational expressions are true or false.
    a) A1 > A2
    b) 3*A2 > A1
    c) 2*A2 + 3 = A1
    d) A1 >= A2 + 4
    e) A1 <= 5*A2 − 1
    f) A1^2 < A2)

2. Determine the values of the following functions:
    a) @IF(A1>A2, 100, 200)
    b) @IF(3*A2>A1, 100, 200)
    c) @IF(2*A2+ +3=A1, 100, 200)
    d) @IF(A1>=A2+4, 100, 200)
    e) @IF(A1<=5*A2−1, 100, 200)
    f) @IF(A1 2<A2, 100, 200)

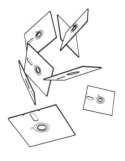

Command Table 8.5   Conditional functions available in Lotus 1-2-3, GoldSpread and SuperCalc 3.

Program	Command	Comments
Lotus 1-2-3 and GoldSpread	@FALSE	Returns the value 9 (false).
	@TRUE	Returns the value 1 (true).
	@IF(cond,x,y)	If condition (*cond*) is true then return the value x; otherwise return the value y.
	@ISNA(x)	Return 1 (true) if the cell address x is NA (not available), that is, it contains no data; return 0 otherwise.
	@ISERR(x)	Return 1 (true) if x equals ERR (error); return 0 otherwise.
SuperCalc 3	IF(cond,x,y)	If the condition *cond* is true then return the value x; otherwise return the value y.
	AND(x,y)	Returns true if both x and y are non-zero, false otherwise.
	OR(x,y)	Returns true if one or both of x,y is non-zero, false otherwise.
	NOT(x)	Returns true if x is zero, false otherwise.
	ISERROR(cell)	Returns ture if contents of cell contain an error, false otherwise.

Hands-on Exercises

1. Write a formula that has the value 0 if A1 is positive and the value 1 if it is otherwise. Use your spreadsheet to evaluate this function if A1 equals -5, 0, 1.

2. Write a formula that has the value 0 if A1 is less than A2 and the value 1,000 if it is otherwise. Use your spreadsheet to evaluate this function if A1 equal 50, A2 equals 100; if A1 equals 100, A2 equals 50.

3. Refer to Section 8.1, Exercise 5. Write a function that equals 0 if the amount of the payments is larger than $300 per month and the amount of the loan is otherwise.

8.3 Applications of Formulas

Now that you have gained some experience in writing formulas, you are ready to use this information to build worksheets to solve typical problems. You might have the impression that spreadsheets can be used to solve only business problems. Nothing is further from the truth. As you will see below, you can use spreadsheets to analyze a number of common personal financial transactions, such as saving for retirement or buying a house or a car.

Even if you're just beginning your career, a spreadsheet can help you analyze your post-retirement financial picture.

Saving for Retirement

One approach to saving for retirement involves setting aside a fixed sum each year and depositing it in a savings account or some other investment that pays interest. Let's use a spreadsheet to analyze this strategy for saving money, and to determine how much money the savings are worth after a certain length of time.

There are two basic variables: the amount to be deposited each year and the rate of interest that the money earns. For simplicity, assume that the rate of interest does not vary over the years. With a view toward varying both the amount of annual savings and the interest rate, store these quantities in cells B1 and B2, respectively. To make the spreadsheet easy to read, label these two constants, as has been done in Figure 8.2. It is a useful

Creating a constants area will help you improve your efficiency in using a spreadsheet program.

Figure 8.2   Saving for retirement.

```
A4:  'YEAR                                                              READY

            A            B           C           D           E           F
 1    AnnSaving    $1,000.00
 2    IntRate          9.00%
 3
 4    YEAR                 1           2           3           4           5
 5    AMOUNT       $1,000.00   $2,090.00   $3,278.10   $4,573.13   $5,984.71
 6
 7    YEAR                 6           7           8           9          10
 8    AMOUNT       $7,523.33   $9,200.43  $11,028.47  $13,021.04  $15,192.93
 9
10    YEAR                11          12          13          14          15
11    AMOUNT      $17,560.29  $20,140.72  $22,953.38  $26,019.19  $29,360.92
12
13    YEAR                16          17          18          19          20
14    AMOUNT      $33,003.40  $36,973.70  $41,301.34  $46,018.46  $51,160.12
15
16    YEAR                21          22          23          24          25
17    AMOUNT      $56,764.53  $62,873.34  $69,531.94  $76,789.81  $84,700.90
18
19    YEAR                26          27          28          29          30
20    AMOUNT      $93,323.98 $102,723.13 $112,968.22 $124,135.36 $136,307.54
20-Jun-86   10:17 AM
```

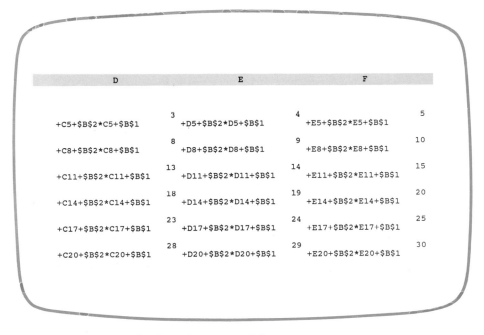

Figure 8.3   Formulas for the retirement worksheet.

technique to accumulate all of the spreadsheet constants in a particular area of the worksheet, called a **constants area**. It is much better to set up a constants area and to refer to the constants as contents of cells rather than to use the values of constants directly in formulas. Indeed, by changing the contents of one cell in the constants area, you can change the value of a particular constant. As we shall see below, this can be a great advantage in analyzing a problem.

Since the spreadsheet is intended to calculate the savings in the account at the end of each year, enter the labels YEAR and AMOUNT in cells A4 and A5, respectively. Across the YEAR row, enter the numbers 1,2,3,. . .,30 to indicate years 1 through 30. In the AMOUNT row, display the amount in the savings account at the end of the given year. This amount is calculated as follows:

Amount at =   Amount at end +   Interest   +   Deposit
end of year   of preceding year   for current
                                                                                    year

For year 1, there is no amount on deposit for the preceding year, so the new amount is just the deposit for the current year, or

   +B1

This is the formula to be entered in B5. For year 2, the amount equals

Amount at   +   Interest +   Deposit for   =   B5+$B$2*B5
end of pre-   current year   +$B$1
ceding year

This is the formula to be entered into cell C5. Note that B2 and B5 are absolute references. That is, in copying this formula, we won't want these references to change; therefore, we we have made them absolute. For the subsequent years, the formula is similar and can be obtained by copying the formula in C5 into the cells D5 . . AE5. The resulting formulas are shown in Figure 8.3.

Once you've designed the spreadsheet, you can use it for analysis. First, set the annual savings amount to $1,000 and the interest rate to .09 (which equals 9 percent). The spreadsheet shows you the build-up of your savings year by year. At the end of the tenth year, your savings are worth $15,192.93. By the end of the thirtieth year, your savings are worth $136,307.54.

By modifying the constants in B1 and B2, you can analyze the effect of different assumptions. For instance, if you raise your annual savings amount to $1,200, the total at the end of 30 years rises to $161,134.61. If the interest rate is lowered to .08, then

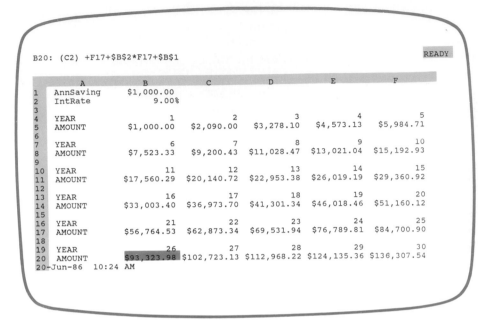

```
B20: (C2) +F17+$B$2*F17+$B$1                                      READY

           A          B          C          D          E          F
 1  AnnSaving     $1,000.00
 2  IntRate           9.00%
 3
 4  YEAR              1          2          3          4          5
 5  AMOUNT      $1,000.00  $2,090.00  $3,278.10  $4,573.13  $5,984.71
 6
 7  YEAR              6          7          8          9         10
 8  AMOUNT      $7,523.33  $9,200.43 $11,028.47 $13,021.04 $15,192.93
 9
10  YEAR             11         12         13         14         15
11  AMOUNT     $17,560.29 $20,140.72 $22,953.38 $26,019.19 $29,360.92
12
13  YEAR             16         17         18         19         20
14  AMOUNT     $33,003.40 $36,973.70 $41,301.34 $46,018.46 $51,160.12
15
16  YEAR             21         22         23         24         25
17  AMOUNT     $56,764.53 $62,873.34 $69,531.94 $76,789.81 $84,700.90
18
19  YEAR             26         27         28         29         30
20  AMOUNT     $93,323.98 $102,723.13 $112,968.22 $124,135.36 $136,307.54
20-Jun-86  10:24 AM
```

(a)

```
B1: (C2) 1200                                                    READY

           A          B          C          D          E          F
 1  AnnSaving     $1,200.00
 2  IntRate           9.00%
 3
 4  YEAR              1          2          3          4          5
 5  AMOUNT      $1,200.00  $2,508.00  $3,933.72  $5,487.75  $7,181.65
 6
 7  YEAR              6          7          8          9         10
 8  AMOUNT      $9,028.00 $11,040.52 $13,234.17 $15,625.24 $18,231.52
 9
10  YEAR             11         12         13         14         15
11  AMOUNT     $21,072.35 $24,168.86 $27,544.06 $31,223.03 $35,233.10
12
13  YEAR             16         17         18         19         20
14  AMOUNT     $39,604.08 $44,368.45 $49,561.61 $55,222.15 $61,392.14
15
16  YEAR             21         22         23         24         25
17  AMOUNT     $68,117.44 $75,448.01 $83,438.33 $92,147.78 $101,641.08
18
19  YEAR             26         27         28         29         30
20  AMOUNT     $111,988.77 $123,267.76 $135,561.86 $148,962.43 $163,569.05
20-Jun-86  10:25 AM
```

(b)

```
B1: (C2) 1000                                                    READY

      A          B           C           D           E           F
1  AnnSaving   $1,000.00
2  IntRate         8.00%
3
4  YEAR            1           2           3           4           5
5  AMOUNT      $1,000.00   $2,080.00   $3,246.40   $4,506.11   $5,866.60
6
7  YEAR            6           7           8           9          10
8  AMOUNT      $7,335.93   $8,922.80  $10,636.63  $12,487.56  $14,486.56
9
10 YEAR           11          12          13          14          15
11 AMOUNT     $16,645.49  $18,977.13  $21,495.30  $24,214.92  $27,152.11
12
13 YEAR           16          17          18          19          20
14 AMOUNT     $30,324.28  $33,750.23  $37,450.24  $41,446.26  $45,761.96
15
16 YEAR           21          22          23          24          25
17 AMOUNT     $50,422.92  $55,456.76  $60,893.30  $66,764.76  $73,105.94
18
19 YEAR           26          27          28          29          30
20 AMOUNT     $79,954.42  $87,350.77  $95,338.83 $103,965.94 $113,283.21
20-Jun-86   10:25 AM
```

(c)

Figure 8.4 Varying the constants in the retirement worksheet. (a) Set the annual savings amount to $1,000 and the interest rate to .09. (b) Modify the constants in cell B1 to $1,200. (c) Set the interest rate to .08 and the annual savings amount to $1,000. Note the effects on total savings.

the total at the end of 30 years is lowered to $113,283.21. Figure 8.4 shows the effects of these modifications on the spreadsheet.

By experimentally varying the constants, you can solve problems. For instance, suppose you wish to retire after 20 years with $1,000,000 in the bank. How much do you need to save each year in order to accumulate this amount? You don't need to know any fancy mathematics to solve this problem. Just experiment with assorted values for the annual savings rate to achieve the desired 20-year total. It is clear that $1,000 a year is not enough. So experimentally raise the amount to $2,000, $3,000, and so forth, until you achieve the $1,000,000 after 20 years. Figure 8.5 shows you some of the experimental values and the results. Note that the $1,000,000 goal can be achieved with annual deposits of $7,400.

Analyzing a Car Loan

At different points in your life, you might want to borrow money to make important purchases, such as a car or a house. Many mathematical problems arise in connection with such loans: What is the monthly payment to repay a particular loan? How much can you afford to borrow if you can make monthly payments of $550?

A spreadsheet can help you analyze the interest and payment options for a car loan, so you will know when you're getting the best deal on your purchase.

```
B1: (C2) 3000                                                    READY

        A            B            C            D            E            F
1   AnnSaving    $3,000.00
2   IntRate          9.00%
3
4   YEAR             1            2            3            4            5
5   AMOUNT       $3,000.00    $6,270.00    $9,834.30   $13,719.39   $17,954.13
6
7   YEAR             6            7            8            9           10
8   AMOUNT      $22,570.00   $27,601.30   $33,085.42   $39,063.11   $45,578.79
9
10  YEAR            11           12           13           14           15
11  AMOUNT      $52,680.88   $60,422.16   $68,860.15   $78,057.57   $88,082.75
12
13  YEAR            16           17           18           19           20
14  AMOUNT      $99,010.20  $110,921.11  $123,904.01  $138,055.38  $153,480.36
15
16  YEAR            21           22           23           24           25
17  AMOUNT     $170,293.59  $188,620.01  $208,595.82  $230,369.44  $254,102.69
18
19  YEAR            26           27           28           29           30
20  AMOUNT     $279,971.93  $308,169.40  $338,904.65  $372,406.07  $408,922.62
20-Jun-86   10:26 AM
```

(a)

```
B1: (C2) 5000                                                    READY

        A            B            C            D            E            F
1   AnnSaving    $5,000.00
2   IntRate          9.00%
3
4   YEAR             1            2            3            4            5
5   AMOUNT       $5,000.00   $10,450.00   $16,390.50   $22,865.65   $29,923.55
6
7   YEAR             6            7            8            9           10
8   AMOUNT      $37,616.67   $46,002.17   $55,142.37   $65,105.18   $75,964.65
9
10  YEAR            11           12           13           14           15
11  AMOUNT      $87,801.47  $100,703.60  $114,766.92  $130,095.95  $146,804.58
12
13  YEAR            16           17           18           19           20
14  AMOUNT     $165,016.99  $184,868.52  $206,506.69  $230,092.29  $255,800.60
15
16  YEAR            21           22           23           24           25
17  AMOUNT     $283,822.65  $314,366.69  $347,659.69  $383,949.07  $423,504.48
18
19  YEAR            26           27           28           29           30
20  AMOUNT     $466,619.88  $513,615.67  $564,841.08  $620,676.78  $681,537.69
20-Jun-86   10:26 AM
```

(b)

Figure 8.5 Achieving a $1,000,000 retirement fund in 20 years. Modify the constants in cell B1 to (a) $3,000, (b) $5,000, and (c) $7,000. (d) Your goal of $1,000,000 can be achieved by saving $7,400 per year.

B1: (C2) 7000   READY

	A	B	C	D	E	F
1	AnnSaving	$7,000.00				
2	IntRate	9.00%				
3						
4	YEAR	1	2	3	4	5
5	AMOUNT	$7,000.00	$14,630.00	$22,946.70	$32,011.90	$41,892.97
6						
7	YEAR	6	7	8	9	10
8	AMOUNT	$52,663.34	$64,403.04	$77,199.32	$91,147.26	$106,350.51
9						
10	YEAR	11	12	13	14	15
11	AMOUNT	$122,922.05	$140,985.04	$160,673.69	$182,134.32	$205,526.41
12						
13	YEAR	16	17	18	19	20
14	AMOUNT	$231,023.79	$258,815.93	$289,109.37	$322,129.21	$358,120.84
15						
16	YEAR	21	22	23	24	25
17	AMOUNT	$397,351.71	$440,113.37	$486,723.57	$537,528.69	$592,906.27
18						
19	YEAR	26	27	28	29	30
20	AMOUNT	$653,267.84	$719,061.94	$790,777.52	$868,947.50	$954,152.77

20-Jun-86   10:31 AM

(c)

A4: (T) [W10] 'YEAR   READY

	A	B	C	D	E	F
1	AnnSaving	$7,400.00				
2	IntRate	9.00%				
3						
4	YEAR	1	2	3	4	5
5	AMOUNT	$7,400.00	$15,466.00	$24,257.94	$33,841.15	$44,286.86
6						
7	YEAR	6	7	8	9	10
8	AMOUNT	$55,672.68	$68,083.22	$81,610.71	$96,355.67	$112,427.68
9						
10	YEAR	11	12	13	14	15
11	AMOUNT	$129,946.17	$149,041.33	$169,855.05	$192,542.00	$217,270.78
12						
13	YEAR	16	17	18	19	20
14	AMOUNT	$244,225.15	$273,605.41	$305,629.90	$340,536.59	$378,584.89
15						
16	YEAR	21	22	23	24	25
17	AMOUNT	$420,057.53	$465,262.70	$514,536.35	$568,244.62	$626,786.63
18						
19	YEAR	26	27	28	29	30
20	AMOUNT	$690,597.43	$760,151.20	$835,964.81	$918,601.64	$1,008,675.79

20-Jun-86   10:34 AM

(d)

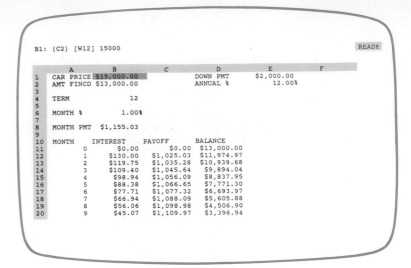

Figure 8.6 A car loan worksheet.

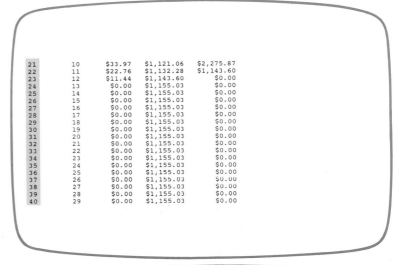

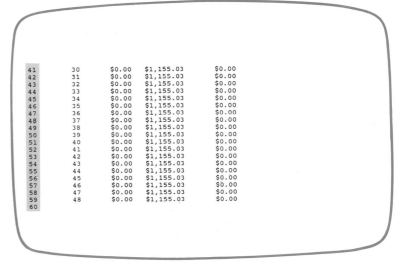

What is the effect on the monthly payment of raising the interest rate one-half percentage? What is the effect on the monthly payment of increasing the length of the loan by a year? How much of this month's payment goes for interest and how much to pay off the loan? Questions such as these can be easily answered using a spreadsheet. We will design two worksheets to analyze various aspects of a loan. The first worksheet will analyze a car loan month by month and track the payments, interest, and loan balance.

The process of paying off a loan is called **amortization**. A table that shows the sequence of balances as the loan is being paid off is called an **amortization table**. The worksheet we construct will contain an amortization table for a car loan with a repayment period not exceeding 48 months.

A car loan is affected by the following numbers:

- The price of the car.
- The down payment.
- The length of the loan (in months).
- The interest rate on the loan (expressed as an annual percentage).

These values are best specified in a constants area of the worksheet so that they may be easily changed to analyze the effect of, say, varying the price of the car, the amount of down payment, or the interest rate.

From the values listed in the constants area, the worksheet will use the function @PMT to determine the amount of the monthly payment. Moreover, the worksheet constructs an amortization table that shows, for each month, the amount of the payment applied to interest, the amount to pay off the loan, and the balance of the loan. Figure 8.6 shows a sample worksheet. The user-supplied numeric data are contained in a constants area indicated by darker color; the worksheet headings are indicated by lighter color. The unhighlighted entries are computed by the spreadsheet from formulas.

To construct the worksheet, begin by entering the titles for the rows and columns in the worksheet, a straightforward task that you should feel comfortable with by now. The amounts for the price of the car, down payment, interest rate, and term (in months) are all filled in by the user. However, in constructing the worksheet, you should format these cells so that the user is presented with data in the most convenient format. The price of the car, the down payment, and the amount financed are formatted as currency, the term as a fixed place number with zero decimal places, and the interest rate as a percent.

The amount financed (AMT FINCD) is the difference between the price of the car and the down payment. Note that the user must enter the annual interest rate (ANNUAL %) as a decimal. For example, a 12 percent annual interest rate must be entered as .12. This rate is displayed as 12 percent. The worksheet computes the monthly interest rate, which is needed for the various computations, by dividing the annual interest rate by 12. The monthly interest rate is also formatted on the worksheet as a percent.

To compute the monthly payment and the monthly balances, it is simplest to use the built-in financial function @PMT. @PMT allows you to compute the payment required for a loan of amount A, with periodic interest rate I and a term of N periods. In our case, the period is a month, the amount of the loan is given in cell B2, the periodic (monthly) interest rate is given in cell B6 and the number of periods is given in cell B4. With this information, the monthly payment may be computed by the function

@PMT(B2,B6,B4)

To compute the monthly loan summary rows, enter the month numbers down column 1. This can be done one at a time or by using a formula, if you are clever (see the Hands-on Exercises in Section 8.3). The worksheet displays months 1 to 48. If you wish to analyze loans lasting more than 48 months, you may extend the worksheet accordingly. The interest for a particular month is computed by using the formula

Interest =   Balance for   *   Monthly
            preceding month   interest rate

The payoff for a month is calculated as

Payoff =   Interest   − Monthly
          for month   payment

The balance for a month is calculated as

Balance = Previous balance − Payoff

if this number is non-negative. Otherwise it equals zero.

This twofold calculation is necessary to avoid recording negative balances. Once the balance reaches zero (when the loan is paid off), the balance for all future months should read zero. The calculation for the balance can be calculated by using the function @MAX:

Balance = @MAX (previous balance − payoff, 0)

It is convenient to enter the initial loan status in a row labeled MONTH 0. For this month, the balance is the amount financed, and there is no interest and no payoff.

```
A9: (T) [W12]                                              READY

        A                  B            C             D
1   CAR PRICE              25000                  DOWN PMT
2   AMT FINCD     +B1-E1                           ANNUAL %
3
4   TERM                    24
5
6   MONTH %       +E2/12
7
8   MONTH PMT     @PMT(B2,B6,B4)
9
10  MONTH         INTEREST            PAYOFF        BALANCE
11         0                     0              0  +B2
12         1  +$B$6*D11          +$B$8-B12         @MAX(D11-C12,0)
13         2  +$B$6*D12          +$B$8-B13         @MAX(D12-C13,0)
14         3  +$B$6*D13          +$B$8-B14         @MAX(D13-C14,0)
15         4  +$B$6*D14          +$B$8-B15         @MAX(D14-C15,0)
16         5  +$B$6*D15          +$B$8-B16         @MAX(D15-C16,0)
17         6  +$B$6*D16          +$B$8-B17         @MAX(D16-C17,0)
18         7  +$B$6*D17          +$B$8-B18         @MAX(D17-C18,0)
19         8  +$B$6*D18          +$B$8-B19         @MAX(D18-C19,0)
20         9  +$B$6*D19          +$B$8-B20         @MAX(D19-C20,0)
20-Jun-86   10:44 AM
```

Figure 8.7   The formulas for the car loan worksheet.

The formulas for the car-loan worksheet are listed in Figure 8.7. The car-loan worksheet may be used in a number of ways. In the simplest application, you may use it to produce an amortization table for the loan. For instance, Figure 8.8 shows the worksheet for a $12,000 car with a $2,000 down payment, financed at 12 percent for 36 months. You can also use the car loan amortization table to determine the interest paid during any loan period. This can be useful in filling out your income tax return, where interest paid during the year can be used as a tax deduction. You may also use the amortization table to determine the balance on the loan at the end of any particular month. You might find that helpful if you want to consider trading the car in for a later model. By consulting the amortization table, you can determine how much cash from your trade-in can be applied to your new car and how much must go to pay off the loan.

Shopping for a House

A mortgage is a loan used to buy real estate, such as a house. The mortgage is paid off in equal monthly installments for a certain number of years, usually 15, 25, or 30. The payments are part interest and part principal. Although the interest rate is quoted as an annual rate, it is actually computed monthly at one-twelfth of

A spreadsheet can be a crucial tool when analyzing a home mortgage or other real estate transactions.

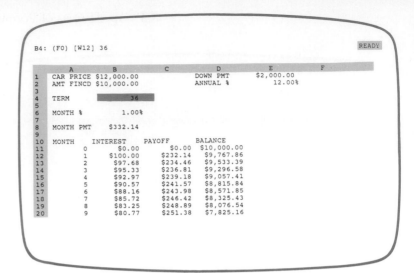

Figure 8.8 An example of an amortization table for a car loan.

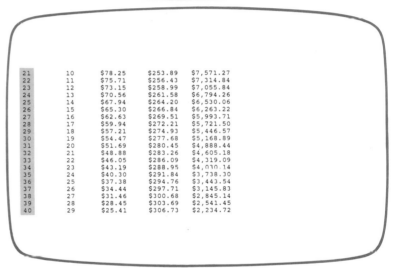

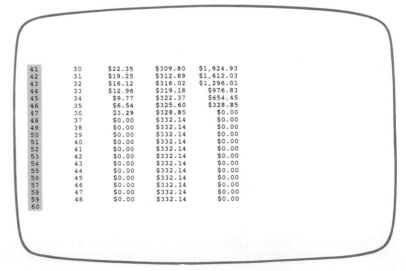

```
A7: (C2) +B2                                                           READY

       A             B            C           D           E           F
 1   IntRate           9.00%
 2   Amount       $100,000.00
 3   Length(Yrs)        30
 4
 5   Percent          9.00%       9.25%       9.50%       9.75%      10.00%
 6   Amount
 7   $100,000.00    $804.62     $822.68     $840.85     $859.15     $877.57
 8   $101,000.00    $812.67     $830.90     $849.26     $867.75     $886.35
 9   $102,000.00    $820.72     $839.13     $857.67     $876.34     $895.12
10   $103,000.00    $828.76     $847.36     $866.08     $884.93     $903.90
11   $104,000.00    $836.81     $855.58     $874.49     $893.52     $912.67
12   $105,000.00    $844.85     $863.81     $882.90     $902.11     $921.45
13   $106,000.00    $852.90     $872.04     $891.31     $910.70     $930.23
14   $107,000.00    $860.95     $880.26     $899.71     $919.30     $939.00
15   $108,000.00    $868.99     $888.49     $908.12     $927.89     $947.78
16   $109,000.00    $877.04     $896.72     $916.53     $936.48     $956.55
17   $110,000.00    $885.08     $904.94     $924.94     $945.07     $965.33
18   $111,000.00    $893.13     $913.17     $933.35     $953.66     $974.10
19   $112,000.00    $901.18     $921.40     $941.76     $962.25     $982.88
20   $113,000.00    $909.22     $929.62     $950.17     $970.84     $991.66
20-Jun-86   09:55 AM
```

Figure 8.9   A table of monthly mortgage payments.

the annual rate. For example, if a mortgage has a 12 percent annual rate, then 1 percent interest is charged on the loan's outstanding balance each month. The interest is added to the amount owed and the monthly payment is deducted.

An amortization table is not the only table of interest in connection with home mortgages. In shopping for a house, one of the key factors to consider is the size of the monthly mortgage payment. You can estimate the monthly payment by using a table like the one shown in Figure 8.9, which gives the monthly mortgage payments for a selection of five interest rates and 14 mortgage amounts.

To use your spreadsheet program to analyze a mortgage, specify the first interest rate in the constants area of the worksheet. The other rates are computed by successively adding one-quarter percent. Then specify the first mortgage amount. The other mortgage amounts are computed by successively adding $2,000 amounts. The table entries give the monthly payment for a mortgage of the given amount at the particular interest rate. The @PMT function discussed in Section 8.2 is used to compute these entries.

Figure 8.10 shows the formulas for the mortgage worksheet. Exercising all the concepts you've learned on spreadsheets, determine an efficient scheme for entering this worksheet. By judiciously

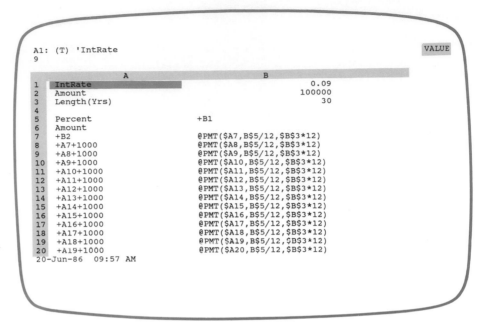

```
A1: (T) 'IntRate                                              VALUE
9
                    A                              B
1    IntRate                                      0.09
2    Amount                                     100000
3    Length(Yrs)                                   30
4
5    Percent                  +B1
6    Amount
7    +B2                      @PMT($A7,B$5/12,$B$3*12)
8    +A7+1000                 @PMT($A8,B$5/12,$B$3*12)
9    +A8+1000                 @PMT($A9,B$5/12,$B$3*12)
10   +A9+1000                 @PMT($A10,B$5/12,$B$3*12)
11   +A10+1000                @PMT($A11,B$5/12,$B$3*12)
12   +A11+1000                @PMT($A12,B$5/12,$B$3*12)
13   +A12+1000                @PMT($A13,B$5/12,$B$3*12)
14   +A13+1000                @PMT($A14,B$5/12,$B$3*12)
15   +A14+1000                @PMT($A15,B$5/12,$B$3*12)
16   +A15+1000                @PMT($A16,B$5/12,$B$3*12)
17   +A16+1000                @PMT($A17,B$5/12,$B$3*12)
18   +A17+1000                @PMT($A18,B$5/12,$B$3*12)
19   +A18+1000                @PMT($A19,B$5/12,$B$3*12)
20   +A19+1000                @PMT($A20,B$5/12,$B$3*12)
20-Jun-86   09:57 AM
```

(a)

```
                    C                              D

     +B5+0.0025                 +C5+0.0025

     @PMT($A7,C$5/12,$B$3*12)    @PMT($A7,D$5/12,$B$3*12)
     @PMT($A8,C$5/12,$B$3*12)    @PMT($A8,D$5/12,$B$3*12)
     @PMT($A9,C$5/12,$B$3*12)    @PMT($A9,D$5/12,$B$3*12)
     @PMT($A10,C$5/12,$B$3*12)   @PMT($A10,D$5/12,$B$3*12)
     @PMT($A11,C$5/12,$B$3*12)   @PMT($A11,D$5/12,$B$3*12)
     @PMT($A12,C$5/12,$B$3*12)   @PMT($A12,D$5/12,$B$3*12)
     @PMT($A13,C$5/12,$B$3*12)   @PMT($A13,D$5/12,$B$3*12)
     @PMT($A14,C$5/12,$B$3*12)   @PMT($A14,D$5/12,$B$3*12)
     @PMT($A15,C$5/12,$B$3*12)   @PMT($A15,D$5/12,$B$3*12)
     @PMT($A16,C$5/12,$B$3*12)   @PMT($A16,D$5/12,$B$3*12)
     @PMT($A17,C$5/12,$B$3*12)   @PMT($A17,D$5/12,$B$3*12)
     @PMT($A18,C$5/12,$B$3*12)   @PMT($A18,D$5/12,$B$3*12)
     @PMT($A19,C$5/12,$B$3*12)   @PMT($A19,D$5/12,$B$3*12)
     @PMT($A20,C$5/12,$B$3*12)   @PMT($A20,D$5/12,$B$3*12)
```

(b)

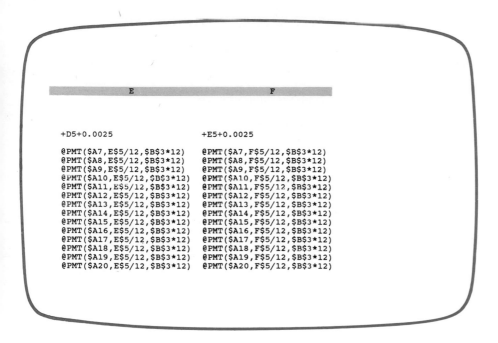

```
         E                      F

+D5+0.0025              +E5+0.0025

@PMT($A7,E$5/12,$B$3*12)    @PMT($A7,F$5/12,$B$3*12)
@PMT($A8,E$5/12,$B$3*12)    @PMT($A8,F$5/12,$B$3*12)
@PMT($A9,E$5/12,$B$3*12)    @PMT($A9,F$5/12,$B$3*12)
@PMT($A10,E$5/12,$B$3*12)   @PMT($A10,F$5/12,$B$3*12)
@PMT($A11,E$5/12,$B$3*12)   @PMT($A11,F$5/12,$B$3*12)
@PMT($A12,E$5/12,$B$3*12)   @PMT($A12,F$5/12,$B$3*12)
@PMT($A13,E$5/12,$B$3*12)   @PMT($A13,F$5/12,$B$3*12)
@PMT($A14,E$5/12,$B$3*12)   @PMT($A14,F$5/12,$B$3*12)
@PMT($A15,E$5/12,$B$3*12)   @PMT($A15,F$5/12,$B$3*12)
@PMT($A16,E$5/12,$B$3*12)   @PMT($A16,F$5/12,$B$3*12)
@PMT($A17,E$5/12,$B$3*12)   @PMT($A17,F$5/12,$B$3*12)
@PMT($A18,E$5/12,$B$3*12)   @PMT($A18,F$5/12,$B$3*12)
@PMT($A19,E$5/12,$B$3*12)   @PMT($A19,F$5/12,$B$3*12)
@PMT($A20,E$5/12,$B$3*12)   @PMT($A20,F$5/12,$B$3*12)
```

(c)

Figure 8.10   The formulas for the mortgage worksheet.

using the COPY command, you can enter the formulas by using very few keystrokes. The key to entering the formulas efficiently is to use the COPY command on the formulas involving the function @PMT. Creating a scheme for entering the data is a good test of your mastery of the COPY command.

Computing Social Security Taxes

You may use a spreadsheet to maintain payroll records and to calculate payroll deductions, such as those for social security taxes, federal and state income taxes, and so forth. In order to calculate deductions, you must be able to write formulas that describe the calculations. As an example, consider the problem of computing payroll deductions for social security taxes.

In 1986, social security taxes were levied at the rate of 7.15 percent on the first $39,600 of income. Computing the tax on a paycheck involves both the amount of current gross earnings (before any deductions) and the total of all previous gross earnings for the current year. For simplicity, assume that the total of all previous gross earnings this year is stored in cell A1 and that the current gross earnings are stored in cell A2. In terms of the values stored in these two cells, try to write a formula for computing the amount

A spreadsheet is a vital tool for employers to use in calculating taxes, payroll deductions, and employee benefit costs.

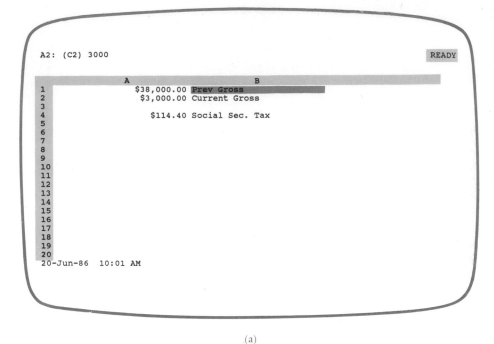

(a)

(b)

Figure 8.11   Computing the social security deduction.

of social security taxes to be deducted. Develop this formula in several steps.

The total amount of gross earnings this year (including the current earnings) is $+A1+A2$. The portion of this on which no taxes are paid is the amount over \$39,600. This amount is calculated as the larger of

$+A1+A2-39600$ or 0

That is, the amount on which no taxes are paid is given by

@MAX(A1+A2−39600,0)

The amount of current earnings that are taxed is given by

$+A2-$@MAX(A1+A2−39600,0)

and the amount of social security taxes is 7.15 percent of this amount, namely

.0715*(A2−@MAX(A1+A2−39600,0))

This is the formula that must be used in the worksheet to correctly compute the social security tax. (See Figure 8.11.)

Computing Income Taxes

Most states and some cities have income taxes. Computing the amount of these taxes poses another interesting problem in developing spreadsheet formulas. As an illustration, consider an income tax that is 2 percent on the first \$10,000 of income, 3 percent on the next \$10,000, and 4 percent on amounts over \$20,000. You need to develop a formula for computing this tax. Suppose that the income to be taxed is stored in cell A1. This is the constants area for the worksheet.

It seems reasonable to compute the tax separately for each of the different percentages and to add the results, so store the results for the 2 percent tax in cell D1, the 3 percent tax in cell D2, the 4 percent tax in cell D3, and the total tax in cell D4. D4 will then contain the formula

@SUM(D1 . . D3)

Now develop the formulas to insert into cells D1 . . D3. The amount subjected to the 2 percent tax is

B1, if B1 is \$10,000 or less

\$10,000, if B1 is more than \$10,000

This amount is computed by the formula

@MIN(B1,10000)

and the 2 percent tax is given by the formula

.02*@MIN(B1,5000)

A spreadsheet can help you accurately calculate your state and federal income taxes.

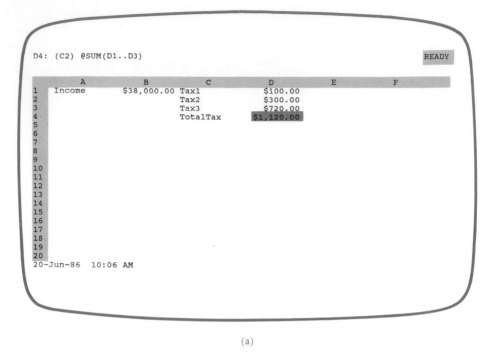

```
D4: (C2) @SUM(D1..D3)                                              READY

         A           B          C            D           E           F
 1  Income        $38,000.00  Tax1          $100.00
 2                            Tax2          $300.00
 3                            Tax3          $720.00
 4                            TotalTax    $1,120.00
 5
 6
 7
 8
 9
10
11
12
13
14
15
16
17
18
19
20
20-Jun-86   10:06 AM
```

(a)

```
B1: (T) 38000                                                     READY

         A           B          C                    D
 1  Income        38000      Tax1       0.02*@MIN(B1,5000)
 2                           Tax2       0.03*@MIN(@MAX(B1-10000,0),10000)
 3                           Tax3       0.04*@MAX(0,B1-20000)
 4                           TotalTax   @SUM(D1..D3)
 5
 6
 7
 8
 9
10
11
12
13
14
15
16
17
18
19
20
20-Jun-86   10:07 AM
```

(b)

Figure 8.12 Computing income taxes.

This is the formula that should be inserted into cell D1. (See Figure 8.12.)

The amount subjected to the 3 percent tax is

0, if B1 is less than $10,000

B1-10000, if B1 is between $10,000 and $20,000

$10,000, if B1 is more than $20,000

The formula

@MAX(B1-10000)

equals B1-10000, if B1 is more than $10,000, and 0 otherwise, which fulfills the first two requirements. You must modify this formula so that if B1-10000 is more than 10000 (B1 is more than $20,000) then the formula yields 10000 rather than B1-10000. This adjustment is accomplished with the formula

@MIN(@MAX(B1-10000), 10000)

and the amount of the 3 percent tax may be computed by using the formula

.03*@MIN(@MAX(B1-10000), 10000)

This formula should be inserted into cell D2. (Refer again to Figure 8.12.) The amount subject to the 4 percent tax is

0, if B1 is $20,000 or less

B1-20000, if B1 is greater than $20,000

This amount may be computed by the formula

@MAX(0,B1-20000)

and the amount of the 4 percent tax equals

.04*@MAX(0,B1-20000)

This formula should go into cell D3.

The procedure just outlined is typical of the way in which complex calculations are described on a worksheet.

Section 8.3: Test Your Understanding

1. Describe how a college registrar might use a spreadsheet program to keep track of the registration of students per quarter and the number of academic credits for which each student is registered.

2. Define amortization.

3. In a certain state, unemployment compensation is paid for by a tax on business payroll equal to 1.8 percent of the first $7,000 of an employee's income. Write a formula to compute the tax corresponding to a single employee.

4. In a certain state, the income tax is 0 on the first $5,000, 2 percent on the next $5,000, 3 percent on the next $5,000, and 4 percent on any remaining amount. Write a formula that computes this tax.

Hands-on Exercises

1. Enter the retirement savings worksheet described in Section 8.3 of the text. To the nearest $1,000, what annual contribution must be made at 9 percent interest to accumulate $500,000 after 20 years?

   a) What will be the total accumulation in the retirement savings account if $1,500 per year is deposited at 11 percent interest?

   b) Now assume that you would like to retire after 20 years and live off the interest earned by the account. How much interest will the account earn per year?

   c) Modify the retirement savings account worksheet to reflect deposits made every three months. How much is in the account after 20 years if $250 is deposited every three months at 9 percent interest? Compare this with the amount generated by depositing $1,000 annually at the same interest rate.

2. Enter the car-loan worksheet described in Section 8.3 of the text.

   a) Determine the monthly payment for a car costing $11,000 with a down payment of $3,500 and a 13 percent car loan. In what month does the loan balance first reach $5,000?

   b) The total amount of loan interest you pay in a year is deductible for federal income tax purposes. Modify the car-loan worksheet so that it computes your total interest payments for months 1 through 12, 13 through 24, and so forth.

3. Enter the mortgage payment comparison worksheet.

   a) Suppose that you are looking at houses priced at $100,000 and are shopping for a 90 percent loan. What will be your monthly mortgage payments if the interest rate is 11 percent? 11.25 percent? 11.5 percent?

b) Modify the mortgage comparison worksheet so that it gives payments as the interest rates vary by one-eighth percent and the mortgage amounts vary by $1,000.

KEY TERMS

value	statistical function	relational operator
argument	financial function	constants area
nested function	scientific function	amortization
named range	conditional function	amortization table
range name	relational expression	

CHAPTER REVIEW QUESTIONS

1. Give an example of a financial function. Provide an application in which the function can be used.

2. Give an example of a scientific function. Provide an application in which the function can be used.

3. Give an example of a statistical function. Provide an application in which the function can be used.

4. Give an example of a conditional function. Provide an application in which the function can be used.

5. List the options for specifying a function argument.

6. Explain the advantage of using named ranges as function arguments.

7. Give an example of a function that can have any number of arguments.

8. Give an example of a function that can have a range as an argument.

9. Give an example of a function for which a range argument would not make sense.

10. Give an example of a function for which multiple arguments would not make sense.

DISCUSSION QUESTIONS

1. To what extent does the collection of built-in functions set limitations on the worksheets you can design using a spreadsheet program?

2. What type of features can be built into worksheets if you are using conditional functions?

APPLICATION PROJECTS

1. The plant manager of Freidman Manufacturing Company's Lincoln, Nebraska, plant is preparing her 1987 production budget. The Lincoln plant assembles video cassette recorders. Some of the manufacturing costs vary directly with production volume, while others remain relatively constant from month to month. Estimated production costs for 1987 are as follows:

Variable Production Costs (per unit produced)	
Materials	$160.00
Direct labor	25.00
Employee benefits	10.00
Plant utilities	2.50
Manufacturing supplies	.75

Fixed Production Costs (per month)	
Supervisors' salaries	$11,500
Property taxes	1,500
Insurance	1,000
Depreciation—machinery	2,500
Rent—factory building	3,750
Maintenance	1,250

Production is expected to remain constant at 1,000 units per month for January through September. Based on an anticipated surge in demand, production is expected to increase at the rate of 10 percent per month for October through December.

a) Set up a spreadsheet with the titles illustrated in Figure 8.13.

b) Prepare a production budget for each month of 1988. Include totals for the year, as shown in Figure 8.13.

c) Freidman's management is negotiating a new contract with the labor union representing the plant's employees. The new contract will probably become effective on May 1, 1988, and is expected to result in a 15 percent increase in direct labor costs and employee benefits. Modify the spreadsheet to reflect this anticipated change.

d) Refer to the original data. Because of uncertainty in the market for video cassette recorders, management has requested supplemental budgets at the following monthly production levels, for each month from January through December:

  1,000 units per month
  1,750 units per month
  750 units per month
  500 units per month

Prepare spreadsheets for each production level.

2. A spreadsheet can be easily used to find the value of a U.S. Treasury bond, which is a debt obligation of the federal government, and its true yield. A bond is originally sold

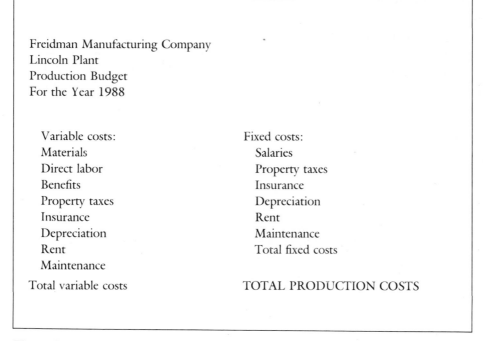

Freidman Manufacturing Company
Lincoln Plant
Production Budget
For the Year 1988

Variable costs:	Fixed costs:
Materials	Salaries
Direct labor	Property taxes
Benefits	Insurance
Property taxes	Depreciation
Insurance	Rent
Depreciation	Maintenance
Rent	Total fixed costs
Maintenance	
Total variable costs	TOTAL PRODUCTION COSTS

Figure 8.13   Freidman Manufacturing Company's production budget.

near its par value of $1,000 and pays a yearly interest amount stated by the bond coupon rate (i.e., a $1,000 par bond with a 10 percent coupon will pay $100 per year in interest). When the bond matures it pays the holder the par value of $1,000. The value of a bond is a function of four variables: the par value, the coupon interest rate, the time to maturity, and the "market" interest rate. The market interest rate, reflecting what an investor is willing to pay for the bond, changes daily in reaction to economic conditions.

a) Create a spreadsheet entitled Values of Treasury Bonds. The second line of the title should read Market Interest Rate—. Insert a market interest rate of .08 in the cell following the dash. Complete the table with the following column headings: *MA-TURITY, COUPON %, PAR, THEORETICAL VALUE, MARKET PRICE,* and *YIELD.*

Enter the following data for the five bonds in your portfolio:

Maturity Date	Coupon	Par	Market Price
1991	8.0%	$1000	$1010
1995	12.0%	1000	1220
1997	10.5%	1000	1142
2001	7.75%	1000	910
2010	8.5%	1000	985

To the right of the spreadsheet beginning in Column H, model the cash flow each bond produces (i.e., the interest payments and par value at maturity), assuming that each one matures on today's date in the year indicated. In the last year, include both the interest payment and par value as one payment. It may help to title each column with the appropriate year. (Lotus 1-2-3 provides a function to do this easily.) To calculate the theoretical value for each bond, use the @NPV (net present value) function, inserting the market interest rate for "int."

Use the @IRR (internal rate of return) function to calculate the yield of the bond, assuming you purchase it for today's market price. To calculate the IRR, you need to insert in Column G the market price of the bond with a negative sign attached, which indicates that you paid the market price for the bond today. The range begins in Column G and extends to the last receipt of interest and principal. The @IRR function asks for a "guess" about the rate of return; in each case insert the market rate of interest.

b) Assume the market interest rate changes to .075 tomorrow. What is the theoretical value of each bond? (If you have set up your spreadsheet properly, you will only need to enter the new interest rate in one location and all bond values will change.)

c) Save the worksheet in a file called BONDS and print the body of the table, excluding the ranges used to calculate NPV and IRR.

The Microcomputer Revolution

In the early 1970s, microcomputing was enjoyed almost exclusively by hobbyists, computer "jocks" who usually had some experience with mainframes or minicomputers and who were fascinated by the possibilities of computers. Hobbyists dabbled in the new technology by purchasing kits, like the ALTAIR (shown here), from which they could construct their own micros. (The Computer Museum, Boston, Massachusetts)

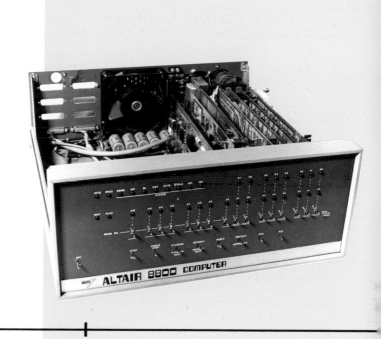

1970

Some visionary computer scientists who foresaw a market need for personal computers took micros a step further. Programmers had long played an important role in computing; for example, in the early 1960s John Kemeny and Thomas Kurtz had invented the BASIC (Beginners All-purpose Symbolic Instruction Code) language for mainframes. In the mid-1970s, Bill Gates , a young program developer, took BASIC into another market by structuring the language for use on microcomputers. (Courtesy of NEXT, bottom right photo; From Michael Trombetta, BASIC FOR STUDENTS USING THE IBM PC, Addison-Wesley Publishing Company, Inc. 1986, page 369.)

In the mid-1970s, upstart hardware and software developers caught the fever created by the potential of microcomputers. In 1977, Steven Jobs and Steven Wozniak assembled their first micro in Wozniak's parents' garage and marketed it under the logo of their newly-formed Apple Computer Company. (Diana Walker/Gamma-Liaison, top left photo; Courtesy of Apple Computer, Inc.)

1975

The Apple was easy and fun to use, and quickly captured a devoted audience. This popularity led to development of a wealth of application programs, such as the VisiCalc spreadsheet program, developed by Bob Frankston and Daniel Bricklin. (Darlene Bordwell, bottom left photo; The Computer Museum, Boston, Massachusetts)

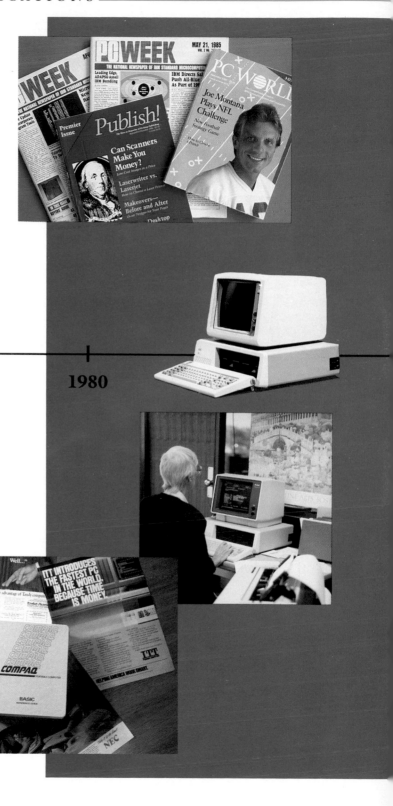

Throughout the '70s and into the '80s, microcomputer users shared programs and demanded more from software developers—creating new markets, new industries, new jobs, and an ever-wider microcomputing audience. (Darlene Bordwell)

1980

IBM broke new ground in the micro industry by focusing its efforts on businesses, helping to create the automated office of the '80s. (Courtesy of International Business Machines Corporation; Darlene Bordwell, bottom photo)

Within the business market, the IBM PC quickly became the standard for other manufacturers to emulate. (Darlene Bordwell)

In the mid-1980s, the growing number of microcomputer users demanded more business-oriented application programs. With microcomputers finding their way into all levels of industry, education, and research, the trend toward increasingly more useful and more powerful software packages is likely to continue well into the 1990s. (Darlene Bordwell, two photos at top; Courtesy of International Business Machines Corporation; Courtesy of Hewlett-Packard Corporation, bottom right photo)

1985

1990's

9 Advanced Spreadsheet Topics

Counting on Spreadsheets to Do the Job

The first census of the American people was accomplished in 1790—entirely on horseback. Now that there are millions more of us to count, the job is staggering. Thousands of field workers must travel by boat, car, mule and plane to reach everyone, at a current cost of $800 million.

Like many private organizations, the U.S. Bureau of the Census has turned to computers to handle much of the burden of its work. Most of this work is so massive, it must be done on large mainframe computers. But much of the day-to-day administrative work of the bureau is now done on microcomputers.

Eugene George, a bureau budget analyst, calculates budget projections for 11 of the bureau's 37 divisions. "Ninety-two percent of what I do involves numbers," George says. He issues monthly internal reports on current spending, to make sure no division is overspending its budget. Large items in the budget include salaries, travel expenses for field operations, supply contractors, printing,

utilities, office space, and equipment. So, naturally, George's most important job tool is a spreadsheet program: SuperCalc 3.

Before he distributes his monthly reports, George edits them onscreen in whatever format he desires. He and his colleagues are impressed that the printout is much more professional and readable than the old handwritten reports.

George finds that the speed of the microcomputer is its biggest advantage. "I could not do what I'm doing now by hand. It would be impossible," George says. Another important factor is the accuracy of a computer's calculations. "It eliminates the mistakes that you'd make on an adding machine," he adds. "That's a very important factor."

Because the micro is so fast, it means there is now time to do appreciably more budget analysis than in the bureau's earlier days. "Much of what we're doing now was never done before because there would never have been time to do it," George says.

A WORKSHEET DESIGN is rarely static. During the worksheet design phase and after the worksheet is put into use in applications, you will want to make alterations. As with word processing, such alterations are called editing.

9.1 Editing and Printing Worksheets

This section discusses the spreadsheet editing commands available to you. In addition, it discusses ways you can format your worksheets to make them more readable, and how to print your worksheets on paper.

Editing the Contents of a Worksheet Cell

Suppose you want to change the contents of a worksheet cell. One method, of course, is simply to reenter the contents from scratch. However, in many instances, you need to make only a simple change—perhaps altering a single digit or adding an expression to a formula. In such cases, it is inefficient to retype the entire cell entry. To help you make more efficient use of your time, most spreadsheet programs have an **EDIT command** that displays the contents of the current cell on the data input line and allows you to edit the cell contents just as if you were working with a word processor. In other words, you can move the cursor along the data input line by using the cursor-motion keys, you can delete characters by using the DELETE key, and you can insert characters at any point along the line. Command Table 9.1 summarizes the operation of the EDIT command for our sample spreadsheets.

Adding, Deleting, and Moving Rows and Columns

When using the MOVE command, remember that the contents of the target range are erased when replaced by the source range.

Some of the most common editing operations involve adding and deleting rows or columns, and moving ranges of cells from one spreadsheet location to another. Here is a survey of the spreadsheet commands that will carry out these operations.

The MOVE Command. In many instances, you will want to rearrange the rows or columns of a worksheet. For example, you might want to alphabetize the income and expense rows of the Jones budget discussed in Chapters 7 and 8. You can accomplish this rearrangement by using the **MOVE command**—the command that enables you to move a range of cells. To accomplish this, specify the range of cells you want moved (the source range), and the range to which those cells should be moved (the target range).

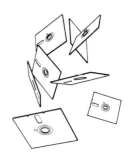

Command Table 9.1 The EDIT commands for Lotus 1-2-3, Gold-Spread, and SuperCalc 3.

Program	Command	Comments
Lotus 1-2-3 and GoldSpread	Press F2. Current contents of cell appears on data entry line, with cursor at first character. You may use CURSOR-MOTION keys to move along data entry line. You may use INS key to turn insert mode on and off in order to insert characters. You may use DEL key to delete characters. To input edited data entry line into the cell, press ⟨ENTER/ RETURN⟩.	
SuperCalc 3	Move cursor to cell you wish to edit. / Edit ⟨ENTER⟩ Use CURSOR-RIGHT and CURSOR-LEFT keys to move to error, backspace to delete characters. Press ⟨ENTER⟩ to end editing. / Edit ⟨cell address⟩ Edit cell contents. See above.	Edit contents of a cell. Go to cell and edit.

The spreadsheet then rearranges the cells as instructed.

For example, you can move the range of cells A1 . . B10 to the range C2 . . D11, as shown in Figure 9.1. In making this move, the contents of A1 . . B10 is erased, and the original contents of A1..B10 becomes the new contents of the range C2 . . D11. It is extremely important to note that, as part of the operation, the original contents of the target range C2 . . D11 is erased. You must be careful when using the MOVE command because you can lose information contained in the target range. The operation of the MOVE command for our sample spreadsheets is summarized in Command Table 9.2.

The ADD ROW/COLUMN Command. In some instances you will want to add a row or column to a worksheet. Suppose that Janet, one of the Jones children, is starting college. The family wants to

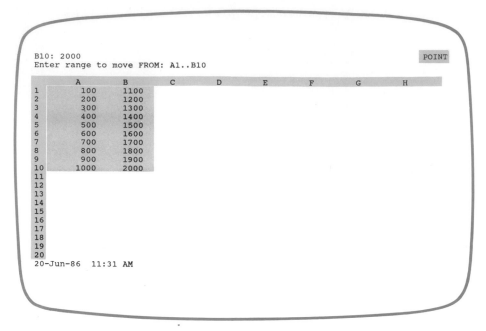

(a)

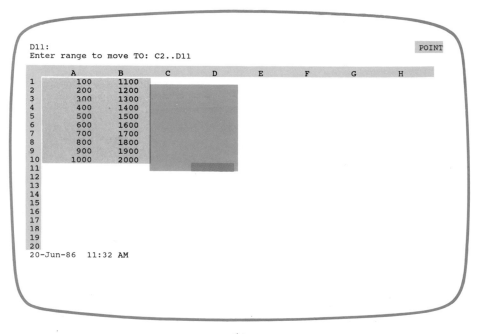

(b)

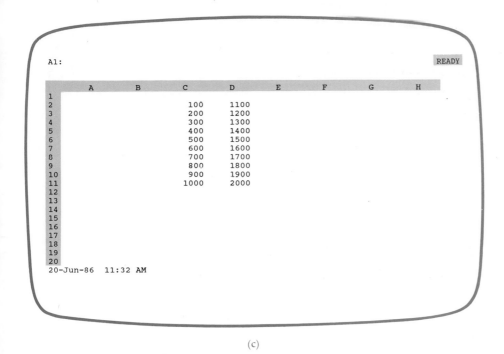

```
A1:                                                              READY

        A        B        C        D        E        F        G        H
 1
 2                        100      1100
 3                        200      1200
 4                        300      1300
 5                        400      1400
 6                        500      1500
 7                        600      1600
 8                        700      1700
 9                        800      1800
10                        900      1900
11                       1000      2000
12
13
14
15
16
17
18
19
20
20-Jun-86   11:32 AM
```

(c)

Figure 9.1 Using the MOVE command. (a) Specify the source range (A1 .
. B10). (b) Specify the target range (C2 . . D11). (c) After you press ⟨ENTER/
RETURN⟩, the source range is moved.

Command Table 9.2 The MOVE commands for Lotus 1-2-3,
GoldSpread, and SuperCalc 3.

Program	Command	Comments
Lotus 1-2-3 and GoldSpread	/ Move Specify range to move. Specify target location.	The range to be moved may be specified either by typing range addresses (e.g., A11 . . B20) or by using cursor to point to range. (e.g., first clear range by using ESC; then move cursor to first corner of range and type a period; then move cursor to end corner of range and press ⟨ENTER⟩.)
SuperCalc 3	Same as 1-2-3.	

```
A8: [W15] 'Entertainment                                          POINT
Enter row insert range: A8..A8

            A           B           C           D           E           F
1                       JAN         FEB         MAR         APR         MAY
2     EXPENSES
3     Rent          $795.00     $795.00     $795.00     $795.00     $795.00
4     Food          $400.00     $400.00     $400.00     $400.00     $400.00
5     Car Loan      $297.80     $297.80     $297.80     $297.80     $297.80
6     Car Operation $135.00     $135.00     $135.00     $135.00     $135.00
7     Clothes       $125.00                 $350.00
8     Entertainment $200.00     $200.00     $200.00     $200.00     $200.00
9     Taxes       $1,272.49   $1,272.49   $1,272.49   $1,272.49   $1,272.49
10    Medical       $200.00     $200.00     $200.00     $200.00     $200.00
11    Tuition     $3,000.00
12    Personal      $200.00     $200.00     $200.00     $200.00     $200.00
13    Decorating                            $800.00     $800.00   $1,000.00
14    TOTAL EXPENSES $6,625.29  $3,500.29   $4,650.29   $4,300.29   $4,500.29
15    INCOME
16    Jim's Salary $2,450.00   $2,450.00   $2,450.00   $2,450.00   $2,450.00
17    Betty's Salary $1,950.00 $1,950.00   $1,950.00   $1,950.00   $1,950.00
18    Bank Interest $300.00                             $300.00
19    TOTAL INCOME $4,700.00   $4,400.00   $4,400.00   $4,700.00   $4,400.00
20    NET        ($1,925.29)    $899.71    ($250.29)    $399.71    ($100.29)
20-Jun-86  11:34 AM
```

(a)

```
A8: [W15]                                                         READY

            A           B           C           D           E           F
1                       JAN         FEB         MAR         APR         MAY
2     EXPENSES
3     Rent          $795.00     $795.00     $795.00     $795.00     $795.00
4     Food          $400.00     $400.00     $400.00     $400.00     $400.00
5     Car Loan      $297.80     $297.80     $297.80     $297.80     $297.80
6     Car Operation $135.00     $135.00     $135.00     $135.00     $135.00
7     Clothes       $125.00                 $350.00
8
9     Entertainment $200.00     $200.00     $200.00     $200.00     $200.00
10    Taxes       $1,272.49   $1,272.49   $1,272.49   $1,272.49   $1,272.49
11    Medical       $200.00     $200.00     $200.00     $200.00     $200.00
12    Tuition     $3,000.00
13    Personal      $200.00     $200.00     $200.00     $200.00     $200.00
14    Decorating                            $800.00     $800.00   $1,000.00
15    TOTAL EXPENSES $6,625.29  $3,500.29   $4,650.29   $4,300.29   $4,500.29
16    INCOME
17    Jim's Salary $2,450.00   $2,450.00   $2,450.00   $2,450.00   $2,450.00
18    Betty's Salary $1,950.00 $1,950.00   $1,950.00   $1,950.00   $1,950.00
19    Bank Interest $300.00                             $300.00
20    TOTAL INCOME $4,700.00   $4,400.00   $4,400.00   $4,700.00   $4,400.00
20-Jun-86  11:34 AM
```

(b)

```
A8: [W15] 'College                                              READY

        A           B          C          D          E          F
1                   JAN        FEB        MAR        APR        MAY
2    EXPENSES
3    Rent           $795.00    $795.00    $795.00    $795.00    $795.00
4    Food           $400.00    $400.00    $400.00    $400.00    $400.00
5    Car Loan       $297.80    $297.80    $297.80    $297.80    $297.80
6    Car Operation  $135.00    $135.00    $135.00    $135.00    $135.00
7    Clothes        $125.00               $350.00
8    College
9    Entertainment  $200.00    $200.00    $200.00    $200.00    $200.00
10   Taxes        $1,272.49  $1,272.49  $1,272.49  $1,272.49  $1,272.49
11   Medical        $200.00    $200.00    $200.00    $200.00    $200.00
12   Tuition      $3,000.00
13   Personal       $200.00    $200.00    $200.00    $200.00    $200.00
14   Decorating                           $800.00    $800.00  $1,000.00
15   TOTAL EXPENSES $6,625.29  $3,500.29  $4,650.29  $4,300.29  $4,500.29
16   INCOME
17   Jim's Salary $2,450.00  $2,450.00  $2,450.00  $2,450.00  $2,450.00
18   Betty's Salary $1,950.00  $1,950.00  $1,950.00  $1,950.00  $1,950.00
19   Bank Interest  $300.00                          $300.00
20   TOTAL INCOME $4,700.00  $4,400.00  $4,400.00  $4,700.00  $4,400.00
20-Jun-86  11:34 AM
```

(c)

Figure 9.2 Adding the row *COLLEGE* to the Jones budget worksheet. (a) Specify the position where the row is to be added. (b) The program creates a space for the row. (c) Enter the name of the new row and press ⟨ENTER/RETURN⟩.

add to their budget (which was introduced in Chapter 7) an expense row labelled *COLLEGE*, as shown in Figure 9.2.

You may insert a row or a column by using the **ADD ROW/COLUMN command**. The spreadsheet program first asks you for the position of the row or column to be inserted. A blank column is then added at the position you specify. Existing rows and columns are renumbered to accommodate the new row or column. The operation of the ADD ROW/COLUMN command for our sample spreadsheets is summarized in Command Table 9.3.

The DELETE ROW/COLUMN Command. You will sometimes want to delete a row or column from a worksheet. For example, suppose that Mrs. Jones decides to quit her job. The Joneses will want to delete from their budget the income row corresponding to Mrs. Jones's job.

You may delete a row or a column by using the **DELETE ROW-COLUMN command**. The spreadsheet program first asks you for the rows or columns to delete. The program deletes them and renumbers the remaining rows and columns to reflect the

Command Table 9.3   The ADD ROW/COLUMN commands for Lotus 1-2-3, GoldSpread, and SuperCalc 3.

Program	Command	Comments
Lotus 1-2-3 and GoldSpread	/ Insert Row or Column Specify location of insert. Type cell address immediately to right of or below column or row to be inserted. Or, position cursor to point to cell. ⟨ENTER⟩	Insert row or column at indicated position.
SuperCalc 3	Same as 1-2-3.	Rows or columns to delete may be indicated by typing row or column numbers rather than cell addresses.

deletion. The operation of the DELETE ROW/COLUMN command for our sample spreadsheets is summarized in Command Table 9.4.

When editing your worksheet, beware of unexpected changes in your spreadsheet formulas! Always save and back up your data in the event of unwelcome mistakes.

Some Words of Caution. You should always save your worksheets before making extensive changes. You should also be careful when adding, deleting, and moving rows and columns. These operations may play unexpected havoc with your formulas. The program accommodates formulas to the changes in the worksheet as best it can. To avoid unwelcome surprises, however, you should understand how the spreadsheet adjusts its formulas.

A spreadsheet adjusts all the references in its formulas by translating them to their new values. Suppose that you add a new column A to your spreadsheet. All existing columns are then moved to the right. A reference to B12 in a formula will be changed to C12; the range A1 . . A10 in a formula will be changed to B1 . . B10, and so forth.

A problem can occur when you delete a row or a column. The spreadsheet rejects any formulas containing references to the deleted cells by displaying an error message in the corresponding cell. For instance, if you delete row 2, then the function

@SUM(A2, D12, E13)

is rejected because of the reference to A2. On the other hand, the function

@SUM(A1 . . A10)

is replaced by the function

@SUM(A1 . . A9)

Because no cell in row 2 is explicitly referenced, the translation proceeds without error.

Text Formatting Features

To increase worksheet readability and appearance, spreadsheet programs incorporate a number of features for formatting text. Many of these formatting options are controlled by special formatting characters preceding the text itself. These characters vary with the spreadsheet. However, most spreadsheets have formatting characters to accomplish the following:

- Define a sequence of characters as a text entry, overriding the usual data classification rules.
- Specify that a text entry is to be centered in the cell display.
- Specify that the character following is to be repeated to fill out the cell.

Defining an Entry as Text. As mentioned earlier, a spreadsheet automatically classifies data as text, numeric, or formula. However, there are circumstances where you may want to override this automatic classification. For instance, if a cell entry begins with a digit, it is automatically regarded as numeric. This means, in particular, that the entry is aligned on the right side of the cell. This sort of alignment is called right justification, as it is in word processing.

Command Table 9.4 The DELETE ROW/COLUMN commands for Lotus 1-2-3, GoldSpread, and SuperCalc 3.

Program	Command	Comments
Lotus 1-2-3 and GoldSpread	/ Delete Specify Row or Column range. Specify rows or columns to be deleted. ⟨ENTER⟩	Rows or columns to be deleted may be specified by using cursor in the same way that the cursor is used to specify a range. Or, they may be specified by typing a range. After a deletion, any remaining cell entries referring to deleted entries will display a value of ERR.
SuperCalc 3	Same as for 1-2-3.	Rows or columns to delete may be indicated by typing the row or column numbers rather than cell addresses.

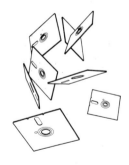

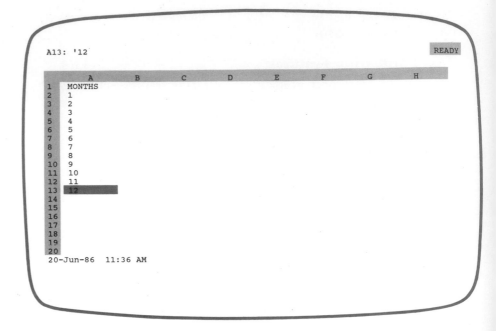

Figure 9.3   Numeric data considered as text.

In some cases, you may want to regard a sequence of digits as text rather than a number. For instance, you want to number months with the labels 1,2,3, . . . , and have them aligned along the left edge of the cells, as shown in Figure 9.3. To do this, you must instruct the spreadsheet to consider the numbers as text. This can be done by starting the cell entry with the **text definition character**. The text definition character varies with the spreadsheet. In Lotus 1-2-3 and GoldSpread, it is the apostrophe character ('). Thus in these spreadsheets, an entry of the form

'125

tells the spreadsheet to treat the entry 125 as a label. In particular, it will be justified on the left side of the cell. Note, however, that when numbers are entered as labels, they may not be used within calculations, either within expressions or as a numeric argument in a formula.

The text definition character can be used in other ways as well. Suppose, for example, that you want to enter a label that begins with the character /. If you simply type the character, it will put the spreadsheet into command mode. However, you may enter the character onto the command line by typing the text definition character first and then typing ⟨/⟩. The presence of the text definition character tells the spreadsheet that what comes next is text and not

Command Table 9.5 The text definition characters for Lotus 1-2-3, GoldSpread, and SuperCalc 3.

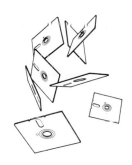

Program	Command	Comments
Lotus 1-2-3 and GoldSpread	'	Any string of characters preceded by single quote is interpreted as text.
SuperCalc 3	"	Any string of characters preceded by a double quote is interpreted as text.

an instruction to enter command mode. Command Table 9.5 shows the text definition characters for our sample spreadsheets.

Centering Text within a Cell. You may greatly improve the appearance of a worksheet by centering the titles in their respective cells, as shown in Figure 9.4. You may center a text entry by starting it with the **text centering character**. In Lotus 1-2-3 and GoldSpread, the text centering character is v̂. So, the entry

    ^JAN

will produce the title *JAN* centered in its cell.

Figure 9.4 Centering text within a cell.

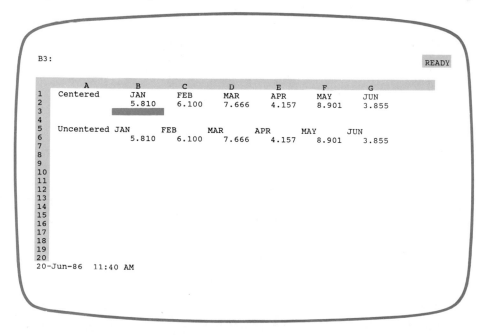

```
B3:                                                              READY

            A         B         C         D         E         F         G
1    Centered      JAN       FEB       MAR       APR       MAY       JUN
2                  5.810     6.100     7.666     4.157     8.901     3.855
3
4
5    Uncentered JAN       FEB       MAR       APR       MAY       JUN
6                  5.810     6.100     7.666     4.157     8.901     3.855
7
8
9
10
11
12
13
14
15
16
17
18
19
20
20-Jun-86  11:40 AM
```

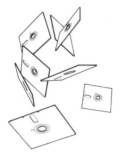

Command Table 9.6   The text centering characters for Lotus 1-2-3, GoldSpread, and SuperCalc 3.

Program	Command	Comments
Lotus 1-2-3 and GoldSpread	^	Any text entry preceded by a caret is displayed centered in its field. If column width is changed, this centering is automatically readjusted.
SuperCalc 3	See Command Table 9.5.	

Note that if you alter the column width, an entry beginning with the text centering character is automatically centered again in its new position. Command Table 9.6 shows the text centering characters for our sample word processors.

Filling a Cell with a Character. The **repeat character** indicates to the spreadsheet that the character following is to be repeated across the cell. This character can be used, for example, to divide a worksheet into sections with single and double horizontal lines, as illustrated in Figure 9.5. You can do this by using the repeat

Figure 9.5   Filling cells with the " = " and " − " characters.

```
A2: [W15] \-                                                          READY

           A            B           C           D           E           F
 1                      JAN         FEB         MAR         APR         MAY
 2     ----------------------------------------------------------------------
 3     EXPENSES
 4     ----------------------------------------------------------------------
 5     Rent           $795.00     $795.00     $795.00     $795.00     $795.00
 6     Food           $400.00     $400.00     $400.00     $400.00     $400.00
 7     Car Loan       $297.80     $297.80     $297.80     $297.80     $297.80
 8     Car Operation  $135.00     $135.00     $135.00     $135.00     $135.00
 9     Clothes        $125.00                 $350.00
10     Entertainment  $200.00     $200.00     $200.00     $200.00     $200.00
11     Taxes        $1,272.49   $1,272.49   $1,272.49   $1,272.49   $1,272.49
12     Medical        $200.00     $200.00     $200.00     $200.00     $200.00
13     Tuition      $3,000.00
14     Personal       $200.00     $200.00     $200.00     $200.00     $200.00
15     Decorating                             $800.00     $800.00   $1,000.00
16     ==================================================================
17     TOTAL EXPENSES $6,625.29   $3,500.29   $4,650.29   $4,300.29   $4,500.29
18     ==================================================================
19     INCOME
20     Jim's Salary $2,450.00   $2,450.00   $2,450.00   $2,450.00   $2,450.00
20-Jun-86  11:44 AM
```

Command Table 9.7 The repeat characters for Lotus 1-2-3, Gold-Spread, and SuperCalc 3.

Program	Command	Comments
Lotus 1-2-3 and GoldSpread	\	Any character preceded by backslash character will be repeated to end of field. If column width is changed, number or repetitions of character is automatically adjusted.
SuperCalc 3	'	Any text string preceded by the apostrophe will be repeated from the current cell across the row to the cell before the next non-blank cell.

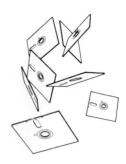

character followed by the characters "–" for single lines or "=" for double lines. In Lotus 1-2-3 and GoldSpread, the repeat character is \ (backslash). So an entry of the form

\ =

produces a double line across the cell. Note that if you change the column width, the number of copies of = is automatically adjusted to fill the cell to its new width.

In SuperCalc 3, the repeat character is ' (apostrophe). Starting a character string with this character causes the string to be repeated across the worksheet until the first non-empty cell is encountered.

Command Table 9.7 lists the repeat characters for our sample spreadsheets.

Printing a Worksheet

You may use a spreadsheet program to prepare printed reports like the one shown in Figure 9.6. Using the PRINT command, you may print the data in any range of worksheet cells, along with titles, page numbers, and row and column titles. This command is usually quite complex because of the extensive formatting options it allows.

Command Table 9.8 on pages 342–343 summarizes the operation of the PRINT command for our sample spreadsheets along with the various formatting options. For more details about printing worksheets with your program, refer to the user manual for your spreadsheet program.

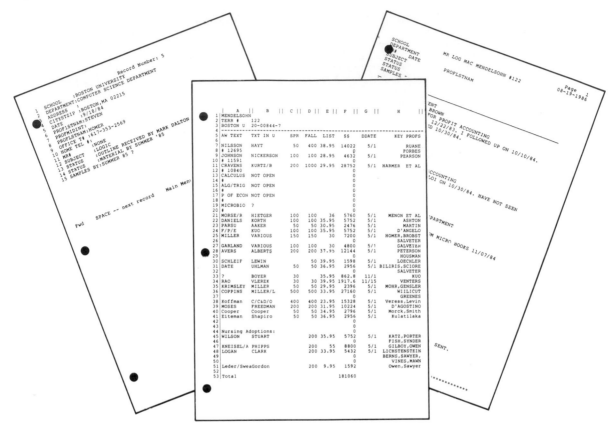

Figure 9.6 A report printed from worksheet data.

Section 9.1: Test Your Understanding

1. Explain how to center a title in a cell.

2. What happens to a centered title if you change the column width?

3. How do you create numeric titles that align along the left side of a cell?

4. What is the repeat character? How is it used?

5.a) Suppose that a column is added to the C position in your worksheet. Explain how the function @SUM(A1 . . F1) is adjusted.

   b) Suppose that a row is added in the 3 position. Explain how the function @AVG(C1, D1, F1, G2 . . H2) is adjusted.

   c) Suppose that row 1 is deleted. Explain how the function C2*D3 is adjusted.

d) Suppose that row 1 is deleted. Explain how the function C1*D1 is adjusted.

Hands-on Exercises

1. Recall the worksheet saved under the file name JONES in the Hands-on Exercises in Section 7.4.

   a) Redo the Jones budget worksheet, centering all titles and adding lines to clearly separate the titles from the data. Also use lines to box off the column totals.

   b) Add a new row under *EXPENSES* with the title *COLLEGE*. Can you position the row so that the formulas do not have to be reworked?

   c) Delete the row describing Mrs. Jones's income. Can you think of a way to do this so that the formulas do not need reworking?

   d) Divide the JONES worksheet into two sections by drawing a double line between the *EXPENSE* and *INCOME* sections.

   e) Center the column titles in the JONES worksheet.

   f) Produce a printout of the entire JONES worksheet.

   g) Use the editing facilities of your spreadsheet to change the title *EXPENSES* to *EXPS* and the title *INCOME* to *INC*.

   h) Use the editing facilities to change the titles back to their original forms.

   i) Enter the formula @SUM(A1 . . A50). Use the editing facilites to modify this formula to read
   @SUM(A1 . . A30,A35,A40).

9.2 More Spreadsheet Features

You use a spreadsheet program to manipulate numeric information in much the same way that you use a word processor to manipulate text. Like a word processor, a spreadsheet includes many commands to make worksheet manipulation easier. This section discusses several of these commands.

Command Table 9.8 The PRINT commands for Lotus 1-2-3, GoldSpread, and SuperCalc 3.

Program	Command	Comments
Lotus 1-2-3 and GoldSpread	/ Print	Print worksheet. Displays the print menu (options described below). After executing GO, you exit the print menu. After executing any other option, you are returned to print menu. To cancel print menu, press ESC.
	Printer vs. file:	Select printing a worksheet range to printer or select printing a worksheet range to file.
	Line:	Advance paper one line.
	Page:	Advance paper to top of next page.
	Options:	Set page formatting.
	Clear:	Clear all print menu settings.
	Align:	Set print parameters to format from top of page.
	Go:	Execute specified print command.
SuperCalc 3	/ Output Select Display Report or Contents Report. Specify range. Specify output device or format parameters. ⟨ENTER⟩	Display Report displays specified range exactly as it appears on screen. Contents Report displays contents of each cell of range, with formulas displayed rather than values. The output devices are the printer, console (screen), disk file. Format parameters are speci-

Merging Worksheets

You may insert a range of cells from another worksheet at a specified position on the current worksheet, as shown in Figure 9.7. In this figure, a range of cells from a saved worksheet in being inserted at the cursor position of the current worksheet. Such an insertion operation between worksheets is called **merging**, and it is accomplished by using the **MERGE command**. Merging is especially useful in organizing large volumes of data in multiple worksheets.

Program	Command	Comments
		fied by requesting setup menu (S). This menu allows you to specify the following parameters: Length (lines) Width (characters) New border character Border printing Auto-form-feed (on/off) Double-space (on/off) End-line-feed (on/off) Set printer control codes Retain printer control codes Print report Various parameters may be set by repeated reference to menu. When they are all set, worksheet may be printed by selecting the print report option on menu.
	Useful special cases of this general command: /Output Display All Printer /Output Formula All Printer /Output Display All Setup {select options} Printer	Printer entire worksheet. Print formulas for entire worksheet. Print entire worksheet, sending printer command to select compressed print. (This allows printing 132 characters across a line instead of usual 80 on an 8 inch wide line. Command to invoke compressed print must be determined from your printer manual.)

Spreadsheets allow a number of different variations related to merging. The simplest merge operation is the one described above, in which a section of the current spreadsheet is replaced by a section from another spreadsheet. Another variation allows a section of a spreadsheet to be added (or subtracted) cell by cell to the current worksheet. For instance, you may want to add together corresponding data from a number of plants to generate figures on total sales or total shipments. This can be done by adding corresponding cells

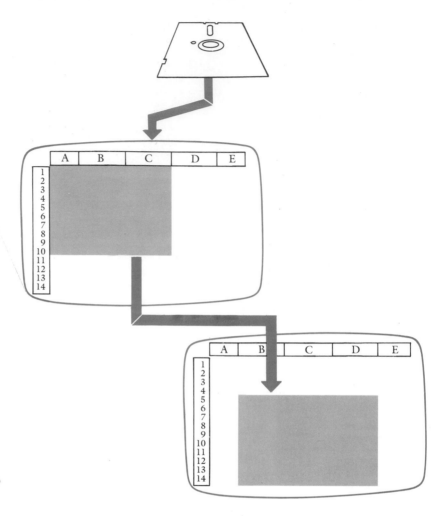

Figure 9.7 Merging two worksheets.

of two spreadsheets. The operation of the MERGE command (including the variations supported) for our sample spreadsheets is summarized in Command Table 9.9.

Hiding and Protecting Cells of a Worksheet

Use the PROTECT command to prevent accidental changes in data that should not be altered.

In using a spreadsheet program to analyze information, you may want to vary certain data items and not others. Using the **PROTECT command**, you can disallow changes to certain cells of a worksheet, and prevent accidental changes to data that should not be altered, such as price lists or tax rates.

The PROTECT command allows you to declare that a range of cells is protected—that is, it cannot be changed. It also allows you to remove protection from a range of cells. When you remove the protection from a range of cells, they revert to their normal status, in which their contents may be altered.

Some worksheet data, such as salary or sales information, may be confidential; in other words, you may want to **hide** rows or columns containing such information. When hidden, a row or

Command Table 9.9 The MERGE commands for Lotus 1-2-3, GoldSpread, and SuperCalc 3.

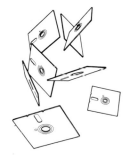

Program	Command	Comments
Lotus 1-2-3 and GoldSpread	/ File Combine	Combine all or part of worksheet file with current worksheet by using the indicated method of combination. Inserted material is placed with its upper-left cell at current cursor position. Original content of combined cells is lost. Substitute current cell contents from specified range. Methods of combination: Copy Add Subtract Add corresponding current entries to entries from specified range. Form differences of corresponding current cell entries minus cell entries from specified range. Combine entire file. What to combine: Entire file Named/Specified-Range Combine only a named range or a designated range. Program will ask for either name of range or specified range.
	Specify name of file to combine. ⟨ENTER⟩	
SuperCalc 3	/ Load ⟨file name⟩ Specify All or Part of file. If Part, specify range to load. Specify location to load first cell from file to.	

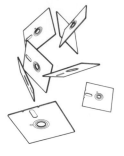

Command Table 9.10   The HIDE commands and the PROTECT commands for Lotus 1-2-3, GoldSpread, and SuperCalc 3.

Program	Command	Comments
Lotus 1-2-3 and GoldSpread	/ Worksheet Global Format Hidden	Hide or reveal contents of all cells.
	/ Range Format Hidden Specify hide or unhide. Specify range. ⟨ENTER⟩	Hide or reveal a range of cells.
	/ Range Protect Specify range. ⟨ENTER⟩	Protect a range of cells.
	/ Range Unprotect Specify range. ⟨ENTER⟩	Unprotect a range of cells.
SuperCalc 3	/ Format Specify level to which format applies. Hide values.	Hides values of a collection of cells. Level specifies collection of cells to which command applies. The various levels are as follows: Global Column range Row range Cell range
	/ Protect Specify range of cells.	Protect a range of cells.
	/ Unprotect Specify range of cells.	Unprotect a range of cells.

column is not displayed on the screen. However, the corresponding data remains in RAM and in any saved copy of the worksheet. You may hide or reveal a range of columns or rows using the **HIDE command**. The operation of the PROTECT command and the HIDE command for the sample spreadsheets is summarized in Command Table 9.10.

Displaying Spreadsheet Formulas

In normal operation, you will want your worksheet to display the current numeric values associated with each of the cells; you will also want these values to be properly formatted. Sometimes, as in the case of checking your worksheet design, you will want the worksheet to display formulas rather than their values. (See Figure 9.8.) Most spreadsheets have a **FORMULA DISPLAY command** for displaying formulas in the worksheet cells. Command Table

```
A2: (T) [W15] \-                                                    READY

              A                    B                 C
 1                               JAN               FEB
 2   ---------------- ------------------------------------------
 3   EXPENSES
 4   -----------------------------------------------------------
 5   Rent                        795               795
 6   Food                        400               400
 7   Car Loan                    297.8             297.8
 8   Car Operation               135               135
 9   Clothes                     125
10   Entertainment               200               200
11   Taxes                       1272.49           1272.49
12   Medical                     200               200
13   Tuition                     3000
14   Personal                    200               200
15   Decorating
16   ===========================================================
17   TOTAL EXPENSES @SUM(B5..B15)        @SUM(C5..C15)
18   ===========================================================
19   INCOME
20   Jim's Salary                2450              2450
20-Jun-86   12:35 PM
```

Figure 9.8 The Jones budget worksheet with formulas displayed rather than values.

9.11 shows the implementation of the FORMULA DISPLAY command for our sample spreadsheets.

Using Multiple Windows in a Worksheet

As you know, your monitor allows you to view only a small part of a worksheet at a time. To expand your view, most spreadsheets allow you to see two different sections of a worksheet simultaneously by splitting the screen into windows. You can split the screen

Command Table 9.11 The FORMULA DISPLAY commands for Lotus 1-2-3, GoldSpread, and SuperCalc 3.

Program	Command	Comments
Lotus 1-2-3 and GoldSpread	/ Worksheet Global Format Text ⟨ENTER⟩	Display all formulas instead of values.
	/ Range Format Text Specify range to format. ⟨ENTER⟩	Display formulas instead of values in specified range.
SuperCalc 3	/ Output Contents Console	Display formulas on screen in a display of cell-by-cell contents of worksheet.

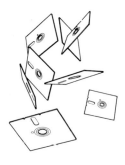

```
B1: ^JAN                                                              READY

            A           B           C           D           E           F
                       JAN         FEB         MAR         APR         MAY
15  INCOME
16  Jim's Salary    $2,450.00   $2,450.00   $2,450.00   $2,450.00   $2,450.00
17  Betty's Salary  $1,950.00   $1,950.00   $1,950.00   $1,950.00   $1,950.00
18  Bank Interest     $300.00                             $300.00
19  TOTAL INCOME    $4,700.00   $4,400.00   $4,400.00   $4,700.00   $4,400.00
20  NET            ($1,925.29)    $899.71   ($250.29)     $399.71   ($100.29)
21
            A           B           C           D           E           F
 1                     JAN         FEB         MAR         APR         MAY
 2  EXPENSES
 3  Rent              $795.00     $795.00     $795.00     $795.00     $795.00
 4  Food              $400.00     $400.00     $400.00     $400.00     $400.00
 5  Car Loan          $297.80     $297.80     $297.80     $297.80     $297.80
 6  Car Operation     $135.00     $135.00     $135.00     $135.00     $135.00
 7  Clothes           $125.00                 $350.00
 8  Entertainment     $200.00     $200.00     $200.00     $200.00     $200.00
 9  Taxes           $1,272.49   $1,272.49   $1,272.49   $1,272.49   $1,272.49
10  Medical           $200.00     $200.00     $200.00     $200.00     $200.00
11  Tuition         $3,000.00
20-Jun-86   12:37 PM
```

Figure 9.9   Horizontal windows.

Figure 9.10   Vertical windows.

```
O2:                                                                  READY

            A           B           C                 M           N           O
 1                     JAN         FEB         1      DEC         YEAR        JAN
 2  EXPENSES                                   2
 3  Rent              $795.00     $795.00      3     $795.00    $9,540.00     $795.00
 4  Food              $400.00     $400.00      4     $400.00    $4,800.00     $400.00
 5  Car Loan          $297.80     $297.80      5     $297.80    $3,573.60     $297.80
 6  Car Operation     $135.00     $135.00      6     $135.00    $1,620.00     $135.00
 7  Clothes           $125.00                  7                $1,225.00     $125.00
 8  Entertainment     $200.00     $200.00      8     $200.00    $3,700.00     $200.00
 9  Taxes           $1,272.49   $1,272.49      9   $1,272.49   $15,269.88   $1,272.49
10  Medical           $200.00     $200.00     10     $200.00    $2,400.00     $200.00
11  Tuition         $3,000.00                 11                $6,000.00   $3,000.00
12  Personal          $200.00     $200.00     12     $200.00    $2,400.00     $200.00
13  Decorating                                13                $2,600.00
14  TOTAL EXPENSES  $6,625.29   $3,500.29     14   $3,500.29   $53,128.48   $6,625.29
15  INCOME                                    15
16  Jim's Salary    $2,450.00   $2,450.00     16   $2,450.00   $29,400.00   $2,450.00
17  Betty's Salary  $1,950.00   $1,950.00     17   $1,950.00   $23,400.00   $1,950.00
18  Bank Interest     $300.00                 18                $1,200.00     $300.00
19  TOTAL INCOME    $4,700.00   $4,400.00     19   $4,400.00   $54,000.00   $4,700.00
20  NET            ($1,925.29)    $899.71     20     $899.71      $871.52  ($1,925.29)
20-Jun-86   12:38 PM
```

horizontally, as in Figure 9.9, or vertically, as in Figure 9.10. Note that both windows show sections of the same worksheet. When you use a split screen, one of the windows is designated as the **active window**, the portion that currently contains the cursor. Any scrolling takes place in the active window. You may change the active window by using an appropriate command.

   Using a split screen, you can view one section of a worksheet for reference as you enter data in or analyze another section. By using the **WINDOW command**, you may split the screen into horizontal or vertical windows, return to an unsplit screen, and control the relative sizes of the windows.

   If you are using Lotus 1-2-3 or GoldSpread, you may split the screen into windows by using the command /WORKSHEET WINDOW. The program then asks if you want to split the screen horizontally or vertically. The split (horizontal or vertical) will occur as marked by the current cursor position (on either a row or a column). For example, to create vertical windows with the left window three columns wide, position the cursor in column 4 and give the command /WORKSHEET WINDOW VERTICAL.

   Most spreadsheets allow you to choose whether or not to synchronize the scrolling of the two windows. For instance, if you have horizontal windows, then synchronized scrolling will guarantee that the same columns are always visible in the two windows. Similarly, with vertically synchronized scrolling, the same rows will always be visible in the two windows. Command Table 9.12 outlines the specific WINDOW commands for our sample spreadsheets.

Section 9.2: Test Your Understanding

1. What is the function of the PROTECT command?
2. What is the function of the HIDE command?
3. What is the function of the MERGE command?
4. Explain the operation of the FORMULA DISPLAY command.
5. Why is the FORMULA DISPLAY command useful?
6. What is a spreadsheet window?
7. Why are spreadsheet windows useful?
8. Explain what is meant by synchronized scrolling.
9. Give an example in which synchronized scrolling would be helpful.
10. Give an example in which unsynchronized scrolling would be useful.

Command Table 9.12 The WINDOW commands for Lotus 1-2-3, GoldSpread, and SuperCalc 3.

Program	Command	Comments
Lotus 1-2-3 and GoldSpread	/ Worksheet Window Choose menu item. ⟨ENTER⟩	Split screen horizontally. Before giving command, cursor must be moved to row where screen is to be split.
	Menu Items: Horizontal	
	Vertical	Split screen vertically. Before giving command, cursor must be moved to column where screen is to be split.
	Synch	Synchronize scrolling of two screens.
	Unsynch	Unsynchronize scrolling of two screens.
	Clear	Return to unsplit screen.
	F6	Switch between windows.
SuperCalc 3	/ Window Choose window command.	Split/Unsplit the screen horizontally. Before giving command to split, cursor must be moved to row where screen is to be split.
	Window commands: Horizontal	
	Vertical	Split/Unsplit the screen vertically. Before giving command to split, cursor must be moved to column where screen is to be split.
	Synch	Synchronize scrolling of two screens.
	Unsynch	Unsynchronize scrolling of two screens.
	Clear	Clear to right or below split.
	Use to transfer between active windows.	

Hands-on Exercises

1. Recall the document JONES, which you edited in the Hands-on Exercises in Section 9.1.

    a) Display all the formulas on the worksheet and then redisplay all the values.

    b) Divide the Jones budget worksheet into two vertical windows. The right window should contain three columns.

c)   Scroll the left window so that the data for April is visible.

d)   Scroll the right window so that the data for December is visible.

e)   Make the right window active. Change one of the expense numbers for December.

f)   Make the left window active. Scroll it to make the December data visible. Note the change you previously made in the other window.

g)   Return to one window.

h)   Divide the Jones budget into horizontal windows. The upper window should have six rows.

i)   Fix the titles in the upper window. Scroll to the bottom line of the worksheet.

j)   Release the titles in the lower window. Scroll the lower window. What happens?

k)   Scroll the lower window back to the top of the worksheet and fix the titles in place. Now scroll the window again. What happens?

9.3   Templates and Macros

There are two other advanced spreadsheet tools that can help you create the most useful worksheets possible in the shortest amount of time. Let's take a closer look at these tools.

What Is a Template?

In building worksheets thus far, you have concentrated on determining the formulas to insert in cells. For the most part, you left blank the cells containing numeric information. This procedure is the normal order in designing "general purpose" worksheets: First you design the worksheet and fill in the titles and formulas; these items stay the same from application to application. Then you enter the numeric data corresponding to a particular application.

A general-purpose worksheet, which contains formulas and titles but no numeric data, is called a **template**. You may accumulate a library of templates for solving a variety of problems. For example, your library may include templates for payroll, project planning, and general ledger. You may even use one template to produce a number of worksheets. For example, a template of expenses may be used to produce a new worksheet to reflect expenses each month.

In a number of examples in these chapters, you have seen how to construct templates. However, you may purchase templates that provide ready-to-use spreadsheets for a wide variety of applications. (See Figure 9.11.) Such templates relieve you of the task of determining the formulas to calculate the required data items. Moreover, ready-made templates often build in data specific to a particular field, such as tables of financial or engineering data.

What Is a Spreadsheet Macro?

Manipulating worksheets often requires that you enter long sequences of keystrokes that communicate commands, formulas, and data to the spreadsheet program. To simplify the entry of keystroke sequence, some spreadsheet programs incorporate **macros**. A macro is a sequence of keystrokes that has been stored for later use. The keystrokes that make up a macro can correspond to any sequence of commands, data items, or formulas.

Figure 9.11   Some ads for commercial spreadsheet templates.

A macro is assigned a name (often a single keystroke). By giving the **MACRO command** along with the name of a macro, the sequence of keystrokes is entered into the worksheet exactly as if you were typing each individual keystroke on the keyboard.

Macros may be used in many ways to simplify worksheet manipulation. For example, you may use a macro to enter repetitive data into a worksheet. Because a macro can include cursor motions, you may use a single macro to enter a sequence of titles—say, a sequence of month names or a sequence of account names. A macro can accept user data by positioning the cursor at a particular cell and asking the user to enter data for the cell. The macro can then continue by moving the cursor to another cell and asking the user to enter data for that cell.

Macros in Lotus 1-2-3 and GoldSpread

To give you an idea of how macros work, let's create and use a macro on Lotus 1-2-3 or GoldSpread. (The procedure is the same for both programs.) Suppose you need to repeatedly recall the worksheet JONES. You can do so by typing the following keystrokes:

⟨/⟩	Enter command mode
⟨F⟩	File
⟨R⟩	Recall
⟨JONES⟩	File name
⟨ENTER/RETURN⟩	ENTER/RETURN key

You can store and assign a name to this sequence, or macro, directly on the worksheet. Then, when you type in the macro name, the keystrokes will be automatically entered onto the data input line, just as if you had typed each of them manually.

You may erase a macro by assigning to the macro name a range that is blank. To store the keystrokes on the worksheet, find a blank section of the worksheet and enter the keystrokes vertically. You can use as many cells as you want. However, if you want to use several cells, arrange them in consecutive vertical order. In our example, there are not many keystrokes to record, so use a single cell, say A100.

To type ⟨/⟩, you must precede it with the character ⟨'⟩ to indicate that the next input is text input. (Otherwise, pressing ⟨/⟩ will tell the spreadsheet to go into command mode.) Moreover, the ENTER/RETURN key is indicated by typing a tilde (˜). So our keystrokes to enter macro data are

⟨'/FR⟩⟨JONES⟩⟨˜⟩

Now press ⟨ENTER/RETURN⟩ to input this keystroke sequence to the current cell. In the cell, you will see the display

/FRJONES˜

The next step is to give a name to the macro data by using the command /RANGE NAME. This command will ask for the range to be named; in this case, focus on the range A100 . . A100. The command will also ask you for the name to assign to the range. To name a macro, you must use one of the names

backslash →

\O,

\A

. . .

\Z

The name /O has a special use that we will describe below. In this example, select the name /A. Type this name and press ⟨ENTER/ RETURN⟩. You have just created a macro with the name /A.

To execute the macro, press the key combination ⟨ALT-A⟩. That is, hold down the ALT key and then press the letter assigned to the macro. The keystrokes will be input to the spreadsheet exactly as if you had typed them. The spreadsheet will respond by recalling the JONES worksheet.

Macros /A, /B, . . . , /Z are associated with a particular worksheet. (After all, the data for the macro is stored on the worksheet.) If you save the worksheet and later recall it, any macros you may have defined will be available to you again.

The macro named /O is special. This macro is executed when the spreadsheet is first started. Thus if we had assigned /O to the macro created above, the JONES worksheet would automatically be recalled each time the spreadsheet is started.

Macros could be one of the most powerful spreadsheet tools available to you. Learn to write effective, useful macros to save time and keystrokes.

Macros are an extremely powerful feature of spreadsheet programs. You can use them to program a spreadsheet to perform many tasks automatically. For example, you can write macros that copy onto a master budget worksheet monthly data submitted to you by different department heads. Such macros can be quite complex and involve a large number of keystrokes. However, once they are written, they save a tremendous amount of work because they are used repeatedly.

In effect, macros constitute a **programming language** for describing worksheet manipulations. Although today's microcomputer application users may not need to write programs in BASIC or PASCAL, they may nevertheless be confronted with using spreadsheet macros to write programs (or, as we shall see later, using database programming languages). Programming for application program users has not been eliminated; rather, it has taken on a different form.

The use of macros is an advanced topic in spreadsheet applications; this chapter has attempted to cover only the basics. However, if you find that you use your spreadsheet for serious modelling, it is well worth the effort to learn more details on writing and implementing macros.

Section 9.3: Test Your Understanding

1. What is a template?
2. What is a spreadsheet macro?
3. Explain in what sense macro writing is the same as programming a computer.
4. Devise three macros that you would find useful in spreadsheet manipulation.

Hands-on Exercises

1. Create the macro /A described in the text.
2. Use the /A macro to recall the spreadsheet JONES you edited in the Hands-on Exercises in Section 9.2.
   a) Create a macro to save the current worksheet under the name JONES.

KEY TERMS

EDIT command
MOVE command
ADD ROW/COLUMN
   command
DELETE ROW/COLUMN
   command
text definition character
text centering character

repeat character
merging
MERGE command
PROTECT command
HIDE command
FORMULA DISPLAY
   command
active window

WINDOW command
template
macro
MACRO command
programming language

CHAPTER REVIEW QUESTIONS

1. Using the commands available for your spreadsheet, write the sequence of commands necessary to accomplish the following tasks.

   a) Print the current spreadsheet.
   b) Print the range A1 . . F30 of the current spreadsheet.
   c) Add a row in between rows 40 and 41.
   d) Delete row 80.
   e) Move the range C100 . . D110 so that C100 is moved to A1.
   f) Copy the range C100 . . D110 so that C100 is moved to A1.
   g) Fill the current cell with the letter x.
   h) Draw a horizontal line along the worksheet from cell A1 to A10.
   i) Display the formulas in the spreadsheet.
   j) Hide the range A1 . . A20.
   k) Protect the range A1 . . A20.
   l) Create horizontal windows with two columns in the right window.
   m) Synchronize scrolling of the windows.
   n) Execute the macro /Z.

2. Several utility programs print spreadsheet data onto paper "sideways." Explain why such programs might be useful.

DISCUSSION QUESTIONS

1. You are the owner of a construction company and need to build a worksheet template to use in preparing construction bids.

   a) Describe the procedure you would follow to construct the template.
   b) Once the template is built, explain how you would use it.

2. In what sense can macro construction be called programming?

APPLICATION PROJECTS

1. Refer to the final JONES worksheet built in the Application Projects in Chapter 7. Add columns to show the percentages of the costs accounted for by each category of component. (There should be seven such columns, one for each set of costs.)

2. Terry Wolcott is a graduating senior in the marketing department of a local state college. During college, Terry developed a strong interest in microcomputers; now he wants to combine this interest with his desire to own and manage a small business.

   Terry realizes that large firms have many employees capable of preparing spreadsheet templates but that a small firm may be restricted in resources. A small firm may have only one owner and a limited number of employees who have neither the time nor capability to prepare spreadsheet templates, even though the firm has the same basic data handling needs as a large firm. Terry has decided to prepare a set of templates that a small retailer might be able to use. He believes he'll be able to turn the sale of these templates, and related training, into his own money-making small business.

One template in particular will be concerned with the inventory turnover ratio—the total sales of an item or group of items divided by the average inventory on hand for the period under review. The inventory turnover ratio is a crucial measure of retailing performance.

Each product will have a "normal" inventory turnover range. A ratio lower than normal indicates that the product is moving slowly and too much capital may be tied up in inventory, or that some inventory may be damaged or unsalable. A ratio higher than normal may mean that stock of the item is too narrow, or that frequent out-of-stock situations are occurring, both of which lead to low sales.

Assume that Terry wants to create a template that he could show potential customers who own clothing stores. A clothing store owner might need to compute inventory turnover ratios for individual items such as belts, for groups of items such as accessories (belts, handbags, gloves, and so on), casual wear (skirts, blouses, and pants), and finally all of the stock in the store.

Design Terry's template for a clothing store. You should have seven columns for data input: one column for the month, and one column each for the monthly sales and inventory on hand for accessories, casual wear, and total stock. You will have twelve rows for data input—one for each month. At the bottom of the screen you should present three inventory turnover ratios.

Hint: Average inventory is simply the total inventory on hand each month divided by 12 (the months in a year).

3. You have just inherited from your rich uncle a stock portfolio consisting of the following securities:

Stock	Shares	Purchase	Price	Dividends/Year
IBM	300	$65	$\frac{1}{8}$	$4.40
AT&T	500	$18	$\frac{1}{4}$	1.20
GM	220	$35	$\frac{1}{2}$	5.05
Boeing	345	$18		1.20
RCA	400	$10	$\frac{3}{4}$	1.08
PepsiCo	75	$21	$\frac{1}{4}$	1.84

a) Set up a spreadsheet titled STOCKS with column headings of *STOCK, SHARES, PURCHASE PRICE, PURCHASE VALUE, CURRENT VALUE, DIVIDENDS PER SHARE, DIVIDEND YIELD, % OF PORTFOLIO, APPRECIATION,* and *INCOME.* If necessary, change the column width to accommodate the headings.

b) Enter the values above in the appropriate columns. Calculate values for the other columns as follows:

Purchase value = Shares * purchase price
Current value = Today's price per share

IBM	$156	$\frac{1}{4}$
AT&T	25	$\frac{1}{2}$
GM	74	$\frac{1}{8}$
Boeing	91	
RCA	63	$\frac{1}{2}$
PepsiCo	88	$\frac{1}{8}$

Dividend yield = Dividend/current price
% of portfolio = % of current value of each stock
     to total portfolio value
Appreciation = (Current price/purchase price) − 1
Income = Shares * dividends per share

Hint: To perform calculations using the share prices, you'll need to convert them to decimal format. The @VALUE command in Lotus 1-2-3 will do this for you.

c) At the bottom of the spreadsheet, indicate the value of the total portfolio, the average dividend yield, and the total income it will provide.

d) Save the spreadsheet as STOCKS and print it.

e) Use *The Wall Street Journal* or your local newspaper to determine the prices and dividends of these securities in today's market. Retrieve the spreadsheet STOCKS and copy your data to a different location on the spreadsheet. Insert today's data, print only the revised spreadsheet section, and save the worksheet in a file named CURRENT.

10 Data Management

Micros Beef Up Sales for Burger King

They say when you're number two you try harder. When you think of burgers and fries, you probably think of McDonald's—but Burger King runs a close second. In its efforts to boost sales, Burger King is peddling hamburgers from mobile vans, called the Burger King Express, which are wheeled to ball parks, colleges, and military bases. Burger King also has more than 900 company-owned restaurants, with scores more operated by franchisers.

Managing these far-flung restaurants is a demanding job that requires assistance by microcomputers. Large mainframes at corporate headquarters in Miami hold extensive databases containing information about every Burger King restaurant in the country. However, daily management of the restaurants is handled by a number of regional offices, all equipped with microcomputers.

In his job as regional accounting manager in the Detroit office, Scott Phillips makes great use of the corporate database on his micro. Communicating with the Miami mainframe via modem, he can find out what he needs to know—from a store's identification number and address to the name of its franchisee, sales volume, and contract infor-

mation. Phillips needs this information to make sales projections, to establish sales trends based on sales histories, and to find out when certain lease contracts will expire so he can budget for new ones.

Phillips depends constantly on the micro and the database. "The computer is on from eight in the morning until six at night," he says. "It's an extension of my right hand." If he wants to further examine any information from the mainframe, Phillips downloads the data to a file for his micro, using programs such as Condor or dBASE III. "I can download it any time at my convenience and get current information," he says, because the mainframe database is continuously updated. For instance, he can download information on store openings, sort it by date, and find out what stores opened in the last ten years. Knowing when a store opened is necessary to calculate its average monthly sales volume.

That kind of sorting can't be done by dialing up the mainframe, only by manipulating data on a micro. "The micro allows for better reporting, because we can sort and track, versus doing individual queries on the corporate database," Phillips says.

D ATA MANAGEMENT PROGRAMS constitute our third major category of application software. These programs are extremely useful in providing facilities for storing, retrieving, analyzing, and summarizing data to help you solve problems and make decisions. This chapter and the next describe the capabilities of data management programs and how to apply them.

10.1 Data Management Programs and Data Files

This section discusses typical data management problems that arise in running a business, and the ways data management programs are used to solve them.

Data Management Problems in Business

Suppose that you have just opened your own business—a large retail pet store with the creative name of Aardvark Pets. In order to manage your business, you will need to handle many forms of data: sales slips describing sales transactions, invoices from your suppliers listing items you have purchased and their cost, inventory records of merchandise you currently have in stock, payroll records listing the salaries paid to each of your employees and the various taxes withheld, price lists for goods and services you purchase, and so forth.

The data involved in your business generates a variety of data management problems, among them the following:

- **Storing data,** or recordkeeping, a major task in any business. In order for your business to function efficiently, data must be accessed quickly and easily. You must thus set up a system for storing records of orders, receipts, bills, payroll, and inventory. As your business develops, new data will be generated in each category; hence, data storage becomes an ongoing operation and your storage system must allow you to store data that have been accumulated for several years.

- **Updating data,** or adding information reflecting your current business activities, such as the day's sales, new orders to suppliers, additions to inventory, and personnel changes. In addition, you may often have to alter existing data, either to correct errors (an incorrect price in an invoice for a boa constrictor) or to record changes (a new mailing address for your tropical fish supplier).

- **Recalling data** for reference purposes, such as tracking a lost payment for birdseed.

- **Summarizing data,** such as total weekly sales for each department: dogs, cats, rodents, birds, fish, etc. This information can help you make good decisions. (Have I stocked more parakeets than I can sell? Do I need to have a sale on puppies because there are too many in stock?)

- **Disseminating data,** or circulating information to colleagues or customers. For example, you may want to send a memo to your employees about a price increase, or a flyer to customers about a sale. The data you circulate must be timely, complete, and in a convenient form.

- **Analyzing data,** or taking a closer look at what the data represents and its implications so you can make sound decisions and determine new directions for growth. (What is the profit for each department on a monthly basis? How many canaries have been ordered from a particular supplier?)

- **Organizing data,** or assembling all data relevant to a particular problem, deleting irrelevant data, and arranging the data in a convenient order. For example, you may want to list dogs in alphabetic order by breed, or all pets by department in order of sales volume.

To help you solve these problems, you can use any one of the many data management programs available for use on microcomputers.

Data Management Programs

The data management tasks of large businesses have been handled by computers for several decades, usually by specialized data processing departments using mainframes or minicomputers. However, the microcomputer revolution has made the same data management capabilities available to small and medium-size businesses. Today's data management programs allow you to use data stored within the microcomputer system itself (on diskette or hard disk), or to use data stored on a minicomputer or a mainframe, translated into a form acceptable to your microcomputer. In a **data management program** (sometimes called a **file management program**), your data is stored in files, called **data files,** on diskette or hard disk. A data management program allows you to create data files and to enter and update data in them. It also allows you to view all or parts of your data on a monitor and to print out data arranged in convenient formats. In addition, a data management program can generate statistics describing your data and answer questions for you.

Types of Data Management Programs

Data management programs can be divided into two general categories: spreadsheet-based and stand-alone. A **stand-alone data management program** only manages data files. A **spreadsheet-based data management program** combines data management with spreadsheet functions by using a spreadsheet to store data. A spreadsheet-based program may even include graphics, word processing, and communications capabilities. Data management in a spreadsheet-based program often lacks the more sophisticated features of a stand-alone system. For our discussion of the basics of data management (in all of this chapter and part of Chapter 11), it makes no difference which type of system you use for hands-on experience. However, some of the features described in Chapter 11 are found only in stand-alone systems.

This book describes the commands for four data management programs: Lotus 1-2-3, GoldSpread, dBASE III,* and R:BASE 5000. Both Lotus 1-2-3 and GoldSpread are spreadsheet-based programs, in which the data management functions are integrated with spreadsheet and graphics functions. Two of the most popular stand-alone data management packages, dBASE III and R:BASE 5000, employ a particular organizational approach to managing data which will be discussed in detail in Chapter 11. Throughout this chapter and the next, these four packages will serve as our sample data management programs.

Installing a Data Management Program

Installing a data management program is a fairly straightforward process. As with the other application packages described, you must make a backup copy of your diskettes (if backups are permitted), and you must install the software, reflecting your choice of video display adapter and printer. You should consult the reference manual for your package to determine the particular steps you must take in order to install the program properly.

The data files produced by data management programs have the potential to be very large. Size considerations generally limit most data management to hard disk systems. You can perform data management tasks on a diskette-based system, but it requires constant switching of disks, which is clumsy and time-consuming.

For purposes of the Hands-on Exercises in Chapters 10 and 11, you will not need to use a hard disk. Since the data files are

---

*Note that dBASE III Plus operates in a menu-driven mode that does not require many of the commands described here. You may use these commands with dBASE III Plus, however. If you switch to the command mode, refer to your software manual for details.

short, you can easily manipulate them on a system with two floppy disk drives.

Section 10.1: Test Your Understanding

1. List seven ways to manipulate business data.
2. What is the function of a data management program?
3. What is the difference between a stand-alone data management program and a spreadsheet-based management program?

Hands-on Exercises

1. Install your data management program.

10.2 Data Files

Before you can learn very much about the operation of data management programs, you must learn about the organization of the data files that they manipulate. Throughout this chapter, let's assume that you are the owner of Aardvark Pets and are starting to set up your own data management system.

A **data item**, a single unit of information (such as the price of a puppy, the date of a sale, or a customer's street address), is displayed on the monitor as a sequence of characters placed within a **field** of fixed **length**. For instance, Figure 10.1 shows the data item *125.83* in a field 10 characters long, and the name *JOHN Q. ARMSTRONG* in a field 20 characters long.

A **record** is a sequence of fields, not necessarily of the same length, used to store a set of data items. For instance, suppose that you want to store a customer list. A typical entry consists of a number of data items: customer name, address, city, state, zip code, telephone number, current balance, customer ID number, and credit limit. To store such a collection of data items, you need to define one field for each data item listed, as shown in Figure 10.2.

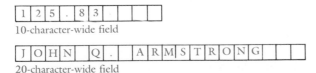

10-character-wide field

20-character-wide field

Figure 10.1   Displaying a data item in a field.

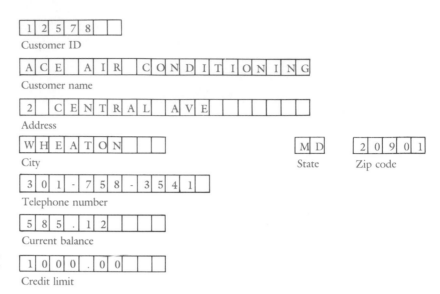

Figure 10.2 Using a record to store an entry in a customer list.

The lengths of the fields are based on the length of the data items.

A **data file** is a sequence of records, all having a common field structure. For instance, Figure 10.3 shows the CUSTOMER data file, which is based on the record structure defined in Figure 10.2. The records of a file are numbered sequentially beginning with one; in Figure 10.3, they are numbered 1 through 10. This same data can be reconceptualized as a table like the one shown in Figure 10.4. Each record containing the data items describing a customer corresponds to a single row of the table.

For the sake of simplicity, our CUSTOMER data file contains only nine records. However, a data file may consist of several hundred thousand records, such as a mailing list for a large professional society.

Figure 10.3 A sequence of records forming a data file.

Data Types and Field Attributes

In some data management programs, you can give a command to limit the type of data that can be entered into a particular field. The allowable **data types** vary with each data management program, but here are some of the possibilities:

- *Text*. Any sequence of characters
- *Real*. A decimal number
- *Integer*. A whole number
- *Logical*. True or false (Boolean)
- *Date*. A calendar date

ID	Name	Address	City	State	Zip Code	Balance	Cred Lim
00001	Gold, B.	6522 Beechwood Dr.	Greenbelt	MD	20910	$358.12	$1,000.00
00002	Marley, C.	1822 Jefferson Pl.	Chevy Chase	MD	20912	$578.85	$1,500.00
00003	Dixon, M.	2 Dabney Ct.	Rockville	MD	20851	$0.00	$2,000.00
00004	Travland, N.	8003 Allentown Rd.	Alexandria	MD	20301	$348.11	$500.00
00005	Samuel, V.	3309 Lancer St.	Columbia	MD	20722	$115.30	$300.00
00006	Matson, A.	30 Victory Ln.	Washington	DC	10001	$582.12	$1,000.00
00007	O'Brien, C.	1703 Gridley Ln.	Silver Spring	MD	20903	$205.40	$800.00
00008	Mathews, F.	12751 Summers Dr.	Beltsville	MD	20744	$500.89	$800.00
00009	Jeffrey, R.	7585 Yellow Moon Pl.	Arlington	VA	20551	$181.33	$1,000.00

Figure 10.4   Viewing a data file as a table.

- *Time.* A clock time
- *Memo.* A sequence of sentences

Figure 10.5 shows some examples of these data types.

Once you specify a field's data type, you can enter data only of that type. For example, if you attempt to enter the number 5.77 into a field of the integer type, then the data management program will automatically reject the entry, because the number 5.77 is a real number, not an integer.

With some data management programs, you can limit access to a particular field by designating it as a **protected data field**. The contents of a protected field are for reference only and can't be changed. You can't write into a protected field, but you can read it. You might want to use protected fields in a personnel file to prevent any inadvertent or unauthorized change in personnel data. (For example, this precaution can prevent someone from changing the ages of all your sales clerks to make them eligible for retirement!)

Figure 10.5   Examples of data types.

Example	Data type
147.38	Real
8325	Integer
$5,325.87	Dollar
John H. Sullivan	Text
10/17/87	Date
14:20:00	Time
Please bring with you all material in the sales kit we sent last week.	Memo

Some data management programs allow you to designate a **confidential data field**. The contents of such a field are stored in the data file but are not shown on the monitor unless the correct password is entered. Certain financial data, such as salaries, might be kept in confidential fields.

Data File Length Considerations

Data files can easily require vast amounts of storage. Each record requires the same amount of storage as all other records of the same file. Roughly speaking, each character of a field requires one byte of storage.

Consider a file consisting of 100,000 records, each containing 50 bytes. Such a file requires $50 \times 100,000$ bytes of storage, or 5,000,000 bytes. That is, the file requires more than five megabytes of storage! However, you should note that data management programs store numbers, times, and dates in an efficient manner so that they usually require fewer bytes than the number of characters in the display.

The extreme storage needs of many data management jobs make a hard disk a must. In fact, data management needs have provided much of the impetus behind the introduction of large hard disks (30 megabyte and larger) for microcomputers.

Section 10.2: Test Your Understanding

1. What is a data file? Give some examples of data files.
2. Describe the structure of a data file.
3. How does a field relate to a record?
4. What are the different types of data that can be stored within a field?
5. What is a protected data field?
6. What is a confidential data field?
7. Suppose that a data file contains 1,000 records with 20 fields, each containing ten characters of text. How many bytes of storage does the data file require?

Hands-on Exercises

1. A company needs to set up a file to store personnel data. A typical record must contain the following data:
   Name
   Address

City
State
Zip code
Date employed
Weekly salary
Job classification
Department
Manager
Performance

a) Based on this data, design the record structure for a data file named EMPLOYEE.

b) For each field, assign an appropriate data type.

c) Which fields should be confidential?

d) Which fields should be protected?

e) Which fields will need to be updated? Under what circumstances?

f) How many bytes will each record of the file require? (Assume that numeric fields require eight bytes.)

10.3   Creating and Updating Data Files

Any data management system requires the creation of many data files that correspond to the different sets of information that must be tracked. In managing Aardvark Pets, for example, you will want to create an inventory file, a personnel file, a customer file, an accounts payable file (for bills you owe), an accounts receivable file (for bills owed to you), and so forth. In this section, you will learn to set up the field structure for a data file and to enter data into the file.

Creating Data Files

The creation of data files is one of the most basic functions performed by a data management program. There are three steps in creating a data file:

1. Defining the file structure.
2. Entering data into the file.
3. Saving the file.

Let's look at each of these steps.

Defining the File Structure

Before entering data into a file, you must specify the **file structure**, usually by defining the structure of a typical record in terms of its fields. At the very least, the description includes the following:

- The name of the field
- The field length

In some data management programs, the description may include additional information:

- The type of data to be entered into the field
- Any **attributes**, or special characteristics, for the field (such as protected or confidential)

In a spreadsheet-based data management program, the file structure is defined by entering column names and specifying column widths. In a stand-alone program, a command is used to define the structure of a data file. Moreover, the structure can be viewed on a monitor, as shown in Figure 10.6.

The methods for defining the structure of a data file for our sample data management programs are summarized in Command Table 10.1.

Figure 10.6   Viewing the structure of a data file.

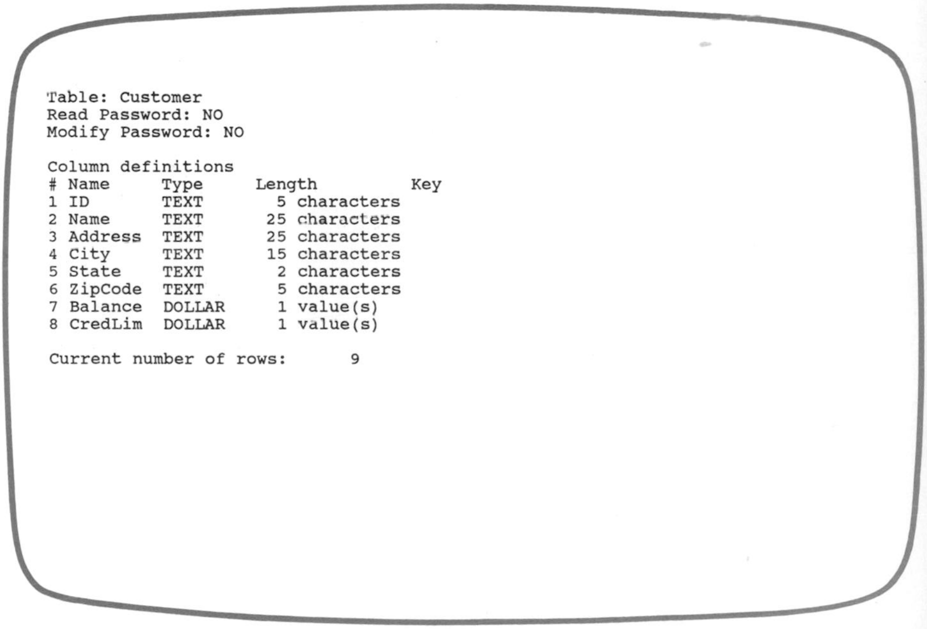

```
Table: Customer
Read Password: NO
Modify Password: NO

Column definitions
# Name      Type       Length        Key
1 ID        TEXT        5 characters
2 Name      TEXT       25 characters
3 Address   TEXT       25 characters
4 City      TEXT       15 characters
5 State     TEXT        2 characters
6 ZipCode   TEXT        5 characters
7 Balance   DOLLAR      1 value(s)
8 CredLim   DOLLAR      1 value(s)

Current number of rows:      9
```

Entering Data into the File

After you define the structure of a data file, you may enter data into the file one record at a time. This is the most tedious aspect of dealing with data files, but it is also the most crucial. For a data file to be useful, its contents must be both *complete* and *accurate*. An omitted record may result in a missed shipment or an uncollected bill. Incorrect data may result in misfiled information that becomes "lost" in the file.

To minimize data input errors, data management programs include the following devices:

A data file is useless if it is incomplete or inaccurate. Be extremely careful when entering or changing data.

- *Input data checking.* Some data management programs check that the data type of each data item matches the assigned type of the corresponding field. If the system detects a mismatch, the data item is rejected. For example, if you enter text data into a real number field, the program will reject your data and ask you to repeat the entry. This is a good method of screening out many errors.

  Some data management programs prevent you from entering data that does not fit into the field. If a field is ten characters wide, then the system accepts up to ten characters as input to the field. Characters after the tenth are rejected. Note, however, that most spreadsheet-based systems allow you to type beyond the field boundaries. You may see on the monitor only what fits into the field, but the spreadsheet retains additional characters in RAM.

- *Use of input screens.* To assist in entering data, some data management programs employ **input screens**, like the one shown in Figure 10.7 on page 372. An input screen displays a single record, allowing you to concentrate on only one record at a time, thus minimizing input errors.

  For each field, there is a field name and a corresponding highlighted area where you may enter field data. A cursor indicates the position of data currently being entered. You may reposition the cursor to enter data or to make changes in any field. When the screen displays the record exactly the way you want it, you may give a command to the program to enter the record into the data file.

- *Use of input prompts.* Some systems use input screens that display **input prompts**, which tell you the kind of data expected in a particular field. In a common arrangement, the bottom of the screen displays a prompt describing the intended contents

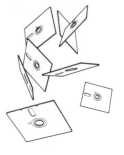

Command Table 10.1   The commands defining the structure of a data file for Lotus 1-2-3, GoldSpread, dBASE III, and R:BASE 5000.

Program	Command	Comments
Lotus 1-2-3 and GoldSpread	None	In a spreadsheet data management system, you define the structure by entering column titles corresponding to the various fields of a typical record.
dBASE III	USE ⟨file name⟩ ⟨ENTER⟩ Specify field structure of file: CREATE ⟨file name⟩ ⟨ENTER⟩ Program displays menu in which to fill in file structure. For each field, you fill in Field name Data type Width Decimal (optional) After each parameter, press ⟨ENTER⟩. When you are finished with all field specifications, press ⟨ENTER⟩. Program will ask you if you wish to enter data	To specify file structure for file, first open database with USE command and then use CREATE to specify structure of each file. The allowed data types are Character (text) Logical (true-false) Numeric (up to 19 digits) Date Memo (for variable length text up to 4000 characters.) The decimal parameter of a field tells number of decimal places of accuracy to keep. This parameter must be coordinated with field width. For instance, to store numbers 9,999 and still allow for two decimal

of the field where the cursor is currently located. Figure 10.8 shows an input screen in which one record of the CUSTOMER file is being entered. Note the prompt at the bottom of the screen that describes the user's current entry.

- *Downloading or importing data*. Entering data is time-consuming and painstaking work. In order to minimize or eliminate this task, you may retrieve data from another computer—even a mainframe or a minicomputer—and store the data on diskette or hard disk for use on your microcomputer. This process is called **downloading**. Similarly, moving data from one data file to another (on the same or another computer) is called **importing**.

Downloading data from powerful mainframes or minicomputers allows you to access and use corporate data files on your microcomputer.

Program	Command	Comments
	into file just specified. Answer Y/N. For data entry procedures, see Command Table 10.2	places, field width of 6 is needed. Entering blank field data ends file specification and returns you to dot prompt.
R:BASE 5000	R>DEFINE ⟨dbname⟩ D>COLUMNS D>col1 type (width) D>col2 type (width) . . . D>TABLES D>tblname WITH col1 col2 ... D>tblname WITH col1 col2 ... . . . Each column definition consists of the following data: Col = column name (1-8 characters) Data type Column width (optional)	In R:BASE 5000, the term *table* is used in place of the term *file* when describing and using a database. A database may contain one or many tables. For this chapter, we will study only databases having a single table. However, multiple table databases are considered in Chapter 11. DEFINE with a database name is used to define a new database. DEFINE may be used without a database name to redefine current database.

For instance, Aardvark Pets may want to acquire a mailing list stored on the mainframe computer of the local Humane Society. By downloading this mailing list into a data file on your microcomputer, you can avoid retyping the list. You may then want to split the mailing list into two data files for use by two employees; importing allows them to transfer data back and forth between their computers and their files.

Note, however, that downloading and importing data are often tricky tasks, since data from other computers may be in a format different from that used by your data management program. Before you can use downloaded data, you must translate it into the proper format.

```
Press [ESC] when done with this data
Customer ID  00011

Name  Brevard, J.
Address  2 Eagleton Ln.
City  College Park
State  MD
Zip Code 20742

Current Balance  587.82
Credit Limit  1000
```

Figure 10.7 An input screen.

Figure 10.8 An input screen with prompts.

```
R>load customer with prompts
 Begin R:base Data Loading

 Press [ESC] to end, [ENTER] to continue
ID        (TEXT   ):00011
Name      (TEXT   ):Brevard, J.
Address   (TEXT   ):2 Eagleton Ln.
City      (TEXT   ):College Park
State     (TEXT   ):MD
ZipCode   (TEXT   ):20742
Balance   (DOLLAR ):587.82
CredLim   (DOLLAR ):1000.00
```

The techniques for entering data into a file and the input data checking available for our sample data management programs are summarized in Command Table 10.2.

Saving the File

When you type data, it is stored in RAM. As you know, however, to retain a permanent record of your data, you must save your data on diskette or hard disk. Some data management programs save records one at a time. However, almost without exception, spreadsheet systems do *not* save to disk until you give a SAVE command. In any case, you should execute SAVE commands on a regular

A power outage or unforeseen error could cause loss of valuable data. To guard against loss, save your data every 15 minutes.

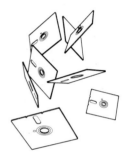

Command Table 10.2   The commands to enter data into a file for Lotus 1-2-3, GoldSpread, dBASE III, and R:BASE 5000.

Program	Command	Comments
Lotus 1-2-3 and GoldSpread	Type a field entry into a worksheet cell.	In a spreadsheet-based data management system, a record corresponds to a single row of the worksheet, with the fields corresponding to single cells.
dBASE III	When using the CREATE command, the program gives you an opportunity to enter data into file. A template listing various fields is displayed. Fill in fields with data and press ⟨ENTER⟩ to indicate a complete record. Pass between fields using the arrow keys. To end data entry, enter a blank record. This will end the CREATE command and return you to the dot prompt.	
R:BASE 5000	R>OPEN⟨dbasename⟩ R>LOAD ⟨tblname⟩ WITH PROMPTS Fill in table data in response to the field name prompts. ESC	Load a table in response to prompts that display field names one at a time. Press ⟨ENTER⟩ to go from field to field and to the next record. Press ⟨ESC⟩ to stop loading and to return to the R> prompt.

basis, at least every 15 or 20 minutes. This puts a strict limit on the amount of data that can be lost if a power outage occurs.

Data files take many hours to create. Protect your investment in time by making several backup copies of your files. Keep one copy available in case the original is damaged by either computer failure or human error. Keep another copy in a different location so it can be used in case of catastrophe, such as a fire or flood. It is a good idea to back up *all* your application programs and data, but it is especially important for your data files because they are so difficult and time-consuming to reconstruct. Command Table 10.3 lists the commands for saving data files for each of our sample data management programs.

After saving your data files, make several backup copies and store them in different locations in case of accident.

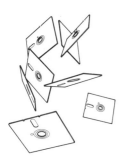

Command Table 10.3   Save commands for Lotus 1-2-3, GoldSpread, dBASE III, and R:BASE 5000.

Program	Command	Comments
Lotus 1-2-3 and GoldSpread	/ File Save ⟨file name⟩	See description of this command in Command Table 7.1.
dBASE III	CLOSE ⟨file name⟩ ⟨ENTER⟩	Closing a file being used saves all as yet unsaved data. Once a file has been closed, you must reopen it with the USE command in order to do further file operations.
R:BASE 5000	CLOSE or EXIT	CLOSE command closes the current database file and returns you to the R⟩ prompt. EXIT closes the current database file and returns you to main menu. Data is continuously saved by R:BASE. The CLOSE command may be used to close a database so that another database can be opened. Normally, the command EXIT is typed at the R⟩ prompt because this command automatically closes the currently open database, which means that the CLOSE command is not needed.

Command Table 10.4 The ADD RECORD command for Lotus 1-2-3, GoldSpread, dBASE III, and R:BASE 5000.

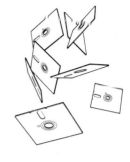

Program	Command	Comments
Lotus 1-2-3 and GoldSpread	Enter data in an additional row of the worksheet.	
dBASE III	APPEND ⟨ENTER⟩ Enter data into records at the end of the file.	Add records to an existing file.
R:BASE 5000	R)OPEN dbasename R)LOAD tblname WITH PROMPTS Fill in table data in response to the field name prompts. ⟨ESC⟩	Load a table in response to prompts that display the field names one at a time. Press ⟨ENTER⟩ to go from field to field and to next record. Press ⟨ESC⟩ to stop loading and to return to R) prompt.

Updating Data Files

Frequently, you will need to update data files. Updating can include the following forms:

- *Adding records*. You will often need to add records to a data file. For instance, Aardwark Pets has new customers and new employees that must be added to the appropriate files. All data management programs have a mechanism for adding records to a file. In spreadsheet-based systems, you simply add a row. With stand-alone systems, you use an **ADD RECORD command**. The details of these commands for our sample data management programs are described in Command Table 10.4.

- *Deleting records*. Sometimes you need to delete records from a file. For example, you may wish to delete from your CUSTOMER file records for customers who have not placed orders in more than two years. Data management programs have mechanisms for easily deleting records from a data file. Command Table 10.5 summarizes these mechanisms for our sample data management programs.

- *Modifying records*. You will often need to change the contents of data fields. For instance, a customer may give you a change of address that requires updating the customer file, which you can implement via the editing commands of the data management program. In a spreadsheet-based system, you can change a data field by typing new data into it. In a stand-alone system, you first call up the record to be changed, then you make any necessary modifications.

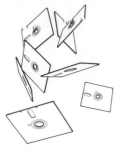

Command Table 10.5 The commands to delete a record from a data file for Lotus 1-2-3, GoldSpread, dBASE III, and R:BASE 5000.

Program	Command	Comments
Lotus 1-2-3 and GoldSpread	Position cursor in row corresponding to record to be deleted. / Delete Row ⟨ENTER⟩	Use spreadsheet command to delete a single row.
dBASE III	Display records using DISPLAY ALL command. Use arrow keys to select record to delete. DELETE ⟨ENTER⟩ PACK ⟨ENTER⟩	If you know the record number of the record you wish to delete, you may omit displaying the records and use the simple command DELETE 6 ⟨ENTER⟩ PACK ⟨ENTER⟩. The PACK command absorbs the space held by the record deleted. This command can be time consuming. If you have a number of deletes to do, perform all DELETE commands first and then give a single PACK command.
R:BASE 5000	R)EDIT ALL FROM tblname	Display contents of table in tabular fashion. Use arrow keys to scroll table in any direction. Point to record to remove. Position cursor anywhere within the row to be deleted by using the cursor control keys. Press the F2 key to delete.
	R)DELETE ROWS FROM tblname WHERE condlist	Delete rows from designated table by satisfying the given list of conditions.

- *Modifying the file structure.* Sometimes you have to modify the file structure by adding or deleting columns from the structure. Command Table 10.6 summarizes how to modify columns in each of our sample data management programs.

Section 10.3: Test Your Understanding

1. What are the steps involved in defining a file structure?
2. What is the advantage of being able to define a data type associated with a field?

3. What is the advantage of being able to protect a field?
4. Give an example of a field that might be protected.
5. List three techniques to minimize data input errors.
6. When might it be necessary to add records to a data file?
7. When might you need to delete records from a data file?
8. When might you need to modify information in a data file?
9. Give an example where it is necessary to modify file structure.

Command Table 10.6 The commands to modify the file structure for Lotus 1-2-3, GoldSpread, dBASE III, and R:BASE 5000.

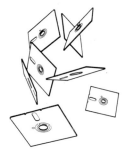

Program	Command	Comments
Lotus 1-2-3 and GoldSpread	To add a field, add a column using / Insert Column. To delete a field, delete the corresponding column using Delete Column. Fields may be rearranged using / Move.	
dBASE III	USE file name ⟨ENTER⟩ MODIFY STRUCTURE ⟨ENTER⟩ Edit the structure.	In response to the MODIFY STRUCTURE command, program displays list of fields and their corresponding parameters. Use arrow keys to move cursor among the fields. Edit entries using the DEL key. In addition, you may use the following key combinations: CTRL-N (Insert field before cursor) CTRL-T (Delete field before cursor) CTRL-W (Save changes to file structure and quit) CTRL-Q (Quit without saving)
R:BASE 5000	R)REMOVE COLUMN col FROM tbl	Remove column from table.
	R)CHANGE COLUMN col IN tbl TO newname, datatype, width	Modify definition of column.
	R)RENAME col oldnme TO newnme IN tbl	Change name of table.

Name	Address	City	State	Zip Code
John Axler	2 Landmark Ln.	Bethesda	MD	20741
Tom Bartholemew	1248 Talbot St.	Baltimore	MD	20411
Al Jackson	38 Stonegate Ter.	Silver Spring	MD	20904
Sue Ribet	4852 Connecticut Ave.	Washington	DC	10211
Martha Cleary	12 Angstrom Ln.	Gaithersburg	MD	20855

DateEmp	Salary	JobClass	Dept	Manager	Perform
12/04/82	$532.00	Maint1	Eng	Blaisdell	A
01/18/84	$733.00	Adv3	PR	Jones	C
05/12/85	$358.00	Clerk	PR	Jones	B
08/15/86	$521.00	Pers2	PERS	Clancy	A
04/12/86	$420.00	Prog	RESRCH	Golding	A

Figure 10.9 The employees of Acme Electrical Repairs.

Hands-on Exercises

1. The following applications refer to the personnel data file, EMPLOYEE, which you designed in the Hands-on Exercises in Section 10.1. Use your data management program to accomplish the tasks below.

   a) Using the information given Figure 10.9, enter data on the five employees in the EMPLOYEE file.

   b) Save the data file under the name ACME.

   c) Add the sixth and seventh employees' data to the file.

   d) John Axler was fired from his job. Delete his data from the personnel file. (In an actual situation, the data are stored in an archive of inactive personnel, so that they could be consulted if necessary.)

   e) In response to a governmental ruling, Acme must keep track of the race of each of its employees. Modify the file structure to add a field that will record race. You might want to create a one-byte code for this, such as 1 = Caucasian, 2 = Black, 3 = Native American, 4 = Asian, etc.

   f) At performance evaluation time, all Acme employees are given a satisfactory rating, except for Sue Ribet, who is given an excellent rating. Record the results of these evaluations in the data file.

   g) As a result of the performance evaluations, all employees are given salary increases of $10 per week, except for Sue

Ribet, who is given an increase of $20. Record the results of these salary changes in the file.

h) Save the modified file.

i) Create a backup of the data file.

10.4 Data Retrieval and Analysis

Once you set up your data file, it is easy to extract information and use it as a basis for business decisions. In this section you will learn how to retrieve information from a data file and how to analyze it.

How a Data Management Program Answers Questions

Data management programs allow you to retrieve information from a data file to answer questions such as the following:

- Which customers have an overdue account?
- Which customers reside in Texas?
- Which customers have not ordered merchandise in the last two years?
- Which customers have a credit limit over $1,000 and an overdue account?
- What is the average annual order for all customers?
- What is the total of all orders for the month of January?
- What is the average dollar amount of orders for customers in New Jersey during the last three months?

You can answer such questions by using a combination of three file manipulation techniques:

1. Field selection
2. Record selection
3. Data file statistical analysis

We shall now look more closely at each of these techniques and how they can be used, either alone or in combination, to answer questions like the ones listed above.

Field Selection

You can use **field selection** to view only selected fields of a data file. Each record of a data file may contain a large amount of information. To answer a particular question, you may need only certain fields in the record. By using field selection, you can eliminate the irrelevant fields for a particular question so that you aren't distracted by too much information. For example, to analyze your current credit policies, you can specify the printing of selected fields, such as *NAME, BALANCE,* and *CREDLIM,* from your CUSTOMER file. (See Figure 10.10.)

Data management programs have a **FIELD SELECTION command**. In stand-alone systems, this command allows you to view only selected fields in the record. In response to the FIELD SELECTION command, the program lets you manipulate the file as if the unselected fields did not exist. You can scroll through the records, edit material, and print out the file—but only on the selected fields that appear on the screen. However, the unselected fields are maintained on disk and can be redisplayed whenever you wish.

On a spreadsheet-based system, field selection works differently. If you give the FIELD SELECTION command, the program writes the desired fields to a different section of the worksheet. This leaves the original records intact, as shown in Figure 10.11. The FIELD SELECTION commands for our sample data management programs are summarized in Command Table 10.7.

Figure 10.10   Selecting fields from the CUSTOMER data file.

```
Name                        Balance           CredLim
--------------------------  ---------------   ---------------
Gold, B.                        $358.12         $1,000.00
Marley, C.                      $578.85         $1,500.00
Dixon, M.                         $0.00         $2,000.00
Travland, N.                    $348.11           $500.00
Samuel, V.                      $115.30           $300.00
Matson. A.                      $582.12         $1,000.00
O'Brien, C.                     $205.40           $800.00
Mathews, F.                     $500.89           $800.00
Jeffrey, R.                     $181.33         $1,000.00
```

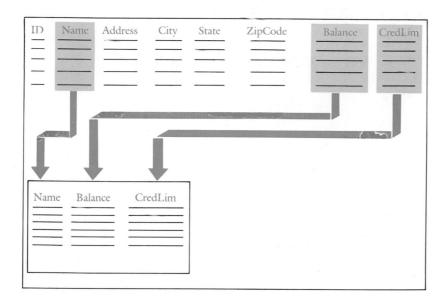

Figure 10.11 Selecting data fields in a spreadsheet-based system.

Record Selection

To answer the questions posed at the beginning of this section, you need to choose records that satisfy a **record selection criterion**. For example, to determine which Aardvark Pets customers are in Texas, you must locate all records with the *STATE* field TX (the abbreviation for Texas). In this example, the selection criterion is

   STATE field is equal to TX

To determine the customers with overdue accounts, you must locate all records in which the *OVERDUE* field is Y (for YES). In

Command Table 10.7   FIELD SELECTION commands for Lotus 1-2-3, GoldSpread, dBASE III, and R:BASE 5000.

Program	Command	Comments
Lotus 1-2-3 and GoldSpread	/ Data Query Select Input range. Select Criterion range. Select Output range.	
dBASE III	DISPLAY ALL ⟨field1⟩, ⟨field2⟩,..,⟨fieldn⟩	Display records including only the listed fields.
R:BASE 5000	R)SELECT col1,col2,..., coln FROM tbl	Display records from designated table including only listed fields. The command refers to current database.

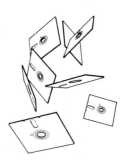

this case, the selection criterion is

> *OVERDUE* field is Y

Numeric fields require numeric selection criteria, such as

> *PAYMENT* field is greater than 100
>
> *ORDERS* field is less than 10
>
> *ORDERS* field is not equal to 0.

How you write selection criteria varies with the data management program. Command Table 10.8 summarizes how to write the

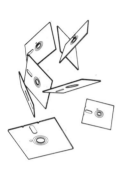

Command Table 10.8   Expressing selection criteria for Lotus 1-2-3, GoldSpread, dBASE III, and R:BASE 5000.

Program	Command	Comments
Lotus 1-2-3 and GoldSpread	=	Equals
	<	Less than (either numeric or precedes in alphabetic order)
	>	Greater than (either numeric or succeeds in alphabetic order)
	<=	Less than or equal to
	>=	Greater than or equal to
	<>	Not equal to
dBASE III	Same as Lotus 1-2-3.	
R:BASE 5000	EQ or =	Equals*
	NE or <>	Not equals*
	GT or >	Greater than*
	GE or >=	Greater than or equal*
	LT or <	Less than*
	LE or <=	Less than or equal*
	CONTAINS	Contains a text value*
	EQA or = A	Equals**
	NEA or <> A	Not equal**
	GTA or >A	Greater than**
	GEA or >=A	Greater than or equal**
	LTA or <A	Less than**
	LEA OR <=A	Less than or equal**
	CONTAINS value	Contains the given text value
	EXISTS	Column contains data
	FAILS	Column has a null value
	COUNT EQ n	Finds nth row in the table
	COUNT EQ LAST	Finds the last row in the table
	LIMIT EQ n	Limit the number of row selected to n

* Compare a column entry with a value.
** Compare two column entries.

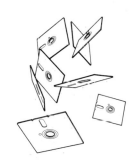

Program	Command	Comments
Lotus 1-2-3 and GoldSpread	/ Data Query Find	Highlight rows in input range matching criteria stated in criterion range.
	/ Data Query Extract	Write in output range a copy of rows in input range matching criteria stated in criterion range.
dBASE III	DISPLAY ALL FOR ⟨condition list⟩ ⟨field1⟩,⟨field2⟩,...,⟨fieldn⟩	Displays the listed fields from the records from ⟨table name⟩ for which each of the conditions in ⟨condition list⟩ is satisfied.
R:BASE 5000	R)SELECT col1, col2,... FROM tbl WHERE condlist	Displays the listed columns from the records from the designated table for which each of the conditions in the conditions list is satisfied.

above criteria for each of our sample data management programs.

The **RECORD SELECTION command** is used to identify all records satisfying the selection criteria. In stand-alone systems, the selected records are displayed on the screen. In spreadsheet-based systems, the records may either be highlighted within the data file itself, or written to a separate part of the worksheet.

The operation of the RECORD SELECTION command for each of the sample data management programs is summarized in Command Table 10.9. For stand-alone systems, you enter the selection criteria as part of the RECORD SELECTION command. In spreadsheet-based systems, you write the selection criteria onto the worksheet in a particular format and give the RECORD SELECTION command the range that contains the criteria.

More About Selection Criteria

The preceding examples used a single criterion to select a record. However, in order to answer more complex questions, you may need to use more than one selection criterion.

Selection criteria that involve several conditions (like those above) are called **compound selection criteria**. They are built from single-condition criteria that use the logical connectives **AND** and **OR**. (Most data management programs allow you to use *and* in place of *AND* and *or* in place of *OR*.) A compound selection criterion may involve several criteria on a single field, criteria on several different fields, or a combination of both.

For example, to for determine Aardvark Pets which customers have a credit limit of more than $1,000 and an overdue account, use the selection criterion

(*CREDIT* field is greater than 1000)

AND

(*OVERDUE* field is Y)

To determine which customers live in New York, California, or Tennessee, use the selection criterion

(*STATE* field is NY)

OR

(*STATE* field is CA)

OR

(*STATE* field is TN)

Data management programs allow you to create compound selection criteria, but the technique varies with the system. Command Table 10.10 summarizes the use of compound selection criteria for our sample data management programs.

Data File Statistical Analysis

In using data files to make business decisions, you often need to look at more than just a selected list of records. To answer some complex questions, such as the ones that follow, you must use statistics derived from the data:

- How many customers live in New York?
- Which customer in Maryland has the largest outstanding balance?
- Which customer in Maryland has the smallest, non-zero outstanding balance?
- What is the total owed by customers in Wisconsin?
- What is the average amount owed by customers in Missouri, Indiana, and Ohio?

The above questions illustrate the five most common statistical calculations, namely:

1. Count the number of records satisfying a certain criterion (*STATE* equals NY).
2. Among records satisfying a particular criterion (*STATE* equals

Command Table 10.10 Compound selection criteria operators for Lotus 1-2-3, GoldSpread, dBASE III, and R:BASE 5000.

Program	Command	Comments
Lotus 1-2-3 and Goldspread	#AND#	Logical AND
	#OR#	Logical OR
	#NOT#	Logical NOT
dBASE III	.AND.	Logical AND
	.OR.	Logical OR
	.NOT.	Logical NOT
R:BASE 5000	AND	Logical AND
	OR	Logical OR
	NOT	Logical NOT

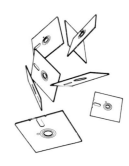

MD), determine the one for which a particular field has the largest value (*BALANCE*).

3. Among records satisfying a particular criterion (*STATE* equals MD AND *BALANCE* is not equal to 0), determine the one for which a particular field has the least value (*BALANCE*).

4. Among records satisfying a particular criterion (*STATE* equals WI), add the values of a particular field (*BALANCE*).

5. Among records satisfying a particular criterion (*STATE* equals MO or IN or OH), average the values of a particular field (*BALANCE*).

In spreadsheet-based programs, these calculations may be performed using the spreadsheet functions discussed in Chapter 8. In stand-alone programs, you can use functions similar to those used in a spreadsheet-based system to answer questions. The answers are displayed on the screen or printed on the printer, at your option. Command Table 10.11 summarizes the operation of these basic data statistical functions for our sample data management programs.

Section 10.4: Test Your Understanding

1. What is field selection?
2. What is record selection?
3. What is a record selection criterion?
4. What is a compound selection criterion?
5. Explain the function of data statistical functions.

Command Table 10.11   The data statistical function commands for Lotus 1-2-3, GoldSpread, dBASE III, and R:BASE 5000.

Program	Command	Comments
Lotus 1-2-3 and GoldSpread		Each of the statistical functions employs three ranges: The input range identifies the database to which the function refers. The column offset identifies the column in the database to which the function applies. Column 0 refers to the left-most column. The criterion range identifies the range in which the selection criteria are stored. This range consists of a set of columns, each identified by one of the field names (column names) for the database in the first row. The remaining rows contain formulas that determine the criteria for selection of records from the database to which to apply the function. The general format for a database statistical function is @Dxxxx(input_range, col_offset,criterion_range), where xxxx is one of the function names COUNT, SUM, AVG, MIN, MAX, STD or VAR. The database statistical functions may be used like other @ functions, either alone or within a formula, to calculate a cell entry.
	@DCOUNT	Count number of non-zero entries in column satisfying the criteria.
	@DSUM	Compute sum of entries in column satisfying the criteria.
	@DAVG	Average the entries in column satisfying the criteria.
	@DMIN	Compute minimum of entries in column satisfying the criteria.

Program	Command	Comments
	@DMAX	Compute maximum of entries in column satisfying the criteria.
	@DSTD	Compute standard deviation of entries in column satisfying the criteria.
	@DVAR	Compute variance of entries in column satisfying the criteria.
dBASE III	AVERAGE	Computes average of a selected collection of data fields.
	COUNT	Computes number of non-zero values in a selected collection of data fields.
	SUM	Computes sum of values in a selected collection of data fields.
R:BASE 5000	R)COMPUTE function col FROM tbl WHERE condlist	Computes given function using rows of designated column from designated table that satisfies conditions in condition list. The various values of ⟨function⟩ are AVE—Computes average of specified column entries. COUNT—Computes number of entries there are among specified column entries. MAX—Determines maximum (numeric or alphabetic) entry among column entries specified. MIN—Determines minimum (numeric or alphabetic) entry among column entries specified. ROWS—Determines number of rows for given column. SUM—Determines sum of specified column entries. ALL—Computes all of the above six functions.

Hands-on Exercises

1. Display EMPLOYEE, the personnel data file you developed in the Hands-on Exercises in Sections 10.1 and 10.2.

   a) Display the names of the employees and their weekly salaries.

   b) In response to a request made by a government agency, you must supply a list showing the name and race of each employee. Prepare this list and print it on your printer.

   c) Determine which employees earn more than $350 per week.

   d) Determine which employees working in the sales department earn more than $350 per week.

   e) Determine the average weekly salary of all employees.

   f) Determine the average weekly salary of employees in the sales department.

   g) Determine the highest salary paid to all employees except those not in the sales department.

   h) Determine the total weekly payroll for employees living in Pennsylvania.

10.5 Sorting

To analyze the contents of a data file, it often helps to sort the data into a particular order. The concept of sorting is not new to you. You have sorted different types of data since you were in grade school, when you began sorting numbers into numeric order and text into alphabetic order. You can perform similar sorting operations on the records of a data file.

The Basics of Sorting

A data file usually consists of records that have a number of fields. A file can be sorted in many different ways, depending on the choice of the **key field**, the category you will use most frequently when performing a search.

To sort a data file, you designate one of the fields as the **primary key**. The contents of this field is used to sort the records into order; it is most efficient to choose a field within which there will not be a great deal of duplication of data. For example, consider once again the data file CUSTOMER. As part of the **SORT command**, designate a primary key. Suppose that you designate

R)select all from Customer sorted by Name

ID	Name	Address	City	State	Zip Code	Balance	CredLim
00003	Dixon, M.	2 Dabney Ct.	Rockville	MD	20851	$ 0.00	$2,000.00
00001	Gold, B.	6522 Beechwood Dr.	Greenbelt	MD	20910	$358.12	$1,000.00
00009	Jeffrey, R.	7585 Yellow Moon Pl.	Arlington	VA	20551	$181.33	$1,000.00
00002	Marley, C.	1822 Jefferson Pl.	Chevy Chase	MD	20912	$578.85	$1,500.00
00008	Mathews, F.	12751 Summers Dr.	Beltsville	MD	20744	$500.89	$800.00
00006	Matson, A.	30 Victory Ln.	Washington	DC	10001	$582.12	$1,000.00
00007	O'Brien, C.	1703 Gridley Ln.	Silver Spring	MD	20903	$205.40	$800.00
00005	Samuel, V.	3309 Lancer St.	Columbia	MD	20722	$115.30	$300.00
00004	Travland, N.	8003 Allentown Rd.	Alexandria	MD	20301	$348.11	$500.00

Figure 10.12 The CUSTOMER file sorted by *NAME*.

the field *NAME*. The contents of this field are used to sort the file, which amounts to arranging the records so that the *NAME* fields are in alphabetic order, as shown in Figure 10.12.

If you choose *STATE* as the key field, then the sorted file appears as shown in Figure 10.13. Note that there are a number of "ties." That is, a number of records have the same *STATE* field. You may arrange these "ties" according to a **secondary key**, which is a field that is sorted after the file is ordered by the primary key sort.

Suppose that you designate the *STATE* field as the primary key and the *NAME* field as the secondary key. Any records

Figure 10.13 The CUSTOMER file sorted by *STATE*.

R)select all from Customer sorted by State

ID	Name	Address	City	State	Zip Code	Balance	CredLim
00006	Matson, A.	30 Victory Ln.	Washington	DC	10001	$582.12	$1,000.00
00001	Gold, B.	6522 Beechwood Dr.	Greenbelt	MD	20910	$358.12	$1,000.00
00003	Dixon, M.	2 Dabney Ct.	Rockville	MD	20851	$0.00	$2,000.00
00004	Travland, N.	8003 Allentown Rd.	Alexandria	MD	20301	$348.11	$500.00
00005	Samuel, V.	3309 Lancer St.	Columbia	MD	20722	$115.30	$300.00
00002	Marley, C.	1822 Jefferson Pl.	Chevy Chase	MD	20912	$578.85	$1,500.00
00007	O'Brien, C.	1703 Gridley Ln.	Silver Spring	MD	20903	$205.40	$800.00
00008	Mathews, F.	12751 Summers Dr.	Beltsville	MD	20744	$500.89	$800.00
00009	Jeffrey, R.	7585 Yellow Moon Pl.	Arlington	VA	20551	$181.33	$1,000.00

R)select all from Customer sorted by State, Name

ID	Name	Address	City	State	Zip Code	Balance	Cred Lim
00006	Matson, A.	30 Victory Ln.	Washington	DC	10001	$582.12	$1,000.00
00003	Dixon, M.	2 Dabney Ct.	Rockville	MD	20851	$0.00	$2,000.00
00001	Gold, B.	6522 Beechwood Dr.	Greenbelt	MD	20910	$358.12	$1,000.00
00002	Marley, C.	1822 Jefferson Pl.	Chevy Chase	MD	20912	$578.85	$1,500.00
00008	Mathews, F.	12751 Summers Dr.	Beltsville	MD	20744	$500.89	$800.00
00007	O'Brien, C.	1703 Gridley Ln.	Silver Spring	MD	20903	$205.40	$800.00
00005	Samuel, V.	3309 Lancer St.	Columbia	MD	20722	$115.30	$300.00
00004	Travland, N.	8003 Allentown Rd.	Alexandria	MD	20301	$348.11	$500.00
00009	Jeffrey, R.	7585 Yellow Moon Pl.	Arlington	VA	20551	$181.33	$1,000.00

Figure 10.14   The customer file sorted by *STATE* and *NAME*.

corresponding to the same state will then be arranged alphabetically according to name, as illustrated in Figure 10.14. Note that designating a secondary key is optional.

Returning to Figures 10.12 and 10.13, these examples show files sorted in **ascending order**—that is, the key fields are arranged in the usual alphabetic order, starting with the letter A. A sort in ascending order also arranges numbers from smallest to largest. In some applications, it is more useful to sort the records in **descending order**, where text is arranged in reverse alphabetic order and numbers from largest to smallest. In most data management programs, the standard order of sorting is ascending. However, you may change to descending order by specifying the order sorting as part of the SORT command.

Using the SORT command allows you to designate a primary key, an optional secondary key, and optional sort orders (ascending or descending) for each of the keys. Command Table 10.12 summarizes the operation of the SORT command for our sample data management programs.

Sorting Techniques

Sorting is time-consuming, even for a computer. The larger the file, the longer the sort time needed by the program.

You could use many techniques to sort file records. For the most part, these techniques are beyond the scope of this book and as a novice user you need not be concerned with them. However, you should know that sorting is one of the most time-consuming of all computer tasks. It is very easy to be lulled into complacency by the speed of computers. However, some tasks are time consuming even for a computer, and sorting is one of those tasks. As the number of records to sort increases, so does the sorting time. Most microcomputers will have difficulty sorting files containing more than a few thousand records. On some slower machines, sorting as few as 500 records may take as long as five to ten minutes.

Using Index Files

To speed up the sorting of large files, some data management programs allow you to use an **index file**—a directory of the records in a file. As an analogy, think of an index to a book as the directory of the book's contents, which helps you to quickly find information within the book. Similarly, not only can index files speed up sorting, but they can be used to access data in response to queries for file update commands. Using an index file to access data improves the efficiency with which you can perform file manipulations.

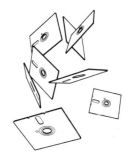

Command Table 10.12 SORT commands for Lotus 1-2-3, Gold-Spread, dBASE III, and R:BASE 5000.

Program	Command	Comments
Lotus 1-2-3 and GoldSpread	/Data Sort Select option from sort menu. ⟨ENTER⟩	The options on the sort menu are as follows: Data-range—Sets the range to sort Primary key—Sets the first column to sort on (the primary key). Secondary key—Sets the first column to sort on (the secondary key). Reset—Cancels all sort menu settings. Go—Perform sorting and exit the sort menu.
dBASE III	Uses index files. See dBASE III documentation.	
R:BASE 5000	R)SELECT ALL FROM tbl SORTED BY col1 = A, col2 = D,... WHERE condl-ist	Displays a list of entries in designated table that satisfy the conditions in the condition list. Entries are sorted by using columns in listed columns as keys. Keys are used for sorting in order in which they are listed. That is, primary key is first, secondary key next, and so forth. =A signifies sorting in ascending order (assumed) =D signifies sorting in descending order

An index file is constructed using the **INDEX command**. As part of this command, you specify a primary key and an optional secondary key, just as if you were sorting the file. The INDEX command constructs a file and lists the numbers of the records, sorted in the order determined by the primary key and the secondary key.

Actual file records may be longer and require hundreds of bytes of storage for each record. To sort such records, the computer needs to physically rearrange the records by recopying them from one place in secondary storage (in unsorted form) to another place (in sorted form), a process that can be very time consuming. In contrast, an index file requires only a small amount of information per record, so the computer can manipulate it much more quickly. Furthermore, when adding or deleting records, you need only to modify the index file; the computer doesn't need to do any physical rearrangement of the file records.

Index files are rarely used in spreadsheet-based data management programs. In these systems, sorting is done by rearranging the worksheet entries. Most stand-alone systems let you use index files, which makes them capable of handling files with large numbers of records.

Section 10.4: Test Your Understanding

1. What is sorting?
2. What is a primary key? Explain how this key is used in sorting.
3. Arrange the following in ascending, then descending, order:
   FRED, NED, ED, TED, DRED.
4. What is a secondary key? Explain how this key might be used in sorting information from a telephone directory.
5. What is an index file?
6. Why are index files used?

Hands-on Exercises

1. Display EMPLOYEE, the personnel file developed in the Hands-on Exercises in Sections 10.2 through 10.4.
   a) Sort the records of the file alphabetically by employee.
   b) Perform a sort by using the *DEPARTMENT* field as a secondary key.

c) Perform a sort by using the *WEEKLY SALARY* field as a secondary key.

d) Sort the employees by weekly salary.

KEY TERMS

storing data
updating data
recalling data
summarizing data
disseminating data
analyzing data
organizing data
data management program
file management program
data file
stand-alone data
  management program
spreadsheet-based data
  management program
data item
field

field length
record
data file
data type
protected data field
confidential data field
file structure
attribute
input screen
input prompt
downloading
importing
ADD RECORD command
field selection
FIELD SELECTION
  command

record selection criterion
RECORD SELECTION
  command
compound selection criterion
logical connectives AND,
  OR
key field
primary key
SORT command
secondary key
ascending order
descending order
index file
INDEX command

CHAPTER REVIEW QUESTIONS

1. Give examples of three data files that can be used in a small business.
2. What is meant by the structure of a data file?
3. List the data types.
4. What is the advantage in assigning data types to fields of a record?
5. List three commonly used ways to check input to a data file.
6. Suppose that a data file consists of 100 records, each containing 50 fields. Of these, 20 fields contain 30 bytes and 30 fields contain 8 bytes.

    a) How many bytes of storage does each record require?

    b) How many bytes of storage does the entire data file require?

7. What is sorting?
8. Explain how using an index file allows you to perform sorting operations more quickly than sorting the file records themselves.
9. What is a record selection criterion?
10. You want to select all the records from a file. In this file, field 1 (*AMOUNT*) is between 0 and 100 and field 2 (*MARRIED*) is F. Write a record selection criterion to accomplish this selection.
11. List the five most common statistical functions used to analyze the contents of a data file.

DISCUSSION QUESTIONS

1. A double-sided, double-density diskette on an IBM PC contains 360K bytes of storage. Suppose a data file consists of 5,000 400-byte records. How many diskettes will this require? What problems in updating, selecting, and sorting can you envision in dealing with files that occupy more than one diskette?

2. Several office workers all need access to the data in a single data file. What problems must be resolved in order to meet such a requirement?

APPLICATION PROJECTS

1. An instructor in a college course wishes to use a data management program to keep track of her students' grades. For each student, she would like to keep track of the following information:

   Name
   Social security number
   Exam 1
   Exam 2
   Exam 3
   Paper 1
   Paper 2
   Final exam
   Semester grade (an average of the six grades)

   Including the final exam, there should be six grades for each student.

   a) Set up a file structure for the data file.
   b) Create and enter data for ten students into the data file.
   c) Use your data management program to determine the class average.
   d) Use your data management program to determine all students who received a grade of 90 or above.
   e) Use your data management program to determine all students who receive 90 or above on Exam 1 but 60 or less on any of the other grades.
   f) Use your data management program to count the number of students having grades in each of the following categories:

   Greater than 90
   Greater than 80 but less than 90
   Greater than 70 but less than 80
   Greater than 60 but less than 70
   Less than 60.

> NAME: Sanborn Weekly Voice
> ADDRESS: 155 Main Street
> CITY: Sanborn
> STATE: VA
> ZIP: 33321
> PHONE: (203)123-4567
> CODE: 2 (Note: 1 = daily newspaper, 2 = weekly newspaper, 3 = free newspaper/advertiser, 4 = independent radio station, 5 = public television station, etc.)
> CONTACT: Nancy Staten
> REVIEWS: 1 (Note: 1 = review plays and need tickets early in the play's run, 2 = do not review plays)
> REACH: 4,000 circulation, delivered only within Sanborn
> COMMENTS: Mostly local news and sports, well-read by subscribers but subscription base is small. Will send reviewer to opening night but quality of reviewers has been poor—frequently they have no theater experience, don't get reviews into print in time to be useful.

Figure 10.15 A sample record from the PUBLICITY file.

2. Harvey Levesque, the Publicity Chairman for the Sanborn Community Theater, is responsible for publicizing the theater's six plays during the season. In addition to signs and posters placed in store windows, the theater also relies on news articles and public service announcements in the local media. Harvey has developed a data file to help him organize the theater's publicity information. A typical record might contain the fields shown in Figure 10.15.

   a) What other fields might be useful?

   b) Explain how Harvey might add, update, or delete records over an extended period of time.

   c) Describe several scenarios detailing how Harvey might sort the data file to get useful information.

3. Midway Pharmacy currently uses a manual system for filling prescriptions. The files are maintained in numeric order by prescription number. The pharmacy is frequently asked

Prescription

Date	Number	Insured	Patient	Physician	Cost
1/4/86	1564	L. Sayers	Leslie Sayers	Anz	$11.55
1/8/86	1565	H. Morris	Casey Morris	Jones	12.80
2/1/86	1566	L. Sayers	Abby Sayers	Anz	21.50
2/3/86	1567	T. Keith	Diane Keith	Smith	32.15
2/7/86	1568	A. May	Lee May	Ott	12.05
3/6/86	1569	L. Sayers	Abby Sayers	Anz	13.36
3/9/86	1570	P. Lane	Paul Lane	Beard	9.02
4/5/86	1571	L. Sayers	Linda Sayers	Anz	22.50
5/5/86	1572	L. Sayers	David Sayers	Anz	47.50
5/8/86	1573	D. Horne	Daryl Horne	Jacks	16.60

Figure 10.16   Midway Pharmacy's PRESCRIPTION data file.

to verify its customers' insurance claims. The insurance claim form requires the following information:

> Insured party's name
> Patient's name (insured party, spouse, child, etc.)
> Prescription number
> Date of prescription
> Prescribing physician
> Cost of prescription

Most insurance companies require a separate claim for each family member. However, many customers do not file claims immediately; in fact, it is common for some customers to file claims only once or twice a year. Those annual claims include the entire family's prescriptions to date. Unless the customer keeps records of dates and prescription numbers, the pharmacist may spend a great deal of time searching through the prescription files.

Betty Shipleigh, the new owner of Midway Pharmacy, has just purchased a microcomputer and a data management package. She now wants to computerize her prescription records. She has the following concerns referring to the data contained in Figure 10.16.

a) Discuss the potential advantages and disadvantages of using a data management package to maintain prescription records.

b) Set up a file structure that will facilitate Betty's verification of customers' insurance claims.

c) Implement the data file using the data in Figure 10.16.

d) On June 1, 1986, Linda Sayers decided to file a claim for her family for the first five months of the year. Retrieve the records of all the Sayers family prescriptions for the period January 1 through May 30.

11 Database Management Systems

The Data Busters

Every season, new shows crop up on television. Viewers in 12 major cities across the country, whose responses are tallied daily by the A.C. Nielsen Company, decide which programs succeed and which don't.

For obvious reasons, these ratings are closely monitored by television producers. Columbia Pictures of Burbank, California, which recently produced *Ghostbusters* and *Starman*, both box office hits, also produces popular TV shows such as "Crazy Like a Fox" and "Mike Hammer."

Douglas Roth, director of research at Columbia's Burbank offices, emphasizes that television ratings are instrumental in deciding which shows stay on the air. "We live and die by these ratings," he says. "The ratings we receive from Nielsen's are the lifeblood of this industry."

Before microcomputers, wading through ratings was a far more ponderous process. Now Roth's microcomputer automatically dials the Nielsen mainframe in Dunedin, Florida, every day, then downloads and stores all the ratings in a database.

A Nielsen software program called Micronode translates the data into readable form, displaying a response every 15 minutes to each station's shows by market. Roth can get eight types of reports from his ratings database. For example, he can query the database about how many viewers watched each prime-time show on all three major networks each quarter hour. Or, he can ask for a report on any Columbia program, such as the 9:00 P.M. movie and compare the show's rating with that of the competition. He can also see how well Columbia's syndicated programs, such as "Charlie's Angels" and "Hart to Hart," are facing up against the vast wasteland of independent stations.

"Say we want to see how 'Hart to Hart' is doing in Los Angeles. We'd type in *L.A.* and *Hart to Hart*," Roth says. "The micro will show a history of the program, and how it's doing every quarter hour."

In the past, all ratings had to be hand-averaged. With Nielsen's new system and a micro, it's all done automatically. The data is then ready for examination by Roth and other analysts to determine which shows sell the best. "Now we're really free to do the work to sell shows," Roth says. "Before we were just punching numbers and averaging."

IN CHAPTER 10, you learned the basics about data file management programs: how to define the structure of a data file, enter data into the file, and update the file by deleting or changing records. The entire discussion centered on the manipulation of a single file at a time.

In applications, you will usually need to store data in a number of different data files and, on many occasions, you will need to manipulate several data files at once. For example, when Aardvark Pets receives a shipment of gerbils, the invoice for the shipment must be entered into the accounts payable file, and the inventory file must be adjusted to reflect the added gerbils.

The files maintained by Aardvark Pets are related to one another in the sense that updating one file (say, the accounts payable file) may require the updating of another (such as the inventory file). This collection of related data files is called a **database**. In this chapter, you will learn how to use a data management program to create a database, which could become your most essential business tool.

As discussed in Chapter 10, there are two types of data management programs: spreadsheet-based and stand-alone. Spreadsheet-based systems are usually not equipped to handle more than one file at a time; for multi-file manipulation, you need a stand-alone data management program. For this reason, we shall limit our discussion in this chapter to stand-alone data management programs; of our sample programs, only dBASE III and R:BASE 5000 are stand-alone programs.

11.1 The Concept of a Database Management System

The related files of a database must be stored in a manner that allows them to be simultaneously accessed. A data management program that can manipulate the related files of a database is called a **database management system**, or **DBMS**. Figure 11.1 shows the organization of a database for the data files maintained by Aardvark Pets.

A DBMS allows you to use the files in a database to update and retrieve data, answer questions, and prepare reports. With a DBMS, you can add new data files and change the structure of existing files. Stretching beyond the simpler data management programs, a DBMS can simultaneously update related data files and assemble answers to questions by piecing together information

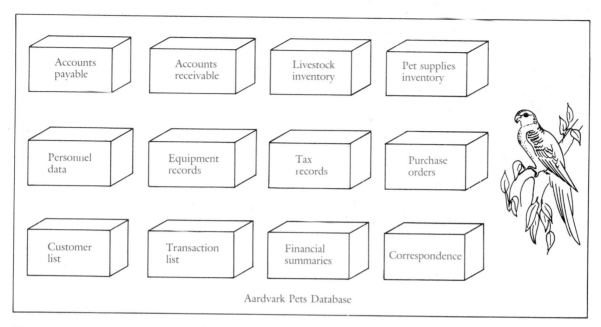

Figure 11.1   Files in the Aardvark Pets database.

contained in those files. The capabilities of a DBMS are summarized in Figure 11.2.

Using a DBMS

Employees with vastly different job responsibilities can use the same DBMS to perform their individual work tasks. For example, the sales manager at Aardvark Pets can use a DBMS to prepare weekly reports on shipments. The warehouse manager can use the same DBMS to answer questions about inventory as they come up throughout a work day. The advertising department can use the same DBMS to prepare a set of address labels to mail notices of a sale on baby rabbits.

Before the era of database management systems, each application required its own program and its own data files. In those days, a company's accounting department had one set of data files, the sales department had another, and the manufacturing department had yet another. As you can see in Figure 11.3, each application required its own custom-designed programs that could maintain files and generate reports. Often, applications developed by different departments within a company used incompatible data files that stored information in different formats—which made it extremely difficult, if not impossible, for one department to use data files constructed by another.

Data files

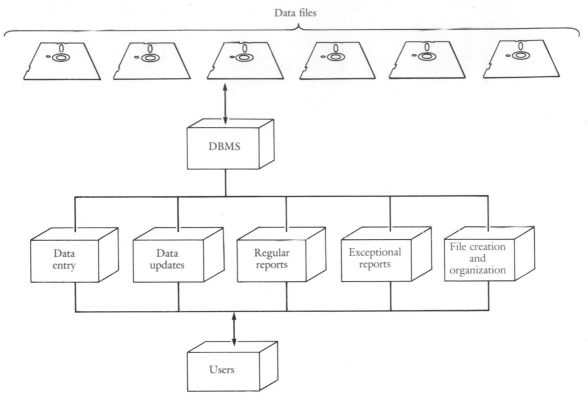

Figure 11.2 The capabilities of a database management system.

As you might guess, these systems were very clumsy. To derive new data from the data files or to present current information in a different format, programmers needed to write new programs, which often meant information could be generated only after delays of weeks or months. Today, such difficulties can be avoided by using a DBMS and its consistent file formats.

Figure 11.3 Pre-DBMS data management.

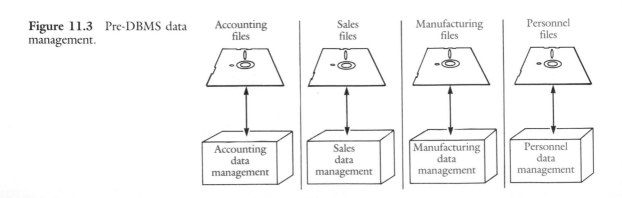

Section 11.1: Test Your Understanding

1. What is a database?
2. What is a database management program?
3. Explain the advantages of using a database management program rather than a custom file-handling program for each application.
4. List some difficulties you may encounter using custom file-handling programs.

11.2 Organizing a Database

You must plan the organization of a database carefully so that the DBMS can supply the information required to make decisions. Let's look at ways to plan and create your database.

Database File Organization Models

The typical database contains many files. A DBMS derives much of its power from its ability to assemble related information from several different files. Both dBASE III and R:BASE 5000 (as well as many other DBMS packages available for microcomputers) employ a relational system—a method of relating files to one another. A DBMS package that uses a relational system is called a **relational database**.

In simple terms, a relational database system might be described as follows: Think of a data file as a table with a column for each field. Each column, or field, has a title. Each row of the table contains a single record of the file. Now consider a database as a collection of tables. Some of the tables in a database can have column names in common, indicating that they contain common information.

Refer to the two tables shown in Figure 11.4. The first table is a TRANSACTION file listing sales to customers. For each sale, the TRANSACTION file records the product name, quantity sold, sales representative's name, date of sale, and amount of sale. The second table, a CUSTOMER file, provides information about customers, including name, address, city, state, zip code, and telephone number. The two tables have a common column labelled *CUSTOMER NAME*. This column, called a **linking column**, provides a link between the two tables, and thus between the two files.

TRANSACTION TABLE

Customer name	Date	Item	Quantity	Amount	Sales rep.

Linking column ↕

CUSTOMER INFORMATION TABLE

Customer name	Address	City	State	Zip Code	Balance

Figure 11.4 The TRANS-ACTION file and the CUS-TOMER file from a database.

You can use a linking column to relate information in one file to information in another. Suppose that a sales manager wants to write a letter of thanks to all customers who placed orders in the last month. He could evolve a mailing list by looking at the TRANSACTION file and determining which sales were made during the last month. Next, he could look up the corresponding customer name in the *CUSTOMER NAME* column and couple that with the address obtained from the CUSTOMER file.

You may be asking, "Why use two different data files to record transactions and customer data? Wouldn't it be simpler to use a single table to record the data?" The answer is no.

Suppose that you did use a single data file to record the information. Each record would be much longer, since each row (representing each transaction) would have to record the address and telephone number of the customer, in addition to the customer's name. However, a single customer might have placed many different orders, which would mean that the customer address and telephone number would be repeated in each transaction record. The size of the data file would be increased and the time for processing most data file activities (such as sorting) would increase.

Data file size is not the only problem with using a single data file to record the information. Consider the problem of updating a data file in the event that a customer moves. If the name and address are kept in a single place, you need to make only one change. However, if you record the address and telephone number with each transaction, then you will have many corrections to make. A simple task thus becomes quite complex.

Yet another problem arises in using a single data file. The customer data is useful information that should be available to many different departments, including accounting, sales, and advertising. If the customer data is buried in the transaction file, it is more difficult to access by other users with different requirements.

You can see that you need to give careful thought to the organization of data within a database. The general principle is to use a large number of simple data files, rather than a small number of complex files.

As you saw, linking columns are used to connect data items in related files. In some cases, however, a single link is not sufficient to connect data items without ambiguity. For instance, suppose that you have two customers named Tom Jones. The linking described above does not distinguish between the two names. One way to avoid this problem is to use more than one linking column to connect the files. For example, you can use *both* the customer name and address as linking columns—a good idea because it will be a unique customer identifier, but it creates the sort of duplication that separate data files are supposed to avoid. Another way out of this dilemma is to identify each customer by a customer number and to use that number as a link between the files. This approach is usually taken in real-world practice.

Using Related Files to Answer Questions

In Chapter 10, you learned to answer questions by selecting rows and columns from a data file. Database management systems allow you to select columns and rows from data files that are related by a linking column. For example, say you're a sales representative for Precocious Software, a small computer software company. You are searching for customer names that appear in both the CUSTOMER file and the TRANSACTION file. You can select all rows from the

Customer name	Balance	Sales rep.	Date
John, J.	385.78	Smith	10/15/86

Rows selected for common entries under CUSTOMER NAME in both tables.

Figure 11.5 Selecting a row that uses a related data file as a selection criterion.

CUSTOMER file that have a customer name corresponding to a customer name in the TRANSACTION file. In effect, this procedure selects rows based on a criterion involving a related file. The resulting list of customers is shown in Figure 11.5.

A database management system can look up data in one file and use it in calculating data for another file. For example, consider again the TRANSACTION file in Figure 11.4. It records the quantity shipped and the amount of the sale. You can use the database management system to calculate the amount of the sale by using the PRICE LIST data file shown in Figure 11.6, which has an entry for each product.

The entry has two fields: *PRODUCT NAME* and *UNIT PRICE*. The PRICE LIST file is related to the TRANSACTION file via the linking column *PRODUCT NAME*. You can instruct the database management system to help enter data for the TRANSACTION file. A clerk can enter all data except for *AMOUNT OF SALE*. The database management system can then use the *PRODUCT NAME* entry to locate the *UNIT PRICE* in the PRICE

Figure 11.6 A PRICE LIST data file.

Product name	Unit price
Index 3	99.95
WP Plus	159.95
Accounting 1	495.00
Accounting 2	495.00
Accounting 3	495.00
Report Writer	159.95
DB Manager	349.95
Hard Disk Manager	49.95
Learning Accounting	99.95

LIST file. The system can then calculate

Amount of sale = Quantity × Unit price

This number is then inserted into the *AMOUNT OF SALE* field.

In a similar fashion, a database management system can use data from related files in computing summary statistics. For example, you can request the average sales for orders shipped to Pennsylvania during the last year. Or you can find the largest sale to a customer in New York in the last month.

Guidelines for Designing a Database

A DBMS gives you power in managing your data. But like most powerful tools, the DBMS must be designed and used properly. If you don't design your database properly, you cannot extract all the desired information from it.

Your DBMS must be well-organized and thoughtfully designed, or it will not work efficiently for you.

No matter which DBMS you use, you must follow an organized procedure to design the database. There are four main steps in the design procedure:

1. *List the information you want to derive from the database*. List the reports you will need and outline their structure. List miscellaneous questions you will want to answer on an irregular basis.

2. *Determine which data items are necessary for providing the information*. A DBMS can base its output on the data that is present in the database. Your design must guarantee that the database contains sufficient information to compile your reports and answer your questions.

3. *Organize the data items into data files*. Make sure that all required data items are contained somewhere in the database. Verify that the necessary linking columns are inserted so that information in different files can be properly related.

4. *List the procedures for accessing information from the data files*. Outline the procedures for making reports and answering questions. This is a test of your data file design. It makes sure that your data files contain both the data and the links necessary for producing the desired output.

Let's implement these procedures by designing a database for the sales department of Precocious Software. The database designer is Laura Spencer, head of the sales department. Sales have been quite brisk and the company's product line has expanded to include four different programs. Laura wants to design a database to provide herself and other company executives with sales data and regular reports.

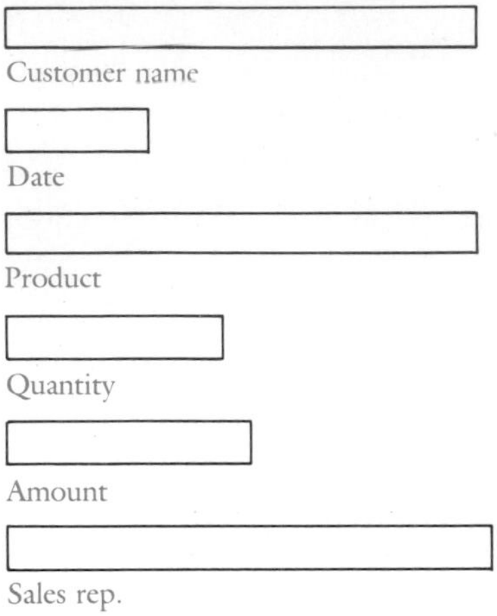

Customer name

Date

Product

Quantity

Amount

Sales rep.

Figure 11.7 The data needed to create Precocious Software's reports.

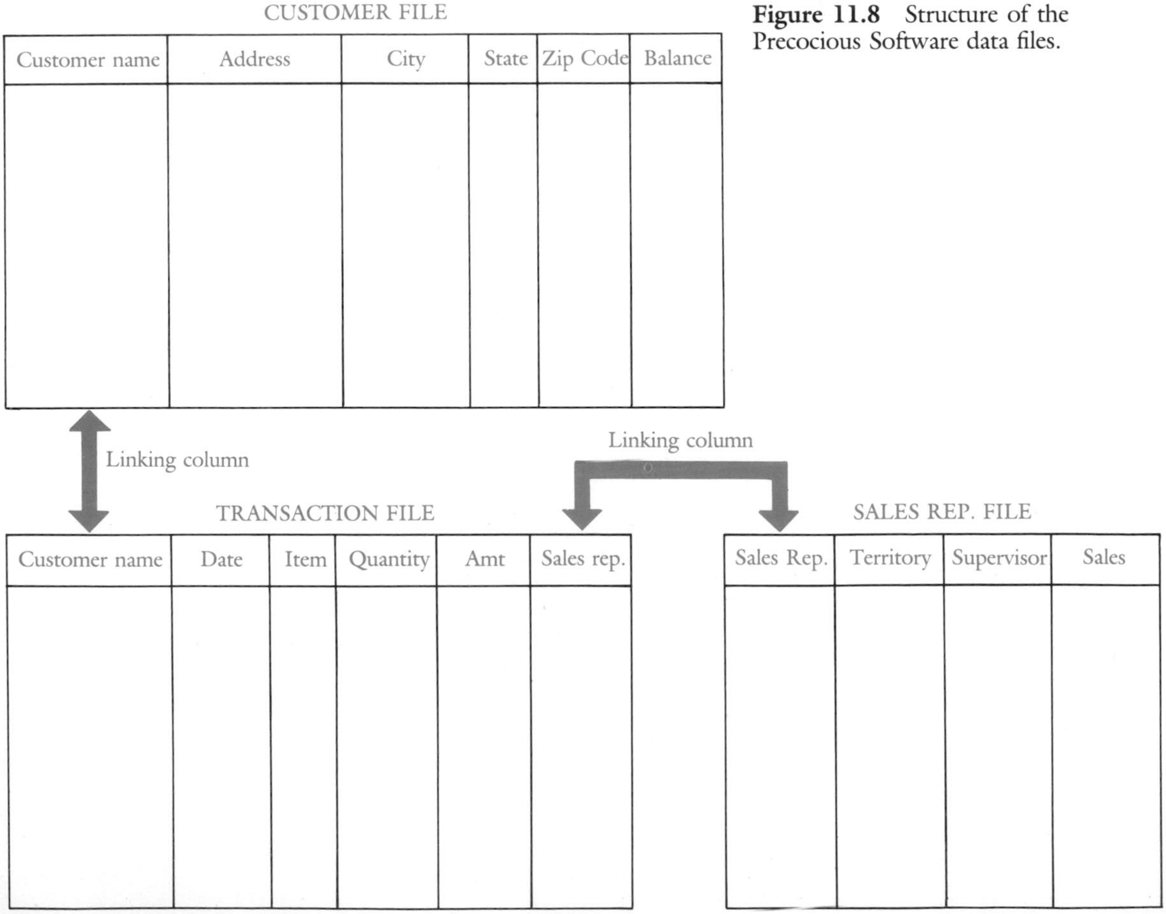

CUSTOMER FILE

Customer name	Address	City	State	Zip Code	Balance

Figure 11.8 Structure of the Precocious Software data files.

Linking column

Linking column

TRANSACTION FILE

Customer name	Date	Item	Quantity	Amt	Sales rep.

SALES REP. FILE

Sales Rep.	Territory	Supervisor	Sales

Her first step is to list the data she needs to derive from the database. She makes the following list:

Weekly sales report
   Number of programs of each type sold
      For the week
      For the year to date
   Comparison with last year
   Dollar volume for each program
      For the week
      For the year to date
   Comparison with last year
   Total dollar volume
      For the week
      For the year to date
   Comparison with last year

Monthly customer report
   Transactions by customer
   List of new customers

Monthly sales representative report
   List of transactions by each sales representative

Step 2 in Laura's database design is to determine the data needed to compile the desired reports. It is clear that Laura needs a list of the transactions that have taken place. In order to tell when a transaction took place, she needs a record of the date. She also needs to record the customer name, the product ordered, the quantity, and the price. To determine which sales representative is responsible for the transaction, she must record the sales representative's name. The data items required for each transaction are summarized in Figure 11.7.

Step 3 in Laura's database design is to specify the data files and their structures. This means dividing the data items into related files. Clearly, there must be a TRANSACTION file. It is possible to put all data about a particular transaction in a single large record, but this is usually a poor design. With an eye toward other uses of the database, Laura could create a CUSTOMER file, a PRICE file, and a SALES REPRESENTATIVE file. Figure 11.8 shows the field structures of these files, which is the fourth step in the database design. The most important point to note is that each of the files must be linked to the TRANSACTION file so that the desired information about each transaction may be compiled.

To complete the database design, Laura must specify how to compile the various reports that will make use of the data files. This process is described in Section 11.3 of this chapter.

Note that the four steps described above do not actually make use of the DBMS. They are design steps only. Once the database design is complete, you may proceed to the next stage, in which you use your design to set up the DBMS.

Implementing a Database

Setting up a database based on your design is referred to as **implementing the database**, a procedure that is summarized in Figure 11.9.

There are four steps needed to implement the database:

1. *Create data files according to the structures worked out in the database design.* As part of this step, you specify the field length, data type, and data attribute restrictions for each data item.

2. *Enter the data into the data files.* You can do this via manual input, downloading from a mainframe, or importing from other data files. Even though data entry is a tedious task, it is one that must be done carefully. Remember, the quality of the data in the database determines the quality of the reports generated by the DBMS.

3. *Specify update procedures and policies.* You must organize the flow of data within your business so that all information needed for the database is actually collected. This may require redoing some of the standard company forms. Your data must be generated with the necessary frequency (daily, weekly, or monthly), and it must be forwarded to the data entry operator in a timely fashion. If a single sales representative is late turning in paperwork, the sales report will be either delayed or inaccurate.

   You may need to use the DBMS facilities to write a file update program. You can use an update program to enter new data into the files, to correct old data, or to calculate data items using the newly supplied data and the data already in the database. As in the above example, a file update program can calculate the amount of a sale as the product of the quantity multiplied by the unit price. The quantity is given as part of the input data; the unit price is found in the PRICE LIST file.

4. *Design reports.* Decide what information from your database needs to go to your colleagues or clients, and what format will be most attractive and easy to read.

5. *Write programs to generate reports.* Use the report writing facilities to create the reports specified in the database design.

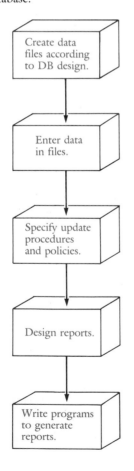

Figure 11.9   Implementing a database.

Section 11.2: *Test Your Understanding*

1. Explain how files in a database are related.
2. What is a linking column?
3. Explain how using related files helps reduce duplication of information.
4. List the steps needed to design a database.
5. List the steps needed to implement a database.

Hands-on Exercises

1. Implement the database described in the text and call it SALES. Fill the files with the data contained in Figure 11.10.
2. Update the database with the information shown in Figure 11.11.

11.3   Output from a DBMS

A major reason for setting up a database is to be able to retrieve its data at some later time, usually as part of a report. Let's examine the reporting process in more detail.

DBMS Reports

DBMS reports are classified into two categories: regular reports and exception reports. A **regular report** is a report that you plan ahead of time. It is usually prepared at regular daily, weekly, or monthly intervals. Examples of regular reports are Precocious Software's Weekly Sales Report, Monthly Customer Report, and the Monthly Sales Representative Report discussed in Section 11.2. An example of a regular report is shown in Figure 11.12.

An **exception report** is a report issued at irregular intervals, in response to a need for particular information. For example, a salary review for a sales representative may require the sales manager to have a complete list of that individual's sales for the last six months. Or a customer complaint about an undelivered order may require a sales representative to look up the date the order was shipped and the mode of shipment.

You may need exception reports for many reasons. Perhaps the information you require is not contained in any regular report,

CUSTOMER FILE

Customer name	Address	City	State	Zip Code	Balance
Jones, C.	2 Broadway	NY	NY	10011	503.12
Chang, E.	3 Bright Rd.	Albany	NY	12102	138.02
Alberts, M.	1250 Alter St.	Albany	NY	12501	112.50

Linking column

Linking column

TRANSACTION FILE

Customer name	Date	Item	Quantity	Amount	Sales rep.
Jones, C.	10/15/86	345	1	103.12	Locker
Jones, C.	10/25/86	588	2	258.14	Locker
Chang, E.	11/1/86	346	1	138.02	Jackson
Alberts, M	11/3/86	340	1	112.50	Jackson

SALES REP. FILE

Sales rep.	Territory	Supervisor	Sales
Locker	NY	Long	58,204
Jackson	Albany	Long	65,809
Taylor	New Haven	Larsen	75,304

Figure 11.10   Data to be entered into the SALES database.

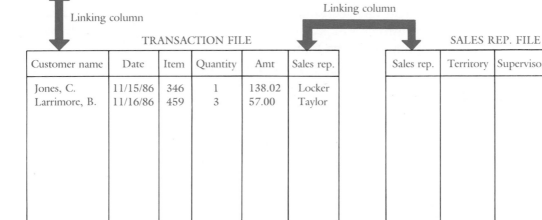

Figure 11.11   Updating data in the SALES database.

Precocious Software Sales Report October 1986

Figure 11.12   An example of a regular report.

	This Year	Previous Year	% Change
Dollar volume	$875,242.48	$650,430.22	34.56
Units moved	12,850	10,420	23.32
Profit	$178,485.12	$151,140.06	18.09
Profit per unit	$68.11	$62.42	9.12

or it may appear in a regular report but it may not be recent enough or comprehensive enough, or it may not be in the correct format.

A report (regular or exception) may contain any of the following types of information, alone or in combination:

- Data retrieved from any of the files in the database. For example, you can list all sales transactions that occurred between October 1 and December 1.
- Data obtained by combining data in related files. You can, for example, list all sales transactions in which the sales representative was not John Jones.
- Statistics generated from data in a single file or in related files. You can, for example, list the average amount of all sales to customers in Nevada, or the total of all sales generated by sales representative John Jones.
- What-if analyses. For example, you can find out what the total sales would have been if New York's representative had increased sales by 30 percent and Pennsylvania's by 40 percent over the preceding year.

Requesting a Report

Most database management systems allow you to request a report in a number of different ways. The simplest method is to use an **interactive report generation command**, achieved by typing a command addressed directly to the DBMS. You tell the DBMS the data to be included in the report and the format in which it is to be displayed. Typing a format can be rather tedious, so interactive report generation is used mostly for exception reports that are to be generated once.

A second method of requesting a report is to use a program written with the facilities of the DBMS. In essence, the program is just a list of the interactive commands that you enter to create the report. However, you can store the list of commands in a data file and have the DBMS execute the commands whenever you want. This approach is extremely useful for generating regular reports or occasional exception reports.

Output of a Report

You may output a report to the monitor, the printer, or a data file. The monitor is most suitable for exception reports, especially for reports used in a what-if analysis. Regular reports are usually printed on paper so that they may be circulated to the people who need them.

When reports are output to a data file, you can circulate them to others via electronic mail. (See Chapter 13.) This is a high-tech way to avoid the ever-higher piles of paper that accumulate in offices everywhere.

Using DBMS Reports

Plan your DBMS reports so that they are useful to others as well as yourself. Regularly survey the people in your company to determine the following:

- Do reports contain all the information they require? Should there be more data in the reports? Should there be less?
- Do reports supply needed information in a timely fashion? Should reports be issued more or less frequently?
- Are reports based on all the latest data? Does the updating schedule mate well with the report generation schedule?
- Is the report circulation list complete? Are there people who should get the reports but do not? Are there people who get the reports but should not?

Based on your survey, you may wish to change database updating procedures, revise the report circulation list, revise the report structure, or even, perhaps, revise the database itself.

Section 11.3: Test Your Understanding

1. What is the difference between a regular report and an exception report?
2. Give two examples of regular reports that a sales manager might prepare.
3. Give two examples of exception reports that a sales manager might receive.
4. What is interactive report generation?
5. What is the most efficient method for requesting regular reports?
6. List three criteria you can use to evaluate the effectiveness of DBMS reports.

PRECOCIOUS SOFTWARE
SALES REPORT

Number of transactions

Dollar volume

Sales by representative

Joe Jackson

Ruth Locker

Figure 11.13   Format for a
regular sales report.

Henry Taylor

Hands-on Exercises

1. Recall the database SALES created in the Hands-On Exercises
   of Section 11.2.

   a) Prepare a regular report based on the report form shown
      in Figure 11.13.

   b) Use the DBMS to determine the total amount of all sales
      made by sales representative Jackson during November.

   c) Use the DBMS to determine the total amount of all sales
      to customer E. Chang in the last six months.

   d) Use the DBMS to determine which sales representative has
      the most sales.

11.4 Database Programming

Communicating with a Database Management System

A DBMS uses its own language, which is different for each DBMS.
You may give single commands to the DBMS via the keyboard,
or you may store a sequence of DBMS commands, called a **DBMS
program**, in a file. Using the DBMS language, you can formulate
commands that will do the following tasks:

- Create a data file
- Specify the structure of a data file
- Enter data into an existing data file
- Change a field in a specific record
- Specify the format of a report

A DBMS program might consist of the following sequence of commands:

Choose the database SALES

Load the files INVOICE and TERRITORY

Prepare weekly sales summary 1

Prepare year-to-date report

Prepare year-to-year comparison

You may direct the DBMS to carry out the commands in the file by giving a single instruction to the DBMS. For instance, the above sequence of commands might be given the name REPORT1. When you give the command REPORT1 to the DBMS, it will execute the sequence of commands. You may need to create a complicated sequence of commands to specify the format for a report and to print the report out, but you can store the sequence of instructions for accomplishing these tasks in a data file so that they may be easily recalled whenever needed.

Creating Stand-Alone Applications

You can create a program to perform a single task, such as preparing a report. However, it is often useful to prepare a single program that incorporates all of the tasks associated with a particular database, called a **stand-alone DBMS program.** A stand-alone program incorporates all routine database management tasks and allows you to prepare all regular database reports.

DBMS programs are generally written by specialists who are experts on the intricacies of the DBMS. Although these programs are not terribly difficult to write, they do require a thorough knowledge of the DBMS commands. From the standpoint of the user, however, it is easy to run a stand-alone program and select the desired task from a menu of choices. Such an arrangement is especially suitable for relatively unsophisticated database users, since it allows routine database tasks to be accomplished by someone who knows very little about the operation of the DBMS.

For example, suppose that you regularly need four different reports to run Precocious Software: an inventory report, a cash flow report, a personnel report, and a customer list report. In addition, you reqularly need to print out mailing labels to send advertising pieces to your customers. You can create a stand-alone application to perform the five tasks (four reports plus the mailing list). Once the stand-alone application is written, one of your sales clerks can run the application and execute the tasks by choosing them from a menu.

Section 11.4: Test Your Understanding

1. What is a DBMS program?
2. What is the advantage of using a DBMS program to perform a task?
3. Are there any DBMS tasks that are best performed by entering commands one by one from the keyboard? Are there any tasks that are best performed as DBMS programs?
4. What is a stand-alone application?

11.5 Protecting a Database

Protect the diskettes and hard disks containing your database as you would all other disks: Treat them with care; save your data every 15 minutes or so; and back up your data regularly.

Database management systems place a tremendous amount of power in the hands of a business user. A DBMS used to organize business data and provide statistics on which to base business decisions represents a huge investment in planning and implementation. However, databases are subject to a number of hazards that you must guard against. If something happens to your database, it may take weeks or months to reconstruct it from source documents, if you can reconstruct it at all! This section discusses these hazards and some ways to protect your database against them.

Physical Hazards

Database files are subject to the same risks as other files stored in secondary memory. Diskettes can be erased accidentally or damaged by mishandling. Hard disks are subject to head crashes. (Refer to Chapter 3 for a discussion on the care of diskettes and hard disks.) For these reasons alone, it is crucial that database files be backed up on a regular basis. You should back up a database after each updating session, so that any database changes are reflected in the current backup.

Databases may be quite large. It is not uncommon to see databases that occupy up to 20 megabytes. Backing up large databases may require that you add a high-speed backup device, such as a tape drive, to avoid the arduous task of copying the database onto 20 to 70 floppy diskettes.

Checking Data Entries

Update your database files consistently and accurately, so that the reports you generate will be reliable.

In designing a database, it is important to build in as many checks as possible on input data. If the contents of a database are to provide a reliable basis on which to formulate business decisions, they must be entered and updated accurately.

Updating Files

It is important to adopt strict rules on who will maintain your database and what sources will be used to update the database files. If the records in a database are to be reliable, then they must be consistent and accurate. The best way to guarantee accuracy is to consistently use the same data sources for updating the files. If any discrepancies in the data files are later observed, then there is a trail you can follow back to the source to determine the correct state of affairs. For instance, if the data files are always constructed from sales invoices, you should save these invoices as a means of correcting errors.

Thievery and Sabotage

You've probably heard many stories about computer crime: A thief steals money or valuable data through entry into a corporate database and then covers up the crime by falsifying information in the database. To deter such crimes, it is necessary to limit access to your database. Most database management systems provide for password protection, which denies access to the DBMS until the user types the correct password. Some systems provide multiple levels of protection through a sequence of passwords, each allowing access only to certain data files.

Limit access to your database through passwords so that only authorized users can gain entry to your files.

Protecting Database Confidentiality

Databases often contain data regarding salaries, medical information, or company trade secrets that require confidentiality. Passwords provide some help in this direction, but better protection can be obtained by using an **encryption system** for encoding the contents of data files. Encryption is the coding of data so they cannot be understood by humans. Some DBMS programs have built-in encryption systems that automatically scramble sensitive data; others allow the user to individually code special encryption routines. Encrypted files can only be decrypted by someone who knows the correct password. Thus, encryption systems protect the confidentiality of a database from unauthorized snoopers.

Protect confidential data by using passwords and encryption systems in your database.

Section 11.5: Test Your Understanding

1. What is encryption?
2. A database occupies five megabytes. How many 360K floppy diskettes will it take to back up the database? Assuming that

it takes 45 seconds to copy data onto each diskette, how long does it take to back up the database?

3. Assume that it takes two minutes to enter data into a single record of a data file. How long will it take to enter 5,000 records? Assuming the conditions stated in Question 2, how long will it take to back up the data file onto floppy diskettes?

4. Explain how unauthorized users might sabotage your database. What precautions can you take against each form of sabotage?

Hands-on Exercises

1. Consult your user manual to determine whether your DBMS has password protection. If it does, determine how the password system works.

   a) Add password protection to the SALES database you created in the Hands-on Exercises of Sections 11.2 and 11.3.

   b) Try to use the database without using a password; now use an incorrect password.

2. Determine if your DBMS has encryption protection.

   a) If it does, encrypt the files of the database SALES.

   b) Try to retrieve data with the files encrypted.

KEY TERMS

database

database management system (DBMS)

relational system

relational database

linking column

implementing the database

regular report

exception report

interactive report generation command

DBMS program

stand-alone DBMS program

encryption system

CHAPTER REVIEW QUESTIONS

1. Outline the steps to follow in designing a database.

2. Outline the steps to follow in implementing a database.

3. What measures can you take to ensure that input to a database is accurate?

4. What measures can you take to ensure that input to a database is consistent?

5. What measures can you adopt to protect the confidentiality of the information in your database?

6. List the functions performed by a database management system.

7. How often should database files be updated?

8. How often should database files be backed up?

DISCUSSION QUESTIONS

1. Discuss the ways in which a DBMS can make a business run more efficiently.

2. Are there dangers if a business over-relies on a DBMS to make decisions? If so, how can these dangers be avoided?

3. Discuss ways in which a DBMS can be used to perpetrate business fraud. What policies can you institute to control such fraud?

APPLICATION PROJECTS

1. You have been operating your company's database for a year and want to determine its effectiveness. Design a survey to query your co-workers about the database and to elicit suggestions for its improvement.

2. Copernicus State College needs to set up a database that will incorporate student records on grades, housing, and financial information. Design a database to store this data.

3. One of the major responsibilities of a sales manager is evaluating the performance of the sales force and helping individuals improve productivity. Frequently, patterns of poor sales practices are hidden in the day-to-day work of each salesperson.

   The typical sales call report contains the company called upon, time of day, length of call, contact person seen, and sales results—as well as information about travel expenses and meals. Such reports are normally filed at the end of each week.

   How might a sales manager use a database titled Sales Calls to help improve the efficiency of the sales force?

4. Alderman Auto Parts, Inc., was established on May 1, 1986. The owner, Ted Alderman, would like to set up a perpetual inventory system for air filters, oil filters, and fan belts. (A perpetual inventory system holds inventory records that are frequently updated to reflect new purchases and sales. The user may retrieve data about inventory on hand on a specific date, as well as data pertaining to sales and purchases for a specific time period.) One approach to creating an inventory system is to establish separate files for sales and purchases, and to use these files to update a master inventory file.

   a) Establish a SALES file, a PURCHASES file, and a MASTER file. Each file should be structured to include fields titled *PART NUMBER, DESCRIPTION, QUANTITY, PRICE*, and *DATE*.

Purchases

Date	Part Number	Description	Quantity	Unit Cost
5/01/86	DSCAF101	Air filter	25	2.25
5/01/86	DMCAF122	Air filter	30	2.75
5/05/86	FSCOF312	Oil filter	15	3.10
5/07/86	FSCFB601	Fan belt	20	5.00
5/07/86	DSCFB500	Fan belt	20	4.00
5/10/86	DMCAF707	Air filter	35	3.15
5/12/86	FSCOF312	Oil filter	30	3.10
5/15/86	DSCAF101	Air filter	20	2.25
5/20/86	DMCAF122	Air filter	25	2.75
5/22/86	FSCFB601	Fan belt	15	5.00
5/25/86	DMCAF707	Air filter	30	3.15

Figure 11.14   Alderman Auto Parts PURCHASES file.

b) Update the PURCHASES file with the data contained in Figure 11.14.

c) Update the SALES file with the data contained in Figure 11.15.

d) Update the MASTER INVENTORY file by using data from the SALES file and the PURCHASES file.

e) Print a report that summarizes the inventory on hand on May 31, 1986.

5. Most full-service brokerage firms offer complete financial services to their clients, including a monthly report on the client's financial position. For example, the Bullish Brokerage Company has a product called a "cash management account," which includes a checking account, a VISA card, and a brokerage account to trade stocks and bonds. At the heart of

Date	Part Number	Description	Quantity	Unit Sales Price
5/02/86	DSCAF101	Air filter	10	3.85
5/04/86	DMCAF122	Air filter	20	4.15
5/08/86	DSCAF101	Air filter	12	3.90
5/10/86	FSCFB601	Fan belt	5	8.35
5/10/86	FSCOF312	Oil filter	8	6.25
5/15/86	FSCOF312	Oil filter	25	6.30
5/26/86	DSCAF101	Air filter	20	4.00
5/28/86	DMCAF122	Air filter	18	4.15

Figure 11.15   Alderman Auto Parts SALES file.

this service is a database management system that keeps track of information for all clients regarding security trades, checks written, VISA transactions, and the daily cash balance in their accounts.

Interview an account executive at a local brokerage firm about the cash management service that firm will provide. Prepare a brief paper describing the following:

a) The regular reports the account executive generates for the client

b) How and where data are input to the DBMS

c) The ability to generate exception reports

d) How the account executive uses the DBMS to assist clients

e) How the information in the DBMS is protected

f) Any other information you believe is unusual or important.

III
More Application Software

12 Graphics

The Buying Picture at Bloomingdale's

One day recently a woman came into Bloomingdale's Manhattan store and bought $2,500 worth of down pillows for a charter boat in the Caribbean islands. This is not an unusual event at Bloomingdale's, a store widely known for its upscale, luxurious items.

What *was* unusual was the way the transaction took place. Instead of using a cash register, the young salesperson, Lennox Oliver, used a microcomputer with a colored screen. The screen listed all the items in his department: pillows, blankets, sheets, towels, and comforters.

Responding to red, green, and blue boxes on the micro's monitor, Oliver touched a light pen to the screen to register items the customer purchased and the quantity of each item. With a box containing a magnetic strip attached to its side, the micro also read the customer's credit card numbers—so Oliver didn't need to key those in, either. The micro quickly added the total, calculated the sales tax, and printed out a sales slip that showed individual item prices, the total, the color and description of each item—even the date and time of the purchase. The whole transaction took only 60 seconds.

Behind the scenes, the micro also logged all the items purchased into a storewide database. Known as a point-of-sale system, this program represents state-of-the-art computer graphics for retailing. Before Bloomingdale's installed a microcomputer system, sales clerks had to enter each and every number on a cash register. Besides being time-consuming, the old system could not control human error. The micro has changed all that. "It takes much less time to do a transaction," Oliver says. "It's fun. I love it. I wouldn't use anything else. If they had to go back to the old system, I think I would leave. I'm serious."

THE MARKETING DEPARTMENT of Precocious Software is planning a presentation of their marketing campaign to sell a new line of computer games. The marketing people have done their homework. Using a spreadsheet program, they have analyzed the potential profit from the sale of the games under various sets of potential market conditions. They have set up a budget for advertising and have plans for a press release and publicity campaign to introduce the games. However, they must first have their plans approved by management.

As a part of their presentation, the marketing group has collected data in the form of a report. They have translated their spreadsheet data, which was many pages long, into a series of graphs. With the help of a microcomputer and a business graphics package, the worksheet information appears in bar, pie, and line graphs that have been printed out on paper and circulated as part of the final report. Their marketing report also contains some sample ads that were sketched using a drawing program. Moreover, the report contains some graphics screens that employ cartoon characters to depict the action of the game.

There will also be an oral presentation: a slide show that uses transparencies created with slide-generation hardware and software to portray information in visual form. The marketing group knows that using graphics makes a presentation more effective. A simple graph that plots the trend of profits for a business can be more easily digested by the human eye than a page of numbers; a colorful cartoon character can tell more about a game program than a page of words.

Today, you too can become an artist by using your microcomputer to prepare graphics directly from data you have stored in a spreadsheet or in a database file. You can output graphics on a monitor, on paper, or on 35-millimeter slides. You can retrieve the data on which the graphics are based directly from the output of other programs, such as spreadsheets and word processors. Moreover, you can store computer-generated graphics on disk for later recall.

This chapter surveys the applications of computer graphics and the hardware you will need to use these applications.

12.1 Using Graphics to Solve Problems

Computer graphics are used in a wide range of fields—from financial analysis to aircraft design. This section will survey the far-reaching applications of computer graphics.

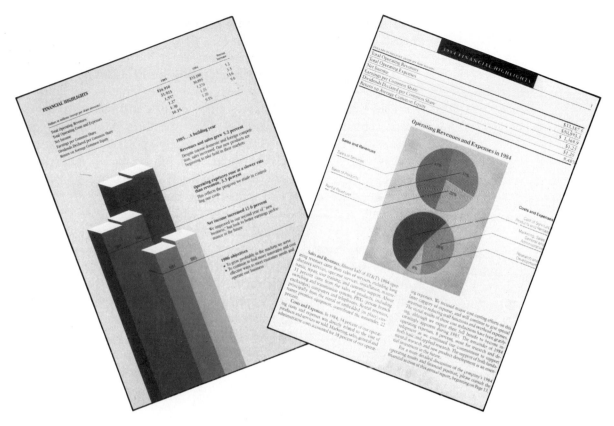

Figure 12.1   Graphics used in a company report.

Generating Graphs and Charts

Business documents are filled with charts and graphs. Stockholders' reports, management surveys, and advertising projects all contain graphics that enliven the presentation of information. Figure 12.1 illustrtes some typical examples. Before computer graphics became commonplace, charts and graphs were rendered by in-house or freelance graphic artists. The expense to an organization, in both materials' cost and labor, was great. Today, any microcomputer user can translate thoughts or data into a variety of graphic presentations that can be produced directly on a microcomputer's monitor. In a matter of seconds, you can reduce hundreds of pieces of data to pictorial form. By examining such charts, you and your colleagues can see trends clearly and use them as the basis for decision-making.

For example, you might use spreadsheet data based on your current work force and order backlog to project average delivery times from your warehouse, as is shown in Figure 12.2. A series of such graphs can help you perform a what-if analysis to determine the effect of different business scenarios.

Graphs such as the one shown in Figure 12.2 can be produced by a **business graphics program**. All types of graphs and charts— from bar charts and pie charts to line graphs and scatter graphs— can be rendered by this program. (The specific types of graphs are discussed in detail in Section 12.3.) Many spreadsheet programs, such as Lotus 1-2-3, GoldSpread, and SuperCalc 3, incorporate graphics functions directly into their packages, making it simple to create graphics based on spreadsheet data. Business graphs and charts can also be produced by stand-alone graphics packages, such as Chart Master, Microsoft Chart, and Graph Writer.

Drawing Pictures on a Computer

A number of programs enable the user to draw pictures on the screen by using either a mouse or a light pen as an input device. Using such programs, you can prepare illustrations for reports, books, and advertising pieces. Figure 12.3 illustrates a typical example.

To render a drawing, you select a shape from the choice bar on the monitor. You can choose lines, rectangles, circles, ellipses,

Figure 12.2   A graph displaying spreadsheet data for analysis.

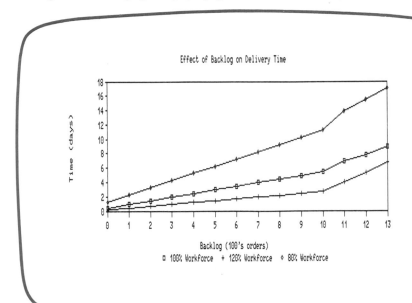

GOLDSTEIN SOFTWARE

12520 Prosperity Dr.

Suite 340

Silver Spring, MD 20904

(301) 622-9020

Figure 12.3   Output from a freehand drawing program.

and freehand curves. Moreover, you can select from a variety of weights and styles of lines, and fill patterns with which to shade different regions. You can place a shape on the screen, move it around, flip it vertically or horizontally, and erase or edit any part of it. Some programs have a feature that allows you to magnify a portion of the diagram to touch-up fine-details. You can even include text in a variety of text styles and sizes within your drawings.

The original drawing program was Mac Paint, available on the Apple Macintosh. Now many similar programs, including PC Paintbrush and PC Paint, are available on MS-DOS machines.

Design Graphics Programs

Many professions have long used graphics to present designs to clients or colleagues. For example, architects prepare blueprints; interior designers prepare space studies (see Figure 12.4); electronics designers prepare circuit designs (see Figure 12.5). Today, they can use **design graphics programs** to create these designs. These programs function much like drawing programs but include the specialized design elements used by a particular profession.

For example, an architectural design program includes components to indicate types of walls and partitions, electrical outlets, lights, switches, and pipes. Architects assemble the components into a complete design with the aid of either a light pen or a mouse. An architect can create and edit the design on the screen and use a printer or a plotter to generate hard copy at any design

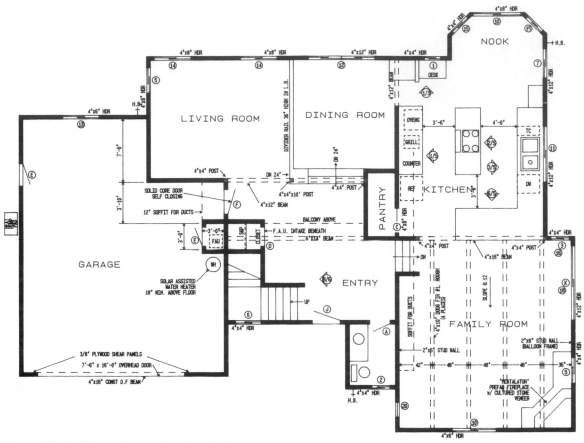

Figure 12.4 Output from an interior design program.

Figure 12.5 An electrical circuit design.

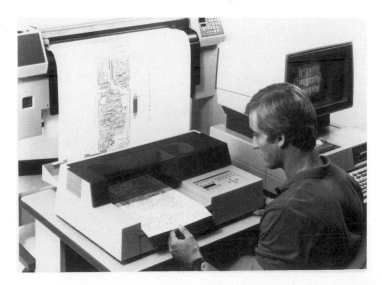

Figure 12.6 An architectural drawing produced on a computer.

stage. Figure 12.6 shows an architect's design produced on a computer.

Design graphics programs are revolutionizing all kinds of professions. For example, office designers can design interior layouts in a fraction of the time it used to take using hand-drawn blueprints. Moreover, changes that formerly required costly manual redesigning and redrafting of blueprints can now be accomplished on-screen with computer generation of the altered blueprints.

A more advanced design tool is provided by **computer-aided design (CAD) programs**. These high-level programs allow engineers and designers to design complex objects such as automobiles and aircraft. An example of CAD graphics is shown in Figure 12.7.

CAD programs give a designer the ability not only to create a design on the monitor, but to change it and analyze it as needed. Most CAD programs allow the designer to rotate objects on the screen so that they appear to be three-dimensional and may be viewed from any angle. Until recently, the complexities of these programs required the power of a minicomputer or a mainframe. However, many CAD tasks, such as design of machine tools and auto parts, can now be handled with microcomputers.

Other Applications of Graphics

Graphics can provide simple and clear illustrations of ideas that may be difficult to describe in words. Accordingly, they are frequently used in educational programs, especially those aimed at

Figure 12.7 Graphics produced by a CAD program.

Figure 12.8 Schoolchildren using LOGO, an educational graphics program.

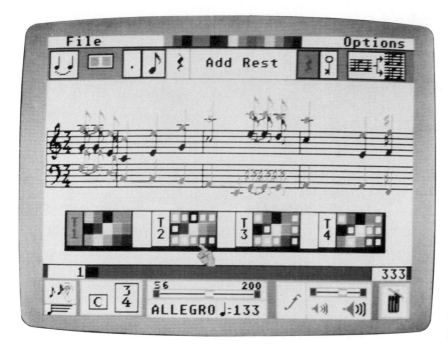

Figure 12.9   A musical score generated by graphics software.

elementary school students. Figure 12.8 shows schoolchildren using LOGO, an educational graphics program.

Graphics software can even be used by musicians. By attaching a music synthesizer to a computer, a graphics program can be used to generate a score as the music is being played and then to display it on a screen. (See Figure 12.9.) What might Bach or Mozart have done with such a tool?

Section 12.1: Test Your Understanding

1. What is a business graphics package?
2. What is design graphics?
3. What is CAD?

12.2 Graphics Hardware

To use graphics application software, you need to know something about graphics hardware and how it works. In this section, you'll find most of the basic facts about graphics hardware that a user needs to know.

Video Adapters and Graphics Modes

Your choice of video adapters and display modes (discussed in Chapter 3) defines the graphics capability of your computer. Each video adapter has a number of display modes with varying degrees of graphics capability. Some video adapters have display modes that allow display of text but no graphics. When graphics displays are allowed, there are usually a number of different display modes supporting differing screen resolutions and color combinations.

A graphics program may require a particular display mode in order for it to function. In that event, a video adapter that supports the required display mode is needed. However, most graphics programs support a variety of display modes and video adapters. As a first step in using a graphics program, you must install the program in order to specify the particular video adapter you are using.

Installing graphics programs. Because most graphics programs are very heavily hardware-dependent, they present special installation challenges. Graphics software must be written for a particular set of hardware (video display adapter, display mode, or output device). To accommodate the wide variety of such devices on the market, most programs support a number of choices for hardware in each category. In order to make a program work, you must install it for your hardware by running an installation program that allows you to select the hardware from one or more menus.

Software developers and researchers interested in graphics are trying to create a graphics standard that will allow software developers to write graphics programs without knowing in advance the particular hardware on which the program will be run. Using such a graphics standard, the programmer can describe, in general terms, the graphics to be drawn. The actual job of translating the description into output is performed by a **graphics driver**, a program that specifies how the graphics features of a particular hardware device work. By using different drivers, one program can output the same picture on a variety of devices. Although a multitude of graphics standards has been proposed, none has yet gained universal recognition.

Monitors

As you saw in Chapter 3, there is an abundance of graphics monitors from which to choose, and all of them vary in their ability to handle graphics and color. It is important to match the capabilities of the video adapter and the monitor, so that the monitor can handle the colors and graphics resolution that is output from the video adapter.

The contents of the video display are stored in a section of RAM called **screen memory**. The amount of RAM devoted to screen memory depends on the particular video adapter and the display mode being used. For example, when using an IBM/PC monochrome adapter, the screen memory is 4K. However, when using an IBM/PC color graphics adapter, its four-color medium resolution graphics mode has a screen memory requirement of 16K.

The video adapter continuously reads the contents of the screen memory and translates those contents into electrical signals which, in turn, are translated into screen pixels. The image on a video display lasts only for about 1/60th of a second, so it must be continuously rewritten by the video adapter. This rewriting must be done at a high frequency, so that no screen flicker will be noticeable.

Here is how screen memory works in text mode: As you will recall from Chapter 3, the screen memory in text mode contains ASCII codes that represent the characters to be displayed. Each character position on the screen corresponds to a single byte of memory. If the byte corresponding to row 5, column 9 contains a 65, which is the ASCII code for the letter A, then an A is displayed there. (See Figure 12.10.)

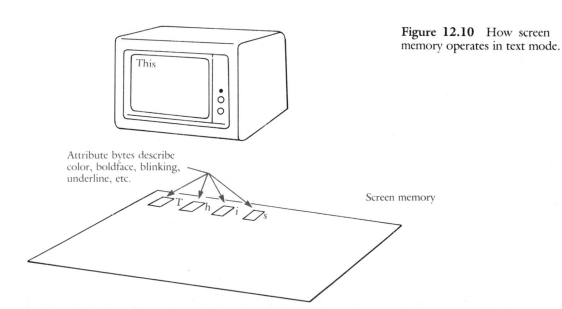

Figure 12.10 How screen memory operates in text mode.

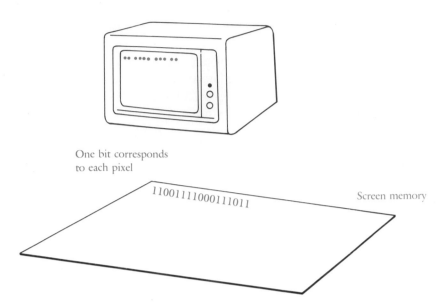

One bit corresponds
to each pixel

11001111000111011   Screen memory

Figure 12.11 How screen
memory operates in mono-
chrome graphics mode.

In graphics mode, the screen memory works differently. A
single byte represents a number of pixels on the screen. For instance,
in a monochrome (black and white) graphics mode, each pixel is
represented by a single bit. A 0 means that the pixel is not lit; a 1
indicates that the pixel is lit. In this scheme, each byte represents
8 pixels. (See Figure 12.11.)

In a color graphics mode, it takes more than a single byte to
represent a pixel. For example, if four colors are allowed, then each
pixel requires two bits of memory. The four colors are then
represented by the four two-bit combinations 00, 01, 10, 11. In
this four-color mode, a byte represents four pixels on the screen.
If 16 colors are allowed, then four bits per pixel are required and
each byte represents two pixels. The more colors allowed, the larger
the screen memory must be.

Graphics modes are often called **bit-mapped** because each
pixel is represented by one or more bits in the screen memory, and
the screen memory is "mapped" onto the screen (as if there were
a highway between the bits of memory and the pixels on the
screen).

Storing Graphics

In many applications, you will need to store graphics data on disk.
For example, illustrations for a brochure might be stored on disk
while awaiting approval or revisions from the marketing department. Graphs generated from spreadsheet data might be stored on

disk so that they can be recalled to the screen for a presentation on the proposed company budget for next year.

The size of the required screen memory depends on the particular display mode. A text mode with 25 lines having 80 characters each requires $25 \times 80 = 2,000$ bytes of screen memory. A monochrome graphics mode having 200 lines of 320 pixels each requires $200 \times 320 = 64,000$ bits $= 8,000$ bytes. A 16-color graphics mode having 400 lines of 640 pixels each requires $4 \times 400 \times 640 = 1,024,000$ bits $= 128,000$ bytes. Figure 12.12 shows how this information is stored on disk and how it relates to screen memory.

As you can see, graphics software exacts a price in the amount of screen memory required. This price rises as you increase the resolution and the number of colors allowed.

Similar considerations apply when you use programs that allow you to store graphics images on disk. The amount of disk space required by graphics depends on the graphics mode in which they were created. A full-screen picture requires an amount of disk space equal to one screen memory. For example, creating a picture in a four-color 320×200 graphics mode requires $320 \times 200 \times 2 = 16,000$ bytes. A 360K diskette can hold only a limited number

Because graphics programs require vast amounts of storage space, it's a good idea to choose a hard disk system rather than diskettes.

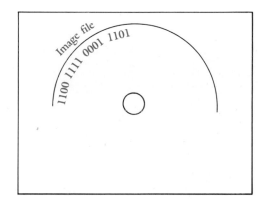

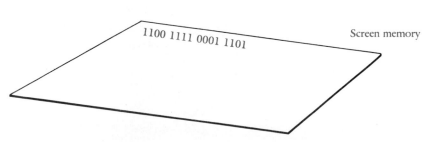

Figure 12.12   Storing graphics information on disk.

(22 as described here) of graphics images. Keep this in mind when using application programs that store graphics images on diskette. Of course, a hard disk is much less limiting than a floppy diskette system. Even a small (10 megabyte) hard disk is capable of storing hundreds of graphics images.

Graphics Input Devices

You can use several kinds of input devices to enter graphics information into a program while it is running. The most common input device is the **mouse**, shown in Figure 12.13. A mouse communicates with the computer either through a special adapter board or through a serial communications port (to be discussed in Chapter 13). By moving a mouse on a flat surface, such as a desk or tabletop, you can position a corresponding dot (or cursor) on the screen. Using the buttons on the top of the mouse, you can communicate with the computer. The way information from a particular button sequence is interpreted by the computer depends on the particular application program. The mouse is used very effectively in painting and design programs.

Another input device is the **light pen**. Resembling a ballpoint pen, it communicates with the computer via a special adapter board. A typical light pen is illustrated in Figure 12.14. When you point to the screen with a light pen, the electronics on the adapter board allow the computer to sense when the light pen is turned

Figure 12.13 A mouse.

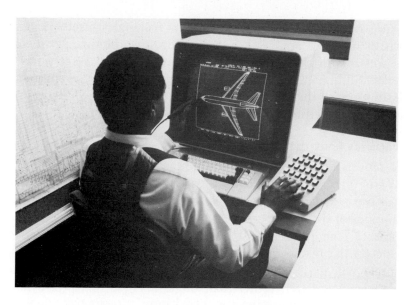

Figure 12.14   A light pen.

on and where it is pointing. You can perform almost the same functions with a light pen that you can with a mouse. However, with the light pen you have the advantage of pointing directly to the screen, which is a less awkward action than moving a mouse around a separate surface.

A **digitizing pad** is a device that reads hard-copy graphics into the computer. (See Figure 12.15.) Like the mouse, this pad communicates with the computer through either a special interface board or a communications port. The pad works by dividing a

Figure 12.15   A digitizing pad.

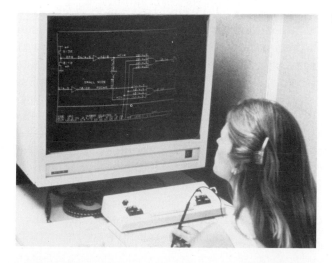

picture on paper into a large grid of rectangles, each rectangle corresponding to one pixel on the screen. The digitizing pad scans the contents of the rectangle, decides whether the corresponding pixel should be lit, and transmits the information to the computer. By scanning all the rectangles of the paper picture, a digitizing pad can turn the picture into pixel form on-screen.

Graphics Output Devices

For reports and memos that will be distributed to colleagues and clients, you will need to produce hard copies of graphs and charts. Most business graphics packages are able to provide hard copy on a number of different output devices, displaying graphics on your monitor. Your printer must be capable of printing dots to correspond to the pixels on the screen. Dot-matrix, ink jet, and laser printers will work, but daisy-wheel printers will not, since they print complete letters rather than single dots (see Chapter 3).

The simplest and most common graphics output device is the dot-matrix printer. Most business graphics programs allow you to copy the contents of a graphics display pixel by pixel onto a dot-matrix printer, with a result something like that shown in Figure 12.16.

Printing graphics is a slow process, especially if you are using a high-resolution graphics mode. On a slower dot-matrix printer, it may take up to ten minutes to print out a single picture. On faster dot-matrix printers and laser printers, the print time can be reduced to one or two minutes.

Another consideration is the horizontal and vertical spacing on a printer, which may not correspond to the spacing on the screen. The printed version of a picture may show horizontal or vertical distortion. Some programs compensate for this by using several printer dots to correspond to a single pixel.

You can produce hard copy of a much higher quality with a plotter. Plotters use one or more moving pens to draw pictures of presentation-quality. Plotters with multiple pens can draw pictures in several colors. Plotters come in a variety of sizes, capable of handling paper sizes from $8\frac{1}{2} \times 11$ inches up to several feet square. The larger paper sizes are suitable for producing posters and blueprints, an example of which is shown in Figure 12.17.

Plotters reduce images to a sequence of lines rather than individual pixels. For example, diagonal lines produced by a plotter don't have the jagged appearance that they often do in printer output. However, you pay a price in speed for the superb quality of plotter output. A single plotter drawing may take 10 to 20 minutes to complete, especially if multiple colors are used.

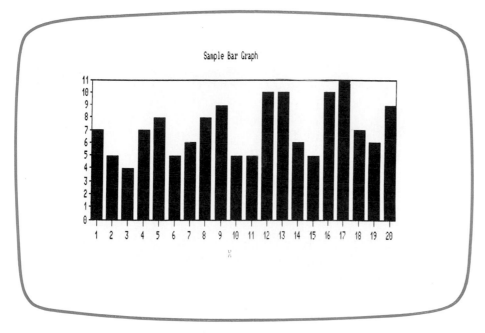

Sample Bar Graph

Figure 12.16 Graphics output on a dot-matrix printer.

Figure 12.17 A blueprint produced on a plotter.

Figure 12.18 Slide output to be used in a presentation.

Some graphics programs allow both printer and plotter output. With these programs, you can use the printer for rough drafts and the plotter for final copy.

Slide output devices that can reproduce graphics displays on 35-millimeter slides can also be used in business presentations. An example of slide output is shown in Figure 12.18.

Section 12.2: Test Your Understanding

1. What is the difference between text mode and graphics mode?
2. What are line graphics characters? How are they used?
3. Explain the operation of screen memory in text mode.
4. Explain the operation of screen memory in graphics mode.
5. How many bytes of screen memory are required for a monochrome 350 × 750 graphics mode?
6. Explain the operation of a mouse.
7. Explain the operation of a digitizing pad.
8. Explain the operation of a light pen.
9. What is a graphics driver?
10. Can you print graphics images on a daisy-wheel printer? Explain your answer.
11. What are the advantages of plotters over dot-matrix printers for preparing hard-copy graphics output? What are the disadvantages?

12.3 Using Graphics to Analyze Business Problems

One of the most important forms of graphics used in business are graphs and charts that depict numeric information. This section takes a look at this type of graphics and how they may be used to analyze and solve business problems.

Types of Graphs and Charts

Let's return to Precocious Software and its new line of computer games for the home computer market. Recall that the marketing department is proposing a marketing campaign to the corporate executive committee. Since they must communicate their ideas in a very short time, they have decided to outline the main features of their campaign in a series of the four basic types of business graphs: bar graph, line graph, pie chart, and scattergraph.

Bar Graphs. A **bar graph** uses rectangular bars to display data. It is a good means for illustrating a few (up to about a dozen) numeric data items. The marketing department is using a bar chart to graph the amount of money they propose to spend each month for advertising, with each month represented by a single bar. (See Figure 12.19.)

Line Graphs. A **line graph** presents data as points plotted on a line. It is suitable for graphing the same type of data displayed in a bar graph. In addition, it can be used to graph data for which the x-coordinates do not occur at regular intervals. The marketing department is using a line graph to illustrate the number of people who will see advertisements at particular times. (See Figure 12.20.)

Pie Charts. A **pie chart** displays data in a form that resembles a pie divided into slices. Each slice represents the proportional share of one data item in the total of all items in the data set. The marketing department is using a pie chart to show the market shares possessed by each of their competitors in the computer game market. (See Figure 12.21.)

Scatter graphs. A **scatter graph** displays data as points plotted without any connection between them. The marketing department is using a scatter graph to show the introductions of various computer games and the total revenues they generated in their first three months of sales. (See Figure 12.22.)

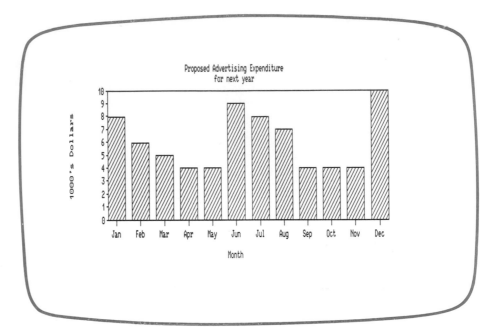

Figure 12.19   A bar graph showing Precocious Software's advertising budget.

Figure 12.20   A line graph showing the number of people who will see Precocious Software's advertisements at particular times.

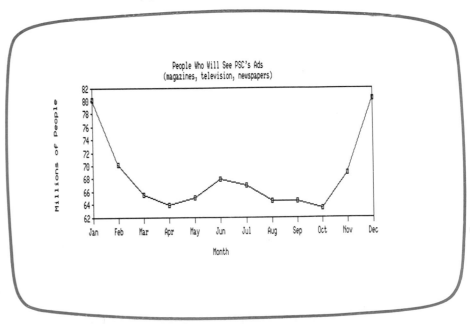

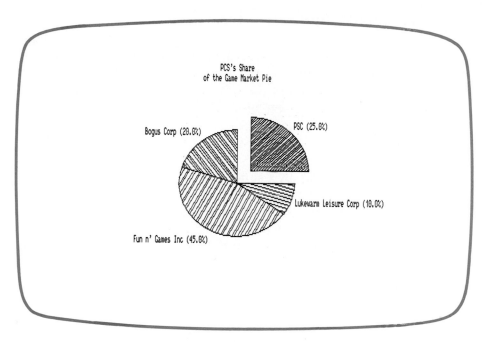

Figure 12.21 Precocious Software's analysis of the competition, as shown by a pie chart.

Figure 12.22 A scattergraph showing the total revenues generated by Precocious Software's introduction of computer games.

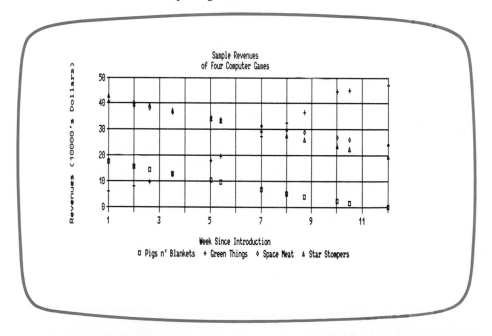

Graphing Multiple Sets of Data

You may sometimes want to display several sets of data on a single graph. For example, the marketing department prepared a chart with two sets of bars—one set projecting company sales after the marketing campaign and the other set illustrating company sales for the same period a year ago.

Graphing multiple sets of data on a single graph can be accomplished by using either superimposed or stacked graphs.

Superimposed Graphs. In a **superimposed graph**, several bars, one from each data set, can be displayed side by side in order to compare sets of data. An example of this is shown in the marketing department's sales comparison in Figure 12.23.

In a superimposed line graph, several lines, one corresponding to each data set, are plotted on the same graph.

Stacked Graphs. **Stacked graphs** display several data sets and illustrate the total effect of adding corresponding data elements. In this type of graph, bar segments corresponding to each data set are stacked or piled on top of each other. The marketing department

Figure 12.23   Superimposed bar graphs.

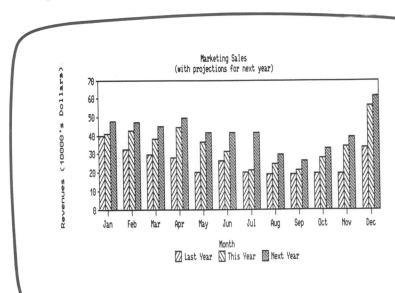

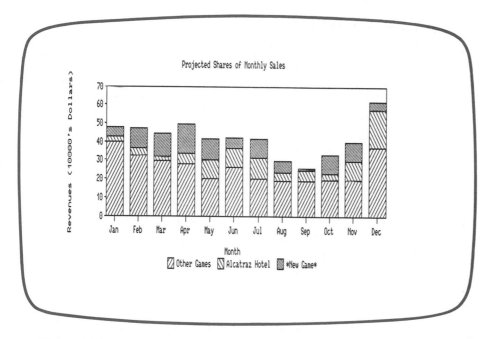

Figure 12.24   A stacked bar graph, illustrating the portion of each month's profits from Precocious Software's new game.

is using a stacked bar graph to show the portion of each month's sales that will be attributed to Precocious Software's new game. (See Figure 12.24).

In a stacked line graph, several data sets are plotted, with each line stacked on top of the preceding one, as in Figure 12.25.

Graphing Trends

When plotting data points, it is important to isolate and display trends. The simplest type of trend, called a **linear trend**, is represented by a straight line. Statistical techniques determine which linear trend best approximates a particular set of data. The most commonly used technique is called **linear regression** and is available in many microcomputer programs, including some spreadsheet packages. Figure 12.26 shows a set of data points that describes the Precocious Software's profits for the last five years and the linear trend obtained by linear regression to approximate the data. Using the linear trend shown, the marketing department can project the profits of Precocious Software for the next year or two.

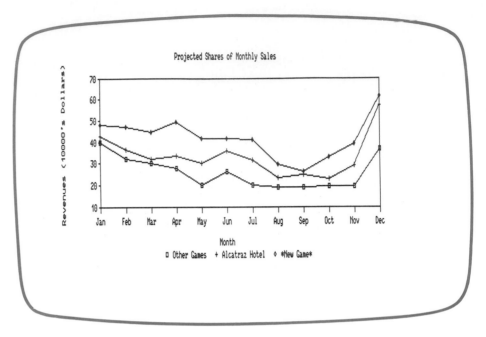

Figure 12.25   A stacked line graph.

Figure 12.26 Precocious Software's profits for the past five years, as shown with a regression line.

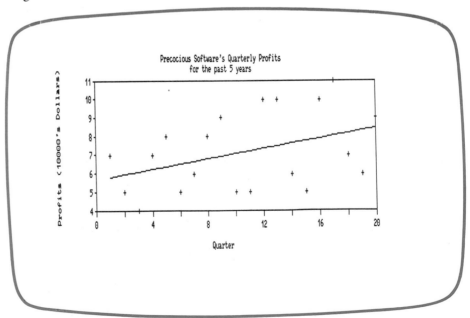

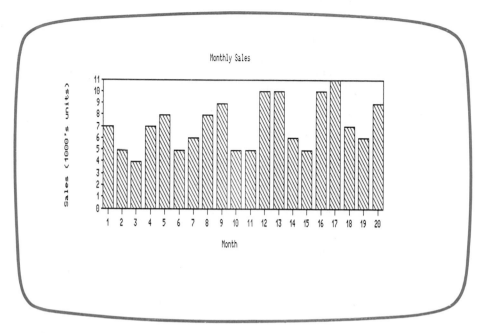

Figure 12.27 Charting sales on a monthly basis.

Creating Business Graphs

The graphs that the marketing department of Precocious Software used in its presentation of a marketing plan can be created by using any one of a number of graphics packages. Some are stand-alone packages whose main function is to create graphs from data produced by other programs, such as database management programs or spreadsheets. Graphics functions are also integrated into some programs, like Lotus 1-2-3 and GoldSpread. Using these graphics functions, you can prepare graphs directly from spreadsheet data without going to a separate graphics program. The next section gives hands-on details about using software to prepare business graphics.

Using Business Graphics

There are many ways that business graphics can improve the quality of your analysis and decisions. For example, to analyze sales trends, you can display a bar chart of corporate sales on a monthly basis. (See Figure 12.27.) You may then project the sales trend to obtain an estimate of sales for the remainder of the year. (See Figure 12.28.) By giving a few simple commands, you can alter the graph, say to compare this year's sales with those for the preceding year.

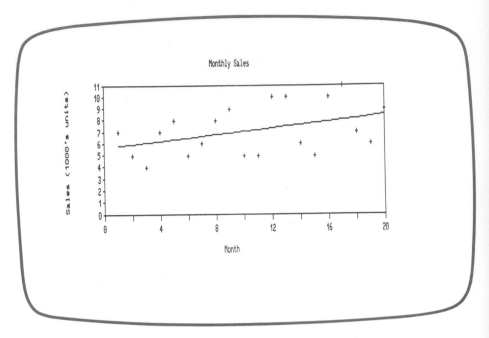

Figure 12.28   Projecting future sales.

(See Figure 12.29.) Or you can display the contributions to sales from each of a number of product lines. (See Figure 12.30.)

The same data can be displayed in different graphic forms. For instance, the contribution to sales from different product lines can be displayed by using a bar chart, a line graph, or a pie chart. (See Figure 12.31.)

Elements of a Business Graph

A business graph is composed of many different elements. In using a graphics program to prepare a graph, you must specify each of the elements to be drawn. Here are the most common elements you need to specify.

- *Graph type*. Line, bar, pie, scatter, stacked line, and so forth.
- *Graph titles*. One or more descriptive titles of the graph.
- *Legends*. Symbols identifying the various sets of data being graphed.
- *X-axis title*. The title of the *X*-axis (e.g., months).
- *Y-axis title*. The title of the *Y*-axis (e.g., millions of dollars).
- *X-axis scale*. The scale of numbers or data titles along the *X*-axis.

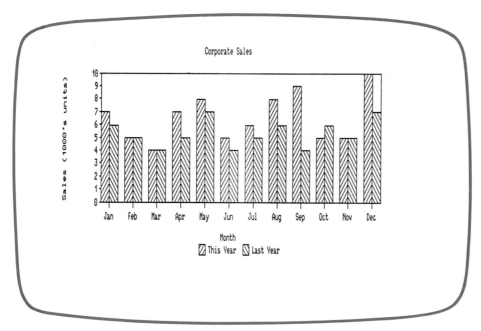

Figure 12.29 Comparing this year's sales with last year's sales.

Figure 12.30 Contributions to sales from different product lines.

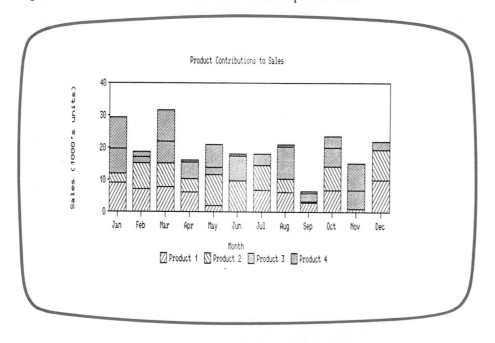

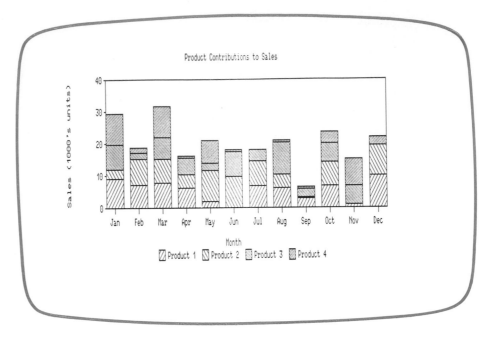

(a)

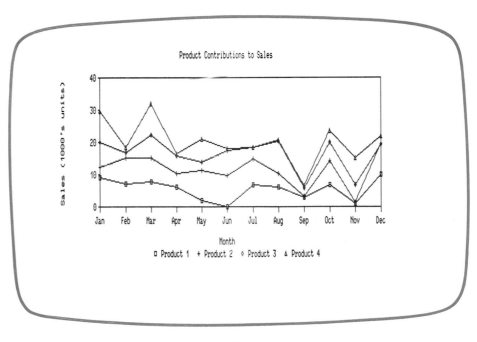

(b)

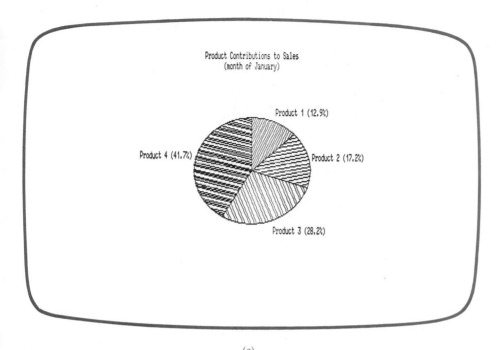

(c)

Figure 12.31   Depicting identical data using (a) a bar chart, (b) a line graph, and (c) a pie chart.

- *Y-axis scale*. The scale of numbers along the Y-axis.
- *Tick marks* (also called **hash marks**). These indicate the positions of the major scale divisions along the axes.
- *Grid*. You may wish to use horizontal or vertical lines to make the values on a graph easier to read. A grid is similar to a sheet of graph paper.
- *Data sets*. The sets of data to be graphed.

Figure 12.32 illustrates some graphic elements in a line graph.

Business Graphics Programs

Many programs can be used to prepare business graphics. In these programs, you must specify some or all of the elements discussed above in order for the program to draw the graph. The typical business graphics program can display a graph on the screen and save it on disk, or use a printer or a plotter to print it on paper.

Business programs differ in the styles of graphs they can produce and the output devices on which they can present them. Some of the more elaborate business graphics programs, such as

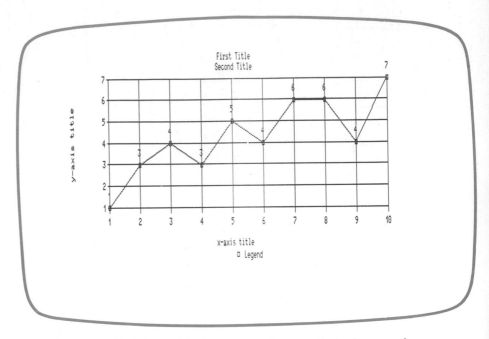

Figure 12.32   A line graph showing the elements of a business graph.

Chart Master, support dozens of variations in style of labelling, shading, grids, and overlays of multiple graphs on the same coordinate system. Some packages, such as Execuvision, allow you to include background pictures selected from a library of images. For example, you can incorporate a picture of an oil derrick into a graph describing oil prices, or a picture of a scientist working in a laboratory into a graph depicting research and development expenses.

Most business graphics programs provide a facility for graphing data that has been generated by another program, say a spreadsheet or a DBMS. This allows you to graph data you generate without re-entering it, thus avoiding a potential source of errors.

Section 12.3: Test Your Understanding

1. Choose the best type of graph to display the following information:
   a) The monthly expenses from a budget
   b) The long-term trend of inflation
   c) The total profits generated by two divisions

   d) Comparison of monthly shipments for last year and this year

   e) Percentage of women working each year since 1900

   f) The total number of workers, arranged into blue collar, white collar, and managerial categories, for each year since 1900.

12.4 Graphing Spreadsheet Data

Integrated programs—programs that incorporate several types of programs in one package—are the most common source of business graphics. A typical integrated package contains, at the very least, a spreadsheet, some data management facilities, and a business graphics program. Lotus 1-2-3 and GoldSpread, the software package available with this text, are both integrated programs. The more elaborate integrated programs, such as Symphony from Lotus Development Corporation or Framework from Ashton-Tate, Inc., incorporate word processing and communication programs as well. Let's look at the ways you can use Lotus 1-2-3 or GoldSpread to graph spreadsheet data.

Illustrating with Spreadsheet Data

To illustrate the procedure for graphing spreadsheet data, recall the worksheet for the Jones budget in Chapter 7, shown in Figure 7.1. We shall now produce a bar graph like the one in Figure 12.33, showing the total expenses of the Joneses for each month of the year. Here is how to construct the graph:

- *Step 1*. Give Lotus 1-2-3 or GoldSpread command /GRAPH. The program displays the submenu shown in Figure 12.34.

- *Step 2*. Choose the GRAPH TYPE option and press ⟨ENTER/RETURN⟩. The program will display a list of possible graph types. Choose BAR (since we wish to display a bar graph) and press ⟨ENTER/RETURN⟩. The program records the graph type and redisplays the submenu.

- *Step 3*. Choose the X option to choose the *X*-axis scale. Press ⟨ENTER/RETURN⟩. The program requests that you choose a range of worksheet cells as names to use along the *X*-axis of the graph. Use the initials of the months along the *X*-axis. These are contained in the worksheet in the range B1 .. M1. Type
⟨B1..M1⟩⟨ENTER/RETURN⟩

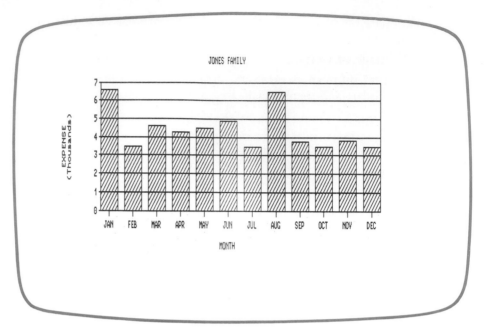

Figure 12.33   A bar graph showing monthly expenses for the Joneses.

Figure 12.34   Submenu for the /GRAPH command.

```
B1: ^JAN                                                            MENU
Type  X  A  B  C  D  E  F  Reset  View  Save  Options  Name  Quit
Set graph type
          A              B           C           D           E           F
                        JAN         FEB         MAR         APR         MAY
1
2      EXPENSES
3      Rent            $795.00     $795.00     $795.00     $795.00     $795.00
4      Food            $400.00     $400.00     $400.00     $400.00     $400.00
5      Car Loan        $297.80     $297.80     $297.80     $297.80     $297.80
6      Car Operation   $135.00     $135.00     $135.00     $135.00     $135.00
7      Clothes         $125.00                 $350.00
8      Entertainment   $200.00     $200.00     $200.00     $200.00     $200.00
9      Taxes         $1,272.49   $1,272.49   $1,272.49   $1,272.49   $1,272.49
10     Medical         $200.00     $200.00     $200.00     $200.00     $200.00
11     Tuition       $3,000.00
12     Personal        $200.00     $200.00     $200.00     $200.00     $200.00
13     Decorating                              $800.00     $800.00   $1,000.00
14     TOTAL EXPENSES $6,625.29   $3,500.29   $4,650.29   $4,300.29   $4,500.29
15     INCOME
16     Jim's Salary  $2,450.00   $2,450.00   $2,450.00   $2,450.00   $2,450.00
17     Betty's Salary $1,950.00  $1,950.00   $1,950.00   $1,950.00   $1,950.00
18     Bank Interest   $300.00                 $300.00
19     TOTAL INCOME  $4,700.00   $4,400.00   $4,400.00   $4,700.00   $4,400.00
20     NET          ($1,925.29)   $899.71    ($250.29)    $399.71    ($100.29)
23-Jul-86  02:53 PM
```

The program redisplays the submenu.

- *Step 4.* Choose the A option to specify the first (and in this case only) data set to graph. To graph the total expense figures in the range B18 . . M18. Type

    ⟨B18..M18⟩⟨ENTER/RETURN⟩

The program redisplays the submenu.

Step 5. To see what your graph looks like at this point, select the VIEW option and press ⟨ENTER/RETURN⟩. The program displays the graph without the titles. Note that the scale along the Y-axis is computed automatically from the particular data you specified. You may set the scale manually, but for now let the program decide it for you. To get back to the submenu, press the ESCAPE key.

- *Step 6.* Add a title to the graph. Select OPTIONS and press ⟨ENTER/RETURN⟩. The program allows you to specify a title for the whole graph and title lines for the axes. Give the graph the title *JONES FAMILY BUDGET*, the X-axis the title *MONTH*, and the Y-axis the title *EXPENSE*. This requires selecting OPTIONS three times, once for each title.
- *Step 7.* Select the GRID option to add horizontal grid lines.
- *Step 8.* View the graph again by selecting the VIEW option. The graph should now look like Figure 12.33.

There are many other features available in the business graphing programs of GoldSpread and Lotus 1-2-3, which are summarized in Command Table 12.1.

Macros

It may seem that you need to expend a lot of effort to produce a single graph. However, you can record the sequence of commands you used to produce a particular graph into a macro, which enables you to prepare the graph by using a single keystroke. (Recall the discussion of spreadsheet macros in Chapter 9.) In this way, you can quickly prepare graphics reports from spreadsheets you regularly maintain.

Graphics and Word Processing

Often, you will need to incorporate graphs and charts into corporate memos and reports. For example, a report on current sales can be greatly enhanced by a graph showing how this year's sales compare with those of the preceding year. Some integrated packages that

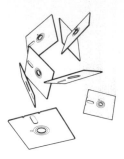

Command Table 12.1   The graphics commands of Lotus 1-2-3 and GoldSpread.

Command	Comments

The graphics commands are accessed via the / GRAPH command, which displays the GRAPH menu.
/ Graph
Select option from the Graph menu.
⟨ENTER⟩
Press ESC to leave the Graph menu.
	The options available on the Graph menu are as follows:
	Type—Select graph type (bar, line, pie, XY, stacked bar, stacked line).
	X A B C D E F—Select graph data ranges. These are specified in usual way as ranges of cells on spreadsheet. X denotes range for X-axis. The contents of the X cells are used to label the X-axis. A,B,C,D,E,F allow you to specify up to six data ranges to be graphed simultaneously. Program automatically scales the Y-axis on the basis of the data given in the Y-data ranges.
	Reset—Cancel all graph menu settings.
	View—Display graph specified by current Graph menu settings. To view a graph, your system must have a video display adapter with graphics capability and the program must be properly installed for your display adapter. When viewing a graph, press ESC to return to Graph menu.
	Save—Save the current graph image in a file.
	Name—Assign and manipulate names for Graph menu settings. You may Create a named Graph menu setting, Use a previously-named Graph menu setting, Delete a named Graph menu setting, or Reset a named Graph menu setting.
	Options—Set various graph options:
	  Legend (assign legends to the graphs A-F),
	  Format (choose format for Line and XY data),
	  Titles (enter the titles for the axes and graph),
	  Grid (specify horizontal or vertical grids),
	  Scale (specify and format numeric axis scales),
	  Color vs. B&W (set or disable color),
	  Data-Labels (assign labels for ranges of data points)
	View graph defined by current Graph menu settings.

Figure 12.35 A document created by integrating graphics into word processing.

incorporate a word processing program also allow you to include business graphics directly into a word-processed document. Figure 12.35 shows an example of how such a document looks.

Section 12.4: Test Your Understanding

1. Explain the use of macros in preparing graphs.
2. What type of printers can be used to print documents containing text and graphics on the same page?

Hands-on Exercises

1. Create and display the graph of the Jones budget shown in Figure 12.33.
2. Create and display the line graph shown in Figure 12.36.
3. Create and display the pie chart shown in Figure 12.37.
4. Create and display the stacked bar graph shown in Figure 12.38.

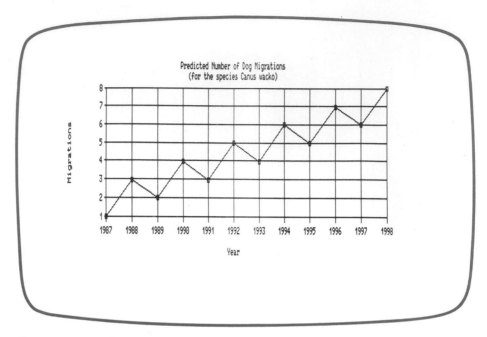

Figure 12.36   A line graph.

Figure 12.37   A pie chart.

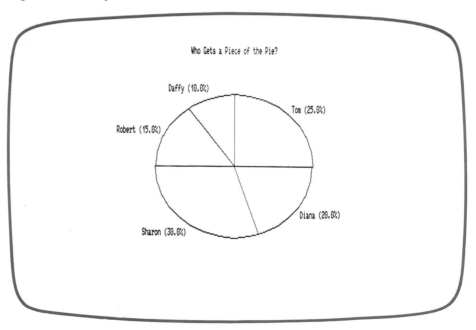

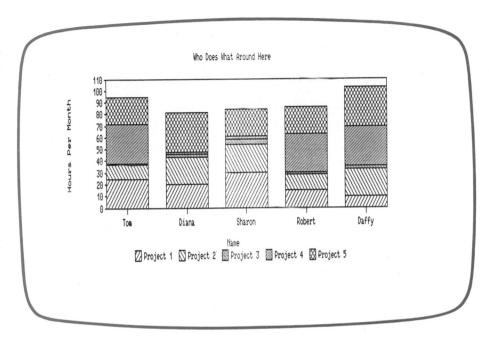

Figure 12.38 A stacked bar graph.

KEY TERMS

business graphics program
design graphics program
computer-aided design
  (CAD) program
graphics driver
screen memory
bit-mapped graphics

mouse
light pen
digitizing pad
bar graph
line graph
pie chart
scattergraph

superimposed graph
stacked graph
linear trend
linear regression
tick marks (hash marks)

CHAPTER REVIEW QUESTIONS

1. Describe the following elements of a graph.
   a) Tick marks   c) X-scale
   b) Grid   d) Y-scale
2. What are bit-mapped graphics?
3. Explain why the use of additional colors requires greater screen memory.
4. Explain why a higher resolution graphics mode requires more screen memory than a lower resolution mode.

5. Name at least two disadvantages of using a dot-matrix printer as a graphics output device.
6. List the types of graphics that you can use in business applications.
7. You are the manager of a landscaping business. Name three applications of graphics software that can be useful to you.

DISCUSSION QUESTIONS

1. What effect does a lack of graphics program standardization have? Can you foresee an effect on you?
2. What applications of computer graphics might be used by the following individuals:
   a) Engineer
   b) Personnel supervisor
   c) Architect
   d) Interior designer
   e) Chief financial officer
   f) Project planner

APPLICATION PROJECTS

1. Determine all the display modes supported by your computer. For each mode, list the screen resolution, number of colors, and the required screen memory.
2. Redo the bar graph of the Jones budget as a
   a) Line graph
   b) Pie chart
3. Assume that you are Vice President of Sales and Marketing for Precocious Software. You have the sales information shown in Figure 12.39, organized by your firm's three salespeople, Adam, Beth, and Carl, and by customer industry for the first quarter of the year.

   Your sales manager is interested in reviewing this data so she can identify problems in the sales force, or reassign salespeople to the accounts with which they have the most success.

   Use your spreadsheet's graphics capability to help make relationships in this data more clear. Create a bar graph of total sales by salesperson, a pie chart of total sales by customer industry, a stacked bar graph of total sales by salesperson to each customer industry, and a line graph of each salesperson's sales by month. What do your graphic representations of the data tell you and your sales manager?
4. "Beta" is an index measure that compares a stock's volatility with that of the market. A beta of 1.0 indicates the stock has the same volatility as the market; a beta greater than 1.0 is more volatile, and less than 1.0 is less volatile. Beta is calculated by regressing a security's return against the return of a market index. Create a spreadsheet with the information shown in Figure 12.40.
   a) Use the /DATA REGRESSION command (Lotus 1-2-3) to produce a regression using the Standard and Poor's 500 return as the independent variable (X) and the return of Emerson Electric as the dependent variable (Y). Beta is the X-coefficient produced by the regression, and the Y-axis intercept is shown as the constant.
   b) Produce a graph of the regression line of estimated Y values against actual Y values. Select the XY type of graph and assign the range of estimated Y values to both the X and A ranges of the graph. Assign the actual Y values to the B range of the graph. Set the format for B to SYMBOLS only. Save the graph file under the name BETA.

Customer Industry	January Sales (in units)			
	Adam	Beth	Carl	TOTALS
Manufacturing	48	76	73	197
Consumer products	39	22	41	102
Construction	60	21	77	158
Monthly totals	147	119	191	457
	February Sales (in units)			
Manufacturing	59	77	67	203
Consumer products	24	10	42	76
Construction	86	65	59	210
Monthly totals	169	152	168	486
	March Sales (in units)			
Manufacturing	69	80	57	206
Consumer products	25	38	25	88
Construction	88	46	46	180
Monthly totals	182	164	128	474
	First Quarter Sales (in units)			
Manufacturing	176	233	197	606
Consumer products	88	70	108	266
Construction	234	132	182	548
Quarterly totals	498	435	487	1420

Figure 12.39   Precocious Software's first-quarter sales data.

Year	Emerson Electric Return	S&P 500 Index Return
1979	−.03	−.13
1980	.25	.17
1981	.32	.14
1982	.11	.04
1983	.10	.11
1984	.14	.11
1985	.78	.24
1986	−.09	−.10
1987	.28	.15

Figure 12.40   Rate of return on Emerson Electric and S&P 500 Index.

13 Communication and Networking

Transmitting the News That's Fit to Print

The *New York Times* has a long tradition of journalistic independence. That independence carries over into the type of equipment—and computers—the paper chooses to use in publishing perhaps the most influential newspaper in the world.

The paper's vice president of information systems, Elise Ross, says that today they "cannot put out the *New York Times* without the use of computers. To the same extent that there is not a *New York Times* without a press, there is not a *New York Times* without computers."

Words—more than 120 million of them yearly—are the core of the *Times*. Until 1982, virtually all of these stories were composed on terminals that were specially designed for publishing, with excellent writing and editing features. The system seemed perfect until the manufacturer stopped making the type of terminal the *Times* had invested in. Faced with a

shortage of terminals, Stanley Kaplan, the news-system director at the *Times*, launched a plan to use IBM PCs—not to replace the terminals, but to work alongside them.

In the main office at Times Square, more than 500 terminals are hooked together in a large local area network, connected to 11 Digital Equipment Corporation minicomputers. Reporters use microcomputers installed in their homes to retrieve previous stories (written by any reporter) on a subject they may be working on. Reporters can also compose on one side of the screen while looking at stories, notes, or edited versions of the story on the other side.

Once the stories are written, the reporters send them via data communication programs to the minicomputer at the home office. There they are edited into the printed version that millions of readers hold in their hands the next morning.

THE PRECEDING CHAPTERS discussed how you can use a micro-computer to generate, store, and analyze data. When using a computer to solve problems, you may also need to communicate data from one device to another. For example, you may want to send the results of your latest spreadsheet analysis to a sales representative in another office. Or, in order to prepare a proposal for a new contract, you may require data stored in a mainframe computer located in another city. Or you may want to send a final draft of your company's quarterly report to a laser printer that will produce typeset-quality hard copy ready for duplication.

All of these scenarios require data to be sent from one device to another, from your computer to another computer or peripheral device. Such transmissions of data are called **data communication**. This chapter discusses data communication from the viewpoint of a microcomputer user.

13.1 Applications of Data Communications

Data communication forms the backbone of many impressive microcomputer applications. Let's begin by looking at some of the applications you are most likely to find useful in solving business problems.

Transferring Data

The ability to transfer data files from place to place in a matter of minutes is a powerful but simple and flexible tool. Workers in distant offices can share data and cooperate on projects. While on the road, salespeople can use a portable microcomputer to obtain sales information from their company's mainframe. Executives can dispatch work from wherever their duties take them and transmit letters or memos back to the office for circulation and action.

Data communication programs and portable computers have created the movable office of today. In a very real sense, your office is where you and your computer happen to be. A portable computer enables you to carry most of your important data and application programs with you and to have access to business information at meetings and sales conferences, in hotels and at home (see Figure 13.1). Some hotel chains have recognized the importance of data communication and have equipped certain rooms with data communication facilities. In at least one major hotel chain, you can rent a room that is outfitted with a microcomputer as well as data communication facilities.

Figure 13.1 While traveling anywhere in the world, an executive can use a portable microcomputer and a communication program to obtain vital data from a corporate mainframe, as well as to transmit data back to the home office.

In many companies, microcomputer users routinely connect into database files kept on the company's mainframe. By consulting mainframe files, local users can get the latest information on sales, recalls, customer support, price changes, and product availability dates. In insurance companies, local agents tap into mainframe data to prepare policy quotations. In automobile dealerships, salespeople use microcomputers to track the manufacture and shipment of automobiles and parts they have ordered.

Bulletin Board Systems

Use an electronic bulletin board to send messages that do not require privacy or security to any user on your bulletin board system.

Bulletin board systems (also called **public access message systems**, or **PAMS**) are electronic versions of the common bulletin board. Electronic bulletin board information is maintained on a computer with data communication facilities. Users can call the bulletin board computer to read the contents of the board or to place messages on the board. Although messages can be read by anyone using the system, a user may address a message to a specific person or to a group of bulletin board users.

Bulletin board systems are widely used to disseminate information. Some computer software developers use bulletin board systems to inform customers of recent updates or reported bugs in the software. If, after consulting the bulletin board notices, users still have problems, they can post a notice on the same board asking for a customer service representative to call or write. Consulting an electronic bulletin board is usually faster and more efficient than sending notices through an interoffice or a public mail system.

Electronic Mail

Electronic mail systems (also called **E-mail**) offer users electronic "mailboxes," which are simply a group of files stored on a computer system. This data communication device allows you to send and receive messages. To send a message, you dial the telephone number of your mailbox and specify the mailbox you want the message to be placed in. You then enter the message that you want to transmit. To retrieve mail, you must first call the electronic mail computer and identify yourself by giving a password. You can then browse through the contents of your mailbox by examining the file names, date and time of transmission, and the originators of the messages. You can transmit selected messages to your own computer, where you may store them on disk or read them on the screen. When you're done with a message, you can delete it from the mailbox.

Electronic mail systems offer much more sophisticated communication options than do bulletin board systems. Most significantly, electronic mail offers privacy. Each mailbox is assigned a password that must be used to access it. Like a traditional mailbox, an electronic mailbox allows unlimited deposits, but limited withdrawals.

You can use an electronic mail system for the simultaneous transmission of a message to several mailboxes. You can, for example, circulate a memo to all the individuals on a departmental mailing list.

A number of commercial electronic mail systems, offered by communication companies such as MCI and Western Union, are run on a subscription basis. Users usually pay a monthly membership fee and a per-transaction amount based on the length of time they are connected to the system, just as telephone subscribers are charged for the use of a phone.

Use electronic mail to send messages intended for only a limited number of users. Just like a post office box, an electronic mailbox can be opened only by the user with the proper "key."

Accessing Remote Databases

You can also subscribe to databases containing information on a variety of subjects. The operators of such databases keep their information current and offer the data on a subscription basis to interested users. Using data communication programs, you can consult a database in much the same way that you consult a reference book in a library.

Communication databases are especially useful for keeping track of information that must be regularly updated. For example, human resources specialists in large companies need to keep abreast of frequently changing government employment statistics and related data. They can subscribe to services that offer regular updates accessible through their desktop microcomputers.

You can easily access remote services—from banking to shopping—and databases by using your home or office microcomputer and a data communication program.

There are many databases that collect research results in a particular subject—from cancer to psychology to space research. A researcher can consult such databases, which act as extensions of the traditional research library, to study the latest theories and statistics.

Accessing Remote Services

Many businesses offer services specifically geared to microcomputer users. To access these services, the user dials the business's computer to carry out a variety of transactions. The list of services available in this format is rapidly growing and currently includes the following:

- *Banking.* You can use your microcomputer to carry out a number of banking transactions, such as transferring money between accounts, making loan payments, and determining account balances. Some banks even allow you to use your microcomputer to pay bills. (See Figure 13.2.)
- *Shopping.* Some database services allow you to shop by computer. The computer can supply you with information from participating stores regarding merchandise for sale, sizes, and prices.
- *Tax returns.* In 1985, the Internal Revenue Service began an experiment in which selected tax return preparers filed their

Figure 13.2 You can use a microcomputer to do a variety of banking transactions—transfer money between accounts, make loan payments, even pay your monthly bills.

clients' returns electronically. If the experiment proves to be a success, you can anticipate using data communication programs to file your returns in the near future. By eliminating paper returns, the IRS hopes that tax return processing can be dramatically speeded up and that refunds will be made more quickly and accurately.

- *Airline reservations and schedules.* You can use a number of database services to consult a master airline schedule to determine the most advantageous schedules and lowest fares. You can even order your ticket by entering a credit card number.

- *Investment activities.* You can receive information on the current prices of securities, monitor the trading on each of the major stock exchanges—even enter trade orders to be executed by a broker.

These services represent only a few of those currently available through microcomputer communication hook-ups; more services are being added all the time.

Section 13.1: Test Your Understanding

1. Give two applications of transferring data files via data communication.
2. What is a bulletin board system?
3. What is electronic mail?
4. How does electronic mail differ from a bulletin board system?
5. List three business services that can be performed at home by any microcomputer user.

13.2 Data Communication Concepts

In order to send data from one computer to another, you need to understand something about data communication hardware, data communication software, and proper user interaction with the hardware and software. Unfortunately, much of data communication is not very user-friendly. In order to operate most data communication programs, you will need to have some knowledge of the hardware and software operation as well as a number of data communication concepts (not to mention the vocabulary of data communication). This section will clarify these issues for you.

Communicating Data between Devices

The basic concept of data communication between two electronic devices is quite simple. At any given moment, one of the devices is sending data (designated as the **sending device**) and the other is receiving data (designated as the **receiving device**). Some devices (for example, keyboards or mice) can only send data; other devices (such as printers or monitors) can only receive data. This chapter is mostly concerned with data communication between computer systems. During such communication, the computer systems can both send and receive data, and the roles of sending and receiving may be reversed (under control of the software), so that the computers can carry on a "conversation."

In order for computers to communicate, both computers must be equipped with **communication devices** that manage the communication process. The communication devices are connected by a **communication link** (see Figure 13.3), which in most cases is simply a telephone line but which may include a microwave or a satellite relay. The data communication process is managed by a **communication program** run by both computers.

Some General Communication Concepts

In using communication programs, you are confronted with terms and concepts relating to the engineering aspects of communication. The following discussion defines the terms you'll need to understand and outlines how data communication programs work.

Transmitting Data

As was explained earlier, data are stored as bytes in a computer's memory. There are two modes of transmitting a byte over a communication channel: parallel mode and serial mode. In **parallel mode**, all of the bits are transmitted simultaneously and each bit travels on its own communication line. In **serial mode**, the bits travel one after another on a single communications line. Figure 13.4 contrasts serial and parallel mode.

Parallel mode, which is faster than serial mode, is used in most communication between a microcomputer and a printer. If you look at the cable connecting your printer to your computer, you will see that there are a number of connections made by the cable. Each connection is used to carry electrical information between the two devices. Some connections carry control information and some carry data. In parallel communication, eight wires simultaneously carry data, one wire for each bit in a byte. In the case of serial communication, only a single wire carries data. Most communi-

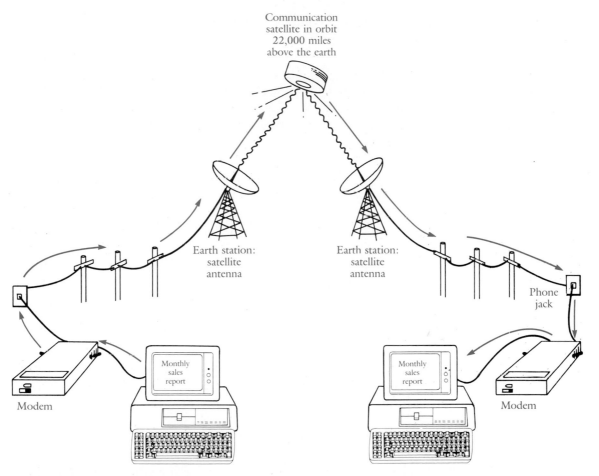

Figure 13.3   The components of a data communication system.

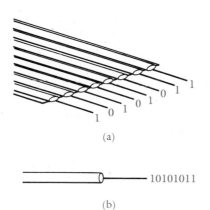

Figure 13.4 Parallel mode versus serial mode. (a) In parallel mode, all bits of a byte travel in a single, simultaneous configuration. (b) In serial mode, all bits of a byte travel singly, one after another.

cation between computers uses the serial mode, since only a single wire is available to transfer the data.

Receiving Data

The receiving communication device must be able to pick out the individual bits as they come over the communication channel. One technique, called **synchronous communication**, is to synchronize the transmissions at either end, so that the receiving device picks up a bit from the communication channel at fixed intervals of time.

Synchronous communication can be used for very high-speed data communication that requires costly equipment and special low-noise communication channels. Large businesses, such as insurance companies or stock brokerages, that need to transfer large volumes of data between offices, usually use synchronous communications equipment to connect their computers.

In **asynchronous communication**, the sending device transmits on its own, requiring no hardware synchronization with the receiver. Asynchronous communication is slower than synchronous communication but can be used with ordinary telephone lines and relatively inexpensive communication equipment. Most data communication involving microcomputers is asynchronous in nature. Figure 13.5 contrasts synchronous and asynchronous communication.

Direction of Communication

When you use a communication program to transfer data between microcomputers, you must choose the direction of communication. In **simplex communication**, data are transmitted in one direction only. One computer is designated the receiving computer and its

Figure 13.5   (a) Synchronous communication versus (b) asynchronous communication.

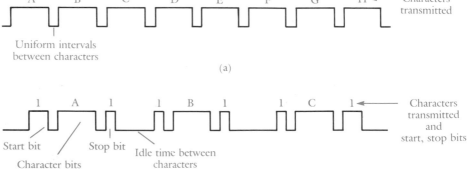

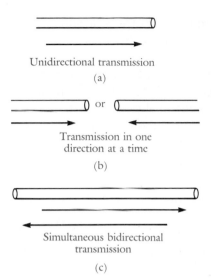

Unidirectional transmission

(a)

Transmission in one
direction at a time

(b)

Simultaneous bidirectional
transmission

(c)

Figure 13.6. The differences between (a) simplex, (b) full-duplex, and (c) half-duplex communications.

role is fixed. It can listen to the sending computer but cannot reply to it.

In **half-duplex communication**, the communication is two-way, but in only one direction at a time. At any given moment, one computer is the sender and one is the receiver. However, the two computers can reverse roles. The situation is similar to communicating via a CB radio. One party speaks and indicates completion with the code word "Over." It is then the other party's turn to speak. Most microcomputer communication uses the half-duplex mode.

In **duplex** (or **full-duplex**) **communication**, both parties can send to each other at the same time. This type of communication is useful in maintaining the flow of data among a number in offices of a large corporation. It allows data to flow simultaneously in both directions. Full-duplex communication might be compared to a telephone conversation in which both parties talk at the same time. In the human conversation, neither party can comprehend what the other is saying; in the electronic conversation, the communication device can easily sort out the signals travelling simultaneously in both directions. Full-duplex communication is rarely used with personal computers. Figure 13.6 contrasts simplex, full-duplex, and half-duplex communications.

Data Form

In using a communication program, you must make a number of choices about the form in which the data are to be transmitted. In order for the sender and receiver to understand one another, they must agree in advance on the form of the data.

The basic unit of data transmitted in communication work is a byte. To aid in decoding transmissions, some communication schemes require that extra bits be added to the byte. One or more **start bits** may be added before the byte. Start bits indicate to the receiving device that a byte is beginning and give the device time to prepare for receiving the byte itself. For example, suppose that you want to transmit the byte 0101 0101. If you and the receiver agree on two start bits, then you will transmit the following sequence of bits:

11 0101 0101

One or more **stop bits** may be used after a byte. These bits create a communication delay to give the receiver time to decode the byte. For example, if you and the receiver agree to one stop bit (and two start bits as above), then to transmit the byte 0101 0101, you would transmit:

11 0101 0101 1

Actually, you don't need to worry about constantly adding start and stop bits. Once you tell your data communication program your choice of start and stop bits, it will add them to your data bytes automatically. However, you must be sure of one thing: You and your receiver must adopt the same choice of start and stop bits. If not, the data received will be interpreted incorrectly, and the transmitted data will be garbled.

Because much of data communication occurs over telephone lines, it is important to realize that phone lines are subject to static and variations in volume. In voice communication, this is rarely much of a problem since the human mind is able to filter out the noise and fill in any missing or garbled bits of the conversation. With data communication, the situation is quite different. Changing a single bit in a communication program may change a spreadsheet cell value, leading to drastic consequences. Therefore, you need to check that your data are received *exactly* as they were sent.

> Data communication using phone lines may be affected by static in the lines that may cause data to be garbled or altered.

> In data communication, the transmitting and receiving users must adopt the same choice of start and stop bits in order to transmit accurate data. Then, they must check the data to make sure they were received correctly.

Checking Data

The simplest data check involves using a **parity bit**, an extra bit added to a byte that indicates the contents of the byte. There are several different parity schemes in common use: even parity, odd parity, and mark parity. With **even parity**, the parity bit is 1 if there is an odd number of ones in the byte. It is 0 if there is an even number of ones in the byte.

For instance, suppose that you are transmitting the byte 1010 1010, and you and the receiver have agreed to use even parity. In this case, there is an even number of ones in the byte, so the parity bit for this byte is a 0, which means that

1010 1010 0

is transmitted.

If the byte to be transmitted is 1110 0101, there is an odd number of ones; thus, the parity bit is 1. In this case, the communication program transmits

1110 0101 1

Note that the parity bit is used in addition to any start and stop bits. Note also that once you make a choice of parity, the communication program adds the parity bits automatically for you. Moreover, the receiving communication program automatically checks the parity bit as each byte is received.

Even parity is only one of the possible parity choices you can make. With **odd parity**, the parity bit is 1 if there is an even number of ones in the byte and 0 if there is an odd number of ones in the byte. With **mark parity**, the parity bit is always 1.

The parity scheme (odd, even, mark) is agreed upon in advance by the sending and receiving parties. The parity bit is set by the sending communication device and is checked by the receiving communication device. If the parity bit is incorrect, then the byte may have been garbled in transmission and the receiver would request that the sender retransmit the data.

For example, suppose that the parity is even and the byte transmitted is 0101 0101, which means that the parity bit is 1. If the byte is received as 1101 0101 (changing a single bit), then the receiving communication program will note that the transmission is erroneous and will request a retransmission.

A parity check is not foolproof. If an even number of ones is changed in the byte, then the computer does not detect a parity error. For instance, in the last example, if the byte is received as 1111 0101, the parity bit will seem correct. However, two zeroes were erroneously received as ones, and the two errors cancel each other out.

Even though a parity check is not foolproof, it is able to catch most errors. After all, a single bit in error is a more likely occurrence than two bits in error. Figure 13.7 shows a parity check being used to determine transmission errors.

Speed of Communication

The rate of data transmission is measured in terms of **baud**, a unit of speed named after communication pioneer J.M.E. Baudot. One baud represents a transmission rate of one character per second. In most microcomputer communication, each byte uses one start bit, one stop bit, and one parity bit. Together with the eight data bits,

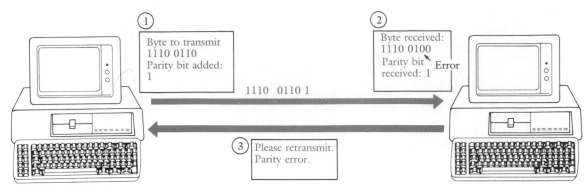

Figure 13.7   Using a parity check to determine transmission errors.

this makes a total of 11 bits. With this communication configuration, a transmission of 110 baud corresponds to 110/11, or ten characters per second.

Most communication devices can be programmed to transmit at different rates. The most commonly used baud rates for microcomputer data communication are 300 or 1200 baud, although transmissions at 2400 baud are being used with increasing frequency. The earliest modems were limited to 300 baud. However, advances in communication technology soon made 1200 baud the more or less standard rate. As of this writing, 2400 baud modems are available. However, the higher the transmission rate, the greater is the sensitivity to static on the line, requiring retransmission of some data. As a result, taking retransmissions into account, the 2400 baud modems are sometimes no faster than 1200 baud modems. Future advances in technology will undoubtedly lead the way to higher transmission rates.

Controlling Transmission of Data

A key to successful data communication is for transmitting and receiving users to use the same communication protocol.

Most microcomputers use asynchronous communication to transmit data. To make up for the lack of synchronization between the sender and receiver, asynchronous communication usually uses an exchange of signals, called **handshaking signals**, to control transmission. These signals form a **communication protocol**, which tells the sender when to start transmitting and when to wait. Some of these standard protocols have colorful names, such as XMODEM, Christiansen, DC1-DC3, XON-XOFF, KERMIT, and EXT-ACK. You don't have to know much about the particulars of any one communication protocol; just remember that both the sender and receiver must agree to use the same protocol. Most communication programs allow you to choose from among several available protocols.

Section 13.2: Test Your Understanding

1. What is the function of a communications device?
2. True or false: Most microcomputer data communication is done in parallel mode.
3. Explain the difference between synchronous and asynchronous communication.
4. Which type of communication allows simultaneous two-way conversation?
5. Explain the function of a parity bit.
6. What is a communication protocol?
7. Are communication protocols necessary in synchronous communications? Explain your answer.
8. What is a baud?
9. What are the advantages of electronic mail over regular mail? Do you see any disadvantages?

Hands-on Exercises

1. Suppose that the byte 00111011 is to be transmitted by using even parity. What is the setting of the parity bit?
2. A certain communication link requires one start bit, one stop bit, and no parity. How many bits are required to transmit one byte?
3. A certain communication link requires one stop bit, no start bits, and a parity bit. How many characters per second are transmitted if the communication rate is 2400 baud?

13.3 Communication Hardware

The basic microcomputer communications device used to transmit and receive data is a **modem**, which translates the electric signals representing bits into an acoustic signal that can be transmitted over a phone line. On the receiving end, a modem translates the acoustic signal back into a stream of bits. There are two configurations for using a modem with a microcomputer:

- An asynchronous communication adapter with an external modem
- An internal modem

Both sets of hardware accomplish the same tasks, but they are organized differently. Moreover, the internal modem is more costly than the combination of external modem and asynchronous communication adapter.

An **asynchronous communication adapter** (also called an **RS232 interface**) is an electrical circuit for outputting and entering data to and from the computer. Some computers have asynchronous communication adapters built into the system unit; others allow for its addition on an optional circuit board. An asynchronous communication adapter can be programmed for a desired baud rate, parity, stop bits, start bits, and protocol. A computer program can then exchange data with other computers through the asynchronous communication adapter.

An asynchronous communication adapter works in conjunction with an **external modem**. As its name suggests, an external modem is a device that plugs into a connector on the asynchronous communication adapter. The combination of an asynchronous communication adapter with an external modem is shown in Figure 13.8.

There are two types of external modems: acoustic and direct-connect. An **acoustic modem**, or **acoustic coupler**, is the original form of modem. Because such modems are very susceptible to static and can be used at communication rates of only 300 baud or less, they are quickly becoming obsolete. An acoustic modem transforms the computer data into tones that are sent into a telephone receiver, which rests in a cradle in the modem, as shown in Figure 13.9.

Figure 13.8   An asynchronous communication adapter and an external modem.

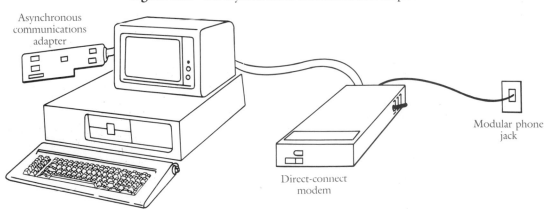

Asynchronous communications adapter

Modular phone jack

Direct-connect modem

Figure 13.9 An acoustic modem.

A **direct-connect modem** translates computer data directly into electrical signals that can be carried on a phone line. This type of modem connects either into a phone set or into a wall phone receptacle. It does not use the phone receiver. Direct-connect modems can be used at rates of 1200 to 2400 baud. Figure 13.10 shows a typical direct-connect modem.

The alternate configuration, an **internal modem**, is a circuit board combining the circuitry of both an asynchronous communication adapter and an external modem. Internal modems allow you to plug your computer directly into a phone instrument or a wall jack, without using any external boxes. This arrangement, shown in Figure 13.11, is particularly useful in portable computers or in offices where desk space is at a premium.

Figure 13.10 An external direct-connect modem. Courtesy of Hayes Microcomputer Products, Inc.

Figure 13.11 An internal modem. Courtesy of Hayes Microcomputer Products, Inc.

Section 13.3 Test Your Understanding

1. What functions are performed by a modem?
2. What is an RS232 interface?
3. Explain the difference between an acoustic modem and a direct-connect modem.

13.4 Using Communication Software

You have now learned the basics about data communication concepts and the hardware needed to implement those concepts. The missing ingredient, communication software, gives you the power to control the hardware and to mesh data transfer operations with all of the components of the system. The next section will put your knowledge to use and give you a concrete "recipe" for carrying out data communication on your microcomputer. The recipe consists of the following steps:

- Choose your communication hardware and install it.
- Choose your communication software and install it.
- Run the communication software to carry out data communication tasks.

Choosing Communication Software

You can choose communication software from a multitude of programs on the market. Some modem manufacturers supply you with accompanying programs; some leave it up to you to select your own communication software. As with most software, communication programs exhibit an expansive variety of features. You really need to research the available software to match the features that are required or desired for your work with the available programs.

Setting Up Your Hardware

You must choose the hardware configuration that's best for your data communication needs. For our discussion, we shall use either an asynchronous communication adapter with an external modem, or an internal modem. For the asynchronous communication adapter, you will need a modem cable to connect the adapter to the modem and, in the case of the direct-connect modem, a telephone cable to connect the modem to your phone system. An internal modem requires only one cable to connect the modem to the phone system.

Installing the Communication Program

You can install an asynchronous communication adapter board or an internal modem in any free expansion slot (see Chapter 3). MS-DOS addresses the board by using one of the device names COM1: or COM2: (COM stands for communication port). This selection is usually carried out by setting one or more switches on the asynchronous communication adapter board. In most cases, you can use the selection made by the manufacturer (usually COM1:). However, if your system has more than one communication adapter, it may be necessary to change the factory setting.

To begin your installation, you must set two important program parameters:

- A specification of the device name assigned to the communication adapter or modem (either COM1: or COM2:).
- A specification of the dialing method.

There are two types of dialing methods available—pulse or tone. Rotary phones use pulse dialing; push button phones use tone dialing. Be careful, however. There are some "designer" phones with push buttons that use a rotary dialing method. You may need to experiment with the setting to determine the actual dialing method of your phone.

Check the dialing method of your telephone before hooking up your modem. If you have a rotary dialing method, you may not be able to transmit data with a modem.

Carrying Out Data Communication

After you install your communication hardware and software, you are ready to carry out data communication with other computers. There are four steps that must be followed in a communication session: specifying the communication parameters, setting up a communications link, performing communication activities, and terminating the communication link.

1. *Specify the communication parameters.* Each computer has a set of communication parameter settings, which are required to establish and carry out communications. Among these parameters are the baud rate, the number of stop bits, the number of start bits, and the parity scheme. For some computers, there is a single set of parameter values that you must use. This is the case, for example, with most commercial databases. On the other hand, you have some leeway in certain communication situations—for example, when you are communicating with another personal computer. You can choose any parameter values as long as both computers choose the same ones. (See Figure 13.12.)

Many communication programs allow you to store sets of parameter values that will correspond to the various computers with which you may be communicating. Thus, you determine the proper values once and then call them up when you need them. (See Figure 13.13.)

Figure 13.12 Specifying parameter values in the communication program Smartcom II.

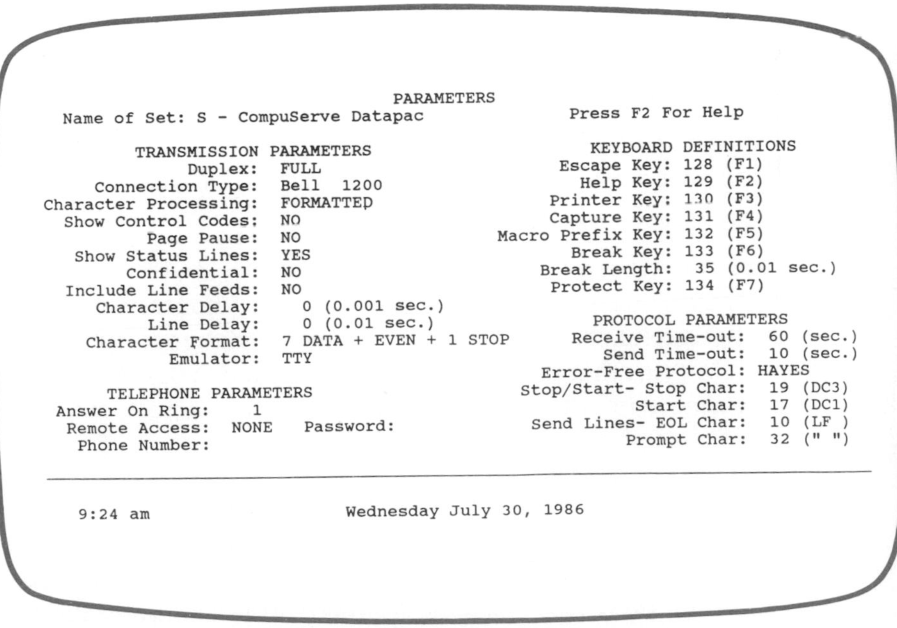

```
                            PARAMETERS
    Name of Set: S - CompuServe Datapac          Press F2 For Help

            TRANSMISSION PARAMETERS                  KEYBOARD DEFINITIONS
                 Duplex:  FULL                     Escape Key: 128 (F1)
        Connection Type:  Bell  1200                 Help Key: 129 (F2)
    Character Processing:  FORMATTED               Printer Key: 130 (F3)
     Show Control Codes:  NO                       Capture Key: 131 (F4)
             Page Pause:  NO                  Macro Prefix Key: 132 (F5)
       Show Status Lines:  YES                      Break Key: 133 (F6)
           Confidential:  NO                     Break Length:  35 (0.01 sec.)
      Include Line Feeds:  NO                      Protect Key: 134 (F7)
         Character Delay:     0 (0.001 sec.)
             Line Delay:     0 (0.01 sec.)              PROTOCOL PARAMETERS
       Character Format:  7 DATA + EVEN + 1 STOP  Receive Time-out:  60 (sec.)
               Emulator:  TTY                        Send Time-out:  10 (sec.)
                                               Error-Free Protocol: HAYES
          TELEPHONE PARAMETERS                 Stop/Start- Stop Char:  19 (DC3)
     Answer On Ring:    1                             Start Char:  17 (DC1)
     Remote Access:  NONE    Password:         Send Lines- EOL Char:  10 (LF )
     Phone Number:                                    Prompt Char:  32 (" ")


        9:24 am              Wednesday July 30, 1986
```

```
Smartcom II              Hayes Microcomputer Products, Inc.

1. Begin Communication   *. Receive File       7. Change Printer Status  (OFF)
2. Edit Set              *. Send File           *. Select Remote Access    (OFF)
3. Select File Command   6. Change Configuration 9. Display Disk Directory (OFF)
A,B,C - Change Drive                            0. End Communication/Program
                         Press F2 For Help
Enter Selection: 1       O(riginate, A(nswer, D(ata: O
Enter Label: S

Communication Directory:

A - CompuServe Direct      J - OAG EE Telenet      S - CompuServe Datapac
B - CompuServe Telenet     K - OAG EE Tymnet       T - DJN/R Datapac
C - CompuServe Tymnet      L - OAG EE UNINET       U - KNOWLEDGE INDEX Data
D - DJN/R Telenet          M - THE SOURCE Direct   V - OAG EE Datapac
E - DJN/R Tymnet           N - THE SOURCE Telenet  W - THE SOURCE Datapac
F - DJN/R UNINET           O - THE SOURCE UNINET   X - Test Set
G - KNOWLEDGE INDEX Tel    P -                     Y - Remote Access
H - KNOWLEDGE INDEX Tym    Q -                     Z - Standard Values
I - MCI Mail               R -


   9:26 am            Wednesday July 30, 1986
```

Figure 13.13   A set of parameter values available to a communication program.

When communicating with a commercial database or with a mainframe computer, you can determine the necessary communication parameters either from documentation or from a database operator's customer service representative. (Most database operators, such as the Source or Dow Jones, maintain a toll-free number you can call for help in using the database.)

2. *Set up a communication link.* After specifying the communication parameters, you are ready to set up a communication link between your computer and the other computer (which is called the **remote computer** since it is usually in a location far from your computer). You can do this by having one computer dial the telephone number of the other, so that the two computers are connected through a telephone line. For the connection to be completed, the two computer operators must first agree on who will place the call and who will answer. They must also agree on the protocol to use. These selections are entered into the computer programs at either end of the communication. Figure 13.14 shows how to set up a communication link.

The communication program in the receiving computer instructs the modem to wait for a call. The communication

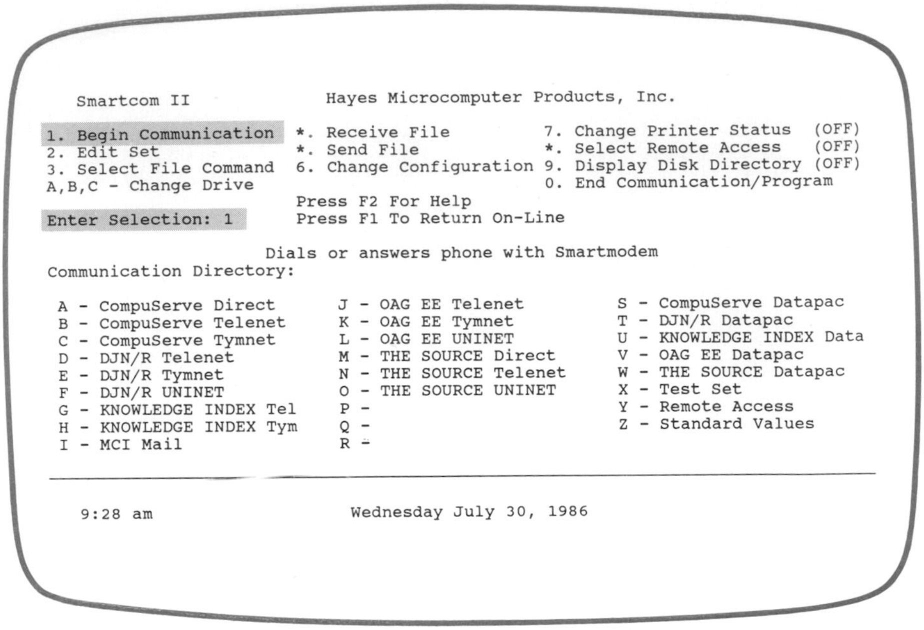

```
    Smartcom II            Hayes Microcomputer Products, Inc.

1. Begin Communication  *. Receive File         7. Change Printer Status  (OFF)
2. Edit Set             *. Send File            *. Select Remote Access   (OFF)
3. Select File Command  6. Change Configuration 9. Display Disk Directory (OFF)
A,B,C - Change Drive                            0. End Communication/Program
                        Press F2 For Help
Enter Selection: 1      Press F1 To Return On-Line

                  Dials or answers phone with Smartmodem
Communication Directory:

A - CompuServe Direct   J - OAG EE Telenet     S - CompuServe Datapac
B - CompuServe Telenet  K - OAG EE Tymnet      T - DJN/R Datapac
C - CompuServe Tymnet   L - OAG EE UNINET      U - KNOWLEDGE INDEX Data
D - DJN/R Telenet       M - THE SOURCE Direct  V - OAG EE Datapac
E - DJN/R Tymnet        N - THE SOURCE Telenet W - THE SOURCE Datapac
F - DJN/R UNINET        O - THE SOURCE UNINET  X - Test Set
G - KNOWLEDGE INDEX Tel P -                    Y - Remote Access
H - KNOWLEDGE INDEX Tym Q -                    Z - Standard Values
I - MCI Mail            R -


   9:28 am             Wednesday July 30, 1986
```

(a)

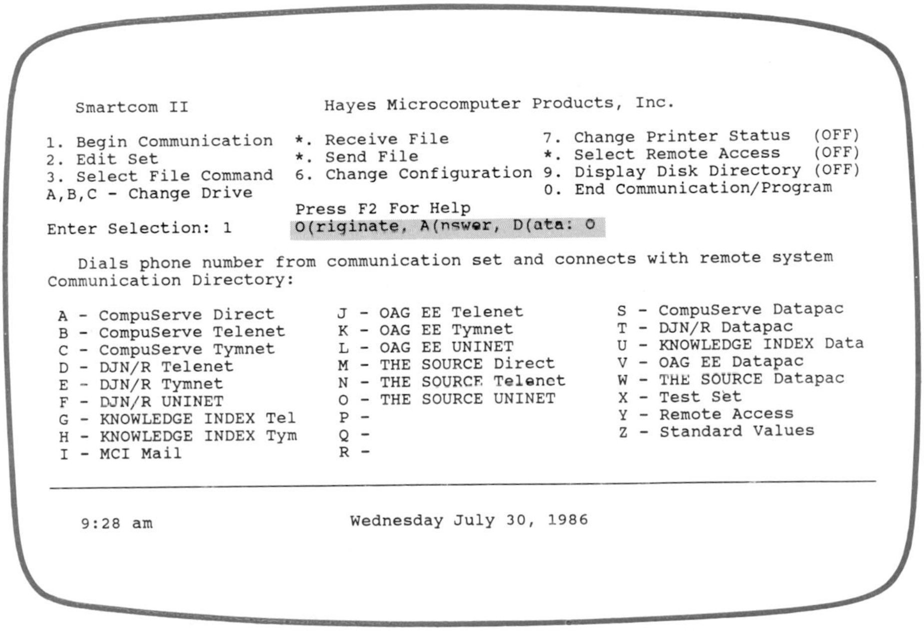

```
    Smartcom II            Hayes Microcomputer Products, Inc.

1. Begin Communication  *. Receive File         7. Change Printer Status  (OFF)
2. Edit Set             *. Send File            *. Select Remote Access   (OFF)
3. Select File Command  6. Change Configuration 9. Display Disk Directory (OFF)
A,B,C - Change Drive                            0. End Communication/Program
                        Press F2 For Help
Enter Selection: 1      O(riginate, A(nswer, D(ata: O

   Dials phone number from communication set and connects with remote system
Communication Directory:

A - CompuServe Direct   J - OAG EE Telenet     S - CompuServe Datapac
B - CompuServe Telenet  K - OAG EE Tymnet      T - DJN/R Datapac
C - CompuServe Tymnet   L - OAG EE UNINET      U - KNOWLEDGE INDEX Data
D - DJN/R Telenet       M - THE SOURCE Direct  V - OAG EE Datapac
E - DJN/R Tymnet        N - THE SOURCE Telenet W - THE SOURCE Datapac
F - DJN/R UNINET        O - THE SOURCE UNINET  X - Test Set
G - KNOWLEDGE INDEX Tel P -                    Y - Remote Access
H - KNOWLEDGE INDEX Tym Q -                    Z - Standard Values
I - MCI Mail            R -


   9:28 am             Wednesday July 30, 1986
```

(b)

Figure 13.14 Setting up a communication link. (a) The sending device user chooses the proper menu selections to begin communication, and (b) specifies it is originating the communication. (c) The sending user then selects the protocol and (d) enters the telephone number of the receiving computer.

```
    Smartcom II              Hayes Microcomputer Products, Inc.

1. Begin Communication    *. Receive File        7. Change Printer Status  (OFF)
2. Edit Set               *. Send File           *. Select Remote Access   (OFF)
3. Select File Command    6. Change Configuration 9. Display Disk Directory (OFF)
A,B,C - Change Drive                             0. End Communication/Program
                          Press F2 For Help
Enter Selection: 1        O(riginate, A(nswer, D(ata: O
Enter Label: S

Communication Directory:

A - CompuServe Direct     J - OAG EE Telenet      S - CompuServe Datapac
B - CompuServe Telenet    K - OAG EE Tymnet       T - DJN/R Datapac
C - CompuServe Tymnet     L - OAG EE UNINET       U - KNOWLEDGE INDEX Data
D - DJN/R Telenet         M - THE SOURCE Direct   V - OAG EE Datapac
E - DJN/R Tymnet          N - THE SOURCE Telenet  W - THE SOURCE Datapac
F - DJN/R UNINET          O - THE SOURCE UNINET   X - Test Set
G - KNOWLEDGE INDEX Tel   P -                     Y - Remote Access
H - KNOWLEDGE INDEX Tym   Q -                     Z - Standard Values
I - MCI Mail              R -


    9:29 am               Wednesday July 30, 1986
```

(c)

```
    Smartcom II              Hayes Microcomputer Products, Inc.

1. Begin Communication    *. Receive File        7. Change Printer Status  (OFF)
2. Edit Set               *. Send File           *. Select Remote Access   (OFF)
3. Select File Command    6. Change Configuration 9. Display Disk Directory (OFF)
A,B,C - Change Drive                             0. End Communication/Program
                          Press F2 For Help
Enter Selection: 1        O(riginate, A(nswer, D(ata: O
Enter Label: S            Phone Number: 302-539-07009

Communication Directory:

A - CompuServe Direct     J - OAG EE Telenet      S - CompuServe Datapac
B - CompuServe Telenet    K - OAG EE Tymnet       T - DJN/R Datapac
C - CompuServe Tymnet     L - OAG EE UNINET       U - KNOWLEDGE INDEX Data
D - DJN/R Telenet         M - THE SOURCE Direct   V - OAG EE Datapac
E - DJN/R Tymnet          N - THE SOURCE Telenet  W - THE SOURCE Datapac
F - DJN/R UNINET          O - THE SOURCE UNINET   X - Test Set
G - KNOWLEDGE INDEX Tel   P -                     Y - Remote Access
H - KNOWLEDGE INDEX Tym   Q -                     Z - Standard Values
I - MCI Mail              R -


    9:29 am               Wednesday July 30, 1986
```

(d)

program in the sending computer requests that the telephone number of the other computer be entered. In response to this entry, the program instructs the modem to dial the number. The modem places signals on the phone line that are identical to the dialing signals placed there by a telephone. On "hearing" the ringing signals, the modem at the other end "answers" the phone and establishes a connection between the two computers.

3. *Perform communication activities.* Once a communication link has been set up, you can perform any number of communication activities, including the following:

- Have a typed "conversation," in which data typed on one computer is displayed on the screen of the other.
- Send a file to the remote computer.
- Receive a file from the remote computer. This file may be displayed on a screen, printed on a printer, or stored on a disk. Any combination of these things may be done.
- Some remote computers allow you access to them without human intervention. This is usually the case with mainframe remote computers that allow users to tap into their facilities from a remote computer. These computers may even allow a remote computer to run their programs. For example, you might use your computer to run mainframe statistical or database programs that write their output to a file (on the mainframe). You could then transmit the file back to your computer for further analysis.

4. *Terminate the communication link.* When you have concluded your communication session, you must direct the communication program to terminate the communication link–a process equivalent to "hanging up the phone."

The Cost of Data Communication

When you carry out data communication, you are using a telephone line just as if you were using the line for a spoken conversation—and you are billed accordingly. If the remote computer is in another state, then you are charged the long-distance rate for your data communication.

Data communication charges can mount up quickly if you are transmitting large amounts of data. For example, a 100K file transmitted at 1200 baud requires approximately 16 minutes of phone time. If the remote computer is on the other side of the country, it could cost several dollars to transmit the file. Of course, this cost should be balanced against the costs of other means of transferring the file, and against the value of having the data available immediately. For many business applications, data communication is clearly the most cost-effective means of transferring data.

Section 13.4: Test Your Understanding

1. Suppose that your communication hardware consists of an asynchronous communication adapter and an external modem. Explain the cable connections required to carry out communications.
2. If your communication hardware consists of an internal modem, what cable connections are required to carry out communications?
3. What are the two methods of dialing?
4. List four communication parameters that you must specify in order to establish a communication link.
5. A certain long distance service charges $1.00 per minute for a long distance call from New York to Los Angeles. How much does it cost to send a file containing 150K between these two cities, assuming that you use a 1200 baud modem connection? (Assume also that each character requires 11 bits to be transmitted.)

Hands-on Exercises

1. Install your communication program.
2. Use your communication program to establish a communication link with a friend's computer.
3. Send a file to a classmate. (A file produced by your word processor or spreadsheet program will do.)
4. Have a classmate send a file to you.

13.5 Microcomputers and Networks

A **computer network** is a group of computers and peripheral devices connected by data communication hardware and software in a way that allows all computers and peripheral devices to exchange information, share files, and make common use of peripherals. The hardware may be located anywhere—in the same

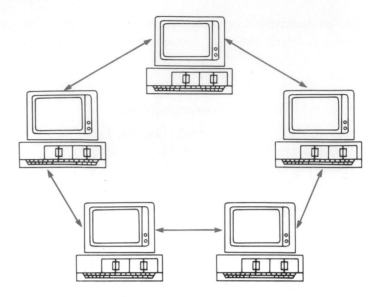

Figure 13.15 A ring network.

Figure 13.16 A star network.

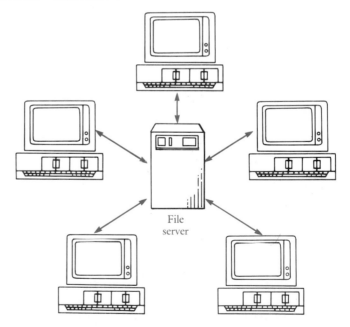

office, in various parts of one building, or at distant sites throughout the country or the world. Data communication programs allow the computers and peripheral devices to function as though they were located in the same room.

Computer networks give you the power to share information. One computer user in the network may be assigned responsibility for keeping certain important files current (perhaps price lists or sales information). All other users in the network can consult these files. One salesperson can consult the price file to determine the current prices to use in a proposal. Another salesperson (possibly in a different location) can consult the sales information file to determine if a particular order has been shipped.

Computer networks also give you the power to share peripheral devices. It may be difficult to justify the cost of some devices, such as a high-speed laser printer or a very large hard disk, if the devices are to be used only with a single computer. However, the high cost may be justified if the hardware is included in a network where it is available for use with a number of different computers.

Network Organization

In some networks, a single computer is designated as the **file server**, or the control computer. The file server manages the network and maintains the order of communication between the computers and peripheral devices. In some networks, there is no file server.

There are four types of computer networks: ring, star, bus, and hybrid. Here are the important features of each.

- *Ring network.* In a **ring network** (also called a daisy chain network), the computers and peripheral devices are connected in a ring formation. There is no file server. Messages are passed around the ring, until they reach their destination. This organization is vulnerable in the event of a breakdown of one of the network components. Moreover, adding or deleting network components usually requires extensive rewiring. Figure 13.15 shows the organization of a ring network.

- *Star network.* A **star network** has a file server in the center and communication links from the file server to the other network components. All communications pass through the file server. The network organization allows for easy addition and deletion of network components but is vulnerable to breakdowns of the file server. Figure 13.16 shows the organization of a star network.

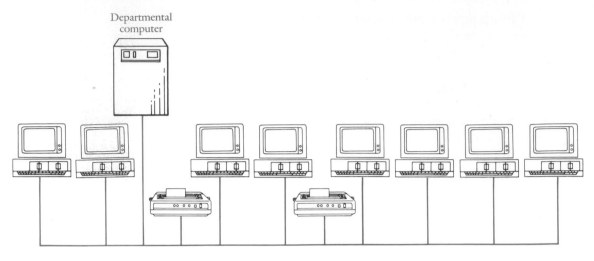

Figure 13.17   A bus network.

- *Bus network.* A **bus network** has a single cable, called the **bus**, which carries all the communication of the network. Each network component is connected to the bus. Each communication is sent along the bus, tagged to indicate its destination. Each network component "listens" to determine whether a particular communication is intended to be received by it. A bus network is easy to modify. Moreover, a failure of a single network component does not cause a breakdown of the entire network. Figure 13.17 shows the organization of a bus network.

- *Hybrid network.* A **hybrid network** is part bus, part star, and part ring. Figure 13.18 shows the organization of a typical hybrid network.

Local Area Networks

Very often microcomputers in a single office or department are connected into a network in order to obtain files and to share devices. A network that has components in close proximity to one another (say in the same building) is called a **local area network** (or **LAN**).

The typical LAN uses a bus structure. Constructing a LAN is a relatively simple affair. Each microcomputer in the network has a network card inserted into one of its expansion slots. The network card has a connector that allows you to attach to the network's cabling. Many LANs use ordinary telephone wire to connect the network computers.

LAN

Some office buildings are currently being constructed with LAN cabling already run through the walls. The tenants of these buildings can construct LANs with great ease because the LAN cabling can be accessed through wall jacks similar to telephone outlets. Moreover, as company needs dictate, the structure of the LAN can be changed by simply plugging and unplugging cables from modular wall jacks.

Network Software

Networks (in particular, LANs) require an operating system that supports multiple users. Currently, MS-DOS is not sufficient. Instead, you must use operating systems such as UNIX and XENIX. (Operating systems were discussed in Chapter 4.)

Some application software must be modified for use in a network environment. Manufacturers may insist on additional fees for software used on a network. If you are planning a network, you must take into account the additional time and costs necessary to convert your current software to versions that will work on the network.

Section 13.5: Test Your Understanding

1. What is a computer network?
2. What is the function of a file server?
3. Describe the organization of the various networks.

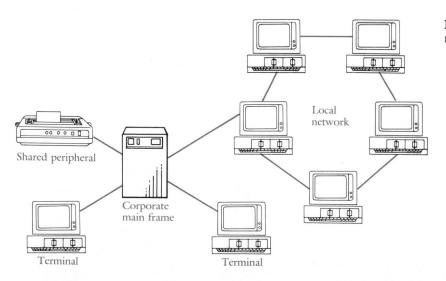

Figure 13.18 A hybrid network.

4. Which network organization is typically used for microcomputer networks?
5. What is a LAN?

KEY TERMS

data communication

bulletin board system

public access message system (PAMS)

electronic mail system (E-mail)

sending device

receiving device

communication device

communication link

communication program

parallel mode

serial mode

synchronous communication

asynchronous communication

simplex communication

half-duplex communication

duplex (or full-duplex) communication

start bit

stop bit

parity bit

even parity

odd parity

mark parity

baud

handshaking signals

communication protocol

modem

asynchronous communication adapter (or RS232 interface)

external modem

modem

external modem

acoustic modem (or acoustic coupler)

direct-connect modem

internal modem

remote computer

computer network

file server

ring network

star network

bus network

bus

hybrid network

local area network (LAN)

CHAPTER REVIEW QUESTIONS

1. Explain the meaning of a data communication rate of 1200 baud.

2. The early teletypes used one start bit, one stop bit, one parity bit, and a 110 baud communication rate to transmit data. How many characters per second is this?

3. Explain the effect of static on a data communication line.

4. What is the function of a parity bit?

5. Suppose that you wish to transmit the byte 0000 0111. What will be the associated parity bit if odd parity is used? Even parity? Mark parity?

6. Acoustic modems are limited to transmission speeds of 300 baud or less. What might you guess is the reason for this?

7. Which type of modems are most useful with portable computers? Why?

8. Which network structure can be most easily modified?

9. Give an example of a situation in which a local area network is useful.

DISCUSSION QUESTIONS

1. What problems might arise if you allow many network users to modify the same file? What network policies might you put in place to minimize these problems?

2. Do you foresee any difficulties if financial activities, such as banking and stock purchases, are transacted from your home? Are there any safeguards that seem necessary to curb potential abuses?

3. What reference materials are most likely to be supplanted by computerized databases?

APPLICATION PROJECTS

1. Many firms have expanded their marketing efforts to include microcomputer order processing. Customers use their microcomputers and modems to contact the selling firm's microcomputer. Customers then review a series of ordering menus, select desired merchandise, and authorize payment by credit card or purchase order.

   The selling firm stores the latest order information on disk and, at the end of the day, sends it directly to the warehouse for shipping and to the accounting department for billing. Manufacturing is also alerted so that future production can be scheduled to replace the purchased units.

   What are the advantages and disadvantages of such a system to each party (buyer and seller) in the transaction?

2. A variety of information retrieval services enable investors to obtain up-to-the minute stock price quotations and a variety of other investment data. The best-known one, Dow Jones News/Retrieval, provides a wealth of information including present and past stock prices, news items, economic forecasts, and airline schedules. Prepare a report indicating the following:

   a) The type of hardware needed to enable your computer to access this service

   b) The software required

   c) The communication protocol to be used

   d) The data available

   e) The cost of this service

   Now prepare a list of other services that provide investment information. Include the fees charged by those services.

14 Other Application Software

Computers Solving Computer Problems

A stubborn robot on an automobile factory floor refuses to start. A technician repeats the starting procedure, pressing buttons in the robot's control cabinet, but still no luck. The robot's arm won't budge.

Then the technician inserts a floppy disk in a microcomputer and taps some keys. The micro displays a menu of questions that list possible causes for the robot's resistance. The technician hits a few more keys, and the display changes to a graphic representing a panel inside the robot's cabinet.

"How many of the five lights are lit?" the display asks. "Three," the technician responds, and the display advises her to make sure that all the safety switches, including one in an out-of-the-way spot, are in the "on" position. When the technician follows this advice, the robot hums to life.

This scene is being played more and more frequently on assembly floors around the nation. One way to handle problems that come up unexpectedly is with a program like the one the technician used on the stubborn robot. The program contains an expert system, a form of artificial intelligence that, unlike conventional programs, does not simply follow a predetermined set of instructions. In-

stead, it interrogates the user and processes the responses to find where the problem lies.

Expert systems are devised through the knowledge of human experts in a particular field. This knowledge is written as a series of "if, then" statements. If something is true, then one or more other things must be true as well. By a process of elimination, the program can pinpoint the most likely trouble spots.

For example, Vision Systems, a computer consulting firm, is designing a microcomputer expert system to help clerks process workers' compensation claims for Allstate Insurance Company. The insurer usually sends out the work to special service bureaus that use a list of some 3,000 rules to determine how much to reimburse a patient. The program, which will incorporate all the variables needed to make such decisions, will save Allstate millions of dollars by cutting the employees and time needed to make calculations.

These microcomputer AI programs need a lot of power to operate—up to two million bytes of RAM might be needed to run a small expert system (the most powerful micros now have only 640,000 bytes of useful RAM). But as micros grow more powerful, you can be sure that AI and expert system programs will become more common in the workplace.

Source: John Holusha, "A System Aids Use of Robots," *New York Times*, April 17, 1986.

THE PRECEDING CHAPTERS introduced a number of different types of application software, but such packages are not the only ones available for microcomputers. The field of microcomputing is still very young, and the applications discussed in this text are those that have achieved prominence thus far in the microcomputer revolution. Many other types of application software are currently available, and countless more will be created in the future. We shall now look at some of these additional categories of application software.

14.1   Integrated Software

The most commonly used business application packages are the ones described in this text: word processors, spreadsheets, database management systems, graphics packages, and communication programs. Another type of application package that is quite popular today is **integrated software**, designed to perform the functions of two or more of these packages. A notable example that has enjoyed enormous success is Lotus 1-2-3, a software package that integrates three programs into one.

The applications included in an integrated package vary with the package. For instance, Lotus 1-2-3 includes a spreadsheet, a data manager, and a graphics capability. Symphony, Jazz and Framework include these same functions, but add word processing and communications.

Advantages of Integrated Software

There are many advantages to using integrated software rather than individual application packages. Most importantly, an integrated package allows you to learn a single, consistent set of commands that perform a wide variety of functions. As you have seen by completing the exercises and application projects in this text, it takes time and effort to master any software package. If you need to use more than one application package, having to learn a separate command set for each can be very confusing and can lead to time-consuming mistakes.

Integrated packages give you the advantage of using a single, consistent set of commands from one program to another. They also allow you to exchange data easily between programs.

It is much more convenient to have a uniform approach for saving and retrieving files, whether spreadsheet, word processing, or graphics files. Similarly, it is convenient to learn only one set of error messages and the proper responses to each. Integrated software offers such a uniform approach.

Another compelling advantage of integrated software over individual application packages is that the integrated package allows the interchange of data between different programs in the package. You can easily incorporate spreadsheet data into word processing documents; you can prepare graphics from spreadsheet data; you can compile database reports from spreadsheet data and then include these reports in word-processed documents.

Compare the simplicity of this type of data interchange with the complications inherent in using separate packages for each application. For one thing, each application tends to store its data in a unique format. To use data produced by one application in another application, you usually must convert the data from one format into another. Some programs are specifically designed to accept data directly from certain packages; some require that you run the data through a conversion program; some make no provisions for accepting data from other packages. If all your application packages are integrated into a single program, you can be sure that the data formats are consistent and that data interchange between applications is a relatively painless affair.

The Dark Side of Integrated Software

A drawback of integrated software is the large amount of RAM the programs require, leaving very little memory for data storage.

"There is no such thing as a free lunch" is a maxim that very much applies to integrated software. Although integrated software offers many distinct advantages, it does have its drawbacks. For one thing, integrated software usually consists of complex programs that require large amounts of RAM. Few integrated packages run in anything less than 256K of RAM, and many require quite a bit more. Moreover, to attach many applications to a single program, integrated software developers must write complex programs. This tends to make the component applications run more slowly than if they were contained in independent, simpler programs.

Another weakness of integrated software is that the package (and its programs) must be chosen as a whole unit. For instance, some of the component applications may lack features you desire from independent programs, or may have features for which you have no use. You may like Microsoft's word processor Word more than the word processor in Symphony. However, by choosing Symphony for its other benefits, you must accept its word processor or lose the advantage of having it integrated into the package. Usually, data management and word processing are the components that tend to suffer the most in integrated packages.

Alternatives to Integrated Software

An alternative to integrated software is offered by **windowing systems**, system software that allows you to divide the screen into several boxes, or windows, each running a separate program.

Figure 14.1 shows the windows in Microsoft's Windows system. You can move the cursor from window to window to perform tasks in each of the programs currently running. You can also transfer data between windows, which gives you the ability to pass data between separate programs.

Using a windowing system, you can create custom-integrated programs. You can combine your favorite word processor with your favorite spreadsheet, for example, thereby enjoying many of the advantages of integrated software without some of the disadvantages.

With a windowing system, you can have the best of integrated software without the disadvantages.

Windowing software is quite complex. It takes a large amount of computer code to keep track of the contents of the windows, manipulate their sizes, and so forth. Moreover, if the windowing system is graphics based (as is the Macintosh software that uses icons to represent programs), the requirements for programming and memory are even greater.

The complexity of windowing software places a heavy computing burden on a microprocessor. In order to keep track of the contents and position of windows, a large proportion of a microprocessor's capacity is consumed, as is a great deal of RAM. For this reason, when slower microprocessors are equipped with a windowing system, windowed programs tend to run very slowly. Accordingly, windowing software has been slow to catch on with

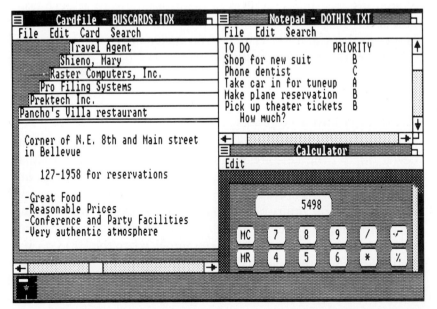

Figure 14.1 The operating environment of Microsoft's Windows.

older microprocessors, such as the Intel 8088 used in an IBM PC. It is quite likely that windowing technology will come into its own only with the "third generation" of microcomputers—those with fast microprocessors, like Intel's 80286 or Motorola's 68020, and several megabytes of RAM.

Section 14.1 Test Your Understanding

1. What is integrated software?
2. What are the advantages of integrated software?
3. What are the disadvantages of integrated software?
4. Explain how a windowing system can achieve many of the same effects as integrated software.

14.2 Utility Programs

A **utility program** is software that provides you with a simplified way of performing a task, such as giving an operating system command. Hundreds of utility programs that perform a multitude of tasks are flooding the market. Some perform rather ordinary jobs, such as reducing the number of keystrokes necessary to give a command; others perform exotic chores, like testing the alignment of your diskette drives or allowing your programs to achieve faster disk access times. Described here are some of the available utility programs that can improve the performance of your computer and relieve you of some frequently repeated tasks.

RAM-Resident Programs

Some utility programs work like ordinary programs, but many newer utility programs are **RAM-resident**, which means they are loaded into RAM and remain there while you run other programs. The program you are currently running is called a **foreground program**, and the utility program is called a **background program**.

Some RAM-resident programs are activated automatically when a particular event occurs (for example, when the DOS prompt is displayed). Others are activated in response to a particular keystroke. RAM-resident utilities remain in RAM until you need them. In the utility survey that follows, a number of the utilities are RAM-resident programs.

Saving Keystrokes: Macro Generators

Most of your interaction with a microcomputer is done by typing on the keyboard, and much of that typing is repetitive. For example, in a particular application, you repeatedly type identical or similar commands. Rather than retype commands each time, you can use a utility called a **macro generator**. As you saw in Chapter 9, a macro is a single command that represents a sequence of commands. A macro generator is simply a RAM-resident utility you can use to assign a macro to a particular key.

Suppose that you must erase a number of files. Rather than repeatedly type the letters ERASE as part of a DOS command, you can use a macro generator to assign the sequence of letters ERASE to a key, such as function key F1. When you press ⟨F1⟩, the macro generator replaces the keystroke F1 with the sequence of keystrokes ERASE. Since the macro generator is RAM-resident, the replacement is automatic.

A macro generator is installed in RAM just as any other program would be. Similar to any RAM-resident program, a macro generator waits until it is accessed (when it detects a keystroke corresponding to an active macro).

You can use a macro generator to create a new macro or cancel an existing macro, even if you are in the middle of running another program. Suppose that you are using your word processor to edit a document. You realize that the work will go faster by summarizing a certain set of keystrokes into a macro. To do this, call up the macro generator. It will write over your document on the screen. However, when you are finished, you can put it away with a single keystroke and your word processing screen is restored exactly the way it was before calling the macro generator.

With a macro generator, you can create and store many macros at a time. In fact, you can keep one set of macros for working in DOS and another for each application program you use. A macro generator allows you to replace one set of macros with another at any time.

You can even rearrange your entire keyboard to suit your needs by using a a macro generator. Suppose that a particular application program uses the function key F1 for a particular command, but another application program uses F10 for the same command. You can construct a macro to replace F10 with F1 in

Macro generators can simplify a program's command structure, thereby making it more user-friendly.

the second program. This rearranges the key command assignments so that they are more consistent throughout the range of applications programs you are using.

Optimizing Disk Performance: RAM Disks

Repeated accesses to a hard disk or floppy diskette can slow down program execution considerably. You may dramatically speed up programs requiring frequent disk access by using a **RAM disk**, another RAM-resident utility. Actually, if you are using a a recent version of PC-DOS, you have a RAM disk available to you. (Indeed, PC-DOS versions 3.0 and later include the VDISK command, which allows you to set up a RAM disk.)

Virtual Disk

A RAM disk creates a fictional disk drive in RAM. Running the RAM disk tells MS-DOS to set aside a specific portion of RAM to function as a disk drive. Then, as far as MS-DOS is concerned, the computer suddenly has an extra disk drive, where you can store data and programs exactly as you would a normal disk drive. However, reading from and writing to this drive amounts to reading from and writing to RAM, which can be done much more rapidly than reading from and writing to a disk drive.

The power of a RAM disk can be gauged with this anecdote: A programmer was developing a 300K program. One operation, which was particularly dependent on repeated accesses to the hard disk, was taking a half hour each time it was performed (which was often). To speed things up, the programmer created a RAM disk to hold all the data for the operation. Using the RAM disk, the operation took 45 seconds!

RAM disks are extremely powerful, so consider using them for word processing and database operations. Indeed, if you have a long document that ordinarily would not fit into RAM, your word processor will need to move portions of the document on and off the disk as they are needed. By keeping the document in a RAM disk, you can dramatically speed up the operation of the word processor, especially operations like scrolling from one end of the document to the other.

A RAM disk, which gives you extra power and extra storage capacity, is very handy in speeding up routine tasks such as sorting.

Similarly, in dealing with a large database, you can keep the entire database in the RAM disk to speed up access to your data. Operations such as sorting—normally a very slow process—can be helped along if you store your database in a RAM disk. Some sorting operations that might take up to an hour can be reduced to a few minutes with the use of a RAM disk.

The RAM used in a RAM disk is not available for any other purposes, so when you set up a RAM disk, be sure that you leave enough memory for application programs. Suppose your computer has 640K of RAM. To run an application program requiring 256K, you can set up a RAM disk having a maximum of 384K.

Remember that RAM is erased when you turn your computer off or lose power. If you use a RAM disk, be sure to frequently transfer its contents to a diskette or hard disk for permanent storage. Whenever you are about to turn the computer off, ask yourself if the contents of your RAM disk has been permanently saved. If you are not careful, you can lose hours of work by simply turning off the power!

> RAM is erased as soon as you turn off your computer. Be sure to save RAM-disk data on diskette or hard disk before turning off the power.

More Disk Utilities

Your computer spends a lot of time reading and writing data to disk. Disks are one of the few mechanical devices in your system, so they tend to slow the rest of the system down. Therefore, whatever tricks you can employ to speed up disk access can pay big dividends in productivity. You may not be able to see particular tasks go faster, but, by saving a second or two on each task, your day at the computer will yield more results.

One way to speed up disk access is to have your disk files well organized. Some utilities use a combination of methods to organize the files on a disk so that they can be found quickly. One method is to sort the disk directory. Just as you can find data more quickly if it is arranged in alphabetical order, your operating system can locate files more quickly if the files are sorted, for example, so that they are in alphabetical order by file name.

A second method involves rewriting the disk so that each file is stored consecutively. Most operating systems store large files on disk, a chunk at a time, wherever the system finds vacant space on the disk. As a result, files are usually scattered all over a disk's surface. (See Figure 14.2.) In reading a file, the computer wastes time while the read/write head moves to retrieve each of the chunks. The more scattered the file is over the disk surface, the more head movement is required to retrieve the file. It is much more efficient if files are stored in consecutive places on the disk, even though this is complicated to do. Thus, utility programs that rewrite a disk so that all the files are contained in consecutive locations can be a real time-saver.

Even if a file is originally stored in continuous locations on a disk, editing operations may cause the file to grow or shrink. When resaved, the file is no longer stored consecutively. For this reason, you need to run the utility program to rearrange your disk every so often, in order to keep your file reading operations at the peak of efficiency.

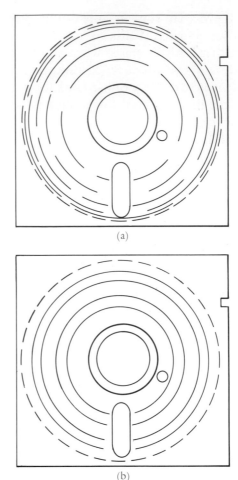

(a)

(b)

Figure 14.2 A file stored in (a) scattered locations and (b) contiguous locations on a disk.

Printer Utilities

A number of utility programs can help you use all of the special features supported by your printer. For example, you can use the graphics capability of a printer to print sideways on a sheet of paper. This is extremely useful in printing out large worksheets that extend horizontally beyond the confines of a single page. You can also choose such features as expanded print, compressed print, and near-letter-quality print, capabilities not usually available in the print sections of application programs. You can access these features by using a print utility designed to work with your printer.

A **print spooler** is a useful program for printing out a number of documents. You may specify a list of documents to print, and the spooler will automatically send the data to the printer.

Improving the Operating System Interface

MS-DOS is not very user-friendly. The MS-DOS prompt provides ← *PCDOS too*
little information other than the current drive. It provides no
information on the amount of space left on the disk or on the
contents of the disk. You can get this information by using the
appropriate MS-DOS commands, but MS-DOS doesn't have built-
in help facilities to assist you if you forget a command's syntax.

Designers have made a number of attempts to make MS-DOS
more user-friendly by building a RAM-resident **shell** around MS-
DOS. The shell is accessed whenever the MS-DOS prompt is
displayed. Instead of the MS-DOS prompt, the shell displays an
elaborate status screen that gives you a visual representation of MS-
DOS.

A number of these shells exist. Figure 14.3 shows the screen
display generated by the utility 1dir from Bourbaki, Inc. On the
left is a list of the files in the current directory of the current drive.
In the middle is information about the status of RAM and the
amount of space on the disk. Along the bottom of the screen are
MS-DOS commands.

To execute an MS-DOS command, use the arrow keys to
point to the command, then press ⟨ENTER/RETURN⟩. If the

An operating system shell can make MS-DOS commands more user-friendly by giving you a visual representation of the operating system.

Figure 14.3 The 1dir MS-DOS shell.

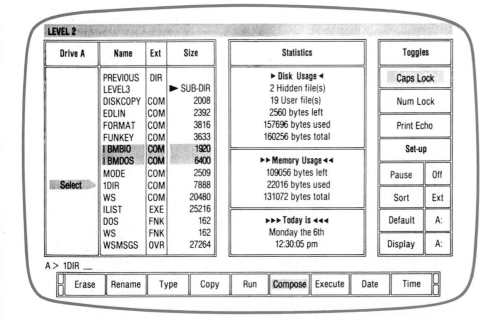

command involves a file (such as RENAME), use the arrow keys to point to the file in the list on the left. With this utility, getting help with MS-DOS commands is a keystroke away.

Some Cautions about RAM-Resident Software

Our discussion of RAM-resident utility programs in this section may have whetted your appetite to buy some of these devices. Before you do, a few words of caution are in order.

RAM-resident software consumes a considerable amount of RAM. The more RAM-resident software you use, the less RAM space you have available for application programs. Your RAM-resident software might easily consume 250 to 300K. Even in a 640K machine, this brings RAM available for applications down to 340 to 390K—barely enough for working with a large spreadsheet or a complex database.

Also bear in mind that some RAM-resident programs may interfere with each other or with other application software. Sometimes, using a RAM-resident utility while you are running a particular program may cause your computer to freeze up, with a consequent loss of data. Whether a particular combination of RAM-resident software and application programs works can be ascertained only by trial and error. In the future, software developers should settle on some memory usage standards to keep RAM-resident programs from interfering with other programs.

Keeping these cautions in mind, try using RAM-resident utilities on an experimental basis with data that are not valuable. It's important to remember that despite these drawbacks, utility programs can increase the power of your computer and your efficiency in using it.

Disk Recovery Utilities

When using a computer for work-related tasks, there are inherent dangers that can affect your data. Simply by giving the wrong command, you can erase a file containing months of work. In case of a disaster, you can use one of several utilities that allow you to reconstruct a file after it has been erased. All such utilities rely on the principle that the ERASE command in virtually all operating systems does not actually erase the data from the storage device. Rather, it removes the file entry from the directory. By reconstructing the file directory entry, the file can be pieced together from the data still in storage, provided, of course, that you have not in the meantime already written over parts of the data. A file recovery program should be an important early addition to every microcomputer user's program library.

Section 14.2: Test Your Understanding

1. What is a utility program?
2. What is a RAM-resident program?
3. Describe the advantages of a RAM-resident program.
4. Describe the effect of a RAM-resident program on memory available to run other programs.
5. Can you have several RAM-resident programs within memory at one time? Explain your answer.
6. Describe a macro generator and two ways it might be used.
7. Explain how a macro generator can assist you in giving a large number of commands of the form
   COPY ⟨filename⟩ B:
8. Explain the operation of a RAM disk.
9. Give an example of an application program whose operation will likely be accelerated by using a RAM disk.
10. Give an example of a program that is not likely to be accelerated by using a RAM disk.
11. When using a RAM disk, what steps must be taken to safeguard its data from erasure?
12. Discuss and compare some printer utilities.

14.3 Pop-Up Application Programs

Section 14.2 introduced the concept of a RAM-resident program and described a number of utility programs of this type. There are several creative application programs that also use the RAM-resident concept. Called **pop-up application programs**, they can be "popped up" on the screen while you run another program. Let's look in more detail at some of these pop-up applications.

Desktop Managers

The most popular pop-up application programs are **desktop managers** (called **desktop accessories** on the Apple Macintosh). These clever programs offer a collection of computer-simulated desktop tools, such as a notepad and a calculator, combined in a single RAM-resident program.

Suppose that you are writing a letter on your word processor and someone calls you for an appointment. Without disrupting your writing, you display your electronic "appointment book" on the computer screen. When you and your colleague agree on a

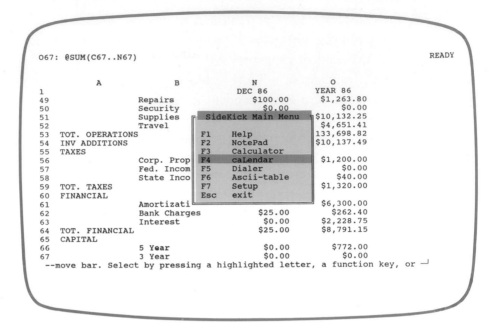

Figure 14.4 The Sidekick menu selection screen.

Figure 14.5 The Sidekick calculator.

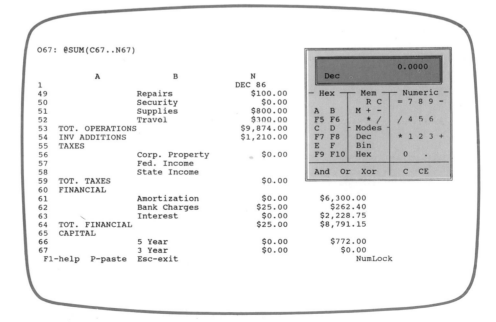

time for the appointment, you type it in and record the altered appointment book on disk. You then "put away" the appointment book, return the screen to the word-processing program, and continue writing your letter.

To illustrate further what you can do with this type of pop-up, we shall discuss Sidekick from Borland International Corporation, a popular desktop manager.

To load Sidekick into RAM, use the command ⟨SK⟩ ⟨ENTER⟩. You may call up Sidekick at anytime by pressing the key combination ⟨CTRL-ALT⟩. The menu selection shown in Figure 14.4 will then be displayed. Select an option by pressing the letter capitalized in the menu choice.

Pressing ⟨C⟩ displays the Sidekick calculator shown in Figure 14.5. This calculator works exactly like a four-function calculator with memory. The calculator can work in decimal, binary, or hexadecimal arithmetic. You can enter numbers by using the typewriter keyboard digits or the digits on the numeric keypad. (The latter allows more rapid digit entry.) To put the calculator away, press ⟨ESCAPE⟩, which returns you to the screen as it appeared just before Sidekick was accessed.

Figure 14.6 shows the Sidekick calendar, with the current date highlighted. You can change months and years by pressing the

Figure 14.6   The Sidekick calendar.

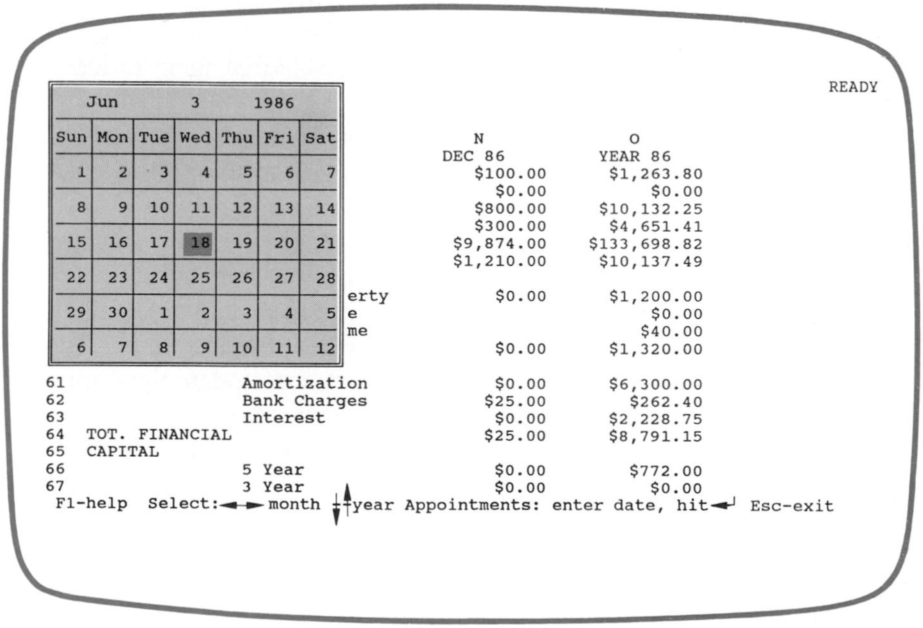

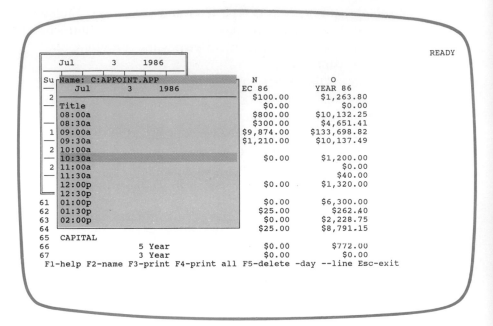

Figure 14.7 The Sidekick appointment pad.

arrow keys. Select a day by typing the numeric date and pressing ⟨ENTER/RETURN⟩. This displays the appointment pad for the day shown in Figure 14.7. Type appointments just as if you were using a word processor. To leave the appointment calendar, press ⟨ESCAPE⟩ to return to the calendar and ⟨ESCAPE⟩ again to leave Sidekick.

Selecting ⟨N⟩ from the main Sidekick menu displays the Sidekick notepad shown in Figure 14.8. You can use the notepad for jotting down notes to yourself or for making a "to do" list. You can save the notepad in a file and maintain many different notepad files that you can recall as the situation demands.

Selecting ⟨D⟩ (for dialer) from the main Sidekick menu displays the Sidekick telephone directory shown in Figure 14.9. The directory is an automated telephone list. You can update the phone list by using the word processing features of the notepad. By giving a person's initials, you can also direct Sidekick to search for that person's telephone number. You may even use Sidekick with a modem to dial your calls directly.

Once you start using a desktop manager, you will realize that it is as an indispensable program that will help you organize your work and make it flow more smoothly.

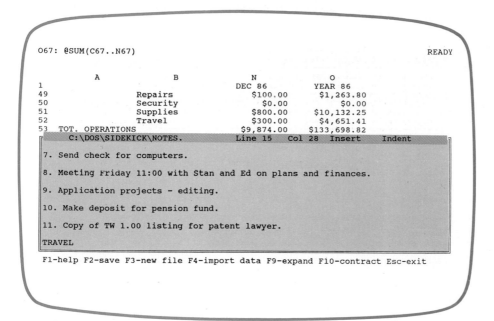

```
O67: @SUM(C67..N67)                                              READY


           A            B             N             O
1                                    DEC 86        YEAR 86
49                    Repairs         $100.00     $1,263.80
50                    Security          $0.00         $0.00
51                    Supplies        $800.00    $10,132.25
52                    Travel          $300.00     $4,651.41
53   TOT. OPERATIONS                $9,874.00   $133,698.82
    ┌─────────────────────────────────────────────────────────────┐
    │    C:\DOS\SIDEKICK\NOTES.        Line 15   Col 28  Insert    Indent
    │  7. Send check for computers.
    │
    │  8. Meeting Friday 11:00 with Stan and Ed on plans and finances.
    │
    │  9. Application projects - editing.
    │
    │  10. Make deposit for pension fund.
    │
    │  11. Copy of TW 1.00 listing for patent lawyer.
    │
    │  TRAVEL
    └─────────────────────────────────────────────────────────────┘
    F1-help F2-save F3-new file F4-import data F9-expand F10-contract Esc-exit
```

Figure 14.8   The Sidekick notepad.

Figure 14.9   The Sidekick telephone directory.

```
O67: @SUM(C67..N67)                                              READY


           A            B             N             O
1                                    DEC 86        YEAR 86
49                    Repairs         $100.00     $1,263.80
50                    Security          $0.00         $0.00
51                    Supplies        $800.00    $10,132.25
52                    Travel          $300.00     $4,651.41
53   TOT. OPERATIONS                $9,874.00   $133,698.82
54   INV ADDITIONS                  $1,210.00    $10,137.49
55   TAXES
56                    Corp. Property    $0.00     $1,200.00
57                    Fed. Income                     $0.00
58                    State Income                    $40.00
┌─────────────────────────────────────────────────────────────────┐
│ CCE         986-7290   Chevy Chase Home Equity  (Cust Service)    │
│ CNB         439-4000   Central National Bank    (Cherry Hill)     │
│ CTL         441-3330   CTL                       (Jim Jones)      │
│ ER    (215) 665-8870   Heffler & Co.             (Accountant)     │
│ FRO   (202) 296-5220   Frommer Travel            (Alice Smith)    │
│ FX          953-3333   Federal Express           (1010-0000-2)    │
│ KPP   (615) 246-7131   Kingsport Press (x214)    (Typesetter)     │
└─────────────────────────────────────────────────────────────────┘
F1-help F2-New file <─┘-dial -scroll search: F3-INIT F4-all F5-stop Esc-exit
```

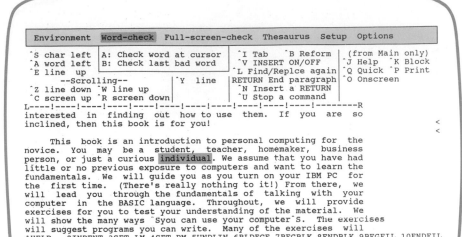

```
┌─────────────────────────────────────────────────────────────────────────┐
│ Environment  Word-check  Full-screen-check  Thesaurus  Setup  Options     │
├──────────────┬─────────────────────────┬──────────────────────┬──────────┤
│ ^S char left │ A: Check word at cursor │ ^I Tab    ^B Reform   │ (from Main only)│
│ ^A word left │ B: Check last bad word  │ ^V INSERT ON/OFF      │ ^J Help  ^K Block│
│ ^E line  up  │                         │ ^L Find/Replce again  │ ^Q Quick ^P Print│
│    --Scrolling--         │ ^Y  line   │ RETURN End paragraph  │ ^O Onscreen│
│ ^Z line down  ^W line up │            │  ^N Insert a RETURN   │          │
│ ^C screen up  ^R screen down          │  ^U Stop a command    │          │
```
L----!----!----!----!----!----!----!----!----!----!----!-------R
interested in finding out how to use them. If you are so
inclined, then this book is for you!   <
                                                                      <

     This book is an introduction to personal computing for the
novice. You may be a student, teacher, homemaker, business
person, or just a curious individual. We assume that you have had
little or no previous exposure to computers and want to learn the
fundamentals. We will guide you as you turn on your IBM PC for
the first time. (There's really nothing to it!) From there, we
will lead you through the fundamentals of talking with your
computer in the BASIC language. Throughout, we will provide
exercises for you to test your understanding of the material. We
will show the many ways ^Syou can use your computer^S. The exercises
will suggest programs you can write. Many of the exercises will
1HELP   2INDENT 3SET LM 4SET RM 5UNDLIN 6BLDFCE 7BEGBLK 8ENDBLK 9BEGFIL 10ENDFIL

(a)

```
          D:IBM.010   PAGE 1  ┌───────────────individual───────────────┐
              < < <           │ Spelling Confirmed Press F2 for Sound Alike Words │
    --Cursor Movement--       └─────────────────────────────────────────┘
 ^S char left ^D char right │ ^G char  │ ^I Tab    ^B Reform   │ (from Main only)│
 ^A word left ^F word right │ DEL chr lf│ ^V INSERT ON/OFF      │ ^J Help  ^K Block│
 ^E line  up  ^X line down  │ ^T word rt│ ^L Find/Replce again  │ ^Q Quick ^P Print│
    --Scrolling--           │ ^Y  line │ RETURN End paragraph  │ ^O Onscreen│
 ^Z line down  ^W line up   │          │  ^N Insert a RETURN   │          │
 ^C screen up  ^R screen down          │  ^U Stop a command    │          │
```
L----!----!----!----!----!----!----!----!----!----!----!-------R
interested in finding out how to use them. If you are so
inclined, then this book is for you!   <
                                                                      <

     This book is an introduction to personal computing for the
novice. You may be a student, teacher, homemaker, business
person, or just a curious individual. We assume that you have had
little or no previous exposure to computers and want to learn the
fundamentals. We will guide you as you turn on your IBM PC for
the first time. (There's really nothing to it!) From there, we
will lead you through the fundamentals of talking with your
computer in the BASIC language. Throughout, we will provide
exercises for you to test your understanding of the material. We
will show the many ways ^Syou can use your computer^S. The exercises
will suggest programs you can write. Many of the exercises will
1HELP   2INDENT 3SET LM 4SET RM 5UNDLIN 6BLDFCE 7BEGBLK 8ENDBLK 9BEGFIL 10ENDFIL

(b)

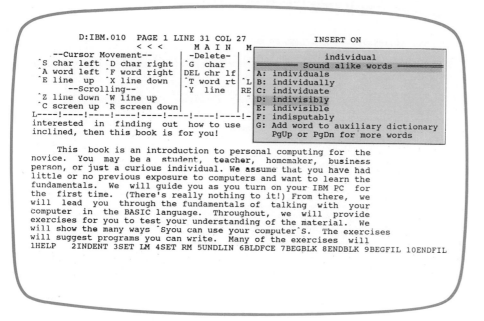

```
        D:IBM.010  PAGE 1 LINE 31 COL 27              INSERT ON
                  < < <      M A I N   M┌─────────────────────────────┐
        --Cursor Movement--    -Delete-  │          individual         │
      ^S char left ^D char right │^G  char     ╞═══════ Sound alike words ═══╡
      ^A word left ^F word right │DEL chr lf │^ │A: individuals              │
      ^E line  up  ^X line down  │^T word rt │^L│B: individually             │
           --Scrolling--        │^Y  line   │RE│C: individuate              │
      ^Z line down ^W line up                 │D: indivisibly              │
      ^C screen up ^R screen down│          ^ │E: indivisible              │
      L----!----!----!----!----!----!----!----!-│F: indisputably             │
      interested  in  finding  out  how to use │G: Add word to auxiliary dictionary│
      inclined, then this book is for you!       │   PgUp or PgDn for more words│
                                                  └─────────────────────────────┘
           This book is an introduction to personal computing for  the
      novice. You  may  be  a  student,  teacher,  homemaker,  business
      person, or just a curious individual. We assume that you have had
      little or no previous exposure to computers and want to learn the
      fundamentals.  We  will guide you as you turn on your IBM PC  for
      the  first  time.  (There's really nothing to it!) From there,  we
      will  lead  you  through the fundamentals of  talking  with  your
      computer  in  the BASIC language.  Throughout,  we  will  provide
      exercises for you to test your understanding of the material.  We
      will show the many ways ^Syou can use your computer^S.  The exercises
      will suggest programs you can write.  Many of the exercises  will
      1HELP   2INDENT 3SET LM 4SET RM 5UNDLIN 6BLDFCE 7BEGBLK 8ENDBLK 9BEGFIL 10ENDFIL
```

(c)

Figure 14.10 Turbo Lightning's pop-up dictionary. (a) Place the cursor on the word in question (*individual*) and choose the menu option WORDCHECK. (b) The program confirms the spelling of *individual*. (c) Press ⟨F2⟩ to see a list of sound-alike words.

Pop-Up Reference Materials

Pop-up reference materials are another type of RAM-resident application program. One popular program of this type features a pop-up dictionary (see Figure 14.10) and a pop-up thesaurus (Figure 14.11). Since these materials are RAM-resident, they may be called from within any program to check on the spelling of a word or to search for a synonym for a word.

Many other reference materials—stock market tables, geographic and statistical information, and almanacs—are candidates for pop-up application programs. You'll soon be seeing programs with these capabilities.

Section 14.3: Test Your Understanding

1. What is the difference between a pop-up application program and an ordinary application program?
2. Give an example of an application for a pop-up calculator.
3. Give an example where the answer from a pop-up calculator may be needed within another application program.

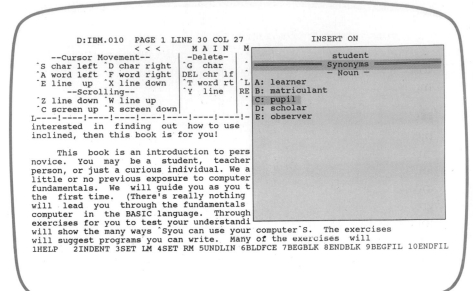

Figure 14.11 Turbo Lightning's pop-up thesaurus.

4. Give an example of an application for a pop-up notepad. What advantage does this approach have over using a pencil and paper? Are there any disadvantages?

5. Give an application for a pop-up calendar.

6. Traditionally, secretaries make phone calls and maintain calendars for executives. Discuss the advantages and disadvantages of using a desktop manager to perform these functions.

7. Give an application of a pop-up dictionary.

8. Discuss the pros and cons of having a dictionary in pop-up form as opposed to including the dictionary as part of a word processing program.

14.4 Project Management Software

When planning and coordinating multi-task projects, **project management software** is an indispensible tool. For example, a builder constructing an office building might use project management software to coordinate the various tasks necessary: drawing up the design, purchasing materials, excavating the lot, pouring the foundation, erecting the superstructure, running electrical wires, erecting external walls, and constructing interior partitions. In such an undertaking, each task uses certain resources (human and material) that are in limited supply. Further, some tasks must be completed before others may begin, and some tasks have mandatory start or completion dates.

Describing the Tasks

Project management software allows a user to describe a job in terms of tasks and resources. The software can add and subtract resources, change assumptions about particular tasks (required resources, prerequisite tasks, start and end dates), and increase or decrease costs of resources. The software can also keep track of the amount of each required resource and the time period for which the resource is necessary. And, the software automatically recalculates the project schedule and performs what-if analyses on costs and resources corresponding to changes in assumptions.

How the Tasks Interrelate

The interrelationships of all the tasks in a project can be graphically described by a **Gantt chart**. This software lists tasks, shows when they are to be performed, and describes which tasks must be completed before others can begin. A typical Gantt chart is shown in Figure 14.12.

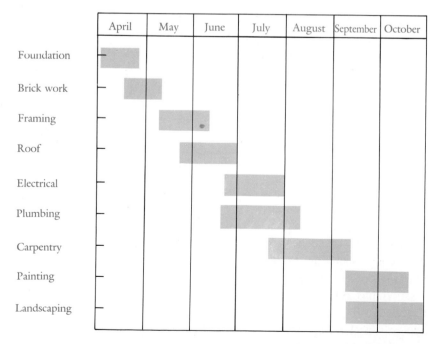

Figure 14.12   A Gantt chart.

Project management software can produce charts that use basic information about a project to keep track of costs by resource and to perform what-if analyses. For example, a builder might ask certain key questions: By adding two more bricklayers, can the construction be speeded up by a week? What will be the cost of having the carpenters work 20 hours overtime per week? What steps can be taken to have the entire job completed by January 15?

Because project management software forces you to think through the phases of a project and to consider how the phases are interrelated, you'll find it useful in many different business settings. Often, by using project management software, you can expose problems in scheduling, design, or budgeting. Even though these problems might be revealed in a manual planning process, the attention to detail required by project planning software encourages you to analyze the project in a thorough, organized way. This type of software also keeps track of relationships that are easy to forget about, especially in analyzing a difficult project.

Section 14.4: Test Your Understanding

1. What is a Gantt chart?
2. Describe the input of a project management program.
3. Describe the output of a project management program.
4. Give two examples of projects that might be planned with the help of project management software.
5. Describe how project management software can be used to monitor an ongoing project.

14.5 Artificial Intelligence and Expert Systems

In science fiction, computers are often portrayed as having the capacity of human thought. In reality, a computer can only perform tasks that humans program it to do. In a strict sense, a computer does not have the ability to "think." However, it has been a long-standing goal of computer scientists to program computers so that they can "make deductions" and "learn." The computer science field devoted to this topic is known as **artificial intelligence** (often abbreviated **AI**) and it is staffed with some of the best scientific minds of our generation.

The field of artificial intelligence has achieved some notable successes. Computers can now challenge—and beat—grand masters in chess. They can aid physicians in performing diagnoses and business executives in solving problems.

Because of the speed and memory requirements of such programs, artificial intelligence was originally confined to mainframe and minicomputers. However, as the capabilities of microcomputers have increased, artificial intelligence is finding its way into microcomputer application programs.

Expert systems (also called **knowledge-based systems**) are application programs that ask the user, or expert, questions that allow the computer to "learn" about a particular discipline. The programs store the data about a particular area of knowledge, and they also store the rules to make deductions about data. Once an expert system is "taught" a particular discipline, it can function as an "expert" consultant in the field.

Some of the initial expert systems were designed to aid in medical diagnosis. In the first step, designers gave these systems all the information about a particular subject, for example, cardiology. The system was taught the questions to ask in making a diagnosis. This required that an expert cardiologist enter his or her knowledge into the expert system. The cardiologist provided the system with a series of follow-up questions to ask, based on the answers to previous questions. The system could then go through a diagnostic session asking questions and, based on the answers, produce a diagnosis (or at least a guess among several most likely diagnoses).

Expert systems do have their drawbacks. They are only able to follow a rigid set of deduction-making rules. This inflexibility does not allow them to make the creative leaps that are often the key to breakthroughs by humans in solving problems.

Artificial intelligence technology will increasingly find its way into microcomputer applications and will make tomorrow's programs more intuitive, and thus more like humans in their problem-solving ability.

Section 14.5: Test Your Understanding

1. What is artificial intelligence?
2. What is an expert system?
3. Where could you use an expert system?

KEY TERMS

integrated software
windowing system
utility program
RAM-resident program
foreground program
background program
macro generator

RAM disk
print spooler
shell
pop-up application program
desktop manager
desktop accessory
pop-up reference materials

project management
   software
Gantt chart
artificial intelligence
expert system
   (knowledge-based system)

CHAPTER REVIEW QUESTIONS

1. What is a macro?
2. Give two applications in which a macro generator might be useful.
3. Suppose that your computer has 640K of RAM. Assuming that your spreadsheet requires 256K, what is the size of the largest RAM disk you can set up?
4. Give examples of three RAM-resident programs that you might like to simultaneously reside in RAM.
5. Explain how an expert system works.
6. Explain how a RAM disk works.
7. What are windowing systems? Why are they useful?
8. What is the purpose of a MS-DOS shell?
9. Give examples of two different types of DOS shells.
10. Explain how rearranging data on a disk can lead to improved file access times.

DISCUSSION QUESTIONS

1. Discuss the implications of desktop managers for improving productivity.
2. How do you explain the acceptance of personal computers by an increasingly diverse group of users?
3. You are an executive who wants to add interesting and useful features to a desktop manager. Which ones would you add? Outline a typical day in your office and specify how each desktop manager feature might help you.

APPLICATION PROJECTS

1. You are a salesperson who has just been given access to an application program such as Sidekick. Explain how your job will be made easier and how you will become more productive.
2. A variety of software packages (such as Sylvia Porter's *Personal Financial Planner* and Dow Jones *Investor's Workshop*) are available for personal investment management. These programs can keep track of a stock portfolio, monitor a budget, write checks, and perform other tasks relating to personal financial management. Prepare an analysis of two financial planning programs. Be sure to evaluate the types of tasks performed, the ease of use, the type of reports that can be generated, and the cost of each.

15 Issues in Microcomputing

Computer Crime Hits Congress

One March evening, an assistant to California Representative Ed Zschau was working late at her office computer when a beep told her that someone had entered her computer system from an outside telephone line. Minutes later, her screen went blank. When it came back on, mailing addresses and more than 200 letters to constituents had been zapped from her database. The culprits had gained entry by breaking one password and two security codes. A similar "break-in" occurred only four days later at the office of Arizona Representative John McCain.

Mr. Zschau said that infiltration of his computer system was "tantamount to someone breaking into my office, taking my files and burning them." Like victims of home and business burglaries, computer break-in victims express a sense of violation and loss. "Because people don't see the files overturned or a pile of ashes outside the door, it doesn't seem as bad," Mr. Zschau explained. "But it is equally as devastating."

The California and Arizona break-ins especially jarred legislators because the targets are members of Congress. Federal and state government officials, already concerned over the proliferation of computer-assisted crimes, stepped up their efforts to pass and enforce

stricter laws deterring such violations of privacy. Because businesses, banks, and government agencies increasingly depend on computers to store and transmit information, computer-literate criminals are focusing their energies on cracking security codes and passwords. Thus computer crime is quickly becoming the crime of the 1980s.

Legislative response has been strong and swift. In New York, Governor Mario Cuomo pressed for a bill making unauthorized use of computers, computer trespassing, and computer tampering crimes with penalties of up to four years in prison or a $5,000 fine. On the federal level, the House of Representatives unanimously passed a bill making the use of computers for fraud, theft, or breaking into other computers felonies. In the past few years, Congress has passed laws regarding computer break-ins that threaten national security or that affect credit and financial records protected by privacy laws.

New Jersey Representative William J. Hughes, head of the House Judiciary Subcommittee on Crime, sums up this new "hard-line" approach to computer crime: "Computer technology has left us with a new breed of technologically sophisticated criminal, whose tools are no longer Smith & Wesson, but IBM and Apple. Unless we act now, computer crime will be the crime wave of the next decade."

Source: "Two Cases of Computer Burglary," *New York Times,* March 21, 1986.

THE WIDESPREAD USE OF microcomputers raises a number of issues regarding procedures, ethics, social responsibility, and law, all of which are explored in this chapter. As you read, think about the way your stance on microcomputing issues will affect your use of microcomputers in the future.

15.1 Data Security

In the preceding chapters, you learned that the microcomputer is a unique and versatile tool. You can easily find microcomputer applications in most aspects of business. Once you start using a microcomputer to perform specific tasks, it isn't long before you are using it for additional applications that you had not even considered.

However, there is a risky side to microcomputer use. By trusting crucial aspects of your work to microcomputer application programs instead of traditional paper files, you increase your vulnerability to particular types of mishaps and mayhem. Microcomputers are generally reliable and safe, but all users should be aware of some potential problems they can create and how to guard against them. Let's take a look at some hazards you should be aware of.

Physical Hazards

It can't be emphasized too much: Protect your data by making backup copies regularly!

It is important to remember that a microcomputer is a machine that can malfunction—but the occasional malfunction need not bring your business to a sudden halt. For example, a new employee erases the only copy of your payroll data for the last five years; or your infant daughter decides to use the diskette containing your masters thesis as a pacifier; or a broken water pipe floods your basement study. In any of these scenarios, you should be able to pick up the pieces and continue your work. The key to surviving disasters like these is to have duplicate copies of all your data. It isn't possible to overemphasize the need to back up your data, and to do it often. No one has ever been disappointed by backing up data too frequently.

To guard against physical hazards that might destroy your computer room along with your backups, keep duplicates of all your most crucial data in a different location. A friend's house or a bank safe deposit box will serve very well as a failsafe data archive.

Remember that RAM is erased when you turn your computer's power off. If you live in an area where power blackouts or brownouts are frequent, consider adding a battery backup that will allow you to shut down your computer without losing data in the event of a power failure. If you don't have an auxiliary power source, save your work every 15 or 20 minutes. That way, even if a power failure does occur, the most you will lose is a small amount of work.

Human Error

As a human with human being shortcomings, you are more likely than Mother Nature to cause a disaster. When you are tired or when you are under stress, it is very easy to mistakenly erase a file or accidentally change some crucial data. It can happen to the most experienced users. When it does happen, it is important to keep your head and work to minimize the damage.

> Stress or fatigue might cause you to accidentally erase or write over your data. Keep your head, and calmly work to minimize damage.

If you accidentally erase some files, don't do anything that might write over those files. That is, don't perform any operations that will write more data to your diskette or hard disk. When you give an ERASE or DELETE command, your data is not physically erased from the disk, but the directory entry corresponding to the data is removed. There are several programs available to you that can recover the "erased" data by restoring the directory entry. Even if you have partially overwritten your data, recovery programs often can retrieve at least part of your file—and something is better than nothing. A data recovery program is a must for every serious microcomputer user.

Another type of mishap occurs when you accidentally change a file, then save the accidental data entry on disk, thereby overwriting your original data. Again, the first step in rectifying the situation is not to panic. Many programs do not erase your original data. They merely rename your original file as a backup file, usually with the file name extension BAK, and keep the file available on the disk for exactly such mishaps. You can use the command to display the disk's directory to determine whether such a file has been saved. If it has been saved, then your original data are not lost and you can recover them from the BAK version of the file.

Sabotage

Probably the greatest danger in entrusting vital pieces of your business to the memory of a microcomputer is the opportunity it presents for theft and sabotage. You've probably read articles about how microcomputers have been used for thefts—how an inventory statement stored on a hard disk covers up stolen merchandise, or accounting statements are altered to cover up a theft of cash.

When a microcomputer is used in a business, procedures must be designed that will minimize opportunities for data to be changed or maliciously destroyed. You can protect yourself by using a variety of safeguards, including passwords to unlock data files, encryption of vital data, and maintaining duplicate records, which can be periodically compared with the main records, to detect irregularities. (See Chapters 9 and 11.)

Be Careful, Not Paranoid

Without being paranoid, you should guard against the dangers of entrusting your important data to secondary storage, where it can be accessed by irate employees or saboteurs.

Don't let the warnings in this section make you paranoid about using a computer. As you've seen, computers are quite reliable and function flawlessly most of the time. It is unlikely that a natural disaster would wipe out your data, and after an initial training period, you should know how to guard against making major errors of your own. In using a microcomputer, take into account the things that *might* happen. Design your operating procedures so that you can recover very quickly when the unexpected strikes. By following these guidelines, your horror stories may be transformed into nothing more than amusing anecdotes.

Section 15.1: *Test Your Understanding*

1. An employee who has recently been fired decides to take revenge by erasing data stored on a hard disk. How can you guard against such an event?
2. How can you stop an employee from entering your payroll records and giving himself a raise?
3. How can you protect your data from a power outage?
4. How can you protect your data against a fire?
5. How can you protect you data against accidental erasure?

Hands-on Exercises

1. Select a diskette containing a word processing file that you no longer need, or one for which you have a backup. Wave a small magnet near the surface of the diskette. How close to the diskette can the magnet come before the file is damaged? (Be inventive to find out if the file has been damaged.)

15.2 Copy Protection and Piracy

As you know, data on diskette is easily copied. Most operating systems have a command to copy files from one secondary storage device to another, which allows you to copy files from a diskette to a hard disk or to another diskette. Most operating systems also have a DISKCOPY command that produces a verbatim copy of a diskette, reproducing not only its files but also the precise arrangement of the files on the diskette.

This capability to duplicate diskettes easily has led to **software piracy**—illegal copying of copyrighted or licensed software without the permission of the copyright owner. Software manufacturers have strongly reacted to this copyright infringement by launching attempts to stop illicit copying. This section attempts to portray both sides of the fierce controversy that has developed between software developers and manufacturers on the one hand, and software users on the other hand.

Intellectual Property Protection

Developers of software can use a number of legal means to register ownership of their creations. Among these means are copyrights, patents, trademarks, and trade secrets. Works based largely on ideas—such as books, plays, music, and computer software—are called **intellectual property** (as opposed to physical property, such as houses, cars, and furniture). Collectively, the means of expressing legal ownership of intellectual property are called **intellectual property protection**.

In the copy protection controversy, software developers and manufacturers want to protect their property from illegal distribution and use.

Copyrights are commonly used to protect literary or musical works, such as written compositions and songs. Obtaining a copyright is quite simple. The work being copyrighted must display the word "copyright," the copyright symbol (the letter "c" inside a circle), and the year in which the work was first produced. To record a copyright, the copyright owner usually completes a form and sends it, along with a copy of the work and the registration fee, to the United States Copyright Office (although this procedure is not necessary in order to claim copyright protection).

If you ignore a copyright by making unauthorized copies, you can be held liable for damage payments corresponding to any revenue lost to the copyright owner. In our litigious society, lawsuits for copyright infringement are fairly common.

In software development, a copyright protects the physical expression of a computer program, preventing someone from copying the literal code of the program. However, creating a program that performs an identical function using *different* computer code could also be considered an infringement of copyright. Computer programs have been copyrighted only since the mid-1970s. At that time a major revision of the United States copyright code extended to computer programs the same protection covering literary works and music.

Under an international copyright convention, most countries (with some notable exceptions) have agreed to respect the terms of copyrights issued in the territories of other nations. This convention enables a work to be copyrighted throughout most of the world.

A **patent** protects the basic idea behind an invention and offers a very broad type of protection. Once granted, a patent awards the ownership of the process to the patent owner. Any other person seeking to use the process in any form can do so only upon obtaining a license and paying royalties to the owner.

In software, patents protect the idea behind a program, not just its specific expression. For a program to be patentable, it must employ a new process to accomplish some specific task. It is actually the process that is patentable rather than the program itself. Like copyrights, patents were first made available to computer programs in the 1970s. Although patents afford a very powerful and broad form of intellectual property protection, they are rarely used to protect software, both because they are costly to obtain and also because their application to software is relatively new.

A **trademark** is a word, phrase, or graphic symbol that represents a product. In your lifetime, you have encountered thousands of trademarks that represent common products you see in advertising. To claim a trademark, you simply need to search through government records to ascertain that the trademark has not already been claimed by someone else. If not, you can then register your trademark with the U.S. Office of Patents and Trademarks.

Computer manufacturers are continuously seeking clever names with catchy trademarks to represent their products. Sometimes, unscrupulous companies attempt to adopt trademarks that resemble the trademarks of established, reliable companies in order to exploit their good reputations. For example, this has been attempted several times with the IBM trademark, which consists of an artistically stylized arrangement of the company's initials. In cases of trademark infringement, the owner of the trademark can sue for damages done to reputation and for loss of business.

The most common method of protecting microcomputer software is the **license agreement**, which dictates the conditions under which a user or group of users can run a program. The typical license requires that the user run the program on only one computer at a time and that any copies made or provided with the software are for backup purposes only and may not be copied or transferred to another party.

The legal theory behind a license agreement is that the program's developer has included in the program some trade secrets that are the developer's own property. The license agreement allows the user to "borrow" the trade secrets under the conditions specified. However, the actual ownership of the secrets rests with the program developer.

The terms of the license agreement are usually found on the outside of the software package or in a sealed envelope containing the software diskettes. By opening the package or the envelope, you agree to abide by the terms of the license. In some cases, a type of license called a **box-top license** is included in the software itself and appears on the screen at the beginning of the program. By continuing with the program, the user accepts the terms of the license agreement. Figure 15.1 shows the license agreement included with Addison-Wesley personal computer software.

Figure 15.1   A software license agreement.

End-User License Agreement

Addison–Wesley Publishing Company, Inc., Reading, Massachusetts 01867 ("A–W") and the party who first uses or copies the enclosed diskette(s) (the "Licensee") hereby agree, that A–W's grant to the Licensee of the right to use and possess the Software shall be subject to the following terms and conditions:

1. Grant. A–W hereby grants a non-exclusive license to the Licensee for the use of the software (the "Software") recorded on the diskette(s) provided herewith (the "diskette(s)") on a single computer subject to the terms hereof. **By using or copying the Software, the Licensee agrees to all the terms of this Agreement, even if the Licensee does not become a Registered Licensee.** A–W may terminate this License at any time if the Licensee breaches this Agreement.

2. License Terms. It is a term of this license that no copying of the diskette(s) is allowed except for the Licensee's own backup use only on one computer, and the Licensee must reproduce all original copyright notices and claims of confidentiality or trade secret rights on all backup copies. The Licensee may not reverse engineer, decompile or disassemble the Software, may not deliver copies to, or rent, lease or sublicense the Software to, anyone else, but may on a single occasion transfer this license, the original diskette(s) and all backup copies to a party who becomes a new Licensee, licensed to use this Software, by signing and sending to A–W a License Transfer Agreement, a copy of which may be obtained from A–W at the following address: License Information: Attention: EMS Division, Addison–Wesley Publishing Company, Inc., Jacob Way, Reading, Massachusetts 01867. Tel. (617) 944–6795.

Affixation of copyright notice(s) and enforcement of the Owners' rights under applicable copyright laws is not an admission of the intention to or fact of publication. The Software is protected by copyright laws, and no copying or distribution of, or other act with respect to, the Software, is allowed that would violate those laws.

The legality of box-top licenses has been questioned, since the user does not have the power to negotiate the terms of the license before opening the package, at which time the license goes into effect. Whether or not box-top licenses do in fact represent legal licenses has not yet been decided by the courts. This issue is so controversial, it would not be surprising to see a case come before the Supreme Court within the next few years.

The Need for Intellectual Property Protection

In spite of the various means of intellectual property protection available to software developers, the simple truth is that a large number of users ignore the legal rights of the developers and make illicit copies. Some estimates indicate that 50 to 80 percent of all microcomputer software currently in circulation was made illegally. These illicitly copied programs represent a loss of hundreds of millions of dollars in revenues to software developers.

In response to the problem, software developers have resorted to **copy protection**, a process that interferes with a diskette's ability to be copied. Many copy-protection schemes are available, and software manufacturers and developers continue to expend resources and energy to invent ever more complex plans to control the copying of disks. However, as quickly as software companies put these protection schemes into operation, software pirates develop and circulate methods to get around them. One of the top-selling programs in 1985 was a program to produce copies of copy-protected software.

The Viewpoint of the Software Consumer

On the other side of the copy protection controversy, software users claim that copy-protected programs are more difficult to use and that the user is left vulnerable if the original program diskettes malfunction.

Copy protection has failed to stop software piracy. Consumers feel that software packages are too expensive and that making bootleg copies of diskettes is justified. Even worse is the burden copy protection has imposed on all software users, whether pirates or not: Users are forced to rely on the one or two copies of the program supplied by the developer, which puts the user in a vulnerable position.

For instance, the disks originally purchased by the user may be damaged and need replacement at considerable cost, not to mention time wasted waiting for new ones to arrive from the manufacturer. Even worse is a situation where the manufacturer goes out of business. Because it may then be impossible for the user to replace a damaged copy-protected diskette, data created with that copy-protected program is rendered useless.

In response to these problems, software consumers have initiated a widespread movement against copy-protected software.

At the same time, software developers feel that copy protection is the only practical alternative available to protect their property from theft. At present, there is no simple way to balance the interests of the software users and software developers.

Section 15.2: Test Your Understanding

1. What is copy protection?
2. Describe the drawbacks of copy-protected software from the consumer's viewpoint.
3. What is the difference between a patent and a copyright?
4. If software is protected by copyright or license agreement, why not drop copy protection and sue the violators?
5. What is a box-top license?

Hands-on Exercises

1. Find a software license agreement and study its provisions.
   a. What rights does this license give the software purchaser?
   b. What restrictions does it impose on the software?

15.3 The Automated Office

This text has discussed the applications of microcomputers, mostly in a business setting. As you have probably guessed by now, the microcomputer is one of the essential ingredients in creating the modern, automated office.

In the first half of this century, the productivity of office workers lagged far behind their counterparts in manufacturing industries. Although modern production techniques, such as the assembly line, drastically increased the productivity of factory workers, most office workers used the inefficient, outdated methods for managing paperwork and for transmitting information that they had used for years.

Thanks to the ingenuity of office equipment manufacturers and designers, new office machines have been regularly introduced throughout the twentieth century. The adding machine, which replaced the pencil-and-paper method for doing arithmetic, was itself replaced by the electronic calculator. Until 1960, secretaries used messy carbon paper or a mimeograph machine to make copies of office documents. The invention of the photocopy machine made both methods obsolete.

As significant as these changes were, however, their effect on office productivity was not immediate or dramatic. Starting in the 1970s, this situation metamorphosed. One high-tech invention after another met office workers' demands to ease workloads and increase productivity. Today these inventions form the backbone of the working environment known as the **automated office**. Let's explore these innovations and their impact on today's office.

The Equipment of the Automated Office

By 1985, approximately 60 percent of all office workers had access to a microcomputer. It is highly likely that by the 1990s most office workers will work at their own microcomputers.

Of course, a major advantage to using a microcomputer in the automated office is the availability of software that helps workers in all occupations do their jobs more efficiently and accurately. Administrative assistants can use a microcomputer and a word processing program to produce reports and correspondence. Executives can use a microcomputer and a database management system to keep track of budgets, employee data, and projects of all kinds. Architects can use a microcomputer to design buildings and interiors.

Printer technology has also contributed to the usefulness of microcomputers in an office setting. High-speed dot-matrix and laser printers are capable of turning out hundreds of pages an hour. The development of revolutionary, low-priced laser printers led to the new field of desktop publishing (see Chapter 6), which has enabled the automated office to internally produce reports, advertising brochures, and presentation materials. In the next few years, the field of desktop publishing will surely grow with astonishing rapidity and turn the tradition-bound printing industry upside down.

Another piece of automated office equipment, the **FAX machine**, can instantly transmit graphic images—photographs, artwork, or contracts—from place to place in much the same way a modem transmits text. A salesperson in the field can request a FAX copy of a sales contract or a bid, signed by the home office, within hours of making a presentation to a customer. Similarly, companies can transmit artwork for advertising across the country in order to meet stringent magazine deadlines. Figure 15.2 shows a FAX machine and a copy of its output.

Modern copy technology is also part of the automated office. The modern copier is capable of enlarging, reducing, repositioning,

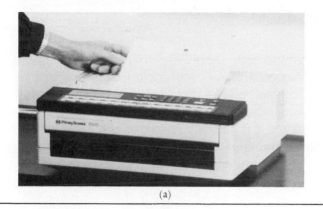

(a)

THE SLEREXE COMPANY LIMITED

SAPORS LANE · BOOLE · DORSET · BH 25 8 ER

TELEPHONE BOOLE (945 13) 51617 · TELEX 123456

Our Ref. 350/PJC/EAC   18th January, 1972.

Dr. P.N. Cundall,
Mining Surveys Ltd.,
Holroyd Road,
Reading,
Berks.

Dear Pete,

    Permit me to introduce you to the facility of facsimile transmission.

    In facsimile a photocell is caused to perform a raster scan over the subject copy. The variations of print density on the document cause the photocell to generate an analogous electrical video signal. This signal is used to modulate a carrier, which is transmitted to a remote destination over a radio or cable communications link.

    At the remote terminal, demodulation reconstructs the video signal, which is used to modulate the density of print produced by a printing device. This device is scanning in a raster scan synchronised with that at the transmitting terminal. As a result, a facsimile copy of the subject document is produced.

    Probably you have uses for this facility in your organisation.

                   Yours sincerely,

                   Phil.

               P.J. CROSS
               Group Leader - Facsimile Research

(b)

Figure 15.2 (a) A FAX machine and (b) a copy of its output.

and overlaying images. Some copiers can produce multiple colors and some can collate and bind documents as part of the copying process. Such copiers are a cross between a duplicating machine, a photography studio, and a print shop.

Modern copiers employ much of the same technology that makes microcomputers possible. Integrated circuits and semiconductor chips form the components of the devices, and ROM inside the copiers contains programs to control the internal microprocessors and allow them to accomplish their copying functions. By 1986, copier technology became so sophisticated that the U.S. government, concerned that copiers could be used to counterfeit currency, altered its printing methods. New currency now includes a special silk thread running through the paper.

Communication equipment (see Chapter 13) forms the final bit of technology found in the automated office. In the past 25 years, communication technology has undergone its own revolution. Today, communication equipment is used to transmit not only voices but also images and data. Modern office telephones employ microprocessors that allow them to "remember" telephone numbers, reroute messages, and set up conference calls. To rearrange a modern office telephone system, it is not usually necessary to rerun wires, only to reprogram the computer that controls the system.

Making the Automated Office Work

To gain the most out of the automated office, a business must plan and coordinate resources, train employees, and develop procedures revolving around the new technology.

Modern technology can dramatically increase the productivity of office workers, but these gains don't come automatically. To get the most out of an automated office, a business must integrate the workers, the technology, and the procedures for using that technology. Business executives must overcome the reluctance of most employees to change established routine. Routine is comfortable, and people are hesitant to change what is comfortable. Moreover, modern technology can breed fear. Office workers who did not grow up with computers and other technological devices may fear the introduction of automated equipment into their work lives. Perhaps they feel that it could reduce the importance of the skills they have worked hard to acquire over the years.

To make an automated office succeed, business executives must bring affected workers into the decision-making process. They must also plan extensive training to overcome workers' fears and to make them comfortable in using the equipment.

Even if workers are comfortable with the equipment and successfully use it, they will not necessarily achieve productivity gains unless the design of the automated office is well-conceived. Before purchasing equipment, a business should appoint a planning committee to decide exactly how the equipment is to be used, who will use it, and how current operating procedures will be affected. Key questions should be asked: Will the new equipment actually improve current operating procedures? Or will new equipment create more work in the office?

New equipment can often be integrated into the office only by redesigning the flow of information within the company and restating office procedures for handling various tasks. As much as possible, this should be a part of the planning process for the automated office.

As part of the creation of an automated office, a company must supply adequate training for its employees— for those involved when the equipment is introduced as well as for new employees hired later. Moreover, if any equipment or software is subsequently updated, there must be a plan for retraining employees and updating office procedures to take into account any changes in operation.

At the present time, no clear body of evidence exists that indicates automating an office will immediately and automatically result in dramatic productivity gains. Like any substantial restructuring of a system, results can be seen only over time. However, it does appear that by taking the drudgery out of some of the most routine and mind-numbing office tasks, the automated office will be populated with happier and more motivated workers.

Section 15.3: Test Your Understanding

1. What is a FAX machine?
2. Explain the resistance of some workers to automation.
3. How can a worker's resistance to office automation be overcome?
4. Describe the process for planning an automated office.
5. List five major technological components of an automated office. Describe the function of each.
6. Explain the different types of training that would be needed, by whom, and when.

15.4 Telecommuting

The spread of microcomputers has had many profound effects on the job market. Old tasks have been redefined and reorganized. Many new job categories, directly and indirectly related to microcomputer usage, have been created.

One of the most interesting developments in the job market is **telecommuting**, a form of employment in which workers perform their jobs at home, maintaining only a loose connection to a traditional office. A mother with small children can use a home computer with a data communication link to pursue a journalism career. A handicapped or ill worker can work at home and benefit from the psychological uplift of performing enjoyable, productive tasks. A programmer can write sections of a program at home, receiving regular guidance and coordination from the office via the telephone, or through periodic conferences at the office.

The Positive Side

Telecommuting was made feasible by the microcomputer. A worker equipped with a microcomputer at home, like the telecommuter shown in Figure 15.3, can perform many of the tasks previously done in an office. Word processing, filing, invoicing, and analysis can be performed in the home and submitted to the office when completed. When workers need information from the office, they can obtain it by visiting the office or by using data communications to tap into the databases maintained in the office computers.

Telecommuting has many advantages. Workers can create an environment specifically suited to their personal tastes. Gone are frictions created by interoffice rivalries. Office politics, which can be annoying and emotionally draining, are eliminated. Telecommuters can structure their days to fit their needs. If the telecommuter wishes to work from midnight until 8 a.m., then so be it. It is very easy to adapt telecommuting hours to the needs of spouse and children. No longer do you need to ask your manager for time off

The benefits of telecommuting: working in a comfortable, familiar environment; meeting parental obligations; avoiding interoffice politics; creating a flexible work schedule.

Figure 15.3   A telecommuter at work.

to attend parent-teacher conferences, school plays, or medical appointments. Telecommuting also fits in well with the obligations of running a home. Work no longer conflicts with waiting for deliveries or repair people. Time and money are saved by not driving to and from work in rush hour traffic.

Telecommuters also report that their presence in the house can have a positive effect on the whole family, even if the telecommuter is busy working. Children may feel reassured to have a parent in the house at all times, even though the parent is occupied. In turn, the presence of the telecommuter at home can relieve parental anxieties over leaving children unattended, or transporting children to and from daycare centers or babysitters.

The Negative Side

It is impossible to accurately predict the long-term effects of telecommuting because it is a relatively new phenomenon. However, even now it is possible to point out some disadvantages that balance the many positive features. For one thing, the telecommuter works, for the most part, in isolation, thereby missing interpersonal contacts that allow the worker to hear several sides of an issue and to "get the creative juices flowing." The feeling of isolation generated by telecommuting can, to some extent, be alleviated by skillfully arranging the work day, perhaps by scheduling periodic phone calls to colleagues to discuss work. Regular luncheon appointments outside the home are almost a necessity.

Another problem is that a telecommuter may be passed over for promotions or special assignments that make promotion possible. Even though office politics can be annoying, it's often a necessary evil for people who want to get ahead in their careers. The telecommuter often cannot establish a peer group or a close relationship with a manager, which causes the telecommuter to be ignored at promotion or raise time.

Telecommuters are never away from their work, which can be a major drawback. The telecommuter may end up working harder at home than in the office. The office environment artificially imposes working hours, at the end of which most people leave their work behind. However, when working at home, it is tempting to return to the computer after dinner for a few hours of extra work—and before you know it, it's past midnight, the rest of the household has gone to bed, and the telecommuter is still working.

Despite these drawbacks, most telecommuters seem happy with the arrangement and would not go back to a standard work day if it were offered to them. It is likely that in the years ahead, many more workers will leave the confines of the traditional office and participate in the microcomputer revolution via telecommuting.

The disadvantages of telecommuting: working in isolation; missing out on important professional contacts traditionally made within the office; never "getting away from it all."

Section 15.4: Test Your Understanding

1. What is telecommuting?
2. Describe the advantages and disadvantages of telecommuting from the employer's point of view.
3. Describe the advantages and disadvantages of telecommuting from the employee's point of view.

15.5 The Future of Microcomputing

This book discussed the microcomputer revolution and the many applications that have been generated by it. The microcomputer revolution is, in a sense, a natural development in the evolutionary chain of computer hardware and software. However, it would be ridiculous to assert that the microcomputer revolution has run its course and that the current state of affairs will be the same in the future as it is today.

Given the level of research and development in microcomputer hardware, software, and applications, we can already see the outlines of new products that will change the world of microcomputers in the years ahead. This final section looks into what the future of microcomputing may hold in store.

Hardware

Microcomputer hardware will continue to evolve at the hectic pace of the last decade. There will be dramatic changes in microprocessors and in storage technology. When the power of microcomputers increases, the number and type of problems they are capable of attacking will also increase. A few years from now, microcomputers will feature microprocessors possessing clock cycles three to five times as powerful as those currently employed in the IBM PC. These microprocessors will be able to address hundreds of megabytes of RAM and to handle data processing that can only be done on a minicomputer today.

Tomorrow's mass storage devices will allow you to store much greater amounts of data than today's hard disks. Disks holding 100, 200, or even 1,000 megabytes of information will be common.

New storage technologies will also be prevalent. **CD ROM technology** will use **compact disks**, similar to the ones used in compact disk stereo systems, to store as much as 500 megabytes of data each. These disks, capable of holding huge databases, will be read by using CD ROM disk drives installed in microcomputers in much the same way that diskette drives are used today.

High-resolution graphics, controlled by new graphics chips, will help create much more realistic and satisfying graphics presentations. Moreover, **interactive disks** will mix computer-generated texts and graphics with high-quality film.

These new technologies and economies of production will give microcomputer users a continuing, rapid decrease in the cost of microcomputers. We can look forward to the day when a computer system comparable to today's IBM PC will sell for $200 to $300. This decrease in the price of microcomputers will encourage their continued proliferation, especially in the field of education. Shortly, computers will be regarded as an educational tool required of all students; we won't give it much more thought than a student's need to use notebooks and laboratory equipment.

Software

Software will change in the years ahead as well. We can look forward to software becoming easier to use and becoming much more intuitive—in other words, tomorrow's software will much more closely parallel our own thought processes. We can also look forward to new applications and to more powerful versions of the applications you studied in this book.

It is impossible to describe the future of microcomputing with perfect precision, but we can be sure of one thing: A decade from now we will look back at today's computers with amusement and astonishment at how primitive they were and how little we were able to accomplish with them.

You ain't seen nothin' yet!

Section 15.5: Test Your Understanding

1. Describe some of the changes that will occur in the microcomputers of the future. How will these changes affect the way we use microcomputers?

KEY TERMS

software piracy
intellectual property
intellectual property
   protection
copyright
patent

trademark
license agreement
box-top license
copy protection
automated office
FAX machine

telecommuting
CD ROM technology
compact disk
interactive disk

CHAPTER REVIEW QUESTIONS

1. List three job activities that can be successfully performed by a telecommuter.
2. List three job activities that cannot be successfully performed by a telecommuter.
3. Name three hazards that may threaten the physical security of your data. Identify the methods needed to protect against each one.
4. Describe three crimes that can be performed with the aid of a computer. What precautions can be taken to foil each one?
5. Explain the difference between a patent and a copyright.
6. What is a trademark?
7. List some typical restrictions of the software purchaser imposed by a box-top license.
8. Name three tasks that you can do more efficiently with the help of office automation.
9. Name three office tasks that you cannot do more efficiently by using office automation.

DISCUSSION QUESTIONS

1. Is telecommuting likely to increase the isolation of workers? If so, how can this isolation be overcome?
2. Give examples of applications that will benefit from the availability of the following:
   a) Faster microcomputers
   b) Larger secondary memory devices
   c) Improved graphics
3. It has been said that microcomputer applications are driven by developments in hardware. Do you agree with this statement? Explain your answer.
4. Should software be copy-protected? Explain your answer.
5. In the mid-1980s, AT&T began manufacturing personal computers and IBM purchased several companies in the telecommunications business. Describe the relationship between telecommunications and personal computing.

APPLICATION PROJECT

A major problem for software publishers is encouraging customers to abide by the software license agreement. This agreement usually states that the software itself belongs to the publisher and that the customer has purchased only the right to use it (and then on only one machine at a time).

Copy-protecting diskettes has not proven to be a very effective deterrent to unauthorized copying. Copy protection makes the software more difficult to use, which angers legitimate buyers. Software publishers need to take the following steps:

Inform the purchaser of the problem and its legal ramifications.

Emphasize the importance of the problem.

Persuade the purchaser to abide by the purchase agreement.

Perform these actions in a positive manner that does not discourage sales or limit the usefulness of the software itself.

What can software publishers do to achieve these goals? Develop an information sheet that might be included in a publisher's software package.

PHOTOGRAPH CREDITS